Other Books Available at Holloway.com

The Holloway Guide to Remote Work
Katie Womersley, Juan Pablo Buriticá et al.
A comprehensive guide to building, managing, and adapting to working with distributed teams.

The Holloway Guide to Equity Compensation
Joshua Levy, Joe Wallin et al.
Stock options, RSUs, job offers, and taxes—a detailed reference, explained from the ground up.

The Holloway Guide to Technical Recruiting and Hiring
Osman (Ozzie) Osman et al.
A practical, expert-reviewed guide to growing software engineering teams effectively, written by and for hiring managers, recruiters, interviewers, and candidates.

The Holloway Guide to Raising Venture Capital
Andy Sparks et al.
A current and comprehensive resource for entrepreneurs, with technical detail, practical knowledge, real-world scenarios, and pitfalls to avoid.

Land Your Dream Design Job
Dan Shilov
A guide for product designers, from portfolio to interview to job offer.

Founding Sales: The Early-Stage Go-To-Market Handbook
Pete Kazanjy
This tactical handbook distills early sales first principles, and teaches the skills required for going from being a founder to early salesperson, and eventually becoming an early sales leader.

Angel Investing: Start to Finish
Joe Wallin, Pete Baltaxe
A journey through the perils and rewards of an finding deals, financings, and term sheets.

D0813439

Better Venture

For Gillian,

Looking forward to having you on the other side of the ocean again soon and to work together on things journalism (King's Review), EVG and hopefully venture capital!

Thank you for your time and hope you find something fun in the book,

Better Venture

IMPROVING DIVERSITY, INNOVATION, AND PROFITABILITY IN VENTURE CAPITAL AND STARTUPS

Erika Brodnock and Johannes Lenhard

A comprehensive guide to diversity and inclusion in venture capital—who funds, who gets funded, and how the industry can change. With history, research, and over 40 interviews with investors and founders that explore the moral and financial needs for a more diverse, equitable, and profitable funding system.

HOLLOWAY

Published in the United States by Holloway, San Francisco
Holloway.com

Cover design by Order (New York) and Andy Sparks
Interior design by Joshua Levy and Jennifer Durrant
Production by Nathaniel Hemminger
Print engineering by Titus Wormer

Typefaces: Tiempos Text and National 2
by Kris Sowersby of Klim Type Foundry

Print version 1.0 · Digital version e1.0.2
doc 4f14bf · pipeline c81f38 · genbook f88066 · 2023-01-30

Want More Out of This Book?

Holloway publishes books online. As a reader of this special full-access print edition, you are granted personal access to the paid digital edition, which you can read and share on the web, and offers commentary, updates, and corrections.

Claim your account by visiting: **holloway.com/print20336**

If you wish to recommend the book to others, suggest they visit **holloway.com/bv** to learn more and purchase their own digital or print copy.

The author welcomes your feedback! Please consider adding comments or suggestions to the book online so others can benefit. Or say hello@holloway.com. Thank you for reading.

The Holloway team

TABLE OF CONTENTS

INTRODUCTION

1 How This Book Came About

Erika Brodnock is an award-winning serial entrepreneur and philanthropist. Following her MBA, she was Research Fellow at King's College London, and is currently finishing a PhD at the London School of Economics and Political Science. Through her work at the intersection of technology and wellbeing, Erika specializes in building products and services that disrupt outdated systems. Erika is co-founder of Kinhub (formerly Kami), an employee wellbeing platform focused on enhancing equity and inclusion in the future of work. Erika also co-founded Extend Ventures,[1] where she leads research efforts that aim to democratize access to venture finance for diverse entrepreneurs.

Johannes Lenhard is a researcher and writer based in London. Following his PhD at Cambridge, he spent three years during his postdoc researching the ethics of venture capital between Europe and the US. His first book, *Making Better Lives*—on homeless people's survival in Paris—was published in 2022. He regularly contributes to journalistic outlets such as Prospect, TechCrunch, Vestoj, Aeon, Tribune, The Conversation, and Sifted. Most recently, he is the co-founder and co-director of VentureESG.[2]

1.1 *Johannes's Work and Research*

My research on the ethics of venture capital (VC) began in the fall of 2017. I started interviewing venture capital investors, first in Europe and then all over the world between Silicon Valley, New York, London, Berlin, Nairobi, Lima, Tokyo, and Paris. Over the past five years, during my post-doctoral research at Cambridge, I've spoken to more than 300 partners in venture capital funds across stages, geographies, and asset classes. Before I began

---

1. https://www.extend.vc/
2. https://www.ventureesg.com/

this research, VC was a place to earn some money on the side for me; I started as a "student temp worker" for a corporate VC fund when I moved to London. Over the years, I have supported and consulted a number of VC investors in areas as varied as reporting, fundraising, and as a deal-flow generating "venture partner."

At first, my interest in VC was abstract: I wanted to use my contacts to shed some light on what venture capitalists do, who they are, and why it matters. It seemed to me not enough scrutiny has been on these "king-makers" of big tech. By 2019 I had already spoken to almost 100 VCs, but it wasn't until I arrived in Silicon Valley that summer that my eyes were opened to the issue at the core of this book: the absurd lack of diversity, equity, and inclusion (DEI) in VC and the related homogeneity across the tech industry.

During my first conversations in Silicon Valley, I always asked about what problems people thought the industry was facing at the time; the biggest issue people pointed out to me (apart from *already* skyrocketing valuations) was DEI. I went back to my own sample of interviews. I was stunned: out of my first 100 or so interviews, five were with female VCs, and even fewer were with people of color. I had also met most of the VCs through "elite networks," as my university and industry contacts provided warm introductions (referrals or endorsements). That was the time when I started to explicitly reach out, first to female VCs, and increasingly to a wider set of investors who weren't either male or white or elite-educated. It was also then when I first started writing about my findings.[3]

When I arrived back in the UK later in 2019, I was curious to compare the European ecosystem to Silicon Valley. I reached out to and asked for introductions to DEI champions. That's how I met some of the people featured in this book, like Maren Bannon of January Ventures; Sophia Bendz,[§14.6] who is now at Cherry Ventures, but at the time was the first female partner at Atomico; and Check Warner,[§15.2] founder of Diversity VC and GP at Ada Ventures. One interview I'd scheduled was with Erika Brodnock, the founder of a company called Kami (and before that Karisma Kidz), to learn from her about intersectionality and racial disparity in the UK tech ecosystem. We connected immediately over the issues, straight away got to write our first piece together for *Sifted*.[4] I was absolutely taken

---

3. https://news.crunchbase.com/news/author/johannes-lenhard/

4. https://sifted.eu/articles/stop-using-the-term-bame/

by Erika's experiences—having raised five children, started two companies, and just embarked on the complicated journey of a PhD at the London School of Economics (LSE)—and had found my match to start working on this book.

And it was an absolutely necessary match, obviously: I am a white, privileged man with ten years at one of the best universities in the world under my belt. Unlike in many other contexts where "expertise" comes with the privilege to speak, in this particular case you might think: why listen to me on questions of gender, racial, and all kinds of other social justice and equality? What do I know about diversity, equity, and inclusion? The good news is that you won't have to listen to my voice for too much of this volume. Not only does my co-author Erika Brodnock *have* all the experiences I am missing (more on that next), this book is first and foremost a book of interviews, the collection of an almost two-year long journey through the worlds of venture capital and tech between the US and EU. My privilege helped us to go on this journey—to get into many rooms, to listen, to ask questions, and to distill what we heard. I hope the result helps you, the reader, gain valuable perspectives and participate in positive change.

1.2 *Erika's Founder Story and Research*

My background is incredibly different from Johannes's; some might say it's the polar opposite. I am a Black female, born and raised in Streatham Vale, South London. I was educated in comprehensive schools and, despite being advanced a year in secondary school for being gifted and talented, I stopped education at A-Levels due to circumstances. I went to university for the first time in 2017 to study for an EMBA at the University of Surrey. Having graduated within the top percentile of my class, I wrote my PhD proposal for the development and deployment of algorithms that would enable an analysis of the allocation of capital by the UK's venture capital ecosystem as pertaining to the perceived gender, ethnicity, and educational background of venture-backed founders. I was offered places at several leading universities and eventually decided to read at the LSE, where I was awarded a fully funded studentship and have been privileged to work with Professor Grace Lordan[§18.1] in the Inclusion Initiative,[5] and

---

5. https://www.lse.ac.uk/TII

am supported by leading figures who are committed to creating tangible change in the venture capital and private equity industries.

Over the last decade, I have been able to co-create two for-profit enterprises as well as two non-profit organizations—one of those is Extend Ventures,[6] where I am co-founder and head of research, alongside the incredible co-founders Tom Adeyoola, Patricia Hamzahee, and Kekeli Anthony. Our research outputs, including the *Diversity Beyond Gender*[7] report, have succeeded in illuminating many of the stark disparities in access to funding, in ways that have not previously been possible. As a result, we have been able to partner with Atomico,$^{\S14.6}$ Nasdaq Entrepreneurial Center,$^{\S21.4}$ JP Morgan, and Innovate UK to support the global analysis of capital allocation to diverse founders. This research has been credited with being a catalyst for many new funds receiving funding that is specifically for diverse entrepreneurs.

Prior to *Diversity Beyond Gender* being released, I had not been able to raise capital for my entrepreneurial endeavors. Even in 2019 and early 2020, when my co-founders at Extend Ventures included an exited entrepreneur, an investment stalwart, and a Bain consultant with degrees from Oxford, Cambridge, and Columbia, while I was at the LSE, as an all-Black team, we needed to bootstrap the first research piece to "de-risk" our proposition. Going back further to 2015 and 2016 when I sought Series A investment for my first company, Karisma Kidz, it was similarly impossible to raise money.

Since the *Diversity Beyond Gender* report, things have improved. We tracked one UK Black female who had raised more than £1M in capital for her venture between 2009 and 2019. That number has risen to more than 16 Black women in the two years since the report was published, however, a significant proportion of the 16 have not been able to raise this money from venture capital funds, having instead to rely upon angel investors who are keen to expedite change.

When Johannes approached me with the opportunity to co-author this volume, I saw an incredible opportunity. This is an issue that goes far beyond just me or the other Black women who are struggling to raise money for industry-altering and immensely profitable ideas. This volume allows us to share the stories of people who bring more diverse experi-

---

6. https://www.extend.vc/
7. https://www.extend.vc/reports

ences to the venture capital and tech industry, as well as spotlight those who promote the fair and equitable allocation of the capital and connections that entrepreneurs need to thrive.

2 Why Diversity in Venture Capital Matters

2.1 *Diversity Issues in VC*

The National Venture Capital Association's (NVCA) 2020 VC Human Capital Survey[8] sampled 2,500 investors in the US, and found that 3% of partners—those with decision-making and check-writing power—identified as Black (compared to 12.6% of the US population[9]); 3% of partners identified as Hispanic or Latinx (16.9% of the US population); 14% of partners identified as women (52% of the US population). In the UK, figures based on a similar sample of around 2,100 venture capital investors mirrors this picture. For the UK, Diversity VC's latest survey from 2019[10] reported that only 13% of partner roles are held by women (compared to 47% of the UK labor force overall), and 83% of all UK venture firms have no women in their decision-making bodies. Further, the number of women on investment committees has not improved since Diversity VC started reporting on these numbers in 2017. The study found that just 8% of all VCs in the UK are Black or of mixed heritage (versus 13% of the population in London, where most of the UK's tech sector is based), while 12% are Asian. As we'll discuss later, these numbers have remained stagnant since 2020, and some have shrunk to even smaller percentiles.

The disparities in other parts of the VC world are similarly pronounced: a 2022 report on the European ecosystem, "European Women in VC,"[11] found that 85% of VC general partners in Europe are male, with the UK (87%), Southern European (90%), and Central European countries (90%) trending even above this average. Even more telling is the "fire power" that certain investor groups have, meaning the overall share of the money in VC; according to the same report, women in Europe control only 9% of capital (5% in the UK, 6% in the Nordics). Indicative numbers

---

8. https://nvca.org/research/nvca-deloitte-human-capital-survey/

9. https://statisticalatlas.com/United-States/Race-and-Ethnicity

10. https://diversity.vc/diversity-in-uk-venture-capital-2019/

11. https://europeanwomeninvc.idcinteractive.net/

for Latin America[12] and Canada[13] tell a similar story. Class is a significant variable as well, and the numbers are staggering:[14] in 2018, 40% of US VCs had degrees from Harvard or Stanford; in the UK, one in five VCs went to Oxford or Cambridge (compared to 1% of the UK population average). As this book will reveal, the closed networks of elite institutions play a large part in keeping the industry homogenous, with many people intentionally locked out.

2.2 *The Consequences of Homogeneity*

For an industry which has for the last 80 years filtered which ideas and technologies reach the market and change the world, this is a disastrous picture. Not only is this group nowhere near representative of the population it makes decisions for, it has neglected to make the best investments to maximize financial outcomes. Increased diversity in investment teams has been shown to contribute positively to the performance of venture capital funds: an authoritative Harvard study[15] based on over 20 years of quantitative data from the US VC industry, for instance, demonstrates the impact a lack of diversity in the investment committee of a VC fund can have. The more similar the investment partners in a fund are, the lower the success rate for acquisition or IPO. To the contrary, if a fund increased their share of female partners by 10%, they had on average a 1.5% higher overall fund return each year and 9.7% more profitable exits. McKinsey & Company have published several studies ("Why Diversity Matters",[16] "Delivering Through Diversity",[17] "Diversity Wins: How Inclusion Matters"[18]) on diversity in more general corporate contexts, which conclusively find that having more women and people from diverse ethnic

---

12. https://lavca.org/vc/women-investing-latin-american-vc-decision-makers/

13. https://www.cbc.ca/news/business/
    women-visible-minorities-vastly-underrepresented-in-canada-s-private-equity-vc-firms-1
    .5192634

14. https://medium.com/@kerby/where-did-you-go-to-school-bde54d846188

15. https://hbr.org/2018/07/the-other-diversity-dividend

16. https://www.mckinsey.com/capabilities/people-and-organizational-performance/
    our-insights/why-diversity-matters

17. https://www.mckinsey.com/capabilities/people-and-organizational-performance/
    our-insights/delivering-through-diversity

18. https://www.mckinsey.com/featured-insights/diversity-and-inclusion/
    diversity-wins-how-inclusion-matters

backgrounds as executives in companies leads to higher financial performance. According to McKinsey's recent study,[19] companies in the top 25% for gender diversity of executives were 25% more likely to report above-average profitability than companies in the bottom quartile. Similarly, companies in the top quartile for ethnically diverse executive teams have a 36% higher likelihood for above-average profitability.

The data and the business case are very clear but—in the converse of the 2020 NVCA report's optimistic conclusions—very little progress has been made towards changing the numbers so far. This book looks both at the history and reasons we are in this position, and provides a first-of-its-kind overview of proven best practices to inspire action towards the change that is needed now.

There are four key reasons why the homogeneity of the VC industry matters:

1. **VCs are the kingmakers of our digital age.** They filter who gets money to build companies and bring ideas to market. Venture capitalists have enabled the success of the world's most highly valued companies, from Amazon, Apple, and Facebook, to WeWork and Theranos. Who these people are and what kind of decisions they make matters to us all.

2. **The VC sector has so far seen very little scrutiny.** Both in terms of DEI but also more broadly within the ongoing "techlash," VCs have been left out of the conversation. While VCs have paid lip service to #MeToo and Black Lives Matter, not much progress has actually been made. This a social justice issue, thus, more external pressure needs to be applied to VCs.

3. **We need to broaden the diversity conversation.** When it is in focus, diversity is often limited to gender and, especially in the US, ethnicity. We need to widen the conversation to include other dimensions of diversity including educational background, socioeconomic background, disability, mental health, sexual orientation, and others—and, most importantly, shine a light on intersectionality, in order to understand the complex interconnections of being excluded in multiple ways.

---

19. https://www.mckinsey.com/featured-insights/diversity-and-inclusion/diversity-wins-how-inclusion-matters

4. **Data doesn't drive change.** While we see the need for data (and more precise data at that) to push the industry to embrace DEI, data so far hasn't made a difference. In fact, data is not something that VCs have historically paid too much attention to in their decision making—"gut feeling" is the strong driving factor. What is key to inspiring change, as even economists have recently picked up on,[20] are stories. This is the main focus of this book: first-hand accounts, best practice examples, and case studies.

2.3 *Ripple Effects in Startups and Tech*

The problem that begins with VC investors invariably extends to the founders of the companies and startups receiving crucial venture capital funding. In 2021, both "European Women in VC"[21] and the State of European Tech[22] reported that all-female startup founding teams received less than 2% of funding (with both reporting approximately 9% went to mixed-gender teams).[23] As *Wired* reported in late 2021, "In a Banner Year for VC, Women Still Struggle to Get Funding."[27] The conclusion: women received *less* money in 2021 than on average across the previous five years. In the US, only 1.2% of VC funding[28] went to Black entrepreneurs in the first

---

20. https://press.princeton.edu/books/hardcover/9780691182292/narrative-economics

21. https://europeanwomeninvc.idcinteractive.net/34/

22. https://stateofeuropeantech.com/chapter/better-ideas-better-companies/article/fuelling-better-more-diverse-ideas/

23. In fact, this is a slight decrease[24] from the 4% funding for all-female teams and 11% for mixed teams that "European Women in VC" reported in 2018 (but more in line with 2019 and 2020). Atomico's annual State of European Tech[25] report tells a similar story of stagnation across the same period: female-only teams earned 1.5% in 2018 and 1.1% in 2021 (and a similar decrease in terms of number of deals, from 5.7% for all-female teams in 2018 to 5.4% in 2021, and from 12% to 10.8% for mixed teams). Only when looking further back, for example in 2011-2012, have numbers significantly increased. See the British Business Bank's "Small Business Equity Tracker 2021".[26]

24. https://europeanwomeninvc.idcinteractive.net/34/

25. https://stateofeuropeantech.com/chapter/better-ideas-better-companies/article/fuelling-better-more-diverse-ideas/

26. https://www.british-business-bank.co.uk/wp-content/uploads/2021/06/Equity-Tracker-2021-Final-report-1.pdf#page=28

27. https://www.wired.com/story/in-banner-year-for-vc-women-still-struggle-to-get-funding/

28. https://news.crunchbase.com/venture/something-ventured-funding-to-black-startup-founders-quadrupled-in-past-year-but-remains-elusive/

half of 2021; just 0.34% went to Black women.[29] The numbers are even more devastating in Britain, where not-for-profit Extend Ventures found that 0.24% of VC funding[30] between 2011 and 2021 went to Black entrepreneurs.[31] The Extend Ventures report also identifies a significant socioeconomic class bias in UK VC funding, with 43% of seed funding going to teams with at least one member from Oxford, Cambridge, Harvard, or Stanford.

Representation, or lack thereof, filters through the fabric of the entire industry, as investors are more likely to invest in those who look like themselves. Richard Kerby writes[32] that the illusion of meritocracy is in fact "mirrortocracy," resulting in adverse effects for diverse startups founders. This is based on similarity bias in investment decision making[33] and the reliance on gut feeling.[34] Given the very limited pool of VC decision makers—mostly white men with Harvard and Stanford MBAs—women, people of color, and those without degrees from elite educational establishments are often left locked out and unable to access the support of venture capital firms.

This is particularly surprising given how clear the business case is for DEI in VC and startups. As PlanBeyond's recent "Bias in US Venture Capital Funding Report"[35] makes clear: more diverse teams are more likely to financially outperform their non-diverse counterparts *and* work on making society better with their companies. As these startups are scaling up to become the next wave of tech behemoths, the biases we see in venture capital and founding teams are filtered downstream and reflected as biases within venture-supported companies. Research[36] from the Kauffman Fellows Research Center similarly shows that while only 20% of cap-

---

29. https://news.crunchbase.com/diversity/something-ventured-black-women-founders/

30. https://www.extend.vc/reports

31. Even more specifically, 1.7% of VC funding went to entrepreneurs who identify as Black, East Asian, South Asian, and Middle Eastern—compared to the 14% of the UK population that identify in these groups. In contrast, 76% of investment went to all-white entrepreneurial teams.

32. https://medium.com/@kerby/where-did-you-go-to-school-bde54d846188

33. https://medium.com/morphais/what-you-are-is-what-you-like-the-dangers-of-similarity-biases-in-the-vc-investment-process-7d1b0c36999a

34. https://journals.aom.org/doi/10.5465/amj.2016.1009

35. https://planbeyond.com/bias-in-venture-capital-report

36. https://www.kauffmanfellows.org/journal_posts/the-pipeline-myth-ethnicity-fund-managers

ital is invested in ethnically diverse founding teams, those teams achieve 30% higher returns than all-white teams. Boston Consulting Group found that female founders generated 10% more in cumulative revenue over five years,[37] and startups with at least one female founder generated $0.78 in revenue for every dollar invested, compared to male-founded startups that generated less than half that ($0.31).

Diversity matters not only when it comes to the business case, but also as a matter of access and participation in shaping the future of economies. Having different kinds of people with unique experiences involved in, for instance, a company board is shown to ensure stronger checks and balances, more thoughtful oversight over company matters, and better performance in times of crisis (for example, when there was female involvement in boards during the financial crisis). When different kinds of people, with different academic backgrounds, different genders and races, from different age groups and geographies, come together, ethical decision-making[38] also tends to be stronger (mitigating the likelihood, for example, of corruption). In contrast, strictly homogenous groups are more likely to show conforming behavior and, particularly for white men, more risky behavior. (The "white male effect" of risk insensitivity[39] is often also connected to generational wealth, another determining factor for whether someone pursues entrepreneurship.)

Thus, the practice of groupthink can be mitigated through the adoption of a more diverse board or leadership structure.[40] Despite all of this data, many, even most, VCs continue to associate more diversity with more risk. Although trillions of dollars have been spent on gut feeling and never returned, it seems diversity is one "risk" some VCs aren't willing to take.

2.4 *Evidence of Slow Change*

Things are changing with awareness, albeit very slowly. Hire and Wire[41] is a movement calling for firms to increase diversity in their workforce and

---

37. https://www.bcg.com/en-us/publications/2018/why-women-owned-startups-are-better-bet

38. http://www.na-businesspress.com/JLAE/DeGrassiSW_Web9_6_.pdf

39. https://onlinelibrary.wiley.com/doi/abs/10.1111/j.1539-6924.1994.tb00082.x

40. https://www.jstor.org/stable/259138

41. https://www.forbes.com/sites/kylewestaway/2020/06/03/
    how-to-support-black-entrepreneurs-hire-and-wire/#3c8439f47794

write checks to a more diverse group of founders in tech. Rather than *yet another* mentorship program or office hours that lead to yet more posts on social media, founders who are not male or white need to simply receive more funding.[42] Over the last years, more and more initiatives have been set up to challenge the uniformity in startup finance and tech.

With All Raise[§15.3] in the US, Diversity VC[43] in the UK, the international Thirty Percent Coalition[44] and the 30% Club,[45] Black Founders,[46] the Female Founders Alliance,[47] and the Latinx Startup Alliance,[48] organizations of investors and founders alike are pushing for more representation in general partner (GP), limited partner (LP), and board roles. At the same time, we are finally seeing a small but increasing number of new funds being raised by long-overlooked GPs, mostly led by women[49] or, as in the case of Base10,[50] Harlem Capital,[51] and MaC Ventures[52] among others, by Black GPs. Concrete solutions, tools, and techniques are being proposed, such as with the Diversity VC Standard.[53]

More and more LPs, from university endowments and pension funds to foundations and family offices, are slowly pushing for change from the top, from the investors' position, too, as we will discuss in our interviews. There is hope.

---

42. https://sifted.eu/articles/female-founders-vc-200-billion-club/

43. https://diversity.vc/

44. https://www.30percentcoalition.org/

45. https://30percentclub.org/

46. https://blackfounders.com/

47. https://femalefounders.org/

48. https://www.facebook.com/LatinxStartupAlliance

49. https://www.fastcompany.com/90567387/women-in-vc-growth

50. https://www.forbes.com/sites/kenrickcai/2022/04/05/base10-becomes-first-black-led-vc-firm-to-cross-1-billion-aum-with-new-460-million-fund-iii/?sh=27fa9a3968d1

51. https://www.forbes.com/sites/alexkonrad/2021/03/31/harlem-capital-raises-134-million-second-fund/?sh=fbb1f492308e

52. https://www.fastcompany.com/90619209/majority-black-run-vc-firm-raises-110-million-seed-fund

53. https://sifted.eu/articles/diversity-vc-standard-launch/

3 The Rise of Venture Capital and Financial Inequality

3.1 *Venture's Connection to Economic Inequality*

A catastrophic cocktail of the coronavirus pandemic, its resultant recession, and the advent of war in Eastern Europe has sent shockwaves through the global economy in a three-year onslaught that has shaken the world into a state of economic insecurity surpassing that of the Great Depression of the 1920s. The crisis has shone an often uncomfortable yet incandescent light on the systemic inequities embedded in the global economy. Those most affected by these inequities have consistently belonged to the most vulnerable communities: lower-income and ethnic households, and those with lower levels of formal education. Disparities in access to support, inadequate health care provision, and undue strain placed on mothers and caretakers have become too-common penalties for those without access to the wealth, education, and employment required to shield them from the downturn.

Securely sheltered from this economic insecurity are those nestled among the world's ever-growing list of billionaires. According to the Forbes billionaire list, seven of the world's top ten billionaires in 2022 are the founders of venture-backed technology companies. Musk, Bezos, Gates, Ellison, Page, Zuckerberg, and Brin are household names. They epitomize the archetypal white male entrepreneur the world has come to associate with world-changing innovation and outstanding venture success. These entrepreneurs create tremendous wealth of their own, which they in turn invest in other venture-backable businesses: the Silicon Valley flywheel. A significant number of the US's 735 billionaires have amassed their fortunes through entrepreneurship and the creation of venture-backed companies.

3.2 *How Venture-Backed Businesses Succeed*

Most businesses begin with an entrepreneur who holds a grand vision, invention, or idea. These ideas are shared with co-founders, team members, investors, and eventually the world when the idea materializes into a product or service offered to consumers at a price. It often requires external finance to fuel that growth as a business grows. To realize this capital, businesses create revenues from sales, borrow money from friends and family, and take loans from banks. These more traditional forms of capital are most suited for companies that will grow rapidly yet steadily in a linear fashion. They can break even within one to three years and provide steady profit and growth.

Venture-backed businesses tend to have a few additional components. They tend to be high-growth, high-risk, high-reward, and, more often than not, tech-enabled businesses that can demonstrate potential for massive scalability. Of the millions of companies that are started each year, only a fraction is considered to have the ability to disrupt industries and achieve the exponential growth required to create returns to investors that are equal to or in excess of the entire fund—often more than £100M—from which they were invested. There are a great many books that delve into the detail of how to create a venture-backable company; each provides overarching principles that determine there must be a robust initial team, a problem faced by a large and preferably ever-expanding market, and a "sticky" product that can solve that problem at a price point consumers are willing to pay, also known as product-market fit. With these components in place, many entrepreneurs create startups they deem to have the potential to achieve the billion-dollar valuations that will propel them onto the Forbes billionaire list.

However, ideas are just ideas without the critical component of capital. A sizable investment, often into the seven figures, is required to fuel early growth and is frequently provided through external funding. Given that these companies are high risk, more traditional forms of capital are out of the question. Startup entrepreneurs increasingly rely upon angel investors or venture capital to provide the boost they need onto the trajectory for exponential scale. Funds flow directly into the company as an equity investment rather than an interest-bearing loan. This is central for early-stage companies with limited track records and little income, for whom interest-bearing loans could be unobtainable, onerous, or even crippling.

3.3 *The Impact of Venture Inequality*

While venture capital enables company expansion that is far less possible with other methods, there are many vehicles and strategies for funding an early-stage company, not least boot-strapping, which is the art of rapidly creating customer revenues that fuel the growth of the company. As we examine who can access venture capital in the modern era and look at those who are invariably excluded from the wealth that venture-backed businesses can create for entrepreneurs, their families, investors, and the communities these players belong to, we acknowledge just how skewed the industry is towards nurturing and perpetuating its existing flywheels. The consequences of these flywheels are explored in this book, along with the substantial returns available from historically overlooked market segments. Investors are missing opportunities for higher financial returns by undervaluing high-performing companies led by diverse groups or by overvaluing white-male-led firms. Moreover, capital allocators may well be infringing their fiduciary duty to generate the most significant possible returns for their investors by not investing in diverse companies that could produce returns as high or even higher than white-male-led companies they are most familiar with backing.

Venture capital (VC) is invested by general partners in venture capital firms, who use their domain expertise to allocate high-risk capital into entrepreneurial ventures to generate significant returns on behalf of limited partners, who are most commonly pension funds, university endowments, state funds, foundations, and insurance companies, who do not usually act as direct investors in startup companies. Venture capital firms are compensated in two ways: annual management fees (usually 2% of the capital pledged by limited partners) and "carried interest," which is a percentage of the profits created by an investment fund (typically 20%). VC funds usually have a lifespan of seven to ten years, and the corporations that fund them frequently manage many funds simultaneously. In terms of payoffs, the venture capital model differs from other types of financing. Returns for venture capital investments do not often follow standard distribution curves but are skewed. The majority of the aggregate return is generated by a few exceptional investments, such as Tesla, Microsoft, Meta, Google, or Oracle.

Funding of this nature has proven pivotal for disrupting the way we work, produce, and live, as technology evolves and advances by investing in high-tech companies that promote the development of industries, support innovation, and drive economic growth. The benefits to society over the years have been described as immeasurable, while the casualties created by technological changes that disrupt labor markets and increase inequity are cited as necessary evils that are far outweighed by the essential innovation that leads to competitive advantage, productivity gains, and increased economic growth over the longer term. Yet, what are the long-term effects of capitalism at all costs? The cataclysmic impact on the environment, society, and governance structures over time are leading all too often towards climates in which wages are depressed as businesses compete on the price, over the quality, of goods; where unskilled workers are incentivized with punishments, over promotions; and where bubbles expand and eventually burst, usually to the detriment of those who are already the most vulnerable in society. Time and time again, these results demonstrate that existing models are not fit for purpose as inequality preponderates and poverty expands. Thus, were these premeditated, globalized, and impeccably organized models ever fit for purpose, or is a shift to a more sustainable modus operandi long overdue? Answering such a question effectively relies on accurate knowledge and examining the foundations upon which venture capital was built.

3.4 *The Overlooked Origins of VC*

Contrary to popular belief, the earliest forms of venture capital can be found long before the whaling industry took off. Other popular maritime money spinners, more commonly known as the transoceanic spice, tea, and slave trades, were instrumental in the creation of several innovations that shaped both modern venture capital and the systems it is inherently reliant upon, such as insurance, productization, leveraging equity and debt, economies of scale, high-risk, high-reward financing, and many more.

Venture capital has been widely accepted as existing in one form or another since the earliest forms of commercialization. Scholars, such as Harvard historian Tom Nicholas in his *VC: An American History*,[54] have accredited the first venture capital style investments to whaling, the transatlantic voyage of Christopher Columbus, and Georges Frédéric

---

54. https://www.hup.harvard.edu/catalog.php?isbn=9780674248267

Doriot,[55] who is seen as being the first venture capitalist to raise money from non-family sources—believing there was a strong business case for investing in entrepreneurs with the vision and acumen to create a future not yet imagined. Among each slightly varying narrative about how venture capital has evolved through the ages, from the financing of whaling ships that were to set sail on perilous waters, carrying precious cargo from one port to another and emblematic of Moby Dick; to the underwriting of risky expeditions leading to the discovery of new territories; and the founding of Doriot's American Research and Development Corporation (ARD) in 1946, the belief in an entrepreneur to execute the completion of tasks in which there is a high probability of failure and the promise of outsized returns if successful is the golden thread running through a complex and intricate tapestry of events.

Most fascinating is that the invention of venture capital is often ascribed to Americans—despite Doriot being French—with much of the activity being focused on post-World War II exploits. The "VC is an all-American invention" narrative essentially negates the part that the Europeans, mainly the British, played in the formation of venture capital and sweepingly omits the transatlantic slave trade, which was the predecessor of the whaling industry and the foundation for the insurance and banking industries to which venture capital has been intrinsically linked and remains heavily reliant upon today.

3.5   *How This Book Can Help*

Given the legacy of these financial industries, it is no wonder that the ethnic wealth gaps persist to the extent they do across the globe. The inequities that persist in society and the economy today can be redressed through the fairer distribution and allocation of venture capital and the potential for higher returns for the investors who choose to pursue the dividends that diversity offers.

This volume does not focus on the apportion of blame or reparations; that is a matter for a different forum. It seeks the commitment of those currently holding the purse strings, who have invariably profited off the

---

55. https://books.google.co.uk/books/about/Creative_Capital.html?id=wgKSot6XuYEC&redir_
    esc=

backs of Black and Brown bodies, to make access to venture capital fair and inclusive going forward.

If and when, for instance, Black and Latinx people enter the venture capital market, and they are unable to progress beyond positions in which they have no decision making power or access to carry, are we recreating patterns where these groups work for the system without being able to profit from it? Black and Brown funds across the globe recount stories of being unable to close their funds. At the same time, their white male and, in more and more instances now, female counterparts regale in the successes of well-funded and well-supported ventures that provide returns.

How can we avoid repeating the same behavioral patterns unless we examine how they arose and are perpetuated?

4 What's In This Book

In this collection of interviews, stories, and research, we use the momentum that has been building in recent years to expand the conversation about DEI, venture capital, and the startup ecosystem, and to inspire more concrete action.

In this book you'll find 43 in-depth conversations with a diverse group of researchers, investors, and entrepreneurs, making it one of the most comprehensive and diverse sets of perspectives on the startup ecosystem ever assembled in one place.

Our intent is that our voices will provide enough guidance and commentary to make sense of what we have heard through these conversations—spanning Europe and the US, and involving more than 85 interview partners.

This is a large collection. We encourage you to read it sequentially, or if you prefer, use the table of contents to find and jump into the conversations you wish to engage with.

Over 80 entrepreneurs, investors, and researchers from around the world were gracious enough to have conversations with us for this guide.

In Part I: History, we investigate the history of the venture capital industry and how we got here. The current homogeneity of VC (and the tech industry) has historical roots in the economic model of VCs—partnerships of GPs that are investing LPs' money—and the birth of the industry from old family money.[56] VCs make early-stage investments based on gut feelings,[57] excitement,[58] networks, and people, rather than market sizes and revenue growth. This facilitates the reproduction of pre-existing networks, often based on families, universities, and other business ties. We dive into how this came to be with two historical retrospectives, interviews with university professors on their research in these areas, and panel interviews with six female investors who came up early on in the US and UK venture industry.

In Part II: Experiences, we seek to expand common uses of the term "diversity" to include not just gender and ethnicity, but immigration status, socioeconomic background or class, educational background, disability, age, sexual orientation, and geography. Drawing on contributions

56. https://pitchbook.com/news/articles/
    whats-past-is-prologue-gilded-age-fortunes-in-vc-and-pe
57. https://www.forbes.com/sites/hbsworkingknowledge/2018/04/04/
    how-investors-use-gut-feel-to-manage-risk/#37e9dd904dc2
58. https://maxcam.socanth.cam.ac.uk/index.php/2018/12/06/
    fieldnote-1-berlin-august-2018-how-excitement-drives-the-venture-capital-industry/

from investors, operators, founders, and journalists, personal stories and narratives provide valuable insights to the situation on the ground through the eyes of those affected. Most importantly, it will become crucial going forward to understand how this kaleidoscope of dimensions intersect, a topic of conversation we pick up in this part, too.

Part III: Best Practices covers concrete action and best practices from a range of operators who have been pushing for change from *within* the ecosystem. Building on the conclusions drawn in Part I: History and the personal accounts in Part II: Experiences, this section provides inspiration for tangible action, based on best practices that have been tested in the industry. In the set of 17 interviews, we dive beyond research and numbers to speak to a plethora of overlooked GPs, ecosystem builders, LPs, and policymakers about their trailblazing experiments, in hopes of inspiring others to follow their lead.

In Part IV: New Ideas, we look beyond the VC ecosystem to share more radical and groundbreaking ideas. While we are confident that internal initiatives and the increased opening up of angel programs will help lead to long-term change, creating completely new flywheels is as important as improving old ones. From interviews with emerging VC managers to initiatives such as Zebras Unite,[20.1] Village Capital,[19.2] or the New Mittelstand,[20.2] a different set of actors is starting to push into the industry from the outside. We also observe how otherwise-established players such as Twitter[21.2] and the Nasdaq Entrepreneurial Center[21.4] have the potential to create new flywheels from outside the VC industry.

We close with a final overview in the conclusion.

◇IMPORTANT   Please note that all interviews have been lightly edited for clarity. We've done our best to preserve both the substance and style of each conversation.

We learned an incredible amount in researching and writing this volume, and the bottom line for us is clear: neither diversity, nor equity or inclusion in VC and tech have come as far as they should have given the intense focus on this area in recent years. Many of the past and ongoing efforts are laudable and have led to some changes, but we need more powerful ecosystem players to engage in more radical and tangible action to make a difference. We hope this volume can serve as one starting point to inspire momentum.

5 Acknowledgments

We want to thank, with all our hearts, everyone—over 80 entrepreneurs, investors, and researchers—who spoke to us so openly.

It was heartwarming that whomever we approached, they were willing to share their ideas and insights.[59] While coordinating calendars between up to six incredibly busy people across multiple time zones wasn't always simple and took effort and goodwill, we made it work collectively. Thank you everyone for believing in the common cause and pushing forward.

A special thanks obviously goes to the team at Holloway; we went from what Johannes thought looked like a scam message on LinkedIn (there are lots of those in this world), to hours and hours spent talking to our phenomenal editors Rachel and Carolyn with lots of freedom, and input from Holloway CEO Josh. Without your support and belief in our unlikely coupling and project, this wouldn't have been possible. Thank you from the bottom of our hearts—also for having such patience with us! A very special thank you also to Eana, who helped us with all the transcriptions forming the basis for the interviews—this book wouldn't have been possible without you!

Lastly, we also want to say a big thank you to our families. For Erika, supporting five children, parents, and a house renovation while dealing with COVID-19, doing a PhD, and running a startup, this was likely one of the toughest periods in her life. For Johannes, Rebecca's endless patience with late-night and weekend work, and loud interview calls over months (while building her own company) was quintessential—thank you! A lot of effort and love has gone into this project and we hope it can inspire at least some people to push for a more diverse, equitable, and profitable funding ecosystem.

---

59. We did have a single disappointing exception of a big-name fund that refused to talk to us. But overall we found unequivocally open doors.

PART I: HISTORY

6 Railways and Whaling Aren't Where VC Started

In an examination of important historical texts relating to the transoceanic spice and tea trades, the transatlantic slave trade, and slave owner compensation payments and their uses, we have been able to piece together an evidence-based account that traces venture capital back to the transatlantic slave trade, while identifying direct links between the regimes and practices, methods, customs, and traditions developed by enslavers, ship captains, and their financiers and how the venture capital and high-growth entrepreneurial industries still operate today.

We've split this historical retrospective between two chapters, one on the East India Company,^{§7} and one on slavery and America's industrial rise.^{§8} This included work from scholars such as Eric Williams and Joseph Inikori, the New York Times podcast series *1619*,[60] and discussions with Professor Nick Draper$^{\S9.2}$ of the Centre for the Study of the Legacies of British Slavery established at University College London, and Professor Terry Irwin$^{\S9.1}$ of the Transition Design Institute at Carnegie Mellon University.

◇ IMPORTANT We do not profess to be historians. While corroborated through the academic literature, this data in no way claims to be a complete examination of the transatlantic slave trade, nor the many horrors within or following it. Dates are generalized by century rather than by decade in some cases, for example.

These first two chapters aim to debunk popularized myths that portray capitalism (including the banking and insurance industries), the 19th-century railroad (US) and railway (UK) era, or the 19th-century whaling industry as the foundation of venture capital. The earliest forms of ven-

---

60. https://www.nytimes.com/column/1619-project

ture capital existed long before that. From the early 1500s forward, the
Portuguese, Spanish, English, French, Dutch, and others fought to control
the resources of the emerging transatlantic world and worked together to
enslave the Indigenous people of Africa and the Americas. The transatlantic slave trade began when the Portuguese initially kidnapped and
packed no fewer than 400 people at a time on ships that sailed from the
west coast of Africa, taking enslaved Africans back to Europe.[61] Pirates
regularly captured ships, and these risk-ridden voyages often ended in
high mortality or theft of the cargo.[62] The system was not primitive, as
is often reported. It was premeditated, globalized, and impeccably organized. Traffickers shared information via written documents, including
letters, lease agreements, bills of sale, logbooks, and passports. Everyone
involved in a slaving venture paid close attention to the materials related
to their business transactions. Often, maritime cargoes were owned com-
munally through the distribution of individual shares. These collectively
constructed legal partnerships opened early transoceanic trading opportunities to a diverse group of traders, colonists, and mariners. They created a decentralized mercantile trade that dispersed profits throughout
communities engaged in the trade of enslaved people. The transatlantic
slave trade and its associated industries created great wealth for many
individuals, families, and countries in the West. It simultaneously
wreaked devastation on the African diaspora, where economic and agri-
cultural development and intergenerational wealth have trailed ever
since.

As Tom Nicholas's recent book on the history[63] of the American VC
industry notes, the founding fathers of venture capital were also connected to the big, white industrial families, from the Rockefellers (the
first money behind the extant VC firm Venrock in Palo Alto in 1969) to
the Phipps and Carnegies (which spun out Bessemer Venture Partners in
the early 1900s). Reproduction of wealth and power has since been at the
heart of the industry, with some of the very early venture funds—Venrock,
Bessemer, and Greylock among them—still operating and making money
for these families today. Again, whose money it is matters: venture cap-

---

61. Saunders, A. C. de C. M. *A Social History of Black Slaves and Freedmen in Portugal,
    1441-1555.* New York: Cambridge University Press, 1982, 11.

62. Bowen, H. V. "The shipping losses of the British East India Company, 1750–1813."
    International Journal of Maritime History, 32.2 (2020): 323-336.

63. https://www.hup.harvard.edu/catalog.php?isbn=9780674988002

ital does not and has never operated on the use of "objective" financial tools such as discounted cash flow, used in investment banking and leverage buyout (private equity). Decisions are made much more on "gut feel" and often "mirrortocracy" (identity-based investing) wins out over meritocracy.

Following our historical summaries, we've included the two interviews with university professors we mentioned above: Terry Irwin on researching the historical inequality of the venture system, and Nick Draper on tracing money from British slave ownership to modern finance and venture capital. We conclude this part with two panels with female investors who are veterans of both the UK$^{\S9.3}$ and US venture ecosystems,$^{\S9.4}$ for their perspective on how the industry has changed over the past three decades.

Overall, Part I: History paints a picture of how VC reached this point: from the misconceptions of its origins and the troubling realities, to the modern history and perspectives within it. This combination of research and interviews sets the scene for opening up the current discussion about diversity, equity, and inclusion (DEI) in venture capital.

7 History of Venture I: The East India Company

7.1 *The World's Most Powerful Business*

Before Tesla, Microsoft, Meta, Google, or Oracle, there was the East India Company (EIC), a company formed in 1599 to establish a British presence in the lucrative Indian spice trade. The EIC rose to become a British colonial powerhouse. It traded and taxed, persuaded and extorted, enriched and looted, and was so profitable and powerful that it single-handedly dominated the majority of the Indian continent, owned an army twice the size of the British Army at the time, and monopolized a plethora of transoceanic trades. By the 19th century, the EIC had earned the title of the world's most powerful business, with control of more than half of Britain's trade.

However, due to years of misrule, malpractice, and the 1770 famine in Bengal, where the company had installed a military dictatorship in 1757, the company's territory revenues plummeted, forcing it to apply for a £1.5M emergency loan from the British government in 1772 to avoid bankruptcy.[64] The EIC was among the earliest in a long line of companies considered "too big to fail." Thus, it was bailed out by the British government. However, that was inevitably the beginning of the end for the company, as scrutiny following the bailout led the government to seek direct control of the EIC. Following a lengthy decline, the British government finally ended the company's rule in India in 1858. By 1874, the company had been reduced to a skeleton of its former self and was dissolved.

By that point, the EIC had been involved in everything from cultivating opium in India and illegally exporting it to China in exchange for coveted Chinese goods, to the transatlantic slave trade (it conducted slaving expeditions, transported slaves, and used slave labor throughout the 17th and 18th centuries). Modern capitalism may have since eclipsed the EIC, but its legacy is still felt throughout the world.

The EIC is significant for three reasons.

First, the EIC was formed as a joint-stock company, an antecedent to the modern-day corporation (with the exception of unlimited liability). The company is owned by its investors, with each investor owning shares based on the number of stocks purchased.[65] Indeed the term investment is first used in the context of investing money as part of a multi-stage process that converts goods or money into an alternate form that can subsequently be used to purchase other goods. As part of its definition of commercial investment ("the investing of money or capital"), the Oxford English Dictionary describes the earliest use of investment as "the employment of money to purchase Indian goods."

Second, the trade being embarked upon by the EIC was novel and risky, with the potential for exceptionally high rewards. The company intended to command market share in the Indian spice trade, which had, until that point, been monopolized by the Spanish and Portuguese.[66]

Third, the company's management was economical, deploying an innovative method of slavery that kept them lean and efficient as they scaled operations. During the first two decades of its existence, the East

---

64. Hooker, M. B. "The East India Company and the Crown 1773–1858." *Malaya Law Review*, vol. 11, no. 1, 1969, p 5.

65. Robins, Nick. *The Corporation That Changed the World: How the East India Company Shaped the Modern Multinational*. Pluto Press, 2012. 24.

66. Robins, Nick. *The Corporation That Changed the World: How the East India Company Shaped the Modern Multinational*. Pluto Press, 2012. 44-45.

India Company was run from the home of its governor, Sir Thomas Smythe, with just six permanent staff. In 1700, 35 permanent employees worked in a small London office. In 1785, it ruled a vast empire of millions of people with a permanent staff of 159 in London. By 1800, the company controlled an army of 200,000 officers who enabled the EIC to both rule and economically exploit India while enjoying a monopoly on all trade along the coast of Guinea, including the traffic in slaves.[67]

7.2 *East India Company's Formation and Financing*

The founding of the EIC at a meeting in September 1599 brought together a group of investors whose participation in risky new overseas ventures drove England's commercial and imperial growth. The establishment of the EIC depended on the investors' decision to entrust their wealth and reputation to a company with no track record, limited state support, and no presence in the Asian markets in which it would operate. Investing substantial sums in the EIC must have been a frightening and highly risky choice, especially for inexperienced investors.[68]

Despite the impact that the EIC would have on finance, investment, and empire over the next two centuries, we continue to treat the EIC as a homogeneous, monolithic enterprise rather than as an organization composed of and dependent upon what is today seen as venture capitalist and angel investor networks—a collective of investors who, either as individuals or collective groups, invest their money into high-risk, high-reward potential companies for an equity stake, which, in the case of the EIC, the company's management team transformed into goods that were vendible or convertible into spices that could be sent back to Europe and sold there.

The EIC's formulation occurred within an intensely interconnected environment that helped create an investing public before the financial revolution, demonstrating that early variants of venture capital-style investments were being made long before the maritime pursuit of whaling. The 1599 petition, which included "the names of such persons to undertake the voyage to the East Indies," mentioned 101 contributions

---

67. Kaye, John. Story. In *Administration of the East India Company: A History of Indian Progress*. Gale Ecco, Making Of Mode, 2010. 110,

68. Robins, Nick. *The Corporation That Changed the World: How the East India Company Shaped the Modern Multinational*. Pluto Press, 2012. 23–24

ranging from £100 to £3,000, and totaling £30,1336. There was a varied cross section of contributors, comprising both new and inexperienced investors and those with significant investment experience. The most common contribution was £200, with 58 investors (57.4%) pledging this sum. The average contribution size was slightly more than £298. Further analysis of the 101 investments reveals that several commitments were from pairs or small groups. Thirty-six of the total contributions (35.6%) were made in this way. Separating these grouped contributions reveals 136 named investors, although the total number of investors would have been slightly higher because some are not named and are merely listed as investing "in company" with another individual.[69]

Diverse types of relationships brought individuals together to invest, and novice investors were likely and able to follow the lead of more seasoned partners. Among the investors, 82 had never invested before, while 54 had participated in previous ventures. Through familial ties, livery company connections, and shared business experience, investors in early-modern London formed overlapping networks that supported the EIC. These networks enabled investors to discuss the trade with seasoned investors, spread their risk with reputable partners, and acquire the necessary expertise to engage in previously impossible ventures. Thus, also allowing the EIC to draw upon the expertise and financial resources of investors including some who had traded, raided, explored, settled, stolen, and fought across much of the globe. This methodology of following experienced lead investors who are able to conduct appropriate due diligence into the company requiring investment persists across venture deals today.

7.3 *Mechanisms of Venture Financing: Funding Individual Voyages*

Composite investment strategies that relied on accumulating small parcels of goods and currency to establish commercially viable cargo financed early capital-intensive voyages. Cargoes were separated into

---

69. Smith, 2020.[70]

70. https://www.cambridge.org/core/services/aop-cambridge-core/content/view/
    9E32D62882F03C60D0115697FDCD34F2/S0018246X2000045Xa.pdf/
    the-social-networks-of-investment-in-early-modern-england.pdf

shares to raise additional finance. Shipowners and merchants used several strategies to limit financial risks and make investments more attractive.

Multiple shareholders owned split shares of a single cargo, defined by allotting proportions of space within the ship's hold. Seamen were often remunerated with free cargo space instead of wages to reduce costs further and keep profits high. Individual investments in cargoes, including enslaved people, were also divided, enabling many people to contribute small amounts to a single commercial mission.

This became a popular way to fund voyages among multiple companies. Articles for the slave ship *Sally*, 1764, listing the names, duties, and wages of each crewman, confirm that Esek Hopkins, the brig's master, was promised £50 per month, plus a "privilege"—a commission—of ten barrels of rum and ten enslaved Africans to sell on his own account. The crew included one "Negro boy," Edward Abbie, understood to be Hopkins's indentured servant.[71]

7.4 *Reducing Risk and Increasing Rewards*

The EIC differed from other enterprises of its time by advancing from merely spending money (for the purchase of Indian goods) from which a profit was expected. Their "investments" put money and goods to another use. It is the transformational power of investment that changes one commodity into another commodity, then into a profit. This productive or "value-added" use of capital was used to drive profitability and provide a substantial return to the company's investors.

According to Thomas Mun, a director of the EIC and author of texts including *A Discourse of Trade from England unto the East-Indies and England's Treasure by Forraign Trade,* it was completely legitimate to procure produce from India at a low cost, transform those produce into English-owned goods, and then sell those "transformed" commodities in Europe at a significant profit to enrich the UK.

He wrote: "It is plain, that we make a far greater stock by gain upon these Indian Commodities, than those nations do where they grow, and

---

71. From the Brown Family Business Records collection[72] at the John Carter Brown Library at Brown University.

72. https://digitalpublications.brown.edu/projects/first-readings-2020/resource-collection/historical-documents

to whom they properly appertain, being the natural wealth of their Countries. ... Wares do not need to "properly appertain" (to belong as a possession) to England for them to represent (or "procure") potential profits for England."

Furthermore, he claimed that "neither is there less honor and judgment by growing rich (in this manner) upon the stock of other Nations, than by an industrious encrease of our own means."

In addition to the transformation of one commodity into another or of a raw material into an artificial product, there is also a transformation of ownership that is justified by (imaginary) English industry. According to Mun, the "natural wealth" of India now "properly belongs" to the English, both materially, as a result of their industry, and discursively, as a result of his own series of substitutions that provide a mirror image of the EIC's complex multilateral trade. Consequently, men from modest origins returned to the UK extremely wealthy, while enlisted men were motivated to fight by the appeal of the money that could be made from pillaging conquered resources.

This business model flowed through the core of the EIC's economic activities, and the West African slave trade was an essential element of ensuring that profits were maximized. The profits gained paid off the debts on factories in Surat, Madras, and Bengal. West African slaves were also integral to the company's success in colonizing St. Helena—an island in the Atlantic Ocean, 1,200 miles off the coast of Angola, which served as a port for the company's Indian Ocean trade. On his first journey, the island's first governor, Captain John Dutton, was told to acquire "five or six Blacks, all able men and women," from St. Iago in the Cape Verde Islands to begin colonizing the deserted island.

The volume of the EIC's slave cargos was another distinguishing factor in its methods of trade. Between 1622 and 1772, the average EIC ship carrying slaves carried only 47 people.[73] A comparative British slave ship belonging to the Royal African Company typically logged 299 slaves embarking and 241 slaves disembarking. In the Atlantic, where slave ships only carried human cargo, the sale of 47 slaves was insufficient to cover the expenses of the transoceanic voyage. However, by layering its slave trade onto its established networks for transporting fabric, spices, tea, and handicrafts, the EIC was able to perpetuate what would have otherwise

73. Allen, Richard Blair. *European Slave Trading in the Indian Ocean, 1500–1850.* Athens: Ohio University Press, 2015. 38.

been an economically unviable trade in human cargo. On the majority of slave-carrying EIC ships, slaves were neither the primary cargo nor the primary goal of the voyage. Small slave shipments through mixed-cargo slave ships aided the company in lowering the enormous overhead costs connected with the slave trade. Mixed-cargo trade and its related advantages became achievable as a result of the company's response to its own internal demand for slave labor, profiting not from the sale of slaves but rather from their productive capacity of slaves within the company. Innovatively, EIC's main benefit from the slave trade was the productivity of its slave labor force.

Smaller slave cargoes allowed the EIC to mitigate the inherent dangers and expenses of large-scale slave trading. Despite the fact that the slave trade might be a successful enterprise—in the Atlantic, the average rate of return for investors was approximately 9%—slave voyages were nonetheless high-cost ventures.[74] Because they required ship modifications, larger crews, and, notably during times of war, more wages, these expeditions had a greater risk and higher fixed expenses than others. The majority of ships used by Europeans to transport slaves in the Atlantic and Indian Ocean trades were not originally designed to handle human cargo, they therefore needed to be adapted to safely transport people. A ten-foot wooden bulkhead, which bisected the ship and used to separate male and female slaves, was one of the most common characteristics of slave ships. The bulkhead might also assist the crew in establishing a strong defensive position in the case of a slave revolt. Modifications such as the bulkhead were not as important for small numbers of slaves in mixed-cargo holds, since the potential of rebellion was far smaller. Avoiding alterations lowered the overhead expenses for slave-carrying EIC ships and provided the company with an incentive to pursue mixed-cargo trading. On one occasion in 1670, the EIC ordered four ships to purchase 40 slaves from St. Iago in the Cape Verde Islands. These ships were the *Unicorn*, the *John and Martha*, the *Satisfaction*, and the *John and Margaret*.[75] Although all four ships were en route to the same destinations, the captains were directed to split the captives evenly among the vessels. If there were only ten slaves

---

74. Anstey, Roger. "The Profitability of the Slave Trade in the 1840s." Annals of the New York Academy of Sciences 292.1 (1977): 84.
75. Letter to the Company's Factors at Bantam, 18 January 1670, India Office Records, Letter Books, E/3/87, fol. 208v,; Today, St. Iago is the island of Santiago in the Cape Verde Islands.

on board, the ships would not have required adaptations to secure the human cargo.

Because carrying fewer slaves reduced the risk of insurrection, company ships were able to sail with smaller crews while maintaining similar crew-to-slave ratios. During the Atlantic slave trade, a ship's crew was often double that of a merchant vessel of comparable size. The expenses associated with maintaining a big crew on a slave ship could account for as much as 18% of the total journey expenses. Smaller slave loads allowed the company to maintain a steady, commercially successful slave trade. Smaller, integrated slave cargoes permitted EIC ships to spend less time in port waiting for cargo. In addition to boosting the voyage's efficiency, minimizing time at port lessened the ship's vulnerability to pirate attacks.

7.5 *Profit Maximization Through the Transfer of Slaves*

The EIC's mixed-cargo slave trade was further distinctive in that not all of the slaves were purchased by the company; many were born into slavery at the company's holdings and then moved to another fort. When EIC directors in London received a request for slaves from one of their agents, they would first look to the slaves they already owned and attempt to transfer them. The EIC's slave trade strategy relied heavily on the transfer of slaves between holdings. According to the estimations of Richard Allen, as many as one-third of the slaves aboard EIC ships were transfers—a sizeable proportion given that transfer requests were consistently smaller than purchase requests. The company authorized at least 77 transfer voyages involving at least 1,040 slaves between 1639 and 1787.

Similar to the mixed-cargo slave trade, the company fused transfers onto its existing trading networks, making transfers both possible and efficient. If the directors deemed a transfer necessary, they would assign it to the next ship that would pass both ports, thereby reducing costs and voyage durations. The transfer of slaves rarely incurred any additional sunk costs, as the ships used needed to pass through both destinations to accomplish its primary objective. The only expense incurred by the company was the captain's wages—typically four pounds per slave.

The EIC was able to reap additional benefits from the specialized skills and knowledge of English culture that its slaves acquired as a result of the reorganization of its non-free labor force that was made possible by slave transfers. At St. Helena, where the company frequently experimented with new crops and goods to maximize the island's productivity and value, these reorganizations were particularly advantageous. During the first five years that the company possessed St. Helena, it sent multiple requests to its agents in Surat, requesting that they send indigo seeds and slaves who "knew how to sow it and then perfect it, and advised the Governor of St. Helena on the particulars." Bencoolen, the company's primary fort on the island of Sumatra, was a particularly dangerous location for EIC employees due to environmental and diplomatic factors, which increased the value of having experienced slaves.[76] The fort at Bencoolen is frequently described in company correspondence as a "sickly" and "fever-infested" location that sent Englishmen "to their eternal homes." Despite the fact that slave transfers reduced the EIC's overall trade volume, they demonstrate the crucial role slavery played in the company's ability to control territory and maximize profits.

7.6 *Weathering the South Sea Bubble*

The South Sea Bubble describes a series of events surrounding the plan to convert a significant amount of British national debt into equity shares of the South Sea Company (SSC) in 1720. The rise and fall of the stock market during the South Sea Bubble is still one of the most heavily discussed events in history.

In 1711, the SSC was founded with a capital stock of more than £9M. It was established to purchase existing short-term government debt and help manage the national debt in a similar way to the Bank of England. The Company also intended to conduct business with the Spanish Empire.[77] Spanish America gained popularity as a more promising trading region than India and the Far East because the market was more accessible and traditional English exports like textile and iron items were more likely to be purchased. Following the conclusion of the Treaty of Utrecht (1712), the SSC was awarded exclusive rights to trade with Spanish America—the so-called South Seas—on behalf of the British government. The SSC also secured a 30-year contract as the sole supplier of slaves to the

---

76. Allen, Richard. "Slavery in a Remote but Global Place: the British East India Company and Bencoolen, 1685-1825." Social and Education History (2018). 155.

77. Section V. A., Scott, 1910.

South Seas, known as the Asiento de Negros. Britain already had colonies in the Caribbean—and consequently, a significant share of the market for slave trading in the Western Hemisphere. The firm appeared to be well positioned in this lucrative new market.

In the autumn of 1719, however, a new war with Spain halted the SSC's trade with the South Sea. Unlike the EIC with its robust Asian trade, the SSC had little room for maneuver. The company's proposed solution to this dilemma was to again attempt to convert government debt into new equity shares. The scale of the proposed scheme was unprecedented, except insofar as it was inspired by the French legal system. By the end of 1719, John Law had successfully converted all French national debt into shares of the newly founded Compagnie des Indes, which monopolistically merged international trade, national banking, and tax collection. Some of Law's system was evident in the SSC's initial proposals, where the conversion of British national debt into South Sea shares was explored with the government, the EIC, and the Bank of England (BoE).[78] The EIC and the BoE, like the SSC, were both "big money" companies, meaning that both had made substantial loans to the government to justify their chartered existences. Exchanging all British national debt for South Sea shares would have posed an existential threat to these companies, so the plan evolved to excluding the debt already held by the EIC and the BoE and converting the remaining national debt into South Sea shares.

The EIC traded slaves between Madagascar and the Western Hemisphere, while the South Sea Company supplied the Royal African Company with slaves from West Africa.[79] The EIC directors were occupied with the outfitting of trading ships and the collection of multi-cargo loads, including bullion that would have to be transported to the Far East by these ships.

As a result of the share-price crash in the United Kingdom, a large number of investors were ruined, and the national economy shrank substantially. The scheme's founders engaged in insider trading by purchasing debt in advance in order to profit from their prior knowledge of the timing of national debt consolidations. Huge bribes were offered to politicians in exchange for their support of the necessary Acts of Parliament for the scheme. Money from the SSC was used to trade in its own shares,

78. Dickson, 1967.
79. Davies, 1957.

and certain individuals who purchased shares were given loans backed by those shares to use for the purchase of additional shares. The public was led to believe that the company would make excessive profits from trade with South America, but the inflated share prices ended up being more than the company's real earnings from slave trading.

According to Chaudhuri (1978), in attempts to reduce the effects of the burst bubble on foreign exchanges, the directors of the BoE and the EIC met in the middle of September 1720 to discuss the shortage of capital in London. By the end of the month, "an international crisis was developing with full force," and in 1721, "the February description of the winter events written by the EIC's Committee of Correspondence contains all the ingredients of a classic liquidity crisis."[80] After the bubble burst, a parliamentary investigation was held to determine the causes, the SSC was eventually restructured and continued to operate for over a century.

The EIC was in a position to weather the storms experienced in 1720 as a result of prior profit maximization and a conservative dividend policy in previous years. Undistributed portions of strong profits earned between 1710 and 1716 were used to fund a reserve. The business continued to operate throughout and after the bubble. After 1722, the company was able to finance its voyages despite encountering greater than usual financial difficulties. Two years of trade losses in 1721 and 1722 led to a decline in cash reserves, but it was not until 1723 that the dividend rate was reduced to coincide with falling interest rates. The years 1717–1727 were turbulent for the EIC, but in the six years following 1727, the company's profits increased by an average of 14.5% annually.

The EIC endured the storm created by the South Sea Bubble. Its shares continued to be actively traded securities. In 1719–1720, £3.2M of stock was owned by around 1,700 investors, by 1723 there were about 1,900 owners of the EIC's stock.[82]

---

80. Chaudhuri, K. (1978). Financial results. In *The Trading World of Asia and the English East India Company: 1660–1760* (pp. 411-452). Cambridge: Cambridge University Press. [81]

81. https://doi.org/10.1017/CBO9780511563263.020

82. Mays and Shay, 2011.[83]

83. https://www.st-andrews.ac.uk/~wwwecon/CDMA/papers/wp1109.pdf

7.7 *Too Big to Fail*

A fundamental belief that economic gain occurred at the expense of others lay at the heart of the EIC and encouraged the annihilation of competitors and the plundering of resources of foreign lands to attain economic supremacy. The company launched attacks and waged war due to the lucrative nature of victory. Officers received annuities and bribes from aligned "leaders" installed on the thrones of formerly noncompliant rulers.

As wars grew more expensive, however, bribery, prize money, and plunder were insufficient to cover military expenses and a series of unresolved wars drained the EIC's cash reserves. Consequently, the business took the next logical step: tax exploitation. Taxation slowed the export of bullion overseas, a significant benefit in mercantilist thought, and maintained a positive balance sheet. This money was also used to fund lobbying efforts to protect the company's monopoly.

The Bengal famine of 1770, which killed ten million people, exacerbated dire financial conditions and heightened public concerns about corruption and despotism in India under British rule. The decision to increase taxes during the famine, in addition to earlier mandates to plant specific crops and regulations against hoarding, further exacerbated the situation and proved to be a step too far on the part of the EIC's leadership. The company's stock price plummeted as investors withdrew funds, and by 1772 the EIC was bankrupt, facing dissolution, and pleading for aid from Parliament.

The lobbyists' response was an imperialist version of the phrase "too big to fail." Insolvency meant the end of the hard-won British dominance in the subcontinent. The argument endured despite France overcoming the Royal Navy's naval dominance to reclaim Indian possessions. The Regulating Act of 1773 stipulated a £1.5M loan and capped dividends. In addition, employees were banned from accepting bribes and illegal donations, and a governor general of Bengal was appointed to enforce the regulations.

Parliament's error was in opting for a compromise and attempting to regulate the company rather than liquidating it, or leaving it, which proved to be unenforceable. Neither the politicians in London, nor the governor in Calcutta, could compel the EIC to comply with government regulations. Fifteen more years of corruption and war ensued. Parliament lost patience after passing additional legislation in 1784 and took decisive action. It impeached Governor General Warren Hastings, who was appointed in 1773. The chief prosecutor was Edmund Burke, who noted:[84]

> *Mr. Hastings's government was one whole system of oppression, robbery of individuals, spoliation of the public, and suppression of the entire system of the English government. … I impeach Warren Hastings for high crimes and misdemeanors … in the name of the House of Commons of Great Britain, whose national honor he has sullied. I impeach him on behalf of the people of India, whose laws, rights, and liberties he has subverted … whose property he has destroyed and whose country he has left desolate. I impeach him in accordance with the eternal laws of justice that he has disregarded.*

Parliament renewed the company's charter for another 20 years in 1793 and exonerated Hastings the following year. Predictably, the outcome was more of the same.

Continued wars in the 19th century, specifically the conquest of the Northwest Territories and Punjab, strained finances and prompted Parliament to intervene once more. In 1813, the company lost its monopoly on all products besides tea and trade with China, and it ceased operations in 1833. The Indian Rebellion of 1857 and the subsequent Government of India Act 1858 led to the British Crown assuming direct control of India in the form of the new British Raj.[86] Just over a century after victory at the Battle of Plassey marked the beginning of British ascendancy, the EIC collapsed.

84. Conniff, James. "Burke and India: The Failure of The Theory of Trusteeship." *Political Research Quarterly* 46, no. 2 (1993): page 300. [85]

85. https://doi.org/10.2307/448889

86. Yadav, Nikhil, Indore Institute of Law. "East India Company Origin and Impact." International Journal of Trend in Scientific Research and Development (2018).

8   History of Venture II: Slavery and America's Industrial Rise

8.1   *The Dawn of the Insurance Industry*

Slave trading was a risky and perilous business. In addition to the dangers posed by the sea in the 18th century, there was always the possibility of a slave revolt. While insurance for suppressing rebellions at sea did not cover losses owing to deaths caused by suppressing the rebellion if fewer than 10% of the enslaved cargo were killed, the insurance industry was established to spread these risks.

Slavery is the most extreme manifestation of the insurance principle of placing a high value on human life. In 1790, the slave trade and the transportation of slave-grown produce from the West Indies accounted for at least one-third of the premiums collected by the London Assurance Company. In the 18th century, insurance flourished and developed its capital accumulation logic, playing a significant role in the rise of finance capitalism in London. The 1720 Act of Parliament, which permitted the formation of two joint-stock insurance companies heavily involved in insuring the slave trade, facilitated the formation of Royal Exchange Insurance, later the Guardian Royal Exchange, and now a subsidiary of AXA, and the London Insurance, which was subsequently merged with Royal and Sun Alliance. The most important business for Lloyd's of London was the West Indian slave trade.[87]

The 1781 tragedy of the British slave ship *Zong* is conspicuously absent from histories of capitalism and venture capital. However, scholars have argued convincingly that the need to insure against losses in the slave trade was a crucial factor in the development of the modern insurance industry, which led to the establishment of the venture capital industry as we know it today.

From Liverpool's docks, the *Zong* sailed to the African coast, where slaves were loaded and transported to Jamaica. The small Dutch ship was purchased by Richard Hanley for William Gregson and others. Gregson had long invested in slavery, and they purchased insurance to cover the shipment of their slaves. For a successful voyage, a capable and sea-

---

87. Inikori. *Africans and the Industrial Revolution in England.* 2002, pp. 313-361; Rupprecht. "Excessive Memories: Slavery, Insurance and Resistance." 2007, pp. 12, 15, 21.

soned captain was required to manage the crew, cargo, and commercial activities. Luke Collingwood's appointment as *Zong* captain marked the beginning of a series of poor choices. Collingwood had completed nine to ten Atlantic voyages, but never as captain.[88] When the surgeon-turned-captain assumed command in Africa, he assembled his crew and loaded slaves using unorthodox methods.

In Africa, crew recruitment was even more difficult than in England. Prior to an already perilous voyage, Captain Collingwood knew few of his crew members. The majority of captains carefully inspected each slave and loaded them in small numbers. Collingwood was inherited by 244 slaves. He had neither chosen nor known them, and they had occupied the ship for months without his knowledge or consent. Collingwood loaded the 110-ton ship with 459 enslaved individuals, despite the fact that ships of that size typically carried only 193.

The voyage across the Atlantic was difficult. First, water containers began to leak, depleting the crew's supply. This complicated their extensive journey. Jamaica was, on average, 61 days away. The *Zong* was at sea for over a hundred days. The captain fell ill, began hallucinating, and lost control of the ship. The crew threw one-third of the chained Africans into the ocean and condemned them to die out of fear that the ship's water supply would run out and the entire cargo would perish without recourse to insurance. James Walvin, author of The Zong: A Massacre, the Law and the End of Slavery, argues that the *Zong*'s crew was conducting the slave trade as usual. Consequently, this crime initially received little attention. However, Gregson and the other Liverpool cargo owners later filed a claim with their insurance provider for the 132 Africans who had died.

The subsequent trial combined sentimentality and humanism to foster abolitionist views in the 19th century, resulting in many Britons viewing the murder of 132 Africans aboard the *Zong* as cruel and immoral. This marked the beginning of the abolition of slavery in the United Kingdom.[89]

---

88. Krikler, J. "The Zong and the Lord Chief Justice." History Workshop Journal, 2007. 64(1), 31.

89. Fehskens, Erin M. "Accounts Unpaid, Accounts Untold: M. NourbeSe Philip's Zong! And the Catalogue." *Callaloo* 35, no. 2 (2012): 407–408.

8.2 *Across the Pond in the Southern Seas*

By the beginning of the Civil War in 1861, more millionaires per capita lived in the Mississippi Valley than in any other part of the United States. Cotton grown and picked by enslaved workers was America's most valuable export. Slaves were worth more than all the country's railways and industry put together. There were more financial institutions per square mile in New Orleans than in New York City. What made the cotton economy boom in the United States, and not in all the other far-flung parts of the world with climates and soil suitable to the crop, was a combination of the UK and America's unflinching willingness to use violence on nonwhite people to exploit seemingly endless supplies of land and labor. Given a choice between modernity and barbarism, prosperity and poverty, lawfulness and cruelty, democracy and totalitarianism, America chose all of the above. By the eve of the Civil War, slave laborers, on average, picked 400% more cotton than their counterparts did 60 years earlier. Undeniably an incredible amount of productivity, the system was pulling as much out of its enslaved workforce as it possibly could.[90]

Enslavers expanded their operations aggressively to capitalize on economies of scale inherent to maximizing crops in America and the Caribbean, buying more enslaved workers, investing in better tools, and experimenting and iterating products to achieve optimal outputs. They established convoluted organizational structures, with a central office staffed by owners and lawyers in charge of resource allocation and long-term planning, and multiple divisional units accountable for different operations. Punishments rose and fell based on the demands of the market—the price of goods in the UK was directly correlated with the level of discipline inflicted on the enslaved to keep their work rates high.

To expand their operations and make more money, they needed more capital. So they took mortgages. The way in which mortgages work is a bank lends the money to buy a house, and against that loan, the asset (typically the house itself) is leveraged. If the loan is not paid in full, the house is seized by the creditor. The concept of mortgages is not new to either the UK or America, yet, the concept of bricks, mortar, or land being leveraged is not where mortgages started. The industry began with enslaved people. Plantation owners approached banks for loans to procure further

---

90. Matthew Desmond, via the 1619 project[91] for the *New York Times*, 2019.

91. https://www.nytimes.com/column/1619-project

land, resources, and slave labor, using the slaves they already owned as collateral.

A newly formed banking industry was used by enslavers to mortgage their slaves to finance the scaling of their operations. The bundling of these debts created bonds that are still used today, and investors were paid dividends from profits made on the mortgaged enslaved people. Today, this is called securitizing debt, and at the time, it ostensibly allowed global markets to invest into the business of slavery. State-chartered banks took slave-backed mortgages from plantation owners, bundled the collective debts into bonds, and sold those bonds to investors throughout the Western world. Thus, when owners made payments on their mortgages, investors received a return. Securitizing debt in this way became an incredibly efficient way of pumping global capital into the American slave economy at the time. Historians have shown that most of the credit powering the American slave economy came from the London money market.

Between 1820 and 1860, approximately 875,000 enslaved people were transported to the western frontier via the domestic slave trade.[92] As men moved westward, credit played a crucial role in their economic success. As shrewd managers of their financial portfolios, planters could profit from the cotton produced by their slaves and use this human property to acquire more land and slaves. Slaveholders frequently pledged the same human property to multiple creditors. The securitization of enslaved people brought these men one step closer to the fortunes that drove them westward in the first place.

Similarly to slaveholders in the Upper South and factory owners or merchants in the North, settlers in the Southwest relied on loans to finance their speculative endeavors and the day-to-day operations of their plantations, such as the purchase of shoes for their slaves, seed for the upcoming season, or new tracts of land. However, this credit system was not as standardized or regulated as it is in the modern day. For elite planters, local merchants known as "factors" provided the necessary loans

---

92. Deyle, Steven. *Carry Me Back: The Domestic Slave Trade in American Life.* Oxford: Oxford University Press, 2005; Tadman, Michael. *Speculators and Slaves: Masters, Traders, and Slaves in the Old South.* Madison: The University of Wisconsin Press, 1989; Gudmestad, Robert H. *A Troublesome Commerce: The Transformation of the Interstate Slave Trade.* Baton Rouge: Louisiana State University Press, 2003.

for cotton production, typically "advances" on the following season's harvest, which elements would sell on commission in the Atlantic market.[93]

Britain officially abolished the African slave trade in 1807, yet Britain and much of Europe continued to fund slavery in the United States until the 1860s. The total slave population in the Americas was around 330,000 in 1700, it was just shy of three million by 1800, and it finally peaked at over six million in the 1850s. Slave-backed mortgage bonds can be traced back to the UK recipients of slave-owner compensation payments. Reparations to the tune of £20M (approximately £15B in today's money) were made by the British government and funded until 2015 by the British taxpayer to those "adversely affected" by the abolition of slavery.

Yes, you read that correctly. The people who were compensated at the abolition of slavery were those who had been enslavers rather than those who had been enslaved. The proceeds of these compensation payments were then used to make investments in railroads, railways, and slave-backed mortgage bonds that provided significant returns and the intergenerational wealth that those associated with the enslavement of people indigenous to Africa and the Americas have benefited from ever since.

In the early 19th century, one in six non-landowning British people derived their wealth from the slave trade. Former slave owners and their descendants were prominent Bank of England directors throughout the 19th century. Merchants in the West Indian trade then evolved into bankers as they responded to the need for credit instruments to facilitate the flow of slaves and tropical produce.[94]

Conversely, enslaved people were subjected to 12 years of further indentured labor and were not compensated in the Caribbean. In just as macabre a reality, their American counterparts were used as mortgage collateral in which enslaved individuals financed the system that perpetuated their subjugation while perversely creating intergenerational wealth for their enslavers and the institutions that enabled them.

"At the height of slavery, the combined value of enslaved workers exceeded that of all the railroads and factories in the nation."[95]

---

93. Woodman, Harold. *King Cotton and His Retainers: Financing and Marketing the Cotton Crop of the South*. 1800-1925, University of Kentucky Press, Lexington, Kentucky, 1967, 3-199.

94. In early institutionalized credit, the "Bill of Exchange" became the most important means of settling commercial transactions and increasing the money supply. (Hall et al., Legacies of British Slave-Ownership, 2014 p.58, 87, 108-11.)

95. Matthew Desmond, via the 1619 project[96] for the *New York Times*, 2019.

8.3 *Bubble, Bubble, Toil and Trouble*

Bonnie Martin argues in her recent work on slave mortgages that this financial practice was the "invisible engine" of slavery. By offering an enslaved person as collateral, men could acquire an enslaved person, a plot of land, or other plantation product without having the full purchase price in cash. In addition to increasing the number of potential borrowers and the acquisition rate of slaves, mortgages enabled slaveholders to maintain their workforce in the fields while also exploiting the same enslaved men and women financially. Without necessarily exploiting an enslaved person's labor in the field or selling an enslaved person outright, slaveholders could still reap a tremendous financial benefit as human property owners. According to Martin's analysis of more than 8,000 mortgages issued after the American Revolution, enslaved people served as collateral for 41% of the loans and generated 63% of the capital.[97]

The Consolidated Association of Louisiana Planters (CAPL) used slaves as collateral to establish a lending institution. The Louisiana state legislature established CAPL in 1827, using the European brokerage services of Baring Brothers of London. European investors purchased slave mortgage bonds from US state governments. This led to an increase in slaves. In 1836, New Orleans had the most bank capital. Following Alabama's example, other states supported banks that offered slave-based bonds to Europe.

The price of cotton continued to rise, and more money flowed into the slave economy, with increasing numbers of individuals in the Western world continuing to invest.

This caused a speculative second slave-related bubble in the Southwest (following the earlier documented South Sea Bubble), which burst in 1839 due to the South's excessive cotton production. Consumer demand exceeded supply and prices began to decline in 1834, resulting in a recession known as the Panic of 1837. Investors and creditors called in their debts, leaving plantation owners in significant debt. They could not sell their enslaved labor force or land to pay off debts because, as the price

---

96. https://www.nytimes.com/column/1619-project

97. Rothman, Joshua D. "The Contours of Cotton Capitalism: Speculation, Slavery, and Economic Panic in Mississippi." 1832-1941. (Paper presented at Slavery's Capitalism: A New History of Economic Development conference, Providence, Rhode Island, April 8-10, 2011); Baptist, "Toxic Debt, Liar Loans, Collateralized and Securitized Human Beings, and the Panic of 1837."

of cotton declined, so did the cost of enslaved labor, and land. The toxic debt caused the majority of state-sponsored banks to fail, but investors still wanted their funds.

8.4 *Too Big to Fail ... Again*

Following the economic downturn, state governments could have raised taxes to redeem the bonds, but their constituents voted against it, and the governments listened. They could have taken possession of the plantations, effectively ending the cotton industry. However, because the cotton industry held everything together, foreclosing on it was equivalent to foreclosing on the entire economy. So they opted for inaction, largely because the cotton industry was "too big to fail."

Eight states, including Florida, defaulted on their debts, and as a result, Southern planters became dependent on Northern credit despite having three million slaves as capital. Northern capital journeyed south to purchase cotton, thereby establishing a new system. The Lehman Brothers (bankrupt in 2008) began as "factors," lending money to slave-owners for future crops and slave mortgages. The term *factory* has its origins in the Portuguese word *feitoria*, the term used from the 15th century to designate a trading post on the coast of Africa. In the context of the transatlantic slave trade of the 19th century, a factory commissioned a locale that "produced" enslaved people and was managed by a "factor."

Brown Brothers, a London-based bank, extended credit to these factors. Numerous household names in the financial services industry began their existence in this manner. The significance of cotton grown by West Indian slaves to the Lancashire textile industry led to the emergence of Liverpool cotton brokers who later rose to prominence in the US cotton broking industry. Slavery was inextricably intertwined with cotton production and cotton trade, spawning numerous parallel business streams.[98]

---

98. Hall et al., Legacies of British Slave-Ownership, 2014, p.98; Baptist, Edward, "Toxic Debt, Liar Loans, Collateralized and Securitized Human Beings, and the Panic of 1837." in Capitalism Takes Command: The Social Transformation of Nineteenth-Century America, edited by Michael Zakim and Gary J. Kornblith (Chicago: University of Chicago Press, 2011), 69 14-16; Mann, Bruce H. *Republic of Debtors: Bankruptcy in the Age of American Independence.* published by Harvard University Press in 2002; Russel, Thomas. "The Antebellum Courthouse as Creditors' Domain: Trial-Court Activity in

In 2019, sociologist Matthew Desmond said that "the enslaved workforce in America was where the country's wealth resided."[99] He was speaking explicitly about the US, however the same was equally true of the UK.

Comparing and contrasting the EIC and cotton bailouts, worrying trends can be identified. Mystifying financial instruments—which conceal risk and connect people all over the world—are used to fuel growth. Scores of paper money are printed on the myth that some institution—cotton, housing, Indian wares, slavery—is unbreakable. Add to this, the intentional exploitation of Black and Brown people. Finally there is impunity for the profiteers when the bubble bursts. The EIC directors were bailed out and faced no penalties in 1772. Similarly, borrowers were bailed out after 1837. Identical similarities can then be noted when the banks were bailed out after 2008.

8.5 *The Decline of Slavery and the Advent of Capitalism*

Capitalism, and indeed the foundations of venture capitalism, began in brutality. Exploitation, plundering, and slavery enabled Britain and the fledgling US to become the powerhouses in the global economy they are today.

Slavery and industrialization fed each other. Many slave traders, planters, and merchants diversified into manufacturing, agriculture, and infrastructure, or kept their money in banks and finance houses that loaned to the developing capitalist economy. Some slave profits were spent on conspicuous consumption, yet, even this helped to boost the market economy. As the slave economy grew, credit, banking, and insurance became ever more important.[101]

As Robin Einhorn has argued, tax codes also reflected the exceptional wealth stored in enslaved people, with virtually every Southern legislature choosing to discount human property assessments that would otherwise

---

South Carolina and The Concurrent Lending and Litigation." The American Journal of Legal History 40, no. 3 (1996), pp. 331-364.

99. Matthew Desmond, via the 1619 project[100] for the *New York Times*, 2019.

100. https://www.nytimes.com/column/1619-project

101. Hall et al., Legacies of British Slave-Ownership, Colonial Slavery and the Formation of Victorian Britain, 2014 p.23, 33.

dwarf all other taxable assets in value.[102] There are several other examples of how practices developed to systemize and maximize profitability during slavery have flowed through to modern venturing. When a CFO depreciates assets for tax purposes, and when work rates are tracked, recorded, and data analyzed for optimal performance rates, it may feel as though we are managing metrics for scale with forward-thinking management approaches, when in fact, many of these operations were developed by enslavers to optimize their plantations. Andrew Carnegie, founder of a company that eventually became part of U.S. Steel, is famed for embodying similar rationality. Carnegie was particularly famous for his industrial activities' "vertical integration." By investing in iron ore and coal mines and railroads to transport the ore and coal to his steel mills, he dramatically reduced the cost of the final product and won market share from competitors.[103]

Though both historians and economists long-contested this point, a broad consensus has emerged over the last several decades that plantation slave labor was a highly efficient system of labor exploitation.[104] Slaves labored under drivers in gangs that gained significant momentum. Between 1800 and 1860, modern "human resources" tactics such as speed-up and measured task working, enforced by the whip and other forms of torture, drove a 400% rise in cotton-picking output in the United States. Industrialization did not reduce the workload of slaves; rather, it increased it as slaves were pushed harder to keep up with the steam-powered processing of harvested cane. A slave picked 200 pounds of cotton a

---

102. Martin, Bonnie. "Slavery's Invisible Engine: Mortgaging Human Property," The Journal of Southern History 76.4 (2010), 866. For more on slavery as labor and a property regime, see: Gavin Wright, *Slavery and American Economic Development* (Baton Rouge: Louisiana State University Press, 2006); Wright, *The Political Economy of the Cotton South*. 41-42; and Robin Einhorn, *American Taxation, American Slavery* (Chicago: The University of Chicago Press, 2006), 111-115.

103. Tomich, Dale W. and Michael Zeuske. "The Second Slavery: Mass Slavery, World-Economy, and Comparative Microhistories, Part I." Review: a Journal of the Fernand Braudel Center, New York, v. 31, n. 2, p. 91-246, 2008; and "The Second Slavery: Mass Slavery, World-Economy, and Comparative Microhistories, Part II." Review: a Journal of the Fernand Braudel Center, New York, v. 31, n.3, p. 251-437, 2008b.

104. Stampp, Kenneth M. *The Peculiar Institution: Slavery in the Ante-Bellum South.* New York: Alfred A. Knopf, 1956, 383-418; Fogel, Robert, and Stanley L. Engerman. *Time on the Cross: The Economics of American Negro Slavery.* Boston: Little, Brown, and Company, 1974; Fogel. *Without Consent or Contract: The Rise and Fall of American Slavery.* New York: W. W. Norton & Company, 1989.

day in 1850; in the 1930s, despite technological advances, a "free" laborer picked just 120 pounds.[105]

Before it was abolished in 1888, slavery had become a central feature of the modern economy. It had its origins in feudal times and helped industrial capitalism take off. Samuel Greg, who opened the first water-driven yarn spinning factory in England near Manchester in 1784, also owned Hillsborough Estate on Dominica. His brother-in-law, Thomas Hodgson, owned slave ships, and his banker brother-in-law, Thomas Pares, made his fortune through slavery. Moses Brown, who made his money in the West Indian provisioning trade, opened the first US cotton mill with mechanical spinning in 1790 in Pawtucket, Rhode Island.[106]

Eric Williams's *Capitalism and Slavery* (1944) essentially asserts that after European elites accumulated enough surplus wealth from slavery to fund the Industrial Revolution, capitalism swiftly superseded slavery. According to Williams, slavery began a rapid decline in the early 19th century after fueling Europe's modernization. As industrial capitalism became the worldwide standard, anti-slavery sentiment grew in favor of a more efficient and less capital-intensive manner of commodity production. Slavery was unnecessary. Ideology followed the economy. Sharecropping and wage peonage continued after freedom, proletarianizing former slaves. Technological development, modern agriculture, and industrial industries replaced traditional anarcho-syndicalism and slavery.

Sidney Mintz argues in *Sweetness and Power* (1985) that slave-plantation sugar fueled European industrialization, urbanization, and class formation. "A transatlantic trade network linked the daily nourishment they put into their bodies directly to the institution of slavery and the slaves who suffered to produce it. Surplus calories from sugar and surplus capital from slavery fueled capitalism's industrial march and unbridled consumption." Slavery produced consumer goods while providing a market for European-made goods. Slaves would be forced to consume before being consumed.

The sugar-slave complex boosted international trade in manufactured goods, raw materials, and foods. Those North American colonies without slave economies earned enough from supplying the slave colonies to correct their balance of payments with Britain. The sugar-slave complex

---

105. Baptist. *The Half Has Never Been Told*. 2015, pp. 164, 332, 426.
106. Beckert. *Empire of Cotton: A Global History*. 2014, p.166.

increased international trade, capital, manufactured goods, and raw materials, as well as the need for shipping and shipbuilding.[107]

Leonardo Marques furthers that America's maritime supremacy grew out of the slave trade. According to him, "the United States became unquestionably predominant" in constructing ships for the slave trade, taking maximum advantage of the country's "abundant supplies of cheap lumber and improvements in the US shipbuilding industry, which saw advances in vessel design theory." This made American ships the best and fastest vessels globally and allowed them to dominate the whaling industry during the early 19th century.[108]

This proffers an entirely new layer of meaning to the phrase "profiting off the backs of others"—it would appear that the transatlantic slave bubbles that were never allowed to burst conveniently provided wealth for the few. This wealth went on to fuel the whaling industry and the Industrial Revolution, which has since filtered down into the wealth gaps that are entrenched in society today.

---

107. Solow. *Capitalism and Slavery in the Exceedingly Long Run*. 1987, p.731.

108. Marques, Leonardo. *The United States and the Transatlantic Slave Trade to the Americas, 1776–1867*. New Haven, CT: Yale University Press, 2016, p. 109.

9 Conversations: Venture's History

9.1 *Irwin: Mapping Inequality*

Terry Irwin (Transition Design Institute, Carnegie Mellon University)

Terry Irwin[109] is a designer, academic professor, and former head of the School of Design at Carnegie Mellon University. She has been instrumental in developing transition design—an area of design practice and research focused on design-led societal transitions away from "wicked problems" and toward more sustainable futures. Terry facilitated the development of systems maps that include the historical foundations of venture capital on behalf of the Nasdaq Entrepreneurial Center'[§21.4]s Venture Equity Project.[110] We discussed her work on this project, how her insights connect to the history of venture capital, and how improving diversity in VC going forward needs to be a systemic solution.

Interviewed October 2021

DEVELOPING THE VENTURE CAPITAL ECOSYSTEM MAP

Interviewer's note: *Terry started by giving me an overview of the project process, in which she and her team researched and mapped the VC ecosystem and its history from stakeholder experiences. According to the project site,[111] the "systems maps" are visual representations of the participating stakeholders' understanding of "the lack of funding for entrepreneurs of color in the US and UK." The stakeholder groups that participated were Black entrepreneurs, capital allocators, community organizers, and researchers. The maps themselves are highly visual and can be explored fur-*

---

109. https://www.linkedin.com/in/terry-irwin-97b4552/

110. https://thecenter.nasdaq.org/vep/

111. https://thecenter.nasdaq.org/vep/vep-project-stakeholder-mapping/

ther through the summary videos on the project site, as well as the systems maps themselves, which are hosted on Miro, a visual collaboration software.

Figure: Historical Evolution Map. (A high-resolution PDF[112] is also available.) Credit: Irwin, Kossof, and the Nasdaq Entrepreneurial Center Venture Equity Project, 2021.

Terry Irwin (TI): The map is not simply a historical bid. We've processed everything, trying to retain the stakeholder voices. Statements from stakeholders are front and center. So much research on problems like this strips away what the stakeholders said. I think that gathering these statements together in one place speaks more eloquently than any researcher synthesis could. So we've tried to make it incredibly visual and nonlinear. We created a demonstration to show how stakeholder ideas can be used to create systemic interventions.

We would like anyone who accesses the data to encounter it as a systems map, so that they get an overview of how complex the problem is and they interact with the stakeholder voices, which have been anonymized.

Key issues are mapped on the left,[113] including things like the history of slavery and the systemic racism that has existed for centuries in the US. Also included is the rise of social media, the internet, and e-commerce, each of which has pros and cons. Then there are policies against immigrants, the unequal distribution of and access to educational resources, along with threads like Black self-determination during the Harlem Renaissance.

Another significant threat, of course, is the history of discriminatory practices in the financial system. But I will say apropos of that, discriminatory lending and financing practices and hiring and metrics is a theme

---

112. https://assets.holloway.com/editorial/images/better-venture/
    nasdaq-board-historical-evolution-of-the-problem-stakeholder-and-research-mapping.pdf

113. As mentioned in the intro, the systems maps[114] are hosted on Miro if you'd like to explore them. The YouTube videos[115] further summarize the project and can walk you through the maps.

114. https://miro.com/app/board/o9J_lwjL4qw=/?invite_link_id=4660134175

115. https://www.youtube.com/playlist?list=PLjMMrMHyxp5loyeJLuIlQOKxFd9HFSadz

that ran through practically every single map, and it's very articulately presented in the problem map and the stakeholder relation maps.

We created analysis and insights that look at high-level timeline themes. So some of the themes that run throughout are enslavement, labor, education, land and property, the financial system itself, and then world views, which, as we know, are the root of all of it. Another theme that emerged recurrently was data, transparency of data, lack of data, and skewed data.

Early themes from stakeholder responses were also documented. Some of those include slavery, history, and systemic issues. Some examples are how traditional routes of funding for businesses are not readily found in institutions used by founders of color, the unequal distribution of access to education, war and forgotten Black veterans, private equity, and VC history itself. We also have some citations from that historical research, because the thing to remember about these historical evolution maps is, ideally they are built by several types of experts. So the stakeholders themselves, but also experts from all sectors like historians, economists, etc.

INSIGHTS ON THE HISTORY OF VENTURE CAPITAL

Erika Brodnock (EB): *Were there any findings around the banking system and the history of venture capital in particular?*

TI: We found that some of the most pernicious issues have to do with data. Some with an acknowledged implicit bias, and some with mirroring and pattern matching. The search for unicorns instead of camels came up as a repeated theme.

Overall, we found that denying funding to minority entrepreneurs does not just affect their business or their ability to launch a new idea that could create an impact in the world, but adversely affects communities that already have a history of being marginalized. What came up again and again was that if you fund Black entrepreneurs, that's a window into strengthening entire communities, lifestyles, and neighborhoods.

EB: *Where did the problem start? And how did the problem start? Understanding the history of venture capital, I believe, holds the key to creating some of the change, because if venture capital came about via the banking and insurance industries that came about via slavery, and the proceeds of slavery were the first funds used to create venture capital, is it happen-*

stance that the descendants of slaves ended up being locked out of venture capital?

TI: The birth of capitalism and the much older enslavement economy arose out of systemic oppression. We tend to think of it more in terms of the large, wicked problems that are clustering. Then it shoots down to a particular area like the one we're looking at. It's one manifestation of these large landscape forces. And money and enslavement just went together.

It's a bit problematic to try and identify the origins of venture capitalism because it's like looking at a river with different currents running through it. We are focusing on trying to show all the different currents intertwining so that everyone who comes to this problem begins to educate themselves about its complexities and different narratives emerge.

INVOLVING ALL THE STAKEHOLDERS, INVESTORS INCLUDED

TI: It is important to involve all of the stakeholders, but getting to all of them at once is virtually impossible, so we need to engage champions. Make a start with the low-hanging fruit. The capital allocators we engaged with through our research have a clear handle on the problem. They completely understand it. So how do we enlist those folks to help create change?

One of the most powerful leverage points for change is to create new narratives and create new networks of help and new sources of funding. Each of these solutions needs to be employed at more or less the same time at different levels of scale, alongside finding champions within each of these sectors who are interested in helping to shift the narrative.

Another thing that we need is to speak to the capital allocators who are invested in not seeing the industry change to understand how much of that is about systemic racism, how much of it is about risk aversion, and how much is about money and power.

EB: *I wholeheartedly believe that, because without capital allocators being involved, things will only ever change at such a glacial pace.*

TI: We only have one or two statements from capital allocators that were very direct and honest. And one was, "I'm afraid, if my firm or I fund minority entrepreneurs, I'm going to get branded as a firm that only does that."

EB: *Every piece of data I've seen says that it's less risky to invest in this way than it is to invest in the status quo. Are investors leaving money on the table for fear of being pigeonholed?*

TI: Some statements did bubble up from stakeholders who were worried that the lived experience of older generations was being put upon the younger generations and [that it has] perpetuated.

OPPORTUNITIES FOR INTERVENTION AND SHIFTING THE NARRATIVE

TI: What also emerged is that two areas for very positive interventions are in data. One is about how we make investment practices more transparent, but that must go hand in hand with interventions about shifting narratives, creating role models, and putting new stories out into the world. Then the other thing is addressing this idea of otherness.

EB: *Could one way be to stop using words like minority, sub, or anything that means less than?*

TI: Yes, coming up with new strategies for terminology. That's all part of shifting the narrative, getting high-profile stories out into the world, creating media platforms.

If we make a concerted effort to make diversity the norm, it will simultaneously solve so many problems, like the one that's manifesting in VC. We've tried to show that solutions in these categories can address more than one issue. This is the very definition of systemic solutions—or an ecology of solutions. If each solution could be connected, we will simultaneously begin to address many issues, and it's precisely the opposite of how solutions are usually conceived.

9.2 *Draper: Venture and the Slave Trade*

Nick Draper (University College London)

Existing literature on the history of VC as an enabler of entrepreneurship is centered on the US—Tom Nicholas's VC: An American History *denotes venture capital as an American invention with whaling as its precursor—resulting in a sustained elision of both slavery and European influences. We sat down with acclaimed historian and co-creator of the Legacies of British Slavery files at UCL, Nick Draper, to understand the influence of European slavery and its multiple mechanisms, not least "carried interest" and "mobilizing pools of investors," on today's venture capital industry.*

Interviewed August 2021

HOW THE SLAVE ECONOMY INFORMED MODERN FINANCE

Erika Brodnock (EB): *I believe that venture capital plays a significant role in creating the products and wealth shaping the present and the future, yet the past is rarely analyzed. I'm keen to learn more about your research and the findings that traced slave-owner compensation payments through to London today.*

Nick Draper (ND): There are two distinct aspects of the slave economy that appear especially relevant to the development of the modern financial system, including venture capital: the first is financial innovation driven by the slave trade, and the second is the capital generated by slave ownership. Slave traders and slave owners were generally separate groups within the British and colonial economies. I will come back to the slave trade, but the work that other colleagues and I have done over the past 10–15 years focused and continues to focus to a large extent on slave ownership. So my knowledge of slave ownership is much deeper and broader than my knowledge of the slave trade.

The work on slave ownership began by looking at the payments made to slave owners in the 1830s, and the compensation payments were looked at for two reasons.

One, it's a very, very vivid expression of the relationship between Britain, the state, slavery, money, and slave ownership. It's just an extraordinary thing to see these payments being made and the circumstances under which they were made. The enslaved people were being cast off into freedom, but with no endowment of anything, no resources, no land, no money, no literacy, nothing. It was as if they were born naked into a new world and had to negotiate and navigate from a zero base, in a world where we know that the ownership of assets tends (as Thomas Piketty showed), over generations, to multiply the disparities that exist.

The second thing is that the records for the compensation process were extraordinary, and they still are. They're in the National Archives at Kew, they comprise an immensely long list of people. You can determine which individuals were connected as owners or mortgagees or annuitants with particular estates and, therefore, which enslaved people were attached to them. The records give complete visibility into the end of slavery and who was holding the bag when the music stopped.

SLAVE OWNER COMPENSATION IS A SMALL PART OF THE TIMELINE

As I have continued to work on slave ownership over the years, I have come to see, however, that the moment of compensation, significant though it is, is in the end just a coda to a story that lasts over 200 years. The money transferred in the 1830s is about a decade's worth of earnings for slave owners from slavery, which had taken place every decade for the previous 20 decades. So we are looking at huge amounts of money in totality. In comparison, while the compensation payments are very visible and very charged, they are still only a small part of the whole story.

Originally the mission was to try and trace, to the extent that we could, the compensation payments and how they flowed into other areas of British life, not just business but also into the cultural fabric of Britain, governance, philanthropic institutions, things that people value highly in Britain today, and we can see that a part of that endowment comes from slavery—there's no question.

We've accumulated thousands of examples, each of them representing micro-histories and, in turn, thousands of specific legacies, and the whole thing seems to me to take on a new life and goes straight back to Eric

Williams's *Capitalism and Slavery,* a text that was in the 1960s taken up and discarded very quickly. The view was that he was wrong on so many counts that there was no point in engaging with him. I think that the work we've done, and the work that other scholars are doing, will reinstate Williams in terms of economic and financial significance.

What we did for slave ownership, a new group of scholars in the UK are now trying to do for slave traders, looking at some of the same questions, which are: where did their capital come from? Where did it go to? Sometimes it was destroyed in business losses, but in other cases, it wasn't, and it was multiplied. Then the question remains, where did it go?

In that context, it is clear to me that the whaling industry is a relatively brief explosion of mobile, entrepreneurial capital and overlaps with the slave trade, as it overlaps too with East India ship owning—there is no doubt. There is a lot of interest in the Venn diagram, which has whaling in a circle. Slave trading is undoubtedly one of those other circles. The same names come up in the intersection. The question is, how significant is that as a whole?

Our work focuses on Britain, and my work focuses on the City of London. It sounds as though there is a thesis in the United States that is relevant to Britain—namely, the connections between the whaling industry and all of these other forms of shipping and ship owning that were going on. It also embraces marine insurance, and I've been trying to think and quantify and get my head around the significance of slavery to marine insurance in the 18th century in Britain.

There seems to be an evidence-based consensus that between a third and 40% of marine insurance in Britain relates to slavery, not only the slave trade but in particular, to the movement of commodities in ships. Originally, of course, these formed a literal triangular trade. The same ships sailing from England to Africa, taking captive Africans across the Atlantic, bring back slave-grown produce. Yet later, the system tends to get differentiated, with people specializing in just bilateral trade between Britain and the Caribbean, and that's where the significant amounts of marine insurance are. That's a very, very important part of the growth of marine insurance and, therefore, obviously connects with [insurance company] Lloyd's. However, it isn't simply a bilateral trade, slavery underpins it all.

THE POSSIBLE CONNECTIONS TO VENTURE CAPITAL

I've never considered this nexus in the context of your specific interest in the venture capital industry. I'm just thinking now about this. The techniques of finance, for the British, are relatively prosaic. They're relatively simple. The Dutch were far more sophisticated. They had created mortgage securities in relation to Berbice, Demerara, and Suriname [then Dutch colonies in South America]. In the 18th century, there were what you would now call general partners in Amsterdam. They were mobilizing pools of investors, buying up packages of securities, and financing the expansion of the slave system. And that Dutch sophistication doesn't appear to be replicated in the case of the British, the British are much more bilateral. A merchant in London, who is a consignee, would advance credit to the slave owner in the Caribbean and will allow that slave owner to run up, often, very substantial debts, the capital being drawn by the merchant in turn from banks and investors in the UK.

EB: *Did the financier in Britain have significant returns? And from those returns, pay carried interest?*

ND: The West Indian merchants in London became bankers for the slave owner. They advanced money to educate their children if they were sent to Britain. They would then pay attorneys in Jamaica and Barbados to manage the estates on behalf of the owners, and those agents were paid, but not in the way of so much carried interest. It appears that in many cases, they were paid a percentage of the value of their crop. So maybe that is indeed analogous to what you describe.

EB: *Carried interest in VC is the payment of a percentage of the value the general partner and company can create.*

ND: Some of the attorney's pay was a fixed salary, and the rest was a percentage. Of course, the consequence is that you incentivized your attorney to focus on this year and next year. He is not interested in the 20, 30, and 40-year perspectives. He just wants to maximize production, which means that he may not be as careful with the lives of enslaved people. He is not concerned about whether the population is healthy and reproduces itself. He just wants to ensure that this and next year's crop is as big as it can be.

EB: *To maximize his returns?*

ND: Yes, there is an incentive that is generated from those percentages.

THE SYSTEMIC IMPACTS OF THE SLAVE ECONOMY

EB: *What then are the systemic impacts of the slave economy?*

ND: Out of the work on slave ownership, I've come to recognize, firstly, that the compensation payments are only part of the story. And secondly, these West Indian merchants in London and, to an extent, Liverpool and Bristol, are the center of the system. It is not the slave trader. It's not the slave owner. It's this mercantile capital in Britain which is the focal point of it. So the question is: A) what returns do they make and B) what do they do with their money?

It's a risky business, and it's clear that a large number of them go bust. Some have spectacular collapses at various points, but others don't. Others create long-term wealth for their families and do with it what British families tend to do. It becomes landed. Often, in that curious blend of both landed money and mercantile money, they'll split it amongst their children. Once that starts, it doesn't evaporate, but it becomes far less spectacular because it's divided between many different families over time.

We have traced some of the money into some companies, railways, and investments across the whole spectrum of Britain. There is no single number to measure how material this cumulative money is, not just from compensation but from the payments and profits made earlier. We came up early on with the suggestion at least 5–10% of the British elites are in the slave compensation records. In many cases, the money flowed away.

In terms of institutional development, we can see that all the big banks in Britain today grew up by consolidating provincial banks and whole networks of smaller banks. If those smaller banks were in Liverpool, Lancaster, Bristol, or London, there's no question they would have done business with slave traders, have done business with slave owners. In some cases, they would have been mortgagees directly on enslaved people. We can generate many examples, and the question again is, how material and how significant is this?

It is clear to me that in the case of Royal Bank of Scotland (NatWest as it is now), many, many of their precursor firms were implicated in this involvement, this entanglement, in slavery. It is a complex tapestry. If, for example, you were a banker in Birmingham, you weren't necessarily involved in trading and enslaving people or owning them. Still, you were financing the manufacturer of guns used in the slave trade. The connections run backwards and forwards like this right across industry.

Joseph Inikori wrote a book 20 years ago, *Africans and the Industrial Revolution*. It is a very important book. At least as important as Eric Williams, yet, it passed more or less unnoticed in Britain. Oddly, you can still pick up literature about slavery and Britain's economy and not see references to Inikori. And others have read Inikori but pushed it to one side. He did an extraordinary amount of work to get to this question of significance by looking into different sectors. There's a lot of important primary research in there. We are working in the shadow of not only Williams but also of Inikori.

DRAWING A LINE FROM OLD MONEY TO MODERN VC

EB: *There's enough to link how venture capital today is structured to how the slave industry was structured. Based on the evidence I have reviewed, I do not doubt that the wealth generated from slavery, both in the US and the UK, has trickled down to create the backbone of venture capital. If we think about the early investors in UK venture capital, it was people who had made money from banking, insurance, etc. There is a lot of old money in the venture capital system. Many people who can angel invest have accumulated wealth that has been passed intergenerationally to them. Indeed, they are not just angel investing, they are sometimes limited partners in funds. Limited partners are often companies, such as J.P. Morgan, or NatWest, who you mentioned earlier, often invest in pension funds, private equity, and venture capital. With this, you can begin to see the clear links between the history of capital markets, the history of slavery, and the VC market that we have today.*

ND: To your point, if you wanted to do business with the City of Chicago in the mid-2000s, you needed to file an affidavit about all kinds of things, including, at the insistence of the city council there, a disclosure about involvement in slavery. Banks did, therefore, commission research into their histories. It was found that Chase Manhattan, which merged with J.P. Morgan, was active in the south and mortgaged enslaved African people in Louisiana. Morgan, in response to that, did set up a small trust fund, I think $5M in Louisiana. There were other banks, at the same time, faced with the same thing. RBS Royal Bank of Scotland also did work at that point. That's one reason why there's more transparency into their lending against, and ownership of, enslaved people than other firms because they laid out some of their histories at that time. Nevertheless, the original RBS reports tended to minimize their involvement—even based on our data at that stage, we knew they were undercounting their involvement.

EB: *The profit that was made from the railway industry, then all marine insurance, but then also the insurance and mortgage of slaves, plus the slave owner compensations, did you follow that money right into the city?*

ND: Yes, but it's not a systematic piece of work, Erika. It's a series of anec-dotal, specific mini-case studies. We haven't been able to do systematic economic work as of yet.

As far as I can see, British insurance companies did not write life insur-ance for enslaved Africans on plantations or estates. That did happen in the US in the 1840s and 1850s. But I think that mass life insurance was developed relatively late, after the end of British colonial slavery. So I think that we found no examples of insurance companies insuring the lives of enslaved people in the Caribbean, although they insured the lives of the slave owners, and they insured the cargoes of captive Africans. The kind of life insurance policies written in the Deep South hadn't been seen in Britain. Fire insurance in Britain, however, is related to sugar refiner-ies. And that is a product of enslaved people's appropriated labor. But the main connections between insurance and slavery are not with life insur-ance, per se, but with marine insurance and fire insurance.

NEXT STEPS NEEDED IN ORDER TO RIGHT HISTORICAL WRONGS

EB: *What, if anything, are your thoughts on what needs to happen next to right some of the historical wrongs?*

ND: I think that there are several dimensions to it. As far as Britain is concerned, at least, we're stuck in a series of culture wars. One of them is about Britain's relationship with slavery, and it's a very bitter conflict. Ten years ago, most people didn't care. They would say, "But it was a long time ago." However, because of the cumulative weight of work by us and many others, the dial has been shifted enough to frighten people who, up until now, have been able to say, "Let's not worry about this. What about the white working class?" "Didn't Africans sell Africans?" Those responses I've had repeatedly, and I'm sure you'd have had, in every public engagement meeting that you've ever been to. But things have moved significantly in the last two or three years, and that's brought a backlash that causes individuals now a difficult time professionally and personally because they are the subject of hate campaigns that social media and mainstream media are capable of launching. The bitterness of that struggle tells me that things are changing a bit.

EB: *So what happens next?*

ND: Ultimately, there needs to be a national commission that acknowledges the many different views but lets us collectively examine the evidence. What does it support? And what does it not support? Until we have more agreement about what the basic history and background were, we're not going to be able to move this from a political conflict into a substantive movement forward.

Only then will Britain be able to articulate a response to the CARICOM reparations movement.[116] Only then will it be able to articulate a response to the British people who've been working for reparations, not on a government-to-government basis, but to say, look, this is not only about Britain and the Caribbean. This is about British society, the structure and the inequalities we have here, and how they've been reproduced over 200 years because of the background of slavery.

Until that point, independent institutions, without doubt, are going to do what they have to do, not what they want to do, but what they have to do, because they are subject to growing internal and external pressures. Take Lloyd's of London and the National Gallery as examples of institutions trying to get their heads around this, to get ahead of the challenge from the public and staff who say, "You haven't even done the work to pre-

---

116. https://caricomreparations.org/

tend to tell us about this history of your connections to slavery." In Oxford, All Souls College, famously the site of the Codrington Library, now has a stone outside which says, for the first time, this represents the labor of enslaved Africans in the Caribbean. All Souls also put some money into a scholarship and made a grant to Codrington College in Barbados. Who's to say that is the right and exhaustive thing to do? Not me, but I think there ought to be someone arbitrating this. There needs to be some check on institutions, so they don't just get to do the bit they want and think they've done it all.

RACISM AS A CONSEQUENCE OF SLAVERY AND ABOLITION

EB: *Just before the issuance of slave owner compensation payments, there was propaganda as to why slavery should continue initially and then why people should be compensated. What are your opinions on the literature used to describe the people that were enslaved? One of the key reasons that venture capital isn't invested in Black people is the perceived risk and a pre-sumption of deficiency. I believe that this started to be propagated through slavery and has then passed down through the ages. What are your thoughts?*

ND: Williams said that racism was a consequence, not a cause, of slavery.

To justify a system of racialized slavery, of course, the slavers had to reconstitute the enslaved people as being less, in whatever way they could. They did this for two centuries and established the basis of all the tropes of racial superiority and inferiority that we see today. But by the 1820s and 1830s, there were relatively few people who would justify slavery by that stage as being a positive good. The view was that this system is not great, but it's here, and there's nothing we can do about it, so we have to live with it. The common sense, by then, was that everybody was *potentially* equal. It was just that the enslaved people have been held back by slavery itself, and maybe one day, enslaved people could reach the same level of civiliza-tion, as you know, the white British.

It's emancipation that shifts that because, by the 1860s, the abolition-ists are beginning to wag their finger at the formerly enslaved and say, "You haven't done what you were supposed to do. You were supposed to become wage labor on the estates. What you're doing instead is becoming a proto peasantry; you're supporting your family, and you're not engaging with the modern commodity world." That then feeds into the much harder racism you describe, which is that it's not about stages of development, i.e., Africa is down here, but maybe one day it will develop with our help and support. Instead, it becomes something more fundamental, which is that it will never happen. The "gap" can never be closed. So I think that maybe racism was not entirely the consequence of slavery; it was the consequence of slavery and abolition. After abolition, the abolitionists began to move toward that fundamentally racist view to say, "No, there's an inherent difference here that isn't working in the way we expected it to, and it is the fault of the 'Negro.'"

EB: *Suppose you take books away from a people for 200 years and provide them with only Bibles. How do you expect them to be at the same level as those who have had resources for 200 years within a couple of years, especially when you allowed an additional 12 years of free (indentured) labor?*

ND: I'm absolutely with you. As I said, this is the whole Thomas Piketty theory, which speaks to your work. If you don't have an asset endowment at the beginning, you'll never catch up because the return on assets is greater than the wage increase over time. If you have nothing, and you're invited to join a race with people who started 100 yards down the course, you're not likely to catch up. In the States, work has been done to quantify the systematic differences in wealth from generation to generation. It's a fact that with zero resource endowment, you can never close that gap as a complete collective.

9.3 *Glover, Karia, Noble: Women in British Venture*

Anne Glover (Amadeus Capital Partners)

Bindi Karia (Molten Ventures, formerly Silicon Valley Bank)

Diana Noble (Kirkos Partners, formerly CDC Group)

What happened in the tech and VC ecosystem in Europe and the UK in the last three decades? We spoke with three of the most senior investors in the space: Anne Glover[117] of Amadeus Capital; Bindi Karia,[118] currently venture partner at Molten Ventures; and Diana Noble,[119] a PE and VC veteran, about the evolution of European venture capital and their experiences as females in the ecosystem. One of the core learnings: you needed to behave like the men (be confident, like sports) to get ahead; while this is slowly changing, deep-seated structural issues, including in-fighting among women, are not truly behind us, even today.

Interviewed February 2021

GROWING INTO LEADERSHIP IN THE UK ECOSYSTEM

Johannes Lenhard (JL): *How has it been coming up in the UK's tech world?*

Anne Glover (AG): I started in venture capital in '89, when I moved back from the States. I had been working there in consulting to small tech companies for a little while. A fundamental difference was there were not a lot of tech investors in the UK at that time. I did all kinds of deals, from retail to leisure to technology. I found that I was much more in my own milieu, because I was talking to people about products and things that I understood, and they understood and could explain to me. I then gravi-

117. https://www.linkedin.com/in/anglover/
118. https://twitter.com/bindik
119. https://www.linkedin.com/in/diana-noble-42b49566/

tated back to tech from general business, because I could establish my credentials and my legitimacy more easily.

Eventually, I joined and was COO of one of my companies for a couple of years, when it was listed on the London Stock Exchange. Sometimes, when I was sitting next to a guy, whoever the guy was, all the questions would be directed to him, even if I was the right person to answer them. When I set up my own firm, those kinds of things improved. Then people needed to converse with me. That was 23 years ago. Overall, I found that tech is actually more welcoming than general business.

Bindi Karia (BK): I have been part of the UK ecosystem since about 2000, working alongside venture or partnering with venture since then. Have I felt barriers as an Asian female? I have. But do I let that stop me? I tend not to. Bruce Lee said this and I did a talk on this about four years ago: "I am like water." If I hit a brick wall, I find a way in, through, around, and over it. That has gained me decent amounts of respect with the men I have worked with. Even to this day, I find that in the network I have, I am getting pretty powerful men approaching me to work alongside them.

I think that partially is because of the culture. I learned working at Microsoft, which was super male-dominated. I was working initially in the sales team, before I joined the startup and ventures team. The guys there were really alpha and very macho, and you had to act a bit like them in order to fit in. I was working in financial services, then tech sales. As long as you proved you could do it and demonstrated you were capable, what I found is I gained their respect. To this day, I continue to get calls to do work.

I see a lot of female entrepreneurs getting funded at pre-seed, seed, and Series A, and I observe that deal flow is definitely increasing. Having said that, I see fewer female founders that are getting Series B and onwards funding. I know that there is a massive pipeline coming from pre-seed to seed and now popping into Series A. But I still see some barriers when you get to the growth stage. With a lot of the growth stage investing, you are looking at the metrics and the scaling possibilities of the business. The challenge is how do you get to that level of metrics that are required at a certain stage of investing in the business.

Diana Noble (DN): The themes that we are talking about here are our ability to gain credibility and respect, and as a result, have influence on our audience. That is largely about two things. It is about the competence you have, and obviously that changes over your career. It also changes based on the knowledge that you bring. It also depends on the person or group of people you are dealing with and whether they have bias against females.

I will quickly contrast the period that I was in private equity, from 1987 to 1999, and then tech VC, which is a relatively short period from 1999 to 2005. During that first period, my confidence per se was low and when I look back I realize I was trying to form judgments beyond my experience and training. I was assessing industries, such as engineering, that I had no real empathy with. All of this created a large credibility gap, both in my own head and also in reality.

Funnily enough, my issue was not with my colleagues at the time. There were actually three female partners out of nine partners, which was very unusual. That ratio would also be unusual today; we have not moved forward that much. And so it did not feel like an intimidating environment internally at all. That's not to say that there weren't the occasional individuals with whom you just felt, as a young woman, it was difficult to have influence. It wasn't about anything explicit, just those subtle inferences that make you feel rather small.

When I moved into VC, with EVentures Softbank, and then Reed Elsevier Ventures, it was different. I was CEO. And so you do start with that credibility with investee teams. You walk into the room and it is your agenda. You are not fighting for credibility. Also, the people I was dealing with were pretty young, West Coast tech entrepreneurs. That generation did not care whether I was female or not, the question was simply, "Do you understand what I am trying to do? Can you speak my language?"

SUPPORTING WOMEN FROM GRADE SCHOOL TO THE BOARDROOM

Erika Brodnock (EB): *Is the world of tech and VC really as bad as it is perceived to be? Why aren't there more women in tech and venture? Are women not trying hard enough? Is that why they are not there?*

AG: If we only go back to what is happening in our careers, we are missing the point. I ended up studying sciences, because my parents were scientists, and I loved it. They made it exciting for me and they treated me as an equal with my brother, who was also an engineer. When I get asked this question by audiences, and I frequently do, I usually say, "How many of you have daughters? What are you encouraging them to study and do when they are nine?" Some of them think about it, and some of them just shuffle in their seats and look awkward.

Your proclivity for tech as a field of interest happens very early. It is down to schools and parents. There are female engineers and they are brilliant, as well as female scientists and mathematicians, but the pool is always smaller. We have to work within the school system to get women more interested in STEM subjects and to get them to realize that these careers can be creative, exciting, and compatible with having a family life. When you look at VCs, it is the compatibility with a family life that is the later problem, but the tech problem happens early.

BK: In career management 101, you are taught, go for a job that is 80% stretch and 20% of what you have done. For women, from my personal experience, I see the standards assigned to us is 80% of what you've done and 20% stretch. Men are more likely to get jobs where it is 80% stretch, because we just have to look at these first-time fund managers who come from the right family and the right background, and they can raise £80M for a first time fund with zero track record. Then, if I went out to raise a fund myself, I would never be able to raise that money, not without someone by my side who has also had that track record.

It is also a confidence thing. I may come across this confident, but I always have imposter syndrome and confidence issues. We are all good at wearing the mask. I am just a venture partner and I am not full-time there. There are times I am in the deal room and I think, "I am not sure if I belong here." It stops me from speaking out and asking questions, even though my own questions are valid and viable, based on 20 solid years of operator experience.

The other thing—and this is controversial—is that I find some of my biggest detractors have been other women, not men. One of my favorite mantras is that sisterhood is not a zero-sum game, there is room for all of us! For a certain generation (mine!), when you get to a certain level, we have been taught that there is only room for one of you at the top. It is the establishment at the top that has historically generated this attitude, and this needs to change. At least, this has been my own personal experience.

But I would also say that is an old-school attitude, and I observe that this is definitely changing (I hope!). Based on the calls I am getting from headhunters and the advent of ESG (environmental, social, and governance) thinking everywhere, I am hopeful that this mindset is at last beginning to shift. That being said, we still have a very long way to go! You just have to look at the recent Diversity VC/BBB/BVCA study[120] to realize this.

MOVING BEYOND "FIT"

DN: This is multi-layered. To answer your question about what has changed is, the very obvious misogynistic, individual behavior is largely gone. In a way, that is easier to identify and easier to get rid of. What remains is a culture of guys feeling comfortable with guys, if I can put it like that. When it comes to who makes partner, who really climbs the tree, there can still exist this inherent bias, which hides behind phrases like "fit." Fit can be used as, "You are like me, I like to have a beer with you. We can talk about football or rugby." That is what starts to exclude and that is going to take a lot longer to break down. It is not necessarily even intentional; it is human to want to surround yourself with people like you because it is comfortable.

BK: I 100% agree with your comment about "fit." If you look at client entertainment, for previous roles I have held we mainly attended sports events. I would go to rugby, I would go to cricket with male clients all day long, or we would take them to tennis or Formula One. We would mainly have the male VC partners in attendance, as this was a form of client entertainment that catered to their tastes. But I would rarely see the female VCs in attendance, as their comments to me were along the lines of, "I cannot go, I have family priorities that come first." Why do we not do something that is more in line with what that audience wants and is slightly more inclusive?

AG: The 80/20 point that Bindi made is exactly right. I ticked every box; I ran teams of people, I did strategic consulting and small company startups before I got into venture capital. Nobody was going to say I had not done it. That is not the path that most guys take—they take the opportunity that a mate of theirs offers them as soon as they can, because they have better networks and people are more willing to take risks on them.

JL: *We heard quite a few people say, instead of trying to make it through the ranks of existing institutions and pushing in there, why not start something else?*

---

120. https://www.british-business-bank.co.uk/uk-vc-female-founders-report/

BK: I sit on the board of the European Innovation Council (EIC)[121] where I am also co-chair of the Diversity and Inclusion working group, so we are exploring this quite closely. For example, the EIF[122] (European Investment Fund) is one of the biggest LPs in Europe. Anecdotally speaking, the number of female-founded funds that have been turned down for EIF funding is eye-opening. Someone wrote me recently, "You have to have the first name Alex to be a fund manager from Germany and you have to have the first name Peter to be a fund manager from CEE [Central and Eastern Europe]." Then she sent me the names of all the general partners of all the funds in Germany and CEE, and the majority of the names are Alex or Peter, I am serious! We are trying to make the point that actually the LPs have got to start thinking about diversity when they invest as well. This is about the entire value chain of investing, from LP to investor to founder. It has got to start from LPs where you ask, can you trust first-time female fund managers because of their other life experience, which means they are going to get this across the line? It is interesting food for thought, and all I know is that things need to change.

RETHINKING "RISK"

DN: That is the phrase that gets to all of this: "Take a risk." Why is it a risk when looked at objectively?

BK: One hundred percent true that they are not a risk. My observation is that there can sometimes be a self-belief that we are a risk (and that can be both internally and externally reinforced). From the internal perspective, this stems back to the confidence thing. We are not a risk; we get things done. We have the right instincts and insights to pick the right investments, and we can get it across the line. Why do we have to spend the time convincing LPs and others of the 80% of what we have done? In tandem, we also have to get rid of that self-belief that we are a risk as well!

AG: I would not have been able to raise a fund had I not partnered with Hermann Hauser, who is a very well-known technology entrepreneur. That was a deliberate choice by him and by me, because all successful enterprises need a team. I am extremely clear about that and so is he. In

---

121. https://eic.ec.europa.eu/index_en
122. https://www.eif.org/

that sense, the partnership worked. We both needed each other. That is how we got things started.

ADVICE FOR FUTURE FEMALE FOUNDERS

EB: *If you spoke to your 25-year-old or 18-year-old self, what would you say about your biggest learnings and experiences growing up as a female in the tech world?*

BK: Be bolder. Have more confidence in yourself; that has held me back constantly.

DN: At 18, that is the time to say to someone, build your substantial knowledge in what you want to do. If you want to be a VC, go out and understand what building businesses is all about, go and work in companies. If you want to work in a tech company, then go and start at the beginning and move around. Learn a function, learn how it works, go and get an MBA. I hate having to say this, but you win by substance, and you win by confidence. This overcomes the barriers, which are still there.

AG: It is certainly belief in yourself. Then frankly, do what you enjoy, if you are going to work hard in this life, just do what you enjoy. Some people are driven by status and money, but I actually think it is better advice to choose what you enjoy.

DN: I would slightly disagree with "do what you enjoy." I tend to say to people, when you are 18 to 24, it does not actually matter what you do. It is who you are working for. Choose organizations that have really high standards, because these standards will stick with you for your whole career and you can apply them again and again. Secondly, make sure you work for people who actually care about you and your learning experience and are generous with sharing their knowledge and input into your career path. You will then get a huge amount out of those early years.

9.4 *Gouw, Perkins, Pfund: Women in US Venture*

Theresia Gouw (Acrew Capital, formerly Accel)

Sonja Perkins (Project Glimmer, Broadway Angels)

Nancy Pfund (DBL Partners)

In early 2021, we met three of the most successful, seasoned, and well-known female American venture capital investors to discuss how they forged careers in the venture world over the last three decades. Theresia Gouw[123] was a managing partner at Accel for 15 years and has since run her own firm, Acrew Capital; Sonja Perkins[124] started investing 30 years ago and is the founder of the famous female angel collective Broadway Angels; Nancy Pfund[125] is the founder of DBL Partners, a firm she has led for the last 13 years. All three of them were very happy to share anecdotes—some of them of annoying experiences, some outright offensive—and their biggest learnings.

Interviewed January 2021

BREAKING INTO TECH AND VC IN THE US

Erika Brodnock (EB): *Each of you spent the last 30 years in VC and tech, and I am keen to understand how it has been for you as women in a historically male industry.*

Nancy Pfund (NP): I was always the token humanities and social science person in the room; I took a different path. I did not know what a venture capitalist was when I was in college—it was not something I dreamed of being and I just evolved to a place where it was what I wanted to do. Bob Noyce, one of the founders of Intel, whom I worked for, needed people that could reach out to broader constituencies in terms of the role and signif-

---

123. https://www.linkedin.com/in/theresiagouw/
124. https://twitter.com/sonjaperkins
125. https://twitter.com/NancyPfundDBL

icance of electronics. That is one of the first jobs in tech I had; I started early and there were no women anywhere.

I did depend on the men that were my bosses or leaders of organizations that saw the need for a different point of view and a different talent set. Clearly, I was not an engineer, and while I felt very comfortable understanding science and engineering, I did not come from that culture. That was liberating, because it allowed me to focus on what I was interested in. But if I had not had the support of people like Bob Noyce; Bill Hambrecht, the founder of Hambrecht & Quist; or Dan Case, the eventual CEO of Hambrecht & Quist, I would not be here today.

Every career, of course, has its highs and lows, but I did really push the specific angle that I brought to bear, which was, how does technology affect society? How do you turn that into a force for good? It has always underpinned my perspective on the industry. I was lucky to find folks who also thought that was important, long before it became popular. The message is that, in the early days, it took a lot of very senior, well-rounded renaissance men to allow someone like me to flourish.

Theresia Gouw (TG): I have an interesting contrast to Nancy. I did take an engineering undergraduate degree, at a time when we were about 10% female at the undergraduate level. No one in my family is from the business world. They are all in medicine, because that was what you did when you were a first-generation immigrant from Asia, at least in my family. That was the path that was expected of you. That was not in the cards for me, but engineering was acceptable to my parents for a college degree, and it was great, because it turns out I love technology.

During my studies, I had some summer internships in traditional industries. I did my first summer internship at a research facility for one of the General Motors parts manufacturing businesses. There were a thousand full-time engineers there, two of whom were women.

While I love technology, I saw that what I wanted was to be the product manager or the business manager for a technology company. [The people who had these jobs I wanted all seemed to have gone to business school, so I decided to get a job after graduating that would help me get into business school.] I went into consulting, which was about 25% female. I was fortunate enough to get into business school, and that brought me to Silicon Valley and out to Stanford. That was where my eyes opened up to the world of startups.

I have always tried to focus on the positive aspects of being different and being the only person who looks like me in the room. Especially early in your venture career, when you are expected to go to these big tech conferences, and to try to meet interesting entrepreneurs and find new companies. I split my time between security and infrastructure, as Sonja does, as well as the more consumer-oriented things that all three of us do.

I went to this technical security conference and I realized very quickly that if they are meeting 25 or 50 VCs a day, it is likely that I am the only one who looks like me. If I can ask a smart question or make an insightful comment about their product or company, and then later when I email them and say, "Hey, I met you at so and so conference," my first name happens to be very clearly female, then the chances that they will remember me is much higher compared to somebody who is emailing them with the first name Jim or John.

At my firm, I worked with more people named Jim or Peter than I worked with females. Early on, I said, "This is going to be something that you can choose to focus on the challenges, or instead choose to focus on your unique potential advantage in being somebody who will be easier to reconnect with, or easier to remember in a meeting or in a larger context."

Sonja Hoel Perkins (SHP): I would say that my experience in venture has been a great one. I also fell into it, like Theresia. I do not have the typical venture capital background. The only operating experience I have is from Symantec (now NortonLifeLock) while also studying at Harvard Business School. I was first hired as an investment analyst at TA Associates in the late 1980s. I was the only woman based in Boston, although there was a female partner, Jacqui Morby, who is famous in the industry. She lived in Pittsburgh.

I was really good at sales because I had to be. I would look for companies that were growing really fast. While at TA, I ended up investing in three companies and all of them went public—all before I was 24 years old. One of them was McAfee Associates. McAfee had just agreed to sell to Symantec for $20 million. I convinced John McAfee, the founder, to sell part of the company and let the rest ride. Today, McAfee is worth over $10 billion.

As a woman in VC, some of my strengths include kindness, compassion, fairness, and just being nice. I like it when everyone wins. People remember me, which has given me a great platform to invest in some amazing companies. I am willing to take risks on people who do not fit the mold. Not all of my entrepreneurs are from "central casting," where they have an MBA, an engineering degree, or experience as a CEO. I love backing the scrappy guy who has a great product who everyone else turned down.

My favorite companies are the ones who do well despite themselves. Having huge growth with an unpolished management team shows me there is a real market. Maybe this comes from being in VC since the 1980s. All entrepreneurs were scrappy then. The founders of F5 and Priority Call Management both had a hard time raising VC, but built multi-billion-dollar companies.

Maybe because I am a woman, I have a different perspective. All the women I know in VC are great at winning deals. It is important to identify markets and to find the best companies in those markets, but the most important thing is to win the deal.

FACING CHALLENGES AND MAKING CHANGES

Johannes Lenhard (JL): *The industry has come quite a long way, but we would love to hear whether being a woman has been challenging. Is there any anecdote or situation you want to share?*

SHP: The problem with being women in our industry is that there are so few of us. If there are any women at all, there is usually just one per firm. Nancy and Theresia's current firms are the exceptions. Theresia and I were the only women in our original Silicon Valley firms (Accel and Menlo Ventures). We did not have networks that truly helped us with our careers.

We would occasionally go have a drink or go out to dinner with each other, but we did not share deals or due diligence. Men network very, very well—they have fun and help each other out with their careers. One of my former partners used to say, "No one is ever going to show you a good deal. You have to find it yourself." I had to work a lot harder because almost no one ever showed me a good deal.

To remedy that, 11 years ago, Broadway Angels was founded. Broadway Angels is a group of the top women VCs, and we share deals and due diligence. Together we have invested in some amazing companies such as The RealReal, 128 Technology, Hint Water, Owlet, and so many more. The RealReal went public and many of us did very well. The CEO was only one of 20 female founders to go public, ever. She had more female investors than men, and many of her investors were Broadway Angels.

Investing in The RealReal showed me how important networks are. I wish I had learned that lesson much earlier in life. In addition to Broadway Angels, All Raise and other groups are working to build strong female networks. These efforts are relatively new but are making strong headway.

TG: That is true, and it is not a surprise for those who study other industries and ecosystems. It's the challenge of the tyranny of one; even when you are a managing partner at a firm, if you are the only person who is in the minority, it creates challenges for deal flow. Whether or not it is an industry that you are interested in and have prior experience in, when you are the only woman in the room, sometimes all eyes turn to you to look at that deal.

Another positive trend, in addition to the creation of these all-female networks, is there are many male allies who want to be part of it. If you just look at things such as the Founders Pledge, this generation of entrepreneurs understands that having diversity of thought—however you want to define that—in your cap table and on your board is actually a competitive advantage.

We see this trend at Broadway Angels, and I see this at my own firm. There are a lot of women, such as Nancy, who was one of the first, and now me and several others, who have gone off and started their own venture funds. Our partnerships look like our networks. At my firm, we are almost 90% women and people of color on the investing team, which is almost a mirror opposite of the average venture capital firm. It was not by design, but because of who me, my partner Lauren, and the co-founders are. What is natural is you end up recruiting and hiring people who either you know or are referred to you by somebody you trust. That is why we look the way we do, and we see it as a huge advantage.

Increasingly, more and more companies are thinking about that advantage. As they think about growing the company management team or increasing their advisory board, they want us to be part of it, because we are going to be additive. Our networks are clearly different from the networks of their other investors on the cap table. It started out being challenging, but now it has actually turned into a competitive advantage in many ways.

NP: Absolutely, it has been wonderful to see the transition and the next generation of professionals that really do appreciate what we do. We can be role models, which is not something that was on our agenda earlier in our career. That is uplifting.

Still, let me share an anecdote that shows the persistence of some obstacles—and what is most shocking is that it was recent, about three years ago. By now, we are all at a stage where we are confident, and we have accomplished many things. We approach the world with some sense of gravitas, we do not go around advertising it, but that is our identity.

What is shocking is that I was on a panel with two male venture capitalists and a male moderator. They are not huge names in venture capital, but they are accomplished colleagues. It was all very friendly and upbeat. At the end, the moderator asked the question,"What is your one secret sauce? What makes you successful as an investor?"

The two men went first. The first panelist said, "I am a super seed, early stage investor. I help the entrepreneur really get through both the day-to-day aspects of starting a company, but also the psychology of it, and I am really good at that." The second VC said, "I am very good at helping our companies to connect with strategic partners and business development, and I understand the psyche of corporations. I knit those worlds together."

Saving me for last, the moderator then turned to me and said, "Nancy, what is your secret sauce? *Is it luck?*" He did not say that to anyone else. I was taken aback, but I decided not to say anything and just answered the question, "We have this double bottom line approach that helps entrepreneurs to build great companies and make the world a better place at the same time."

When everyone had gone home, I said, "Do you realize what you did there? You diminished me by saying everything good that has happened to me is just luck. And yet, you were interested in the substance of the two answers from the other two panelists without pre-judging them." His face just went pale, and it was obviously an unconscious bias. He apologized, but then the funny thing was that he said, "I went home and told my wife what happened, and she was furious with me." It was a teachable moment for him. I find it humorous now, but it was a bit of a shock that such an old double standard would still exist so far into our careers.

SHP: Related to that is the MeToo movement, and how the venture capital industry was involved in it. I did not realize harassment was going on in our industry until relatively recently. I did not experience it personally. I just could not believe that our industry of high-standing and high-minded individuals changing the world through technology would behave that way. It was pretty shocking and I was very disappointed.

TG: I was only a few years behind you both coming into the industry, but I was not surprised. This is partially because of personal experiences earlier in my career, but also because I had heard from several of my female entrepreneurs.

NP: I was not that surprised. What is different now is that people talk about it. MeToo made that acceptable and has played a huge role in the evolution of getting to the point where diversity is a huge value add.

CHANGING INDUSTRY ATTITUDES—FOR BETTER AND WORSE

EB: *Looking back at the last three decades, what has changed the most, and would you say that it has been for better or for worse?*

TG: The biggest positive change has been about the understanding of the economic value of diversity—not just the societal value, which as humans and citizens in the world, hopefully we all see, but the economic value of having diversity, as measured by all the things that one can measure outwardly, in your investor group, management team, and on your board, is pretty clear. Thirty years ago, I am not sure if people were studying and measuring it. Even ten years ago, the data was out there but people did not just intuitively believe it. Perhaps people thought that it was the right thing to do, but they did not necessarily think it was the right thing to do for their shareholders. I have seen a light bulb change. I would say it has probably happened within the last five years, in a very meaningful way.

Alongside that, with the rise of more people starting their own venture funds or angel investing, such as Broadway Angels, we have also seen more diversity at early-stage funding. You start to see the beginning of a virtuous cycle: someone who has a different set of networks becomes successful as an entrepreneur, they become an angel investor, maybe they join Broadway Angels so that they can have a network to do that, and they invest in their networks. This starts to create the virtuous cycle of different networks and types of people both having access to venture funding, and being funders of startups. It really is one ecosystem.

NP: I would point to the Harvard study[126] that was done after MeToo, that showed that where there are 10% more female partners in firms, there was an almost 10% increase in profitable exits and a 1.5% spike in overall fund returns each year. It is fabulous to have that data, which we never had in the beginning.

Our awakening came in our double bottom line practice back in 2006. We were a pioneer in measuring various social dimensions, including the diversity of our workforce and our management teams. We were sitting around a table and going through our annual report draft, and I said, "We have a lot of female CEOs or founders. How many do we have? What is the national average?"

It took a month to find one study from Babson College that said that 2% of venture-backed companies had women in their founding or C-suite teams. You cannot believe how hard it was for us to find something on that. Our percentage of women was 26% at the time and I said, "Wow, we are really doing better than the national average, but that national average is pathetic." That began an odyssey of measuring, which we still do to this day.

Now, we are always around 50%. We were focused on other metrics, as well, but it popped off the page that there was something different about our portfolio. The rigor of measurement and the license to talk about it acts as a megaphone for these changes that need to be made. It is all happening, and happening in ways we could not have predicted.

SHP: The advent of the iPhone really changed the industry tremendously. Now billions and billions of people had a computer in their hands, and the market for VC-funded companies grew tremendously. The billion-dollar valuations and billionaire venture capitalists attracted a different kind of person. Profits have become more important than good.

I only invest in "people and companies that matter." I ask myself: If the company went away, would the world miss it? VC has attracted a different person—one who is a lot more profit and greed-oriented.

ADVICE FOR THE NEXT GENERATION OF FEMALE FOUNDERS

JL: *Growing up female in this world over the last three decades, what have you learned that you wish you would have known in the beginning and that you can now share with the next generation?*

---

126. https://hbr.org/2018/07/the-other-diversity-dividend

NP: It is okay to be you. It is okay to be different. Be smart about it, do not walk into a room and make it obvious how different you are, but use it as a tool of distinction that adds to your effectiveness. If you stay true to what you really care about, and are able to be friendly, upfront, and cooperative, you are going to be able to open doors that you never knew existed.

SHP: Networks matter. It took me a while in my career to cultivate meaningful networks, especially with women. I wish I had started earlier. The other is, live your values. Do not do the deal just because it is going to be profitable. Don't invest in a company if you would not let your kids use the product. Live your values at work and at home.

TG: What I would say to my younger self is, at the right time, do not be afraid to bet on yourself.

NP: So true. That first phrase is important: at the right time. You do not have to do it the day you graduate from college!

TG: Part of what gives you confidence in those moments is when you can look at other people before you—that you can relate to for whatever reason—and say, "I can do that." I agree with Nancy, and I am certainly not thinking right out of college. For myself and a lot of other women of my generation, we have done the opposite.

I saw a sociological study that was based on MIT cohort data, which looked at what percentage of MIT graduates started their own companies 10, 20, and 30 years out. The difference was dramatic in the percentages of female graduates versus the percentages of male graduates. In general, women were waiting 10–20 years longer before making those changes. I hope that the next generation of entrepreneurs and VCs closes that gap.

PART II: EXPERIENCES

10 Deepening Our Understanding of Diversity

Diversity has been talked about in business circles for decades, at least since the 1980s.[127] As early as the 1990s, we started to explore the "business case"[128] for diversity. However, what is mostly addressed when people use the word diversity, even today, are only two categories of it, and they are the ones that are only "skin deep": gender and ethnicity. Most VC coverage, in both reports and journalistic[129] outlets, is limited to these two kinds of diversity, and often just to gender diversity. The excuses for this blatant lack of complexity are often simple: we are either not allowed to collect certain kinds of data (such as data on ethnicity in Germany and France[130]) or the data isn't easily obtainable (plus people may be hesitant to declare personal data such as sexual orientation or ethnicity). The results are devastating: in many ways, what isn't measured (or at least talked about) doesn't count, so anyone who isn't a woman or a person of color is underrepresented in conversations about diversity, including in venture capital. Not only is this a blatant issue of social justice in and of itself (and one that is easily attacked by critics, such as the *Woke, Inc* author[131]) but we are also missing out on many of the important possible benefits of diversity: without radically broadening our definition of diversity and especially without taking intersectionality into account, we might be "coloring" VCs and board rooms, but we aren't really making them truly accessible or diverse in opinions, expertise, and background.

In this part of *Better Venture,* we want to consequently open up the meaning of diversity, not with quantitative data and numbers but with

---

127. https://go.gale.com/ps/i.do?id=GALE%7CA6682115&sid=googleScholar&v=2.1&it=r&
    linkaccess=abs&issn=00410861&p=AONE&sw=w&userGroupName=anon%7E66158ff5

128. https://journals.aom.org/doi/abs/10.5465/ame.1997.9709231661

129. https://staging.sifted.eu/articles/diversity-data-european-vc/

130. https://www.theguardian.com/world/2020/jun/16/
    france-and-germany-urged-to-rethink-reluctance-to-gather-ethnicity-data

131. https://www.vivekramaswamy.com/woke

personal histories and narratives from different people in the VC and startup ecosystems. These conversations touch on numerous dimensions of diversity, and help us think about barriers beyond gender and ethnicity.

We start exploring diverse perspectives[11] by acknowledging the documented underrepresentation of women[132] and people of color[133] among VCs and founders. In our conversation with two Silicon Valley natives, Claire Díaz-Ortiz and Maren Bannon, we trace what it means to be women in the tech world, spanning their various roles, including founder and investor, from the West Coast to Europe. The second chapter[11.2] adds another facet to this picture: what does it specifically mean to be a female *founder*? What are the challenges faced when fundraising or working with a founding team? Nandini Jammi and "Maria" (another fantastic female founder whose identity we are protecting given her experiences) were willing to add some color to that conversation. Maria explains the end of her first venture (she has since successfully started another company!) with the following devastating words:

> *I was very much in an environment where my co-founder had his vision for the company and saw me as an extra pair of hands to execute that vision. I did not actually really have a say in where things were going. That became more and more clear the larger we grew. The way things ended with that venture was that I had talked to my co-founder and said, "You know, this equity compensation isn't fair, and this environment isn't feeling like one I can flourish in."*

After hearing several horror stories (and successes) of a similar kind, mostly from experienced female tech founders and investors, the remaining conversations in this section drastically broaden our understanding of what diversity means and what we should include when we talk about it. We start with June Angelides,[11.3] founder of Mums in Tech turned VC investor; she retells the story of how hard it was—and in many ways, still is—to have parenting responsibilities in the tech sector and shares ideas of what can be done to make VC and tech more family friendly. In the next conversation,[11.4] we spoke to Jolina Hukemann, possibly one of

---

132. https://www.europeanwomenvc.org/_files/ugd/de30d6_
     52430eabd0fc4714872ca67265f83b6b.pdf
133. https://www.dropbox.com/s/ducejd5jpjn0piv/BLCKVC%20State%20of%20Black%
     20Venture%20Report.pdf?dl=

the youngest serial entrepreneurs we ever encountered. Jolina demystifies some of the stereotypes when it comes to *being young* (and a woman) in startup-land, and shares some of the challenges she has faced. Our conversation[§11.5] with Emma Lawton, co-founder of More Human, brings up another crucial question: how does a physical disability impact a tech career? Emma brings a phenomenal amount of optimism to her work and to her venture every day, and in fact turns her Parkinson's into what she describes as a kind of superpower:

> *I have insider knowledge on accessibility and what makes a product work. I'm living with complicated stuff every day, and that gives me a greater insight. I think because of that I can go with my gut instinct a lot more than perhaps some other people can when it comes to making decisions. Because if you design for accessibility challenges, it's going to work for everyone.*

With Lorenzo Thione, managing director of angel community Gaingels[134] (and co-founder of StartOut[135]), and Gary Stewart, investor (most recently at Techstars[136]), founder of FounderTribes,[137] and Yale Law School professor, we spoke[§11.6] about an invisible dimension of diversity: being LGBTQ. The two share their stories about how they were treated differently in different countries and how, fortunately, it has become easier over the last 20 years to be openly gay in tech.

The last two conversations[§12] in this section raise awareness about some overlooked aspects of diversity. The first, and possibly most crucial aspect, is class.[§12.1] We asked British Patient Capital[138] LP Ian Connatty and Balderton[139] GP Suranga Chandratillake about the invisible barriers class puts in front of people trying to "break into VC" or become a founder. Suranga argues really strongly that class needs to become a much bigger focal point, including in its intersectional relation to other factors:

> *As someone who's managed to traverse systems, industries, and places, I'm constantly struck by how similar people are in each*

---

134. https://gaingels.com
135. https://startout.org
136. https://www.techstars.com/
137. https://www.linkedin.com/company/founder-tribes/
138. https://www.britishpatientcapital.co.uk/
139. https://www.balderton.com/

field, and yet how enclosed they are in each group. ... Social and cultural capital are the largest gaps I see in the VC industry. Social capital is very simple. Many people just have no knowledge of venture capital at all. Given that so many people use the products of venture every day, the gap is ridiculous.

In the aftermath of COVID-19, we have finally been talking about founder mental health.[140] We spoke§12.2 with VC Matthew De Jesus, expert on mental health for startups Kristina Barger, and founder Øyvind Henriksen about the prevalence of mental health issues, another invisible dimension of diversity that is crucial to take into consideration. In our conversation, we unearth a variety of concrete tips for founders who struggle with their mental health to stay afloat.

The conversations in this section reveal how complex diversity is; even just broadening the conversation slightly takes us to both new problems, but also new benefits—and we are far from comprehensive here. Yes, we need to start somewhere, and gender and ethnicity are great, and obvious, points to begin with. However, the work—and the benefits that come from this work—can't stop there. By focusing solely on these visible dimensions of diversity, we are risking further marginalization of many other groups, and also lose out on one of the major benefits of diversity: bringing people with truly divergent experiences and backgrounds to the table. VC decision making won't be much improved (and there won't be more money going to underrepresented founders) if we only have a few women on the table, who themselves all have Oxbridge, Harvard, or Stanford degrees, or grew up on the Upper East Side. Further opening up the diversity conversation is hugely beneficial to venture capital, as well as the right thing to do from a perspective of representation and social justice.

---

140. https://www.forbes.com/sites/marenbannon/2020/02/10/
    startup-founder-mental-health-why-it-matters-and-how-to-boost-it/

11 Conversations: Diverse Perspectives in Tech

11.1 *Díaz-Ortiz, Bannon: Female Tech Veterans*

Claire Díaz-Ortiz (VC3 DAO, angel investor)

Maren Bannon (January Ventures)

Claire Díaz-Ortiz[141] and Maren Bannon[142] are true tech veterans. Both have been working in the technology sector—from high-caliber operator roles at Genentech and Twitter to recently becoming investors themselves—for the better part of the last two decades. We talked to them about their experience "growing up female" in the tech world during these years, about investing in diverse founders and the importance of opening doors, and about male VCs who say they want to widen their pipeline but don't want to put in the work.

Interviewed November 2020

EXPERIENCES AND CHALLENGES AS WOMEN IN TECH

Erika Brodnock (EB): *You have both worked in the tech ecosystem for more than 15 years in various roles as operators, founders, investors; you span the whole spectrum, which I have to say is inspirational. How has it been? What are your experiences as women? And how has the industry evolved over time?*

Maren Bannon (MB): To contextualize my experience, I was an engineering major in university. I remember that feeling of sitting in class surrounded by men. Unfortunately, since then, I don't think the numbers have gotten that much better when it comes to computer science (CS) and technical degrees. That feeling of being an outsider in the class because of

---

141. https://twitter.com/Claire
142. https://twitter.com/Maren_Bannon

my gender left an imprint. I remember my first CS class; it was all about coding video games. I thought: this is not for me, I'd never been interested in video games. CS just wasn't taught in a way that showed you the diversity of things you could build. Instead, it felt like it was taught for a certain profile of a person, and so I came away from university with my engineering degree, but didn't actually go work as an engineer.

I ended up spending the first half of my career in health tech. I worked at Genentech, which was actually very evenly split between men and women, probably 50/50; the head of the department that I worked in was a woman. I cold emailed her to get the job; she hired me. It was a very positive work environment with a great culture. I think that was a good thing, having my early career be in that environment. I remember there was one man in our department who sexually harassed somebody, and he got fired very swiftly. I think it was a very healthy culture. I feel fortunate that I had that early in my career, but that's probably not the typical experience in tech.

In general, I don't think the culture for women in tech more generally has changed that much, unfortunately, in the last 15 years. There's a lot more talk now—and I think social media amplifies all of the talk about this topic—but I don't know if the numbers and the environments and the feeling on the ground for female founders or female employees has really changed that much in 15 years.

Claire Díaz-Ortiz (CD): For me, it's weird because I grew up in Silicon Valley, in Berkeley, and then went to Stanford, all during those hot years. So it's strange that I didn't feel I was a part of the tech scene until I was about 28. But looking back, we went to a party as freshmen at the Napster founder's house. And you know, the guy who crashed on my kitchen floor with his girlfriend (on top of a blanket, no mattress) when I studied overseas in Italy is the chief product officer at Facebook. You know, it's like all of that was happening there, but I wasn't aware of it. Joe Lonsdale, who started Palantir, was in my 80-person freshman dorm; we called him "Muscle Man Joe."

But in general, I was just not aware of the extent of the white tech privilege I was raised into. And I really wasn't in tech in any real way until I sort of happened to stumble into it. I had some random career for the first five years out of college, living in random countries doing freelance stuff, and then ended up with a blog that became really successful. At the time, blogs were mostly held on blogger.com and the folks that created Twitter were the folks that had worked at Blogger. Twitter was spun out of a two-week side project. After they had made my blog popular, they invited me to join Twitter. They put us on the homepage and then wrote a blog post about us joining. My best friend and I were traveling around the world at the time. Then we had a non-profit in Kenya, and Maren came out and volunteered. That's how Maren and I met 12 years ago, when Maren was in business school.

So I became basically an early Twitter influencer, because there was no one on the platform at the time, certainly not from Kenya and no one tweeting about "tech for good" stuff. This is how I ended up joining Twitter as an employee. My experience at Twitter was pretty positive, but very gendered. I showed up, I started as an intern at the very end of my MBA, and there were about 50 people there—and they were mostly men. At the time, there were two bathrooms, one for the women and one for the men. But it was really frustrating because the men always used the women's bathroom. My first salary negotiation was like a complete joke. The person I was negotiating with had just told me how he had been grossly overpaid at his past job in tech, but the reason I should only earn $65K, after both an MBA and a Master's degree from Stanford and Oxford, was because I should feel lucky working for Twitter because it was like a "golden ticket." But then I was told I wouldn't even get that deal at first, and first I had to start as a contractor for $20 an hour with no stock options. I remember trying to negotiate that with the (contractor) female recruiter out in the hallway, and she was like, "Uh, yeah, there's no room to go up." It's wild to look back on.

I had a good experience with the company. But I began to see how a lot of the issues of discrimination, against women in particular, were oftentimes a matter of disorganization—or lack of organization, you could say—in terms of HR and legal systems put in place to protect employees at companies that grow really fast. For a long time at early explosive startups—in those days, at least—no one was thinking of how to best put in policies in place; it was just bros coding, and then the company exploding, and then everyone was off to the races. And in those days, we were way less aware of the negative consequences of our work—hence the entire premise of that Netflix documentary on social media.

Johannes Lenhard (JL): *What is the most awkward, annoying story or experience that you're willing to share?*

MB: I can share an experience when I was a female founder back in the Bay Area. I think the process of fundraising as a female founder is quite an interesting one. It's definitely what led me to co-found January Ventures [her own VC fund] because I think there's a lot that's wrong with the way VC is structured.

In the early days of building my startup, I was pitching a very well-known male investor. He heard my pitch and said, "I like you. I'd love to invest in you, but I'm just not interested in your business [which was like a class pass for kids' activities]. If your startup were for hedge funds or golf, I would invest." It's fine that he wasn't interested in my business, but calling out that hedge funds and golf were more exciting to him than kids' activities felt a little obnoxious.

THE LACK OF FEMALE INVESTING PARTNERS IN VC

CD: So I can talk about some more recent experiences of getting into VC. We know VC is bad for women, and I saw that from the beginning. I started angel investing while doing other stuff after leaving Twitter; it was really when I started thinking about a job in VC about two years ago that I came to understand many of the systematic issues at play. When I decided to enter VC, I took about a year to talk to most of the firms in Latin America, where I live. As an author of a bunch of books, I process things through writing. During that time, I took many months to write a long piece for *TechCrunch*[143] that looked at a lot of the numbers in terms of female founders and VCs in Latin America. Some of these numbers no one had actually put together before in a digestible form. So the results are dire—in Latin America, only about 7% of VC check writers are women, so only 7% of investing partners are women.

There were two themes I saw again and again. First, senior level women are consistently on the operating side, not on the investing side of the VC firms. That is the classic way for a firm to say they have a woman in leadership. It is amazing to me how little understanding there is of this, even among the women. Recently, a woman was promoted to partner in one of the top funds here, but it was an operating partner. And every-

---

143. https://techcrunch.com/2020/02/06/
    latin-america-takes-the-global-lead-in-vc-directed-to-female-co-founders/

one was congratulating her; obviously, it's a wonderful accomplishment! Big congrats! But as I was talking about it with another female investing partner [there are less than 20 of us in LatAm], I realized that even she didn't fully understand the difference between the two roles. And she's a VC! Imagine what chance a female founder has of understanding that a woman on the operating side is not likely to help get her a check!

Secondly, when talking to funds, I kept hearing again and again: "half our team is women" when the women work in administration, or "the first people that review our deals are women." Yeah, because they're analysts. Junior, junior analysts! So the idea that women are there, when they don't have power, and have these really junior roles, is a real issue that hides that problem.

There is a list of all the women investing in LatAm that someone put together. And there's a question in the list that says: do you have decision making power? Everyone on that list checks "yes"! I want to empower young women investors, but it's important also to understand what "check-writing ability" and "decision-making power" in a fund really mean!

I think that the number one thing is that when you get a woman investing partner, she really is two to three times more likely to invest in a female-founded team. That's the big lever. We just need different types of investors with different backgrounds to spot outsized opportunities.

FUNDS NEED TO WIDEN THEIR PIPELINES

EB: *Thank you so much for sharing these insights, both of you. I am really keen to hear what you think could be done differently.*

MB: I definitely agree on the more female investors; I think 30–40% of the check-writing team needs to be female to have a better chance to invest in more female founders. I think being the only female partner is a hard position to be in. Funds can promote women at these funds into check-writing roles, or hire them into those roles. Another promising path is more female-led funds. We're seeing more and more of that, because I think the path to work your way up at some of these big funds is a slog, especially for a woman, unfortunately.

The other thing is that you have to widen your pipeline, you've got to get out of your networks, you've got to stop relying on the warm intros. Recognizing the gaps in your pipeline is the first step; then design a process to remove the bias from it. It would be helpful to see more funds actually setting goals around this. If you're a fund with outside LPs, you can't necessarily set a quota, but you could set a goal. If you don't set a goal, you're never going to actually change. A lot of these initiatives don't feel like they're serious because there aren't any metrics. It is just PR.

SUCCESS STORIES FROM DIVERSE INVESTING

JL: *You are now both in roles where you are investing at least part of your efforts giving money to women and diverse founders. What results are you seeing? Can you already share success stories?*

MB: I can share some of the stats about our portfolio: we've invested in 33 companies, and 90% have a female founder, 50% have a founder of color, 39% have an immigrant founder, 70% are outside the Bay Area. It's a much more diverse group of people that we're investing in, a different type of founder than the typical VC. If you look backwards at who founded the current unicorns, it would cause you to invest in a lot of white men. But we believe that the next decade is going to have a very different person founding these big companies. It's going to be people all over the world, from many different backgrounds.

CD: I think what is perhaps most interesting is just the concept of planting a flag with this kind of work; we are saying we want to invest in women or founders of color. That in itself is really, really important, particularly in emerging markets like LatAm. This ensures that founders will come to you and pitch their business knowing it's a safe space, where we're not gonna discuss "what it's like to be a woman with a baby starting a fintech company," and instead we'll just freakin' talk about your fintech company. The thing you see in emerging markets is that the first step in VC funding is always the easier step, which is investing in all the founders that have these stamps of approval: they grew up in Nairobi or Buenos Aires, yes, but then they went to GSB [Graduate School of Business] at Stanford and got into YC [Y Combinator]. In Latin America, we're at least seeing moves towards the second step. I'm in a fund where we do a lot of investing in founders who aren't on the typical road.

There's an author and investor, Nathalie Molina,[144] and I saw a quote she had about how great mentors don't just guide you, they actually open

---

144. https://twitter.com/NathalieMolina

new doors for you. And I think of that a lot in terms of investing in female founders and emerging markets. I think what a lot of these women need is to be more accessible, for them to reach people overseas.

Let me give you an example. Maren and I are in this intimate angel group of women VCs in different geographies I put together, who invest in female founders across borders. We call ourselves the Angel Collective, and it's been a great way to co-invest with trusted investors through our funds or as angels. So there is this one founder from Uruguay, and she is awesome. But Uruguay is a small country that not everyone has heard of. She's called Ximena; she doesn't have perfect English, but I think she's really strong. There's another investor in our group from Hustle Fund, Elizabeth Yin.[14.3] Elizabeth had done one deal at that point in Latin America, which had come out of 500 Startups (where she worked before). Again, you want the stamp of approval.

When our fund decided to invest in Ximena's company, Prometeo, basically a Plaid for LatAm, I thought this deal was an Elizabeth kind of deal. They already had a lot of revenue. It was really interesting to me, the founder's experience when she talked to Elizabeth's partner, Shiyan. Ximena was very nervous about the call; this was her first US investor. But they ended up really hitting it off and Hustle Fund invested. And that same founder, I sent her to one of the best funds on Sandhill Road [in Silicon Valley] and told them they needed to talk to her. Their feedback? There was "cultural dissonance."

ADVICE TO VCS ON DIVERSIFYING INVESTMENTS

EB: *We talked about goal setting for funds and the issue with quotas. What other practical advice would you give VCs to do better when it comes to investing in diverse founders?*

CD: I see the pipeline issue as a real issue, but not in the way people think. For example, there was this VC who tweeted recently about how only a very small percentage of the people applying to him are women and that he would like to increase this number. It's a good thing to say that on Twitter, but it's also a stupid thing. You're the one that should go out and find them! You go get that pipeline—it's waiting for you!

MB: I find those comments irritating because they feel lazy. You could go out and hire diverse people on your team; there are all these different organizations and schools and events where you can meet people to change your pipeline. But it takes work. It's complacent to say, "This is our pipeline, we did our best, and we're just not seeing these founders. There's a lot you can do if you actually want to take action; find a bunch of female scouts, for instance.

11.2 *Jammi, Anonymous: Female Founders*

Nandini Jammi (Check My Ads, formerly Sleeping Giants)

Maria (name changed for anonymity)

We spoke with two female founders—Nandini Jammi[145] and Maria, whose name we changed for anonymity reasons—about their experiences. While the range of different stories and experiences is endless, we take what Nadini and Maria tell us about co-founder betrayal, bias, and dishonesty as exemplary—and possibly one of the biggest barriers—of bad role models keeping others from even considering joining the ecosystem.

Interviewed January 2021

INEQUALITY AND BETRAYAL IN CO-FOUNDING RELATIONSHIPS

Erika Brodnock (EB): *Nandini and Maria, you both had a really tumultuous time with co-founding ventures in the past. Can you tell us a bit more about that?*

Maria: A couple of years ago, I co-founded a FinTech company. I was coming right out of school, and I met a co-founder who had a similar idea to mine. He was already working on the early version of it and asked if I wanted to be involved as a co-founder. It was in a space I was really passionate about as well, so I said yes. I turned down a job offer and took the riskier path of becoming an entrepreneur.

However, I was really new to everything with entrepreneurship; I did not know about cap tables, I didn't really know about how to build co-

---

145. https://twitter.com/nandoodles

founder relationships. I did not know what I should be looking for. It is interesting because sometimes I look back and blame myself and say, I was naive. That's how I ended up in a less than ideal situation. But on the other hand, I think that in situations where we don't know a lot, we hope that we can put trust in the people around us and in the systems in place working well enough, to protect us from getting into a more vulnerable position. Anyway, I digress. Essentially, we built this company over a multiple-year period, we scaled it to three or four countries, we had millions of dollars coming through our platform and were on a high.

Things started to change when we started raising our first official round of funding. Investors started saying, "Wait a second, the fact that you only own 2% of this company is a really bad thing." By this point, I had come to learn what a cap table was and understood what fair compensation should resemble, and had realized this for myself too. In many companies, what I had was the equivalent of an early employee. I asked to shift things around, but my co-founder was not particularly keen on it.

I also started to realize my voice was not really being heard either. I was very much in an environment where my co-founder had his vision for the company and saw me as an extra pair of hands to execute that vision. I did not actually really have a say in where things are going. That became more and more clear the larger we grew. I decided that I wanted to leave, and the final conversation I had with my co-founder was after we had met with a number of investors who started to say they would invest if the cap table changed. A few even said they would invest if we switched roles, and I became the CEO. For me, it was cool, because I had felt very small, but then these external investors, looking at the company, were validating that I had done a lot of the work to get us to where we were, which is what encouraged me to have the courage to move on.

Nandini Jammi (NJ): A lot of that sounds familiar. In November 2016, I was working as a marketing manager at a small tech company. A couple of weeks after the 2016 elections, I visited Breitbart.com, this website that I had been hearing about, that I knew was a vector of disinformation, but had never seen for myself.

The first thing I noticed as a marketer was that it was covered in ads—this is probably how they were making so much money and doing so well. They were publishing incendiary content, fake news basically, and then monetizing it through programmatic advertising. The first thing I did was write a piece on Medium explaining the relationship between Breitbart and their advertising revenues. I talked about how Breitbart, a rightwing media outlet, was being run by Steve Bannon, a white nationalist, and that he was now set to become chief advisor in the White House. I pointed out how important it was that we do not support this financially in any way. I noted that the only way that we could do that as a community was by adding Breitbart.com to our exclusion list in Google. I then urged marketers, particularly those in charge of running Google ad campaigns, to exclude the website from media buy. I included a help desk article from Google. Then I took a screenshot of an Old Navy ad on Breitbart, posted it on Twitter and tagged Old Navy in the post: "Old Navy, did you know your ads are on Breitbart?"

I just started this thing on my own. The very next day, an anonymous Twitter account called Sleeping Giants contacted me saying, "Oh my God, how cool that you're doing the same thing that we're doing." That was how I learned that the Twitter account and I had basically the same idea, although he had started a week earlier than I had. Within a day, we were in touch over the phone. We had a lot in common, it turns out. We were both copywriters from Maryland. We both had a similar outlook, vision, and way of thinking. It felt very natural for us to team up and work on this thing together. He ran the Twitter account; I ran the Facebook page.

Together, we coordinated and worked on Breitbart. This campaign initially was just taking screenshots of ads on Breitbart ourselves and tweeting at the companies. As we grew, because it was such an accessible thing to do, people wanted to join us, and it quickly turned into a crowdsourced effort. Very soon, we had thousands of people contacting companies with screenshots they had taken while visiting Breitbart. Companies were coming back, sometimes within hours or even minutes, to say that the ad placements were unintentional, and they were taking steps to block the site from their media buys. We grew to several hundreds of thousands of followers.

During the time we were anonymous, he was the de facto leader to me, because the name Sleeping Giants was his idea. I felt that because I had joined "his" effort, that he was entitled to that leadership position and to have the final say. There were other factors at play: he was 15 years older than me, he had more experience than I did. I believed that was reason enough to defer to his judgment. Although we worked relatively independently, I would check in with him if I wanted to try something.

We also had that dynamic when it came to speaking to the press. Early on, he asked that I give him all of the press requests, just so that we could "stay on message." I agreed to that, believing that it did not really matter because we were anonymous.

Then in July 2018, we were outed. The Daily Caller identified him as the founder of Sleeping Giants. Knowing this was coming, he contacted a *New York Times* reporter to get ahead of the story and asked me if I'd like to also join him in that. I said yes, because I was ready to come out. I wanted to do more advocacy work around adtech but had really been hamstrung by our anonymity. In the article, we had two pictures side by side, as equals, and it did not quite identify us by any titles. There was a bit of nebulousness to that.

After we came out, we had a lot of attention coming our way. The next few days and weeks, I found that he was taking interviews on his own without giving me a heads-up, and he would take interviews as the founder of Sleeping Giants. At first, I did not think it was a big deal, because I did not necessarily want the attention, nor did I feel as though I needed it. But as these interviews kept appearing, I realized that the way that I was being portrayed, the way that he was talking about me was like an assistant, or as a helper in the relationship. I was really uncomfortable with that.

I called a meeting with him to discuss it, and I said, "I need a title too, and we need to find some ways to make this situation work for me, because I don't want to look like your helper." I outlined the things that I wanted, and he said, "Yes, sure, we'll make sure you get all the credit you deserve." Shortly after this conversation, we agreed that I would take on the title "founding organizer." It was a silly title, but it was the best thing I could come up with that was not "co-founder," which he had explicitly rejected.

Days and weeks passed, and nothing changed. He continued taking interviews on his own. We had a few follow-up calls where I would bring up concerns that I was being shut out of vital communications and left out of major media opportunities. I was also helping sell SG merchandise and had no insight into how that money was being spent. During each call, he would make vague commitments and never follow up with my asks. In the meantime, he was able to build an entire profile for himself through Sleeping Giants, which he was able to translate into real-world influence—speaking at the big conferences, having a seat at the table. People would contact him first and not me. Because why would they? I was not seen as a leader in this effort ... or seen at all.

Exactly one year later, he went to Cannes [Lions International Festival of Creativity] and sent me a picture of himself accepting a Gold Lion, the media and communication industry's biggest award! I had no idea he was going. I had no idea we were even nominated for a Gold Lion. I was obviously not there and I feel I was kept out of it purposefully.

This was a really difficult time for me, both personally and professionally. I was still trying to find my footing career-wise. Sleeping Giants took up so much of my time and paid nothing, it was a volunteer gig. I was working as a freelancer, but it was really hard to build a career in the same industry you're openly and vocally critical of. So I had been working on trying to build my profile as an activist. I wanted to try and support my work through speaking engagements and consulting.

So for me to be left out of the industry's biggest award was an enormous betrayal to me. Not just personally, but on a professional level. That event would have created a significant opportunity for me to network with the right people and get my foot in the door. My career matters too. I should have been there. I no longer trusted him at all.

That was the moment I decided I needed to change something or leave. But I wasn't willing to leave my own campaign, particularly because I would never be able to pursue my career aspirations without it. So instead, I went rogue. I changed my title to co-founder and started taking on all press requests that did not specifically ask for him. I started to take some influence back, write under my own name more often, and claim my own wins rather than feed them to him to post as Sleeping Giants. Then in the summer of 2020, I left Sleeping Giants and started my own new venture.

EXPERIENCING EXPLICIT AND IMPLICIT BIAS

Johannes Lenhard (JL): *How much of your experience do you think was shaped by the fact that you are female? Or that you are not the white male founder and investor archetype?*

NJ: To me, it is pretty clear that the fact that I was not white and male completely changed my trajectory when we came out to the public in the *New York Times*. The pictures were equal in size right next to each other, and it is clear that people saw one of them to be a leader and the other wasn't, and that was me. In the following months, it became clear that my experience was completely different from my partner's. I was not being approached for interviews. Nobody was asking for me at all. To me, it is clear that my co-founder fit the archetype of "white savior." It was almost as though they were looking for that person. They were looking for someone to fill that role ... and they found it in him.

JL: *We see that in the numbers. That's what this whole world is made up of, right? White men supporting their own kind.*

NJ: White men supporting the campaign against bigotry and sexism being led by a white male. They somehow managed to center even a story like that around a white male.

Maria: Me being a woman definitely impacted how my co-founder perceived me, how investors, at least in the beginning, perceived me. What was interesting was that by the end, the investors, as I mentioned, were starting to see me as the person who could lead the company.

In my own experience, my being a woman definitely shaped the dynamics with my co-founder. Actually, I saw this with all the women who joined our team, there was this really toxic dynamic where the men could always make executive decisions. Even at a more junior level. If a man was speaking, that was the voice the room listened to. The other women in the team were initially just in customer service, which my co-founder saw as the lowest rank, and in meetings would yell at them, verbally, raising his voice, and calling them out in front of the team for doing something "stupid" rather than giving valuable feedback one on one, or creating a constructive environment.

There was this negative culture in our team, and it sometimes felt very male versus female. It made me really curious how many early-stage startups have this dynamic, because I do think there is a general idea that women know less or are more soft-spoken, or more gentle, and don't have things to bring to the table.

After leaving, I learned that one of the women on our team was actually sexually harassed by someone on our team. That was a shock and made me think, "I knew that environment was bad, but I had no idea how bad until after I left." It really made me wonder how many early-stage startups have cases of sexual harassment or a toxic internal culture. At an early stage, you don't have diversity and inclusion practices, you don't have HR yet. In many ways, these could be the most dangerous environments for women to be in. Especially as there are no consequences if things do go wrong.

CREATING AND MAINTAINING A SAFE ENVIRONMENT

EB: *What specific things are important to think through when setting up your business? What do you think people could learn from some of the experiences you have just detailed?*

Maria: One is thinking about discrimination and harassment policies from day one. At the new company I am now a part of, we are thinking about how we can create a really safe environment from the beginning. We have been doing a lot of reading, and it just seems like startups totally missed the boat on all the things HR policies, especially for women, whether that's anything from maternity leave, to work-life balance, to actually the really important, challenging discrimination policies.

We have put those in place at the new company and are working hard to ensure we are an inclusive and safe place to work. If all of this had not been so poor at my last company, I would not have learned how important it is to do that. I am really proud of the safe culture that we are creating as a result of this challenging learning.

The second thing I would do is create really clear processes in general. For example, if we have a codified system of how to give feedback and what that looks like, then we could put that into practice more easily. That's something I've really been trying to do in my new role, documenting all the processes, especially when it comes to culture, so that all new hires have guidelines for how to do things. That is something that was really missing at my last company. If we had best practices in writing, it could have really changed a lot of behavior. But then again, you also need a team that is willing to do that too.

TAKE CREDIT, GIVE CREDIT

NJ: The first thing I've learned is that when it comes to any new idea or concept (the way a lot of startups start), take credit and give credit, freely and generously. One thing that I wish that I did earlier was, and there wasn't really a possibility to do it when we were anonymous, but I should have at least made a note of my own ideas and my own wins. That would have made negotiating later about what my job title or my role should be much easier. Taking that credit, as well as giving it, is one of the things that I do now.

The venture we are building now is very much a consultancy. Right now, it is me and my business partner, Claire, and we are very much invested in each other's success. The way that we demonstrate that is by always elevating each other on social media. We take that extra time to elevate and promote, and it makes us both look more powerful and more unified.

ADVICE TO FUTURE FOUNDERS

JL: *If you could give a piece of advice to your own 18-year-old self, what would it be?*

NJ: I have two things I'd like to say. One is, I got lucky. My current business partner, we were friends first. We have an existing relationship and we have had a lot of upfront conversations about where we want to be and what our expectations are for ourselves, in our personal lives and our professional lives. We have asked each other whether we are on the same page as far as the longevity of the company and what it would take for us to sell out.

That has helped build and create trust because it is one thing to be friends, of course, but it is another thing to go into business together. Luckily, through these conversations and in working together, we have found that we have different and complementary core competencies. We have split our duties that way. The other thing is that we have different personal interests. That means that if there is something that she is better at, or an opportunity she is better suited for, that helps us decide who gets to take it.

Finally, we are really careful about who we work with and who we associate with. We have had people approach us for partnerships or to be our clients. If we feel that they don't have the level of integrity we are looking for, we turn them down. This allows us to make time and space for people who are supportive of us, our mission, but also of women in general. We take the time to look at their social media profiles and to talk to others, and we use our whisper networks to see who is worth elevating and working with before we get involved with them.

Maria: One piece of advice is really practical, and it is to be a solo founder. At least be a solo founder until you find someone you are really sure about.

The expectation of co-founders has been set by YC [Y Combinator], and a lot of early-stage incubators or programs. They say you need a co-founder to be able to build something successful. But often since the tech world is really dominated by men, and many men who tend to naturally flock toward working with other men, it is hard to find a co-founder in the first place. Then maintaining healthy relationships with them can be difficult.

I've heard a lot of other women with stories like mine, and Nandini is yet another, and I think: as women, we are strong and powerful. A lot of us have it in us to build something alone. That's a really practical piece of advice I would give my younger self.

The second would be to surround yourself with the right people. I know that is easier said than done. But this is something, especially in building my company, that I have been super careful about. We really want to know the character of a candidate before working with them. We want to make sure they have the right skill sets, but knowing that they are a person of integrity, of trust, who is kind and willing to collaborate, is crucial. I haven't been afraid both on hiring team members and on the investor side of things to say no to people who I don't feel have that kind of culture-fit that we are looking for in these early stages.

The third piece of advice would be: I'm capable, I have good ideas. That is something that I really struggled with at my last company. I listened when my co-founder would say, "I'm the one to speak in the investor meetings." I would have prepared everything and written all the notes and made the entire presentation, but I trusted that I did not know enough to be able to answer the questions. To my younger self, I would definitely say: "Your voice matters, and you have earned that seat at the table, so own it."

11.3 *Angelides: Mothers in Tech*

June Angelides (Samos Investments)

June Angelides,[146] MBE, started Mums in Tech[147] back in 2015, while on her second maternity leave working for Silicon Valley Bank. June has since become a venture capital investor herself, at Samos Investments, and received an MBE for services to women in technology. Together we explored her experiences as a parent in tech and the considerations the industry needs to make to become more family-friendly.

Interviewed October 2020

OPENING THE DOORS OF THE TECH WORLD TO MUMS

Johannes Lenhard (JL): *What was the goal of Mums in Tech?*

June Angelides (JA): The goal was to teach mums about what it was like to work in a tech company, to really break down tech work and to show them that it was more than coding. I wanted to create an educational platform for mums that could help them break into tech. Over eight weeks, mums would learn about product, UX, Agile, HTML, CSS, JavaScript, and learn how to present their ideas. I think a lot of the time when people hear tech, they think coding, they think sitting in a dark room at a computer all day. My whole mission was to demystify tech, and really put it into practical terms by experiencing tech. I brought these mums in to spend time with Microsoft executives, with tech teams, heads of digital and heads of engineering at startups and scaleups. I wanted mums to experience tech professionals and have access to them so that they could ask all those questions that they have about working in a tech company. And at the end of it, I wanted them to build something. Everyone, at the end of the program, built a website or a prototype of an app. They had something to

---

146. https://twitter.com/JuneAngelides
147. https://www.linkedin.com/company/mums-in-technology-ltd/

show for it at our graduation and they would present it with a sense of ful-fillment.

CREATING SPACE FOR MUMS TO DEVELOP TECH SKILLS

JL: *How did you come to start Mums in Tech. Was it based on your personal experience? What was the idea and what did you set out to do?*

JA: I was on my second maternity leave, and I guess I had lots of time to think because I had a C-section for my second child. That resulted in two months of not really being able to go anywhere, with lots of time to reflect. I started to think about what I wanted my return to work to look like. The one thing I knew was that I didn't want it to be a repeat of what happened the first time. After having Adam, my first child, I had been on the venture debt team [at Silicon Valley Bank] and wanted to return to work three days a week, and was told that I couldn't and that this specific role couldn't be done part-time. That was a big blow to my confidence, because I loved that role; it was perfect and I enjoyed it. When I went back and did start part-time, I joined a brand-new team. That was really hard to accept, first of all, because I never expected that. I literally felt like a complete beginner. But then there were all these expectations that I knew certain things, not only because of a new role but also because as far as they were concerned, I should have come back as I left in terms of my up-to-date knowledge. But in my head, so much had changed and I had just devoted a full year to Adam, to being the best mum possible. I think baby brain had really set in and I felt a little bit uncomfortable and low in confidence.

I was very determined that this experience wouldn't repeat itself with my second child. I wanted to make sure my brain was engaged the entire time, and I wanted to do something for me. At the time of reflecting on this, I had the realization that I was working with all these great tech companies, yet I wasn't able to have these deep technical conversations with them, because I didn't have the technical skills. So, still on maternity leave, I decided that I wanted to learn and see what it was like to build an app. I just wanted to go through the motions and see what it was like, so I went on Freelancer.com to hire a developer and I remember writing a mes-sage saying, "I'm looking for a developer, I've only got £150." They laughed me off the site. I was completely naive, and way too optimistic about how these things work. So I decided to go one step further and wanted to learn about coding, because coding kept coming up in all of my conversations with tech founders and startups. I went on Codecademy, did a couple of classes, and very quickly realized that I wanted to learn with other people. I wanted a proper community. I wanted to have an instructor in front of me, where I could ask questions when I got stuck.

At the time, I couldn't find anything out there that was doing this, particularly not with a focus on my situation of being a mum. [There was Tech Mums, but they weren't focused on programs where you could bring kids on site.] When you googled classes for mums on maternity leave, all you got were mummy and babies singing and dancing classes, or weaning classes, and I thought, wow, there's nothing for us to learn. My initial thinking was to reach out to Amali de Alwis, who was CEO of Code First: Girls. I knew they were a girls' coding school, so I asked if there was any chance we could do something for mums. She really inspired me to think about starting something, and also kindly organize us a space. She really helped me think through the curriculum, and shared the curriculum from Code First: Girls. I started Mums in Tech as the first child-friendly education program for mums. It was all about bringing the babies.

In my network, I had these amazing people who've done similar things before—starting a company, crafting a syllabus—and they helped me to do it. The most important thing, however, when crafting the program was: these are mums who are busy, who maybe have the school run in the morning, in the afternoon, worrying about how to feed this baby in the class—how do I design an educational syllabus on technology in such a way that it is inclusive, so that they feel comfortable, they feel safe?

Another thing that was important was childcare on site. I wanted mums to have their hands free during classes. It's really hard trying to hold a baby and type. I wanted Mums in Tech to be three hours in the morning that mums could have to themselves, but with the babies. If they needed to feed, they could have the baby and then give the baby back to the nanny, but the baby is right there in the room, in a very relaxed space. I wanted people to feel that coming to Mums in Tech means we're going to have fun, meet nice people, and learn.

For the first cohort, I had about 100 people apply and I whittled it down to 30. Very quickly, I realized that that was a lot of people to have in one room. I wanted to make sure that I helped these 30 people. We made sure that we had the right space in place—we ended up starting with meeting rooms at the Thoughtworks and M&S [Marks and Spencer] corporate HQ in central London—and most importantly, that the right people came to teach. I was expecting these engineers to give up three hours of their day and thankfully so many did, very willingly. We had the head of engineering at M&S, leading the program and in fact designing it with me. We would look at the M&S website during the program and they would show us live as bugs and interactions were happening; it was amazing to get a real feel for how they would deal with problems. Everything was very practical in this sense.

I think for the people teaching, it was fascinating for them, too, just to see so many incredibly talented women who also were looking for new opportunities. A lot of them were looking for new careers, so those conversations were happening. We were exploring whether it was possible to enable work experience for the women, which ended up being tricky at the time. That would have made the program even stronger—learning how to do a tech job and then immediately putting it into practice.

SUCCESS STORIES OF MUMS IN TECH

Erika Brodnock (EB): *What were your biggest successes with Mums in Tech?*

JA: If I had to tell you the story of one of my mums, the one that stands out the most is Sarah. Sarah was part of the pilot program, and as part of the pilot, we would go on field trips. So we went to the BBC, Makers Academy, and Tech Will Save Us. When she went to Makers Academy, she loved it there, and straight after the talk, she said to me: "June, I love it, I want to do it. I know now after that session that I want to code," and she signed up there and then. For me, that was just so incredible; because she had been made redundant, she wasn't sure what she was going to do next. She did the course while breastfeeding, and her husband did the first shared parental leave at Credit Suisse; he took six months off so that she could do the Makers Academy program. I just thought: wow, she is nailing it. She ended up building her own app and is still going strong while managing to raise investment (for a completely remote team of mothers, which I absolutely love).

Mums in Tech gave her a chance to have that taster, which was always the aim: to give mothers a taste of what it's like to work in tech.

JL: *What kind of activities did mums get involved in at Mums in Tech?*

JA: The courses ran for three hours, once a week, for eight weeks. The first week covered: what is a (tech business) idea? How do you go from an idea to a product? The next week we would focus on user experience design (UX design). During the three hours spent with us, mums would have a lesson, an exercise, and the chance to ask questions. Each week, mums would produce something tangible that would lead them to their final project. They would learn about testing, customer research, idea validation, and different coding languages, such as HTML, CSS, and JavaScript. They would actually do coding in the class as well. Outside of class, they had access to a Slack group, so we would group them into cohorts. They had access to all of the instructors, as well as to each other, to help and support with the homework.

COVID, CHILDCARE, AND OTHER CHALLENGES FOR PARENTS

EB: *How would you say that COVID-19 is changing the landscape for mums? And what do we need to do about it?*

JA: For as long as the schools are open, it's okay, but I would say, when the schools were shut, it was hard. And I think many mums felt it the hardest, because they felt that homeschooling fell on them. Their work was suffering as a result and they felt like they had to overcompensate. So once the kids finally went to bed, they found that they were logging back on, and just working really ridiculous hours trying to show that yes, I have worked, even though the reality was they were so burnt out.

So for me, it was a constant balancing act. I had to be very upfront with my team and say, I'm not going to be able to work the usual hours; it's just impossible. But we had that conversation very early, because I didn't want to start disappointing them. I said, I will get as much done as I can, but really, in this time without our nanny, I'm going to have to spread out my work day and also my weekly schedule. Like me, I think a lot of people felt a massive sort of tug of war between guilt and their own expectations, and what they know they're capable of delivering but can't physically do, because there's just not enough hours.

EB: *COVID-19 obviously is only one kind of emergency, making being a mum in tech very complicated. What do you think needs to be done to better deal with such issues systematically?*

JA: I think a lot of it is down to childcare. So it's fine as long as we have schools open, and if not, I think employers should be asking the mums in their teams what they need to help reduce their workload, whether it be a nanny for a couple of hours a day with costs borne by the employers if the schools are closed. They should be offering childcare to parents so that they can work effectively, or they should tell them to feel free to reduce their day and do what they can, without cutting their pay.

EB: *What about from a mental health perspective?*

JB: I think everyone should be offered therapy. I don't think I could have survived COVID-19 without my coach. She doesn't realize how much of a therapist she's been to me. Mental health needs to be prioritized because a lot of people are feeling isolated, on top of having this strange workload. On top of that, many people are working harder to distract themselves. I know I was doing it for a while, because I didn't want to deal with this crazy environment that we find ourselves in, I was putting a lot more on my plate than I normally would. Because it was too much, I had really bad anxiety at the start of it. So I thought, "I'm going to distract myself as much as possible."

In these situations, employers have a duty to make sure they are paying attention. My boss several times would say to me, "June, you're not allowed to work on Friday, you're not allowed to work on Monday. Don't reply to any emails." He was paying attention. Employers need to set an example and, for instance, not send emails at the weekend, which I really think is important. My employers don't send emails to me on non-working days, and that helps me to switch off because I feel they are respecting my time and not putting unnecessary pressure on me.

THE KEY TO ENTREPRENEURIAL SUCCESS FOR PARENTS

JL: *So, independent of COVID-19, what are the key pieces of advice you would offer to an entrepreneur that either is a parent already, specifically a mum, or wants to become one. What is the key to success?*

JA: The key is, you have to put yourself first. You need to give yourself time to regroup, because there is a lot going on. Self-care is so important.

Make time for yourself, because the kids are around quite a lot. Particularly now, kids are not able to burn off as much energy as before, because all their after school activities have gone on hold to reduce transmission of COVID-19. So, when they go to sleep, give yourself that time to just be, be still, whether it's yoga you do, or reading, or talking to friends, do something for you. I've started carving out 30 minutes to do something that makes me happy every day. I have blocked it in my diary, from 8:30 to 9 a.m. Sometimes it's tidying up my room, because that will make me happy. Sometimes it is something as silly as just listening to music or dancing in my room, or it might be yoga, or it might be listening to a book, or even washing the dishes that I put off. But it's something that will make me reduce my stress in some way.

MAKING VC MORE WELCOMING TO MUMS

EB: *Now, you have switched to become a venture capital investor recently. What is it like to be an investor as a mum?*

JA: As an investor, you constantly have this fear of missing out. At the moment, we don't have the usual events that we might go to, to speak to entrepreneurs in person. So, we're really relying on maintaining connections to other investors or sources of deal flow. I've had to be creative about how I maintain that and about what channel works, [such as] having phone calls instead of Zoom calls, because there's a lot of Zoom fatigue, and maybe having a walk while taking the call. I am trying to be super flexible so I'm not burnt out by having ten calls a day. I think it's a time where we all have to be a little bit more flexible and open to meeting people through various channels, including Instagram, which is different. People are coming from various channels and I think just be very open to that idea that these opportunities can come from anywhere.

JL: *To finish off, let's briefly talk about the responsibility or at least the influence that investors have. How do you think VCs can support making the tech industry a bit more family and mum friendly?*

JA: The best thing you can do as an investor is help founders feel comfortable; be your authentic self. Hopefully, an investor is a nice person that creates an environment where the founder feels safe. This feeling can also come from you being vulnerable as well. For example, I've had meetings where people are pitching, and I get my kids coming into the room, and

I don't send them off. They're there and I get them to say hello. It's about just being very normal about it. I also always start the conversation with "how are you?" Because it's more than a transaction, in my opinion. You're building a relationship, and you want to get to know them. I'll often carry on the conversation on WhatsApp, I'll follow them on Instagram, get to know them as people, but bring that vulnerability into the conversation early, and find that human connection.

11.4 *Hukemann: Young Founders*

Jolina Hukemann (Student)

Jolina Hukemann[148] *is one of the youngest founders we encountered—she entered her first startup competition when she was 13. We talked to her about her experiences learning about entrepreneurship at such a young age, the impact of her gender on her experience, and how complicated it was to find a co-founder in her early teens.*

Interviewed August 2020

STARTING A COMPANY AS A 13-YEAR-OLD

Johannes Lenhard (JL): *You started working on your own company in 2018—when you had just turned 13. How did that happen? Where did the idea and the initiative come from?*

Jolina Hukemann (JH): I watched the German version of *Shark Tank* (*Höhle der Löwen*) on television. I really enjoyed the format. It taught me that if you understand a problem and analyze it enough, anyone is able to solve a problem—that was the biggest learning I got from these shows where founders pitched investors. My idea came from my own experience: I was playing a lot of girls' soccer at the time and we always had an issue with not having enough referees. Usually, what happened is that a parent or the trainer of the visiting team took over that role; obviously, that was

---

148. https://twitter.com/JolinaHukemann

not exactly fair. That really bothered me. I thought back to these shark tank shows and started thinking about a possible solution.

Initially, I started writing things down—like what is the problem, what are possible ways forward. First, I in fact did a referee course to understand the issue better and dive deeper into that part of soccer. I knew I wanted to solve the issue entrepreneurially and one of my first mentors told me about Startup Teens. I signed up to one of their "thinking workshops" (Denkwerkstätte) to pitch my idea for the first time. I was still all over the place at the time, so not everyone understood exactly what I wanted to do, but I learned a lot.

Back home, I started building a prototype with Adobe XD. With that, I went back to the annual competition of Startup Teens—as one of about 1,500 others. I needed some money to really build an app because I don't have strong computer skills. While the voting put me in an ungrateful fourth place, the jury gave me their wildcard and I was invited to the Axel Springer House in Berlin to pitch again. Overall, I was lucky I won the second prize in the Entertainment and Games category, but unfortunately didn't receive any capital. However, the network that I started building at these events was enormously helpful, and I met my first co-founder through it. The feedback from other people was also really helpful. Everything was slowed down a little bit with COVID—and the lack of soccer games—but I am still working on it and it still gets me thinking.

JL: *How was it as a girl, for instance at the Startup Teen Challenge?*

JH: In fact, the Startup Teen challenge participants were really balanced in terms of gender. I thought in the beginning that it really was a boys' thing but it turned out to be quite different. When I first watched the pitch videos, I thought, wow, these are always going to just be boys. And I was afraid that I wouldn't want to talk to anyone, but it was really great. There were lots of girls there—but I was one of the youngest; that did get me quite a bit of attention, but only positive so far. It was all fine; I had a really easy time talking to people and they came to me as well. It was really cool; I was really happy about that.

JL: *When it comes to money, how have you managed that so far?*

JH: I mean, I started to work on the Startup Teen challenge to win the 10K—but the second champion unfortunately did not get any money at all. But fortunately, there wasn't too much need, really, for big investment.

So far it was really my family and my mentors and myself that worked on this together.

I have since found someone that started working on the app pro bono so far; I would really love to pay that person in the future and that's why I would love to continue going to contests and possibly get an investor on board, too, so that we can really get going. But before that we need to test the concept, really, and because of COVID, it is quite complicated at the moment [in 2020]. But my network is great already and I am not too worried about getting money in once I need to.

ENGAGING YOUNG PEOPLE IN POLITICS

JL: *And you already started working on a new endeavor, a kind of Zoom-streamed expert-debating club to bring people your age closer to politics.*

JH: It might sound as if I am already starting too many things, but COVID has really slowed things down on the soccer app side of things. Now, on this new idea, I am working together with some friends. We noticed that way too few people our age think about political issues properly. In the last local elections, only 38% of people voted. That number really scared us—this is a big part of our democracy! We really want to make it a crucial part of people's lives again, politics. They need to understand how important it is. In fact, the question starts even earlier: what even is politics? Even being involved on a school level counts, I believe. So what we are trying to offer is a kind of Zoom-powered debating club. We will invite different experts from different kinds of political organizations and levels. The good thing about this project is that I can extend my networks even further, into politics. I just finished an internship in that sector. We will do this via Zoom first, because of the pandemic, but over time we hope to take this to in-person meetings soon. Another pillar will be a website where we can show videos, blog posts, and photos to promote the topic of local-level politics to youth in my area. We want the readers to really get engaged!

ADVICE FOR GIRLS INTERESTED IN ENTREPRENEURSHIP

JL: *What would you say to other girls if they wanted to become an entrepreneur? What should they do?*

JH: I would tell them: have courage—just do it! You have to just think about one thing: what is the worst that could happen to you if you dare to do this thing now? What is the worst that could happen if I have an idea and write something down and start talking to people? What is the worst that could happen? Somebody says no and another one says, "I don't care." But really, is that bad? No, not at all. You might sleep badly one night—but that's it. Later, you perhaps have a family with children, you might have a house that you need to pay a mortgage for or other things like that. In that case, you just fall deeper and the risk is higher.

You really should not think that just because you are a girl you can't do this. Then you should always keep in mind: if that was true, no man should be able to become chancellor in Germany again. It's just stupid. You really shouldn't hold back. Every gender has its strength, sure, but when it comes to entrepreneurship it really doesn't matter. And a mix of everything—gender, nationality—fuels creativity; it makes everything better, really. I don't differentiate when it comes to that.

SUPPORTING YOUNG ENTREPRENEURS WITH COMMUNITY AND MENTORSHIP

JL: *What do you think is needed in terms of support in order to get more young people into this world?*

JH: The biggest issue I am facing is how to find a co-founder. I was hoping to find one with all the pitching; I was hoping that I would find somebody that would want to do it with me. With a co-founder, things are much easier, it's quicker, you balance each other off. Things just work better. But so far, I haven't been able to find somebody long term. I don't know what a systemic solution to this is, but perhaps we need more spaces where young people that want to work on startups can meet and exchange ideas.

I in fact was working with somebody that I really liked in the beginning, but it didn't work out after some months; she didn't really put effort into the project. So, I called my mentor and talked everything through with her, and she helped me to figure out how to end the relationship. That was the toughest thing I went through so far; ending that relationship was really hard. You have to really learn how to manage this. I learned a lot from that, but this kind of mentorship is really important and isn't available to many people, really. More of that—in whatever institutionalized form—would be helpful if it was more widely accessible.

11.5 *Lawton: Founders with Disabilities*

Emma Lawton (More Human)

Emma Lawton[149] is the co-founder of More Human,[150] a startup to help community leaders scale their communities. Emma has pink hair and one of the most outgoing personalities we encountered during the research for this book. She also has Parkinson's, a brain condition that affects her movement. We spoke to her about her experiences founding and running a tech company while managing her disability, the ups and downs, and the superpower she's made of it.

Interviewed January 2021

EMMA'S JOURNEY INTO ENTREPRENEURSHIP

Erika Brodnock (EB): *What made you decide to take the leap into entrepreneurship, and what were you doing prior to this?*

Emma Lawton (EL): Before this whole entrepreneurship thing, I had just taken on a new job at Parkinson's UK (the Parkinson's Disease Society of the United Kingdom), leading the design team. I had ended up doing a variety of different jobs there, some technology roles and some outreach over the last few years before taking this full-time role with them. At the same time, I was doing a blog project where I did something new every day for a year. And one of the things I decided to do was apply to Zinc, a business accelerator in London. I gave it very little pre-thought if I'm being honest!

I guess, I've always had a slightly entrepreneurial spirit; I've always kind of set things up on my own. I've always dabbled with small ventures—I have had little Etsy shops and made stuff. As a family, we're quite entrepreneurial in that sense, too. If we need money, or we've got an excess of something, we'll make something with it. My parents, when I was younger, used to make soft toys and chess sets and things like that.

---

149. https://twitter.com/ems_lawton
150. https://www.more-human.co.uk

So, I guess I was brought up in that type of environment. But I'd never thought I'd really start an *actual* company. I never thought that would be something I'd do, especially not seven years into having Parkinson's! But I applied to Zinc and when I started looking into it more I wanted to do it. I was actually really surprised when I got accepted.

Overall, I think I like working for myself. I've done a lot of freelance work in my time. I like making decisions about things. I like strategy. And I just saw all of these things coming together in entrepreneurship. In my company now, we've got quite a flat structure, we kind of do a bit of everything. And I really like that every day is quite different. I think that's one of the great things about being an entrepreneur: you never know what's gonna hit you in the morning!

HOW DISABILITY CAN ISOLATE

Johannes Lenhard (JL): *Can you tell us a little bit about how this entrepreneurship journey and your journey with Parkinson's have gone together?*

EL: So Parkinson's is quite weird, because there is a lot of information out there, there's lots of resources, but it's very difficult as someone who's young with Parkinson's to actually find people similar to you. You have to really search them out. I did quite a bit of hunting, but it was actually my nurse who put me in touch with some other young people, which was really helpful. So had it not been for her, I think I probably would have really struggled. It's that whole thing about having your tribe and knowing these people are in a similar situation to you, that stops you from feeling lonely. If you don't know who's got your back, and you don't know people the same as you, you can feel lonely even in a room full of people; it is quite a weird experience. I think that's one of the reasons why we decided to start More Human; we've all struggled with loneliness and know firsthand how important communities are in fixing that.

EB: *Are you happy to share whether having a disability specifically impacts the way in which you work with others, thinking back before COVID-19 in particular, but also now?*

EL: It is often a challenge, because Parkinson's is one of those conditions that doesn't really stay the same. If I had something that was consistent, I'd just get to know where the goalposts are and I could tell people what to expect from me. I think people expect me, after seven years of living with it, to be able to say "I'm gonna be bad on this day" or "I'm going to struggle with this at that time"—it doesn't work like that for me. When I had just started working with my (now) co-founders, I was supposed to go in to do a pitch and my feet started cramping in the morning, and I knew I was going to miss it. I thought: "What do I do? They're gonna think I'm unreliable, it's not a great start to our working relationship." I wanted to be there with them. I wanted to talk about our business and be proud. And in the end, Duncan, my co-founder, had to do it on his own. I just felt really bad. I knew that this was something I couldn't have controlled. But actually, the not knowing really frustrated me, the fact that I couldn't tell him for sure whether I'd make it on time or not. I'm easily worried that I'm letting people down, so sometimes I push myself through things. But actually, that's not good for my body, it's not good for me.

There's an expectation that in business you have to turn up on time, you have to constantly be professional, you have to give your best in usually a small window of opportunity or you miss out. Recently, I did a pitch to some friends and family to practice and fill them in on what I've been working on. And I knew I didn't do a good job because my Parkinson's was terrible. I could barely think straight, and I was in so much pain. I kicked myself the rest of the day, but I shouldn't do that because actually, there's nothing I can do about it. Everyone said it was fine. But I knew I could do better than "fine."

There is this fine line between not expecting too much from myself, not drowning in pressure, but pushing myself just enough to feel proud. For many people who've got a disability, actually just getting out of bed and going to work in the morning is considered to be inspirational in a way; I want to push past that and do more than what's expected of me. I don't want to ever stop expecting more from myself.

DISABILITY AS A DRIVER OF INNOVATION AND CONNECTION

JL: *Obviously, as you just made very clear, this disability comes with a lot of challenges. Are there ways it helps you?*

EL: It definitely does in a number of ways. Firstly, I have insider knowledge on accessibility and what makes a product work. I'm living with complicated stuff every day, and that gives me a greater insight. I think because of that, I can go with my gut instinct a lot more than perhaps some other people can when it comes to making decisions. Because if you design for accessibility challenges, it's going to work for everyone. I sort of have that inbuilt.

And the other thing is very different. When you're a startup founder, a lot of it is about being in the right place at the right time and meeting the right person—just being lucky. I think I am kind of memorable, you know, the shaky girl with pink hair is likely to be the one that stands out in a meeting. I went to a virtual breakfast thing with some VCs and other founders a while ago, and I turned up with my bright yellow dress and my pink hair and talked about Parkinson's, and I thought, "Well, being memorable, that's not a bad thing."

It's also a great leveler. I've met some incredible people that are really high up in some really big companies, who've actually sat on the floor to talk to me; they physically and emotionally come to my level. Having something that outwardly shows my weaknesses and challenges makes other people reveal theirs to me too, and it helps me to make connections on a deeper level. That in turn makes any business we do together more meaningful.

WHAT THE INDUSTRY NEEDS TO DO TO SUPPORT FOUNDERS WITH DISABILITIES—AND EVERYONE ELSE

EB: *What would you say is the most important change that we need to make in the tech industry to make it more accessible for people with disabilities, from your own perspective?*

EL: At the moment, the startup industry has a really bad reputation for people pushing themselves too hard and not resting properly. When you have a disability, you sometimes need to take time for yourself, you need to actually just do things at your own speed. Sometimes I'll have to completely put down tools because I can't do the things that I'm required to do on a task at that time. That's incredibly frustrating. But the world doesn't end when I don't do it, I'll do it eventually. Slowing the pace down a little bit and being a bit more flexible, you see people as people rather than machines. Whether they have physical challenges or a family to care for or other priorities, there needs to be balance. At More Human, we're trying to make sure that we're being good employers, making sure that the human needs of our employees are looked after as well as their work needs. We're trying to break some of the bad habits that we got into when there were just three of us.

EB: *I get that—looking after people's human needs is absolutely fundamental; to ensure that people feel included. But then how do we get more people to apply or create the jobs that need to be there in a way that means that people from all backgrounds, including people with all levels of ability, are able to apply?*

EL: Firstly, you need those of us that are actually doing it to be more visible and do more to share the fact that it is possible. I try and do as much as I can to make that point, to make sure that people know that you can have a disability, you can be a woman and you can be semi youngish, and you can co-found a tech startup. If I can do it, anyone can do it. Those of us that are living that life whilst managing other challenges need to make ourselves more available to people looking to do the same, so they can see themselves reflected in the industry. And it's particularly important to me when it comes to hiring. I'm asking myself, "Actually is there some way that I can open the door to someone like me to join our business?"

11.6 *Stewart, Thione: LGBTQ Founders and VCs*

Gary Stewart (Techstars, FounderTribes)

Lorenzo Thione (Gaingels, StartOut)

Gary Stewart,[151] *the founder of FounderTribes,*[152] *and Lorenzo Thione,*[153] *co-founder of StartOut and now managing director of Gaingels,*[154] *spoke to us about their experience being gay in the world of tech and investing. The bottom line: it really matters where you are (the UK is less networked than Spain or the US) and whether you find your safe group that allows you to be yourself at all times. Holding together really helps—and will eventually allow you to spread the privileges you and your group have achieved.*

Interviewed January 2021

LGBTQ COMMUNITIES IN DIFFERENT COUNTRIES AND IN TECH

Erika Brodnock (EB): *You've both worked in the tech ecosystem in various roles as founders and investors—how has the experience of being part of the LGBTQ+ community in tech evolved during that time?*

Lorenzo Thione (LT): There would be so much for me to say primarily, not just because I've lived my own identity as LGBT and as an entrepreneur, but also because I've really worked to affect and to improve the dynamics of how LGBTQ and entrepreneurship as identities meet. When I started my first company, I had just come out maybe two or three years prior to that. It wasn't so much on my mind at the time, but I perceived it being an obstacle for a lot of other people who I knew and who were not out to their boards or to their investors or within their companies. It has

---

151. https://twitter.com/garystew

152. https://www.linkedin.com/company/founder-tribes/

153. https://twitter.com/thione

154. https://gaingels.com

certainly impacted me to think about why that was. Especially in places like San Francisco, which were extremely open and accepting, there was a dynamic that was characterized by the feeling of not knowing what you had to gain from coming out. I saw the myopic approach in that, I thought there was so much to be gained by not constantly looking over your shoulder and worrying. Not only that, but there's also something to be gained for everybody else, because you're all of a sudden becoming a visible, real role model; you show through representation what's possible, what jobs and professions are possible. The value of representation is so, so important. We know this from entertainment, we know it in so many different circumstances. That was largely why I cofounded this nonprofit, StartOut, shortly after the exit from my first company. StartOut is very much focused around creating not just a safe space, but also an edge, something to gain. For people to understand that the moment that they did come out and embrace their own LGBT identity and entrepreneurial identity together, they had a community to rely on, they had resources to rely on, they had a shared experience and a shared background.

Gary Stewart (GS): I've been gay in three different countries. I think being gay in New York in the 1990s was just really scary. It was at the height of the HIV/AIDS moment. America was a very homophobic country. Being at Yale Law School, in the 1990s, I studied a lot about sexuality, but I was nervous about it; I was afraid to even be associated with homosexuality in any case. At the time, it was still technically illegal for gay men to have homosexual sex. I mean, sodomy was illegal in a lot of states and the Supreme Court had ruled that such discrimination did not violate the US Constitution. So that was America. It was a large part of the reason why I left. I didn't feel it was a place where I would ever be allowed to be myself; if you are gay and can choose where to live, you might not have chosen America in the 1990s. And especially being a Black Jamaican man, there were additional pressures and discrimination to deal with.

When I first moved to Barcelona, Spain, and my friends came to visit, they called it "Gaycelona." Gay men were holding hands and kissing in the streets, which was really weird and transgressive to me. I quickly found a gay mentor, who still is one of my best friends. Everybody was just so open and accepting. And that explains probably why I lived in Spain for 14 years, because maybe from an economic point of view, it wasn't the best place. But it was where I felt like I belonged, without judgment. Spain was really, really free and accepting. Even when I went to work for a business school run by old-world Spanish aristocrats, it was very welcoming. The dean was openly gay. And when I left Barcelona to go to work at a big telco called Telefonica where everyone looked like they came out of a Polo ad, I was worried. Everyone kept saying how they would be super Catholic—and yes, people were super Catholic, but they were still really accepting of me. On the whole, it didn't really seem to be an obstacle, being gay in Spain.

When I came to the UK, I thought, whereas in Spain homosexuality was really embraced and discussed, in the UK it didn't really feel like it was something that was as visible. In the tech scene, I saw people starting to try and create "gay in tech" organizations, and I'd try to support them. But it just doesn't seem like a gay movement exists in tech like it might in Spain or in the US. When it comes to lots of elements of personal identity, it seems like the UK prefers to pretend that a lot of things don't exist and keep it moving. Whereas I feel identity politics seems to be part and parcel of being American. And definitely not something that Spanish people shy away from either.

THE IMPORTANCE OF REPRESENTATION AT EVERY LEVEL OF VC

Johannes Lenhard (JL): *Lorenzo, how and why did you become involved in Gaingels?*

LT: So I should be precise that I did not found Gaingels; I was on the board of StartOut with my friend, David, who started Gaingels with Paul in 2015–2016. I was busy with writing and producing a musical that would go to Broadway, as well as a new social media company I had founded. Back then they came to me and basically said, "Look, we want to create a group for LGBT investors to invest in LGBT entrepreneurs." At the time, that was definitely missing from the equation. I made it clear that I couldn't do it with them but that I would be a big cheerleader and supporter. And then a time came when things had shifted a little, in 2018. My personal situation had shifted, the show had closed, my social media company was largely on autopilot; I could basically focus on other things. We started talking about the fact that there was more that could be impactful in the ecosystem and that could have a positive effect for social change, rather than only focusing on a narrow view of diversity when it came to LGBT leadership. We talked about how important it is to go beyond the founders, to address also the C suite, the boardroom, all the other layers in the venture ecosystem where decisions and value intersect. We started to focus on making sure Gaingels could add value beyond investing—we developed a recruitment tool and established an internal practice for our companies to help them identify great board members that come from diverse backgrounds, including LGBT.

Building a diverse investing ecosystem means also to address the issue of who is benefiting financially from the value that is being created in the ecosystem. If you looked at how this was decades (or even just a few years) ago, both decision power as well as the wealth value would remain within insular groups largely made of people that all looked the same and came from the same socioeconomic backgrounds and the same educational and financial circles. Bringing more diverse investors, investing in more diverse teams, pushing the conversation into valuing diversity and inclusions across all axes, all this can only happen once you're at the table. So we focused on delivering value, and creating access opportunities, and over time Gaingels really evolved into what it is now, a venture investment syndicate made of thousands of individual investors who index very high across many diversity axes, that are able, collectively, to back and invest in companies that embrace diverse leadership at all stages of growth. This is because of our collective commitment, the value we deliver, and the fact that we bring and represent the LGBTQ community and its allies on the venture cap table, to help push forward the conversation on why inclusion and representation is important, even in venture. In the last three years, we went from an angel group that had invested $3M or $4M across a couple of years to having invested almost $150M in the three years since.

MAKING YOUR OWN ROOM TO GROW PROFESSIONALLY

EB: *Gary, what made you start FounderTribes? Was there a particular moment or incident that made you decide to leave your career behind at Telefonica?*

GS: What I found is Spain was really great for me, because I was an American first and Black second; like that, America is great, because as long as you are good at what you do, there's a way, and they really prioritize and love winners of all colors, even though it might be a little bit more difficult to win if you're Black, or gay, or both. Then I found in the UK that it's a societal system that's the most stultified; it's like you're fighting against almost 1,000 years of dynastic history. It's not as fluid as say, Spain, which is ultra-liberal after shedding Franco in the 1970s, or the US, which is still a relatively young country. In the UK, everything is a bit more rigid. So long story short, I found that in Europe, and in the UK in particular, there wasn't really room for me to grow professionally, unless I was willing to create something myself. Certain doors would be closed to me, because in many ways I am a perpetual outsider who is allowed in to visit but never really welcomed to stick around indefinitely, at least not at the level that would match my ambitions. The reason that I created FounderTribes was to see if I could do something about this.

In 2021, it can't be that we still live in a system that rejects 99% of would-be founders in no small part because of race, gender, and other considerations that should be irrelevant in this context. And it's not just about race; particularly in the UK, it's also about class and geography. There are just so many different reasons why people are locked out of the system. Entrepreneurship is not exempt from the rules of society at large, which still privileges upper-middle-class white men who went to certain schools and are based in London. We can't sit around for another 10 years talking about how 1% of founders in the US that get funding are Black or 2% are women, or that in the UK, those numbers are 0.24% for Black founders and not much better for women. I don't even know what percentage are gay. I wanted to use technology to focus on this problem, to give more people access to the feedback, networks, and capital that they need to start up and scale up their businesses, all from a mobile phone.

THE WORK IS NEVER DONE: LGBTQ ACCESSIBILITY AND INTERSECTIONALITY

JL: *Where do you think the accessibility for LGBTQ folks is not yet given? Where is the ecosystem particularly closed? And where do we still need to work harder?*

LT: So, there are two really important dimensions to take into consideration there. But one is obvious: geography. It's not the same everywhere, even within a certain country. Obviously, San Francisco and New York are very different realities than rural America and the South, or even the Midwest. There are still a lot of discriminatory laws in place in states that are just simply not as open. But the other dimension to look at is intersectionality. While things may have gotten better in many areas for gay white men, the issues are compounded for LGBT women, for BIPOC LGBT folx, and especially for trans individuals. I would say that the reality is that for trans men and women in the workforce, as employees in a tech company or a VC, we are in an absolute way much farther behind then where we gay men were 15 or 20 years ago. Issues range from open discrimination to constant microaggression and unconscious bias. The reality is—and the shortest way to say this is—the work is never done. We have to take some of the progress and the privilege that derives from say, even for someone who's a member of the LGBT community, being male and white, and use it to advance the state of things for many others. How do I leverage that power to help create more equity, both through representation so that it becomes normal and through more direct access and opportunities, for anybody else that is not yet at the same sort of place in that forward movement as we are?

EB: *On two occasions now, Lorenzo, you've said that this isn't just about the LGBTQ community, it is about making sure that the door is open for everybody that needs to come through it, which is commendable, and in my opinion, the true definition of allyship. Gary, do you want to answer that question as well?*

GS: Before I get to intersectionality. I still feel that for me, being gay still needs to be focused upon. These two parts of my identity, being Black and being gay, present themselves differently. Being Black is something that I can't really avoid—everyone knows it. So I have to deal with that element of my identity always. Whereas being gay, you can hide it. The struggle is different, precisely because it can be hidden. So for instance in the UK, I don't see that many other openly gay entrepreneurs and I believe many of them might not be out of the closet. And that makes me ask the question, in this day and age, why are people still afraid to come out? And so as much as I think the intersectional bit is important, I think it's also important to still remember that just because gay people can now marry and there are gay characters on TV, it doesn't mean that anti-gay prejudice has magically disappeared. There's still lots of things that gay people can't do. Up until recently, gay people couldn't even donate blood, or at least it was treated with suspicion, because of the AIDS crisis. Gay people can't really have kids the same way, and in the UK, I still don't think you see so many public displays of affection between gay people. I also have a transsexual friend, and I have to say, her struggle is real. Just because people watch

Pose doesn't mean that they don't have issues with transgender or trans-sexual women, for example.

DEALING WITH—AND DEBUNKING—PRESUMPTIONS AND PREJUDICES

EB: *To focus slightly more on your intersectional identity, has either being Black or being gay ever hampered any of your progress?*

GS: Definitely! Like I said, being Black is different, because I can't hide it. People won't always say what they think about it to my face. Being Black in the UK is a really interesting experience, in the sense that even though I'm not from here, there are certain presumptions that I can't seem to over-come. I just wasn't born into the right family. My last name could be an "acceptable" last name if I weren't Black. That is heavily tied to race, but not limited to it. I think that's also about class. Maybe that's why Meghan Markle felt a little bit uncomfortable as an American here. Whereas I think being gay has been less of a factor. I can choose when I want to share it, and I must admit that I don't always choose to share it.

EB: *Lorenzo, what are your thoughts on this—has your sexuality ever been a superpower for you in any way?*

LT: First of all, it's somewhat easy to affirm that my identity as a gay entre-preneur has had an impact on both my choices and my outcome, since it's what makes me who I am, but it's hard to say whether or not it has made things necessarily better or worse. It definitely has carved a path, and I've chosen to walk one set of choices and one set of things that I've leveraged that way, that would not have been the same if I hadn't been gay. Any ingroup/outgroup dynamic—whether it is about sexual orienta-tion or ethnicity or being a Stanford grad—can be helpful and leveraged for advantage, however. It is not something that is specific to either race or sexual orientation, I can guarantee you that for Stanford graduates, it's easier for them to raise money from Stanford graduates. You leverage the shared identity and experience with an ingroup to create more affinity to leverage the fact that they have a vested interest in your success just by virtue of association.

The impact, though, can be certainly negative for people who have to deal with individuals, because of their work or because of where they live, who have prejudices against them. I don't believe that has happened to me specifically. But I've also really tried to create visibility for my own successes and for the things that I was doing, so that it would both help others to see what's possible, as well as debunk the prejudices that may be holding back certain groups of people. I often tell the story of having dealt with a college roommate who came from a very conservative family. I wasn't out when I first lived with him. He was a little younger, and I was doing really well academically and had certain successes that clearly created a certain positive relationship. When I came out to him, which was not easy, it broke down all of the things that his family or his background had created for him: "Wait, wait, wait a second. This is a person who I know, who I respect, who I admire, who I want to emulate in so many other ways; how is this the same person as what I've been told that a gay person is going to do or represent in society?" And whereas that might be a very specific example, I really believe that creating mold breaking examples and stories where you show people what's possible has both a positive impact within the group, because it creates representation and visibility for them to see what they can do, but also outside the group, debunking and breaking down prejudices. It's the same rhetoric that can bolster the acceptance of immigrants in a lot of groups where immigration is seen as something that conservative movements have depicted as leech-like or taking and not giving, it breaks down that narrative by showing what success and what positive impact to society immigrants can have.

ADVICE ON BEING OPEN ABOUT SEXUALITY IN TECH AND VC

JL: *Let's touch on how to best navigate the tech and VC ecosystem when it comes to being open with your sexuality. What would you tell people now? What is the best takeaway that you've learned that you can share?*

GS: My best tip is definitely to find your tribe. I always like to have a group where I feel really safe. At my last job, for instance, there was a group of us who were early-stage investors and we were all gay, some out of the closet, some a bit more closeted. We spent a lot of time together, hanging out, and having all those conversations that normally you can't have when you're in mixed communities, because you're worried about being "too gay" or whatever. It is good to have that community where you have that safe space, and then just navigate it the best that you can; you don't have to be out with everybody if you don't want to be.

LT: So I think it's very similar to what Gary said, but let me focus directly on the relationships; so if we're thinking, for example, about entrepreneurs navigating the world of VC, which largely means looking for investors, employees, or partners. That is quite similar to dating; if you were to date someone and go on a few dates but you felt like you had to hide all of these things about yourself, most likely, that's not going to be a relationship that's going to work out. I see it similarly for the entrepreneurs now; there are enough groups that are dedicated to removing a lot of the specific barriers you might face and connect you with other like-minded people. It helps if you weed out the people that you might not want to be in business with, specifically not for a long relationship between an entrepreneur and an investor. I say, find *your* tribe. If the venture partner that you might want to take a big investment from really has a problem with you being gay, guess what: you do not want them to find out at a later point after they've signed that check.

12 Conversations: Overlooked Barriers

12.1 *Chandratillake, Connatty: Class and Social Mobility*

Suranga Chandratillake (Balderton Capital)

Ian Connatty (British Patient Capital)

Social mobility and class are topics not talked about enough in DEI con-versations. We discuss both with Suranga Chandratillake[155] (GP at Balder-ton[156]) and Ian Connatty[157] (LP at British Patient Capital[158]), two key people in the UK ecosystem who are passionate about social mobility, class, and inclusive practice in venture. Together they bring to the table a multi-faceted view, from the perspectives of founder, GP, and LP. Chandratillake started, scaled, IPOed, and exited his company Blinkx in 2014. He then became a GP at Balderton. From the LP perspective, Connatty has been with the British Business Bank and British Patient Capital, two of the most important UK LPs, since 2010. Given their own backgrounds—both went to state schools in the UK—they are extremely passionate about social mobility and class, which is why we brought them together in this panel.

Interviewed November 2020

SOCIAL MOBILITY IN THE UK AND IN VENTURE CAPITAL

Johannes Lenhard (JL): *Let's start with the basics: what is social mobility and socioeconomic class? Let's think about it particularly in the context of DEI, which has been defined mostly by gender and now increasingly by eth-nicity. What does class have to do with it all?*

---

155. https://twitter.com/surangac
156. https://www.balderton.com/
157. https://www.linkedin.com/in/ian-connatty-54973619/
158. https://www.britishpatientcapital.co.uk/

Ian Connatty (IC): In terms of economic literature, social mobility and socioeconomic class start with income distribution. Imagine stack ranking everyone's income in five equal groups; the question is how likely are you to move from one group to another, both up and down? In the UK, it is actually quite unlikely that people move from the very bottom to the very top.[159] Particularly, people in the North East of the country felt in a recent survey[160] that they had few chances to do better in life. The UK also has higher levels of inequality compared to some other high-income countries, as measured by the Gini coefficient.[161] In the 1950s, just after the war, there was a much higher amount of mobility, which slowed down in the 1970s.[162]

In the private equity industry, 69% of people went to an independent school [which you don't have to pay for].[163] The problem of "social immobility" is particularly pressing when it comes to elite professionals, including venture capital.

When you look at the literature that describes the mechanisms at work, one theory assumes there are several types of capital that all individuals have. One is economic capital. For example, if I want to learn more about quantum computing, I can take a course that I pay for. Money and wealth are the enablers. The second kind of capital is social; if I want to know about quantum computing, I ask Suranga, who's very learned on the topic. In this case I am using my network, built throughout my life, my upbringing, my education, and the work experience that I've had. But there's a third capital that's slightly more subtle. Cultural capital includes the way we behave, the words we use, the clothes we wear, norms of behavior, cultural references, books we've read, or the arts that we enjoy. All of these act as signals to indicate effectively what group we belong to in society. As practitioners, this framework is helpful for thinking about what we can actually do when it comes to social mobility and class.

159. Social Mobility and Its Enemies (2018), Lee Ellio Major and Stephen Machin, p. 32.

160. https://www.theguardian.com/society/2020/jan/21/
social-mobility-decline-britain-official-survey-finds

161. Social Mobility and Its Enemies (2018), Lee Ellio Major and Stephen Machin, p. 36.

162. Social Mobility and Its Enemies (2018), Lee Ellio Major and Stephen Machin, pp. 5-8.

163. ,[164] pg 8

164. https://www.suttontrust.com/wp-content/uploads/2020/01/
pathwaystobankingreport-24-jan-2014.pdf

Erika Brodnock (EB): *We know that you are both very passionate about increasing social mobility within tech and also venture capital. Is that all based on your personal stories or is there something else behind that?*

Suranga Chandratillake (SC): Before VC, I was in the technology industry, building tech companies. Tech has plenty of issues, but it doesn't have as starkly a socioeconomic issue as does venture. Since entering the venture industry, I've been anecdotally staggered by what Ian's describing, in a statistical way. From a social economic perspective, venture capital is a narrow group.

As someone who's managed to traverse systems, industries, and places, I'm constantly struck by how similar people are in each field, and yet how enclosed they are in each group. There are friends of mine, growing up in inner city Manchester, who I would never expect to stumble across in venture capital in London or tech in Silicon Valley. Equally, I wouldn't expect the people I knew in the Bay Area to stumble across the other two fields. There's absolutely no reason why these individuals couldn't be successful in these different areas, considering raw skill, ability, or ambition. Like what Ian's described, people typically start and stay in the place where they began. Amongst developed nations, the UK and US are very mediocre when it comes to this challenge, far worse than the Nordic countries, Germany, Canada, or Japan.[165] This annoys me personally and is a big motivator in the things that I do.

Tech is now incredibly influential in the world that we see created around us. The lack of different perspectives and diversity in the tech industry is a real problem, because technology is increasingly the thing that defines how we access many services outside what we would normally think of as tech. It is no longer a hidden-away industry that only does very specific things—it's all reaching, all encompassing, and it finds its way into every aspect of our lives. If the people designing it, funding it, thinking about it, and shaping it don't have a broad range of experiences in life, then they will likely craft something which is incredibly narrow in its perspective. And that worries me as well.

IC: My parents are from the 1950s, and benefited from post-war social mobility. Our family is very rooted in working class culture, albeit that my parents managed to get some upward movement and trajectory. But when

165. https://www.visualcapitalist.com/ranked-the-social-mobility-of-82-countries/

I was around 10, our economic circumstances changed very quickly in the recession of the 90s. That is a trauma I've never really recovered from; it has effects to this day. For instance, when I'm in the office in London, people see me filling up my thermos flask, because I resent paying for a cup of tea in a café outside. Things like that never really leave you.

Overall, I was very lucky; we managed to keep our house and I went to a good school. But allowing for all of that, when I went to university and work, the gulf between me and lots of other people I encountered was enormous in terms of all three measures of that capital. At age 18 I thought we were a normal family, but I hadn't really met anybody outside of my bubble. I had no idea that such wealth existed; I had no idea that you could be anywhere near as well-connected as the people I met. That sense of imposter syndrome, I suppose, has never left me even now.

EB: *The word "bubble" is an interesting choice you used. I think about our bubbles from the perspective of COVID-19. The pandemic was often referred to as "the great leveler" in the early days. But from what you've just described, it has the potential of making people stay in exactly the same spaces, be around the same people, and create less opportunities for social mobility.*

IC: If you take some of the recommendations that folks in the social mobility commission have made, they talk about helping people physically move areas. To access an elite professional in venture capital, chances are you must move. But now with remote working, people can stay in the place they grew up and not have to travel. We could all think about how to encourage remote working in a way that gives us access to a much broader pool of talent, beyond the people who can afford to live in a certain zone.

But you're absolutely right. The pandemic could also go the other way, where we stay in our echo chambers and our bubble. There's still time to influence the outcome of the discussion, but there is a real danger that it could accentuate current trends.

FILLING IN THE GAPS OF SOCIAL AND CULTURAL CAPITAL

JL: *Let's have some more concrete conversations about what it means to be more inclusive to people from different socioeconomic class backgrounds, and particularly thinking about the venture world.*

SC: Originally, the big focus at Diversity VC$^{§15.2}$ was around gender. The reality is that gender diversity, or lack of gender diversity in venture, is disastrous. We always approached our strategy with a view that over time, it would extend into ethnicity, then socioeconomic differences—which interestingly, people find hardest to agree on. We're now at the point where we're beginning to really crack through.

Social and cultural capital are the largest gaps I see in the industry. Social capital is very simple. Many people just have no knowledge of venture capital at all. Given that so many people use the products of venture every day, the gap is ridiculous.

Future VC is a large internship program for premier venture capital firms. The whole point is to drive into groups that would never have considered venture capital. More importantly, for each one of those 20 interns, 20 more get exposure to the fact the industry exists. Even if they don't join the industry, we now have new people who know about it, will ask questions, kick it around, and debate it.

Cultural capital is really about inclusion. Once interns join the firm, inclusion means helping them understand how to navigate the venture world. Internships at Future VC have structured education and constant informational feedback to help interns build cultural capital. It works—interns from that program are now in venture so building inclusion can be done.

IC: At the heart of inclusivity lies recruitment and retention, in terms of seeing beyond what people are like as a result of their background. Instead, we must focus on what people have the potential to become, when given the right setup. For example, at British Patient Capital we open days to give people the opportunity to learn more about our organization, without having the formality of an interview or structure process. We think very carefully about the wording of our adverts, where we put those adverts, all these little things that make a difference.

I encourage Suranga, and all GPs, to really work with your portfolio companies. It's one thing to think about our own investment industry, but there's a huge impact when thinking about the number of people that your portfolio company interacts with. This is a slow journey because these are not easy things.

EB: *You've outlined an approach that says people start at the bottom and work their way up to the top. I'd like to see how your thoughts juxtapose the* *fact that we are worried about that ability to climb nowadays. Let's delve into the impact of internships and associate positions over decision-making positions.*

SC: From my point of view, social mobility is a valid challenge. I look at the day-to-day reality of what I see around me—my firm, the industry, and even outside the industry, there are sometimes few choices, given the pressure put on us by LPs. For example, when deciding when to support a GP, they look at track record extensively. All of those things point to a structure with some aspects that clearly feel out of date. I've never had the luxury to genuinely think, how could I rebuild this system entirely? What would that look like? Instead, my attitude has been, how do we start to change the structure?

Internships are actually very interesting to me. I have seen a much more targeted focus on recruiting a diverse junior team across internships, and also into associates, principals, and so on. The senior members of the industry realize there's no great difference between these new people and the people they would have perhaps traditionally hired. But it will take a while. Of course you worry that you're reinforcing the same structure. But I personally struggled to imagine how I would change that in the short term.

SCALING THE VC COTTAGE INDUSTRY INTO INCLUSIVE FIRMS

JL: *Thinking about your respective roles as a GP and LP, what is the number one measure that you would change fundamentally about the venture capital that would create a more inclusive industry for people with different socioeconomic backgrounds?*

IC: The single biggest impact is in the activities of the portfolio companies. When it comes to the LPs, now there's real focus on the broader societal impacts of investments. Focus on ESG [environmental, social and governance] isn't just [ticking boxes], but it embeds into the way they think about the world. This includes how much we pay people—are we paying living wages? Having people around the table that are very conscious of these topics, that have a completely different worldview, is helpful.

For LPs, fundamental change means creating structure around topics. How do you think about interest in your own firm? Who gets the carried interest and where does it go? How do you think about share options and remuneration in your company, all the way through the organization and not just the management team? As a result, how do your investments actually contribute towards the goals of society?

SC: One frequent topic of my European boards is share options. For portfolio companies, share options are often thought of as the reserve of more senior people in the team. The excuse is that junior team members in European companies don't understand or want options; they'd rather have $2K more in salary this year. While that's probably true, share options could change their lives. Giving more options, to say a 26-year-old in Berlin, is better for the company because it will engender better loyalty in the business.

Another change is quotas. Quotas are very hard, because it is not easy to define them. What are the metrics on which you find them? But let's say you could do that somehow, at the very, very base layer to give people access to venture capital. While Ian's right that the ultimate impact is in the work the portfolio companies do, my anecdotal observation is portfolio companies are actually a lot more thoughtful about inclusion than most VC firms. I actually think they have less of a problem, frankly. That's why, internally, the whole firm is behind this idea that we should get our own house in order first, before we go off and preach to a bunch of people who actually are slightly ahead of the curve compared to us, in many cases. And then secondly, money is power. If you can change these organizations that control the choices of who gets money and who doesn't, that trickles down dramatically.

Not enough people from diverse groups know about venture or have any understanding of its impact. Everyone, regardless of who they are or where they started, should have access to an insight into venture, through an internship, work, or experience early on in life. Many of those people would then self-select out because of disinterest, which is absolutely fine. But at least they understand what this opaque industry is about. Knowing the industry would lead to a much more diverse feeder base of talent. Inclusion has to start with enabling maximum exposure at the early stage for awareness. Down the line, this leads to a more diverse industry and decision-making, which then impacts the flow.

IC: One of the challenges we see is that venture capital is a series of relatively small partnerships—a stark contrast to something like the accountancy industry, which has four very large firms. You can think very hard about how these big firms do and put pressure on them more easily and publicly. Looking at social mobility in league tables, accountancy firms do quite well.[166] I do think some of this is to do with scale. For small VC partnerships, how could GPs work together?

SC: We shouldn't forget that the VC industry was, until very recently, a tiny cottage industry. Silicon Valley did exactly that: it created silicon chips and picked between four or five different companies each year. Its outsized impact started in the last 10 to 20 years. Because it was this cottage industry, it didn't have any of the things you're describing; it is surely one of the reasons why people hire people who have done it before. In Silicon Valley, many successful VCs exist because their dad was a VC—to find the best talent available across the United States of America, the family business model doesn't make logical sense.

Venture capital doesn't work well as a large corporate structure. Firms lose something when they grow big; they lose the essence that comes from the manual, unstructured nature of building a company. So how does VC scale, in an industry where the participants are probably always going to be subscale? The recent Diversity VC Standard[167] addresses this question. The Standard is an assessment of venture capital firms to promote best DEI practices and helps both funds to understand their own issues (and possible solutions) and aggregates data on the industry level. That is a tool that will push the industry forward over time, the kind we need more of.

---

166. https://www.socialmobility.org.uk/2020/11/
     top-75-uk-employers-for-social-mobility-revealed-2/
167. https://diversity.vc/diversity-vc-standard/

12.2 *De Jesus, Barger, Henriksen: Mental Health*

Matthew De Jesus (Talis Capital)

Kristina Barger (Cognitive and behavioral psychologist and coach)

Øyvind Henriksen (Checkfirst, formerly Poq)

Since COVID-19, there has finally been more discussion about mental health for founders.[168] *We spoke with Talis Capital VC Matthew De Jesus,*[169] *expert on mental health for startups Kristina Barger,*[170] *and founder Øyvind Henriksen*[171] *about the prevalence of mental health issues in tech. This is another invisible dimension of diversity that is crucial to take into consideration and normalize. In our conversation, we unearth a wealth of tools and tips for founders who struggle with their mental health.*

Interviewed April 2021

NORMALIZING AND EXPANDING THE MENTAL HEALTH CONVERSATION

Johannes Lenhard (JL): *Øyvind, you have talked about your journey into being a startup founder and being caught in between competing spheres of life: family, running a company, dealing with employees, and more. It is normal for many founders and VCs to be stretched thin. How is mental health not a big topic of conversations, given these circumstances are so normal and normalized?*

Øyvind Henriksen (OH): I was the CEO of a software service company for about nine years. When my wife and I had kids, the dynamic of work and my whole life really changed in many ways. I suddenly had a hard stop at

---

168. https://www.forbes.com/sites/marenbannon/2020/02/10/
startup-founder-mental-health-why-it-matters-and-how-to-boost-it/

169. https://twitter.com/the_De_Jesus

170. https://www.linkedin.com/in/kristinabarger/

171. https://twitter.com/ohenriksen

the end of every day, six o'clock. I found myself not having enough time to follow up on meetings. I was rushing to do the follow-ups in a taxi home from work, standing outside my front door, finishing one last email before coming in to the kids. Then it was family dinner with screaming babies, my wife was grumpy because I was late, it was an abrupt transition. It was hard to adjust to this new reality. I found it difficult to reduce my own expectations of my own output and to be able to fit work into a narrower window.

There are three reasons why I started getting into trouble. As the company grew up to 100 people, the role of the CEO changed. In the beginning, you are creative, you are out there, you are understanding customers, and you know everyone personally. The whole company is a movement and much less of a machine. There is a whole lot of chaos, but you know everything that is going on, and I was very comfortable with that. When we approached 100 people, the role changed. You are much more of a manager of managers of managers. It is more of a machine and less of a revolution. I enjoyed the work a lot less.

We had just raised a lot of money and we had an ambitious expansion plan to go into many areas. A lot went according to plan, but some things did not, and it needed to be dealt with. I found myself with less time available, not enjoying the work as much, and spending my time on things that were not going according to plan. That is a difficult position to be in. That was also my first experience with being really tired. Our kids never slept well, so I was not sleeping through the night, with two-hour sleep periods. I felt at some point that the company was driving me, rather than the other way around.

Thankfully, I had built up a support network. I had a lot of tools that had been set up around me that helped me deal with that situation before it was too late. I found that it was very much the support available around me that helped, but it really felt like I was flying close to the trees. I want to speak about these things because if there is anyone else in a similar situation, I want to tell them that there are good solutions out there, so you do not have to stay in that situation. But you have to act decisively, because if you do nothing, bad things are going to happen.

EB: *You are currently working on Mindframe. Could you share some best practices and what has worked for you? What are you sharing with other founders in terms of being able to support this area?*

OH: Mindframe is a mindful productivity app that allows you to separate between work and life, by improving the boundaries of your working day. When you finish up your day, you write down what you are working on, write down your experience of the day into a quiet place, and then leave work and be more present with your family and disconnect properly. The next day you can pick it up and get started. During the pandemic, life has become a blur, and it feels as if we are always at work. I have tried to distill some of the mindfulness and productivity practices I have learned as CEO for the last few years into an app.

Erika Brodnock (EB): *Kristina, you have done a lot of work in the past with coaching startup founders. What is your journey into supporting the mental health of these leaders?*

Kristina Barger (KB): I used to be a psychotherapist full time and I am also a cognitive psychologist. I now work in behavioral change, designing behavioral change software, and focus on decision making and mental health. I have been coaching and providing therapy to founders for six years. I do not actively recruit anybody now, but Y Combinator (YC) sends alumni in London to me. I work with Amy Buechler on that, she is YC's psychotherapist and coach. I have also worked with some other startup accelerators, such as Zinc, which is where I met Erika.

I also wrote a study on founder mental health in 2019, with 271 founders. It was the first of its kind with a reasonable sample size, and was actually presented to the UK All-Party Parliamentary Group on Entrepreneurship in 2020. There were questions about founder mental health, psychological stress, and many other things. From that, I helped someone else build a business that targets providing mental health support to VCs, because we think that VCs are a better entry point into accessing healthcare for founders. I have a broad overview of founders, accelerators, VCs, and mental health, and how all these things fit together.

There are a couple of reasons why, even though we know mental health is important, we do not do more about entrepreneurship and mental health. One is that startups are relatively new. Mental health becoming less and less of a stigma is very new. It is a bit further along in the US, where "everybody" has a therapist. London is coming along more in the last two to three years, but it has only been in the last few years that there have been popular mental health campaigns. It is all coming along, just a matter of catching up.

Another factor is a particular stigma around founders: founders have this idea that they need to be very strong and that they cannot show any weakness. They need to present confidence and convince the VCs that everything is going to be great. If they show any cracks in that vulnerability, then potentially their funding will decline as a result. There is very much an incentive built into the system for people to pretend that they are okay.

Another aspect to consider is that mental healthcare is considered a very individualistic thing. It is something you must do yourself and you go in private to a therapist. This is the traditional view. Being a founder is also very similar. It is very much a solo endeavor, much of the time. These people have so much on their plates, and so little structure around, and they do not have HR, nor a culture built into the company. They just do not have extra time to self-monitor and even realize something like, "Things are getting bad and I should look for support." Those are three of the main reasons, in addition to many others, that contribute to the situation.

EB: *Matt, can you tell us about who you are and what you do?*

Matthew De Jesus (MDJ): I'm the operating partner at Talis Capital and I have been with them for seven and a half years now. It has been a good journey to see how founders have progressed during that time from personal investment to where they are now with growth stages. As Øyvind mentioned, managing a team of 100 is very different to managing a team of 20 or under. Different geographies also have different impacts. I am from a VC background. Fundamentally as VCs, we have an inherent responsibility to look out for our founders first and foremost, because it is the right thing to do. It is also good for business. The pandemic has accelerated or exacerbated different issues. There has been a lot of talk about how this pandemic has had an economic impact on the startup as a company, but not a lot of highlights on the founders themselves. They are seen as an entity rather than individuals.

As Kristina mentioned, there is stigma to admitting that one has poor mental health, because that is, unfortunately, still seen as a type of weakness, which it is not. There are expectations of what founders must feel about themselves and they must believe everything is okay. They have their own role, the role of what people look up to them as, and then the role external investors expect of them. They have also got their role in their personal lives, which is the most important aspect, but everything is all-encompassing as a founder of the business. There is an associated glamour that destabilizes the ability to be able to speak out about mental health. Founders are always working at 150% and the environment that we have been in has created more alienation for founders. People are reluctant to talk about it.

Øyvind is an exceptional example of being able to self-regulate and be self-aware; many founders are not. Founders have the Maslow hierarchy of needs flipped. They think, "Do I have time for mental health or self-care?" Mental health is not a quick fix at all. Everything else that you do for a business seems to have an output and a physical tangible result that you can work towards, but mental health is very difficult to quantify, touch, and hold. Founders have an inherent fear that if they do not say that everything is going well, then VCs are going to uninvest. We have put our money into you and we can't just take it out. We always start off our conversations with our founders about this and suddenly, you can see that their shoulders go down a little bit and they are a bit more open. If a VC ever did take money out for that, I doubt they would last long at all.

MENTAL HEALTH STRATEGIES FOR FOUNDERS

EB: *Øyvind, from the founder's perspective, what do you do when things are going wrong? Have you ever worked with anyone externally, such as a coach or psychotherapist? What would you say has been most helpful?*

OH: There are a couple of things that I do differently from other people. I try to be very open with people and build relationships in that way, rather than being the charismatic persuasive boss. There are different styles for different people, and it is both good and bad—it can get you into trouble, because sometimes you are a bit too open. What I ended up doing was trying to see myself as more of an athlete, where they have a support system on all aspects. I had some issues with my hips from taekwondo, so I started working with a physical therapist. I then got a personal trainer and a business coach, those were amazing. Later on I also got a psychotherapist. She was very helpful, we would go for walks and talk about practical things, that was a style that I was comfortable with. I have labeled this "Team Øyvind"—a great group of people around me that I can check in with regularly.

I also have two peer groups. I had a more professional, facilitated, expensive thing where we would go away for a few weekends a year, and hang out and learn more about other CEOs. Then we had a founder group with people who raised Series A at the same stage as us. We meet every month and talk about startup life. It is incredibly helpful to hear that everyone else is going through similar struggles. Being part of these communities and having the individuals support me on a regular basis has been great. It is very helpful to be proactive in setting yourself up for success. Startup life is a roller coaster, and you can limit the impact of the downs by having a support system.

JL: *Many people would be totally comfortable having a coach but then would not want to go to a psychotherapist or anyone that is a medical professional.*

OH: I am grateful for our head of people who joined our company around Series A, she was a very vocal advocate for being open and transparent around mental health. That was five years ago, before it became more mainstream. Having it be within the culture of the company was helpful in me deciding to take that step and being open about it. I believe in making this a very public conversation, so that everyone knows that these things are very normal.

In terms of the coach versus therapist, I go to my coach about balancing home and work, and how to level up as a CEO. It tends to be much more about work, more about how and what to do, and forcing me to come up with my own answers. When I interviewed the coaches, some of them were a bit like psychotherapists, so there is a range in terms of styles. When I speak to my therapist, it is much more personal. She does not know that much about business, and it tends to be much more about me personally.

THE DIFFERENT ROLES OF COACHING AND THERAPY

JL: *Kristina, what key findings came out of the founders survey? How do you think mental well-being should become a key strategic priority, both for the investors and the founders? Are there risks involved if that does not happen?*

KB: The most pronounced was probably the gap between need for support and seeking out of support, especially qualified support. I am both a coach and a psychotherapist, and I have been straddling the space for six years. I have many people coming to me with the belief that a psychologist or psychotherapist is someone who looks only at the past, and that a coach is someone who helps them unlock and unblock and move forward. I have seen a lot of coaches doing what I would call Wild West psychotherapy. I am not always pro-coaches when it gets into that space; good coaches are great for business issues, but many are not properly trained and do not have the same amount of ethics or regulatory oversight that psychologists have. Most coaches are required to have a five-day certification, and then they have to have 20 paid hours of work, with some varied supervision. Then they are certified. A psychologist or a psychotherapist should have at least an undergraduate, a master's degree, potentially a PhD and multiple years of supervised training with both the master's and the PhD. As a client, you are potentially getting the same type of activities, but a different tool set and different ethics coming from one to the other, so often the outcomes can be very different.

A lot of people do not like the idea of going to a psychologist or psychotherapist, because that has a connotation of "something is wrong." That is a stigma. So they go to a coach. I don't recommend that. Coaches excel in skills training, but they aren't trained in brain functioning, attention, memory, et cetera. They aren't highly trained in communication skills and relationships, or development and growth. For mental health, it's really better to go to a healthcare professional.

OH: My coach taught me this idea of writing things down pertaining to my business at the end of the day to clear my head, and then I would be more present with my family and evenings. She taught me how to prioritize better and focus more. My therapist convinced me to take a holiday; that was a much simpler approach of, "It does not matter what work is like, you need a holiday." She taught me about this idea: "Think about yourself as having a tank of energy, and you need to find things that will fill your tank, and if your tank is empty, then whatever you do, you are going to feel exhausted and tired." They had different approaches. One gives you more tools around work and so forth. Both are very useful, and there is overlap.

KB: What goes on in your session will depend on the person, and different therapists have different styles. Different coaches have different styles, but the training and the background is much more extensive on one side.

FOUNDER STRESS AND ISOLATION

KB: For our research, the 271 founders were sourced online, so they were people who elected to fill out the survey on their own. It was about two-thirds female and most of them were UK-based. This was in 2019 and pre-COVID. Seventy-eight percent of them said that they felt lonely as founders. How much more isolated are they now after COVID? Many more are. There is much more pressure.

In addition, 96% of them had at least four symptoms of physical or psychological stress that they experienced monthly; 70% physical and 78% psychological. Headaches, backaches, upset stomach, insomnia, and others were in the physical category, and then worry, anxiety, low mood, feeling depressed (different from clinical depression) went into the mental health category. Seventy-eight percent reported feeling low and anxious as well.

Those stats are incredibly high. They are reflective of society, but also very much reflective of founders. London was considered the loneliest city in the world that year, and the founders were five and a half times lonelier than the average person in London. There is a lack of support. We know from all the psychological research that social support is one of the biggest buffers for essentially anything you go through, whether it is a life issue, a psychological disorder, or a psychiatric disorder, good social support helps mediate all of that and improve outcomes. Social support can be your family, colleagues, going into the workplace. It can be Team Øyvind. It is anyone helping you giving you social energy and support.

OH: The stress is very valid. With any startup, there are bad times and good times, often in the same day. The problem is that founders are very forward looking, so if you are going up or down on that day, it is going to make a big difference to your daily mood. Another thing that investors can do: is there education around, for example, how to deal with the stress or practice mindfulness? For me, the idea of writing things out at the end of the day really cleared my head and allowed me to sleep better. There are many commonly accepted and helpful best practices and a lot of education around the topic.

THE ROLE OF INVESTORS IN MENTAL HEALTH SUPPORT

EB: *From your perspective, would it be helpful for investors to take some responsibility for ensuring that all founders are provided with tangible support? Is there a difference between being a first-time founder versus someone who has founded before?*

OH: It is common among second-time founders to give advice about taking care of one's health. First-time founders know nine out of ten startups fail, but they are the one where everything is going to go well. A founder is optimistic and ambitious, right? You cannot tell them what to do. If I hear it from enough people, I might listen, but it is difficult.

EB: *If there was something that they can dip in and out of as they needed to, like a resource group, that might be different to being told what to do.*

OH: You also cannot get too close. There is this stigma around being open about stress. This is real and many investors are going to have this unconscious stigma. When things are going well, you can talk about your problems, but if things are going badly, investors are not the ones who should be helping you. Many founders will be uncomfortable being too close to investors. You can still facilitate that people get the support system, but investors would not do it directly.

KB: If I were an investor, I would have all founders go to a psychologist once a week or at minimum, monthly. It would be a condition of investment. People need social support. Typically, subclinical anxiety and depression are these features that we all have under times of intense stress. They creep up, are insidious, and lead to burnout. It is very much a slow drop off. If you start having support early, you prevent yourself from going down into that deeper decline. Once you get down, it takes a lot more work to get back out of it. It is a financially low investment to see a psychologist one time a week. If you see that person and you think you do not need them, it does not hurt anything to just go anyway.

Sixty-three percent of people said they had seen severe conflicts between co-founders, which creates stress and problems. On the one hand, if co-founders are on good terms, there is a sense of safety and openness, even if you feel that you must put on a brave face for your employees and for your VC. On the other hand, there is often a lot of conflict. If you have a psychologist or a coach, there will be confidentiality. My ideal would be the VC will say, "We'll give you money and you've got to go to a psychologist once a week. What you talk about is between you and the psychologist, and we have no idea. I want you to go to have support because everybody needs support."

In Øyvind's experience, he already had family, so there was support in place. The founders that struggle the most are the ones that have the least support. This is particularly true for younger founders. Second-time founders may also realize that they need more support and that they cannot do everything on their own. Younger founders are less likely to have a family around and are less likely to realize that needing support is normal. They are the ones that I would support even more and encourage to look for support even more. They might also be the most resistant, but they still might be the ones who could benefit from it the most.

MDJ: We are about to implement our mental health support program. We took a step back and said, we know that there is an issue here; it is a big one and overwhelming to approach it. First and foremost, investors do not necessarily know how to approach a conversation like this in the first place. There is an issue where you want to do much more than just "pay."

The first step for us, which is a first step every VC firm should do, is to do an anonymous survey of our own founders. We want them to give feedback to us to understand how we can help. We had three key takeaways from this. The first is that there is an appetite for mental health support from investors among founders: 53% do not use small groups or mental health services, but said they would like to. Interestingly, 30% do not think they need any kind of service, which again, is another point to address.

The second thing was there are a lot of barriers to accessing mental health services: 42% believe that the therapy is too costly, 24% say they do not have time for therapy or life coaching, 30% were not sure what they needed—which is a big issue because how would we know what is needed for founders if they do not know themselves?—12% did not think they needed it, but that is the minority.

The third theme we saw was that our founders were not training themselves or their leadership to navigate it in the workplace. Sixty percent of our founders would appreciate access to mental health training or workshops to understand their own and their team's issues. Investors need to know how to approach the conversation and acknowledge and understand their portfolio and what they need to do. There are limitations, but you need that support there. You need to understand what your limitations are before you can start on this journey with your founders.

KB: Everybody is trying to figure out how to provide mental health, but there are psychologists. That is what psychologists do. Psychologists assess people and see what they need to help their mental health and their performance. A psychologist is the one who works together with their client to understand what their goals are and helps them then achieve those mental health and wellness goals. I always find this in startups and VCs, and I do not understand why everybody is trying to figure it out themselves. This is what a psychologist would do. The first session with someone is an assessment and needs assessment of what they believe they want and how they can be supportive. I do not do that work personally anymore, so I am not building that platform for myself. I am saying that we are here. We have been studying human behavior and wellness for a hundred years, while also being relevant and updating our knowledge.

OH: Most people do not know the different designations of what the different roles are, and the entry point into it is fuzzy. Leadership training needs to level up and learn about how to lead your team and mental health is a part of that. The other aspect is being part of a community of other people in the same portfolio. That is a way that people could jump into it and stay in it because they see other people doing it. This makes it more mainstream.

EMERGING BEST PRACTICES FOR INVESTORS

JL: *Matthew, what best practices have you come across from your perspective? What are we not doing very well and need to do much better on?*

MDJ: The first stage for us is mental health training in the workplace. We do not deliver it as VCs, but we facilitate it and make sure it is done. To Kristina's point, we believe experts are needed. For us, it was understanding what the needs are and then to facilitate the first action plan. The second phase is arranging peer groups between founders and founder development to include mental health. VCs are not part of that group, because the point is founders helping themselves and each other. We are there to support you, but we cannot be part of that conversation you have with others, in order for it to work more effectively. Another thing VCs can do is make a point of having one-to-one catch ups that are not about prepping for board meetings, but about life outside of business.

Every time you speak, it does not have to have a result at the end of it. It does not have to be result orientated. It is about the connection, because currently investors do not know where to start when they feel they do not have the right connection with a founder. It is important to encourage a culture that is supportive of self-care by, for example, having 15 minutes of mindfulness to recalibrate before a board meeting. Do not use it to try to get something done. It is quite simple, but it is the small points that count.

VCs forget that though we are focusing on founders, the culture must be in their own investment team as well, and they need to focus on their own mental health to make sure they are in a good mindset. There is internal work to do. I have struggled during lockdown;[172] I like to meet with people, and the absence of that has been difficult. I have been going to a great internal support group that we have monthly where there are one-to-one catch-ups as a team with our seniors. It is a very open conversation.

As investors, we also must learn the warning signs of burnout. It does not mean that we are experts, but there are certain things founders have told us that they have noticed themselves, or people have told them, that is an indicator. If a founder is being erratic or quiet in meetings, it could be to do with mental health or other things. Those can be triggers. As an investor, those are things that you need to pick up on. The interactions with the founders should be human, authentic, and vulnerable. We are people, not machines. We need to genuinely listen, and not have our laptops out when someone is speaking.

As VCs, we want to understand how the world works very quickly, we have short attention spans, and we try to problem-solve immediately. Mental health is not something that you can fix in the short term. For founders, peer groups are hugely important, where you can be with like-minded people without investor input. That is your time to work with others. These aspects have been part of our groundwork, and we think other VCs should be implementing them as well.

KB: Social support is incredibly important, and it comes from the teams as well. Having one-to-ones that are human and are not about KPIs goes a long way. Peers, psychologists, coaches are all forms of social support. I hope you convince all the other VCs to also provide more support. Confidentiality is also critical, and it is important to create a safe space for the founders as much as you can. If they feel that what they say is going to get back to you, they may not feel safe enough to open up. Having safe spaces or close relationships help facilitate that, though very often you will still see people put up brave faces.

---

172. This interview was conducted in 2021.

MDJ: If something is exposed, trust is gone. When the trust is gone, the relationship is gone. We should never underestimate the power of confidentiality.

KB: There is also an asymmetrical relationship between VCs and founders. Many founders perceive a big power difference between themselves and the investors. They are going to tell you what you want to hear more, and they are going to hide more, because they are afraid. It is important to be aware that the level of comfort that you have in the relationship is not the same as the level of comfort that they have. They are naturally going to be intimidated.

OH: The default state is that you are pitching the progress of the company to make sure that they follow on the next round. The idea of having regular one-to-ones with founders is something that you have to be careful not to impose, because people will show up to it out of politeness and see it as overhead. In my experience, many investors try to be helpful, and there are specific aspects that investors are excellent at advising on. On the other hand, there is a lot of superficial knowledge, and someone may have a better experience working with a psychotherapist about some things and an industry advisor about other things. It is important to be helpful, but there is only so much you can do to help. Imposing on time must be carefully thought through. Imposing one weekly session with a psychologist can be a lot for people, and they will balk at that level of time commitment. It will be hard to justify for people who might not see it as important. We need to figure out the right level of asking people to commit a certain amount of their time for support.

PART III: BEST PRACTICES

13 How the Industry Is Already Changing

When we started the research for this book, our goal was not to put together a critical and theoretically inspired book that practitioners would be unable to use. Instead, we wanted to unearth concrete ideas on how to *change behavior*, in a book that would not only inspire, but that would also be full of practical and tangible advice that could be easily applied. So, who else to ask but the people who are already doing things differently? Part III: Best Practices, which turned out to be the most substantive, is hence all about presenting the voices of investors and people within the ecosystem who have decided to practice what everyone else is preaching. We sought people who have already proven to be change makers—both in a small or systemic way, as a founder, funder, or funder-of-funds—to inspire change. Conversations range from learnings from VC and founder education programs and the influence of data and journalistic writing, to elaborate "how to" tutorials on increasing inclusion in a fund or running an angel investor program with a diversity focus.

The first section^{§14} of conversations covers VCs who are doing things differently, looking at established players in the ecosystem and their decisions to tweak the traditional VC approach. We set the scene with a story of two VCs that have over recent years become famous in their own right. Mac Conwell, or "Mac the VC," raised his first fund, RareBreed Ventures,[173] completely on Twitter, and publicly documented the process, which involved thousands of calls with potential LPs. Mac was joined by Thea Messel, one half of Unconventional Ventures,[174] a Scandinavian early-stage fund that has been fighting for more diversity in the Nordics for years. With Unconventional Ventures (UV), Thea has raised money to invest in "tech for good" startups with underrepresented founders; UV is also raising awareness and transparency in the Nordics ecosystem with

---

173. https://www.rarebreed.vc/
174. https://www.unconventional.vc

their annual Startup Funding Report.[175] In our conversation,[§14.1] Mac and Thea shared openly about the ordeal that fundraising is (or at least can be) if you are not a white male with a "strong network."

In the next interview,[§14.2] we focus on an American story (with parallel stories in some European countries like France or the UK) about where investment money flows: predominantly to Silicon Valley, New York City, and Boston. Mucker Capital's William Hsu and Monique Villa, alongside one of their portfolio founders, Allan Jones of Bambee,[176] talked to us about their explicit focus on investing *outside* of Silicon Valley. At the latest, since AOL founder Steve Case has been making this point[177] (including with actual investment dollars[178]), we have been seeing a slight diversification.[179]

Elizabeth Yin,[§14.3] co-founder and GP at Hustle Fund[180] in San Francisco, recounts her trials starting her own business and her journey to partnership at accelerator 500 Startups (now 500 Global[181]) in 2014. At Hustle Fund, Elizabeth not only writes VC checks differently (earlier, quicker, to a wider pool of people, without warm introductions), she is on a mission to democratize wealth through entrepreneurship and furthers this with her fantastic Twitter threads[182] explaining the world of VC to the public.

The next conversation[§14.4] features a power couple truly deserving of the name; Mitch Kapor and Freada Kapor Klein have been leading the charge of diverse investing for several decades, with a focus on funding companies that close the gaps of access and opportunity for underrepresented groups, like low-income communities and communities of color. As Mitch explains, Kapor Capital[183] has proven that it can be done, not

---

175. https://www.unconventional.vc/report/
176. https://www.bambee.com/
177. https://www.startupgrind.com/blog/
     steve-case-building-silicon-valley-outside-of-the-valley-at-techcrunch/
178. https://www.businessinsider.com/
     steve-case-revolution-investing-shearshare-freightwaves-2018-12
179. https://techcrunch.com/2021/12/08/
     silicon-valleys-share-of-us-vc-funding-falls-to-lowest-level-in-more-than-a-decade/
180. https://www.hustlefund.vc/
181. https://500.co/
182. https://twitter.com/dunkhippo33
183. https://www.kaporcapital.com/

only in a financially successful way, but also in a way that inspires social change:

> *Talent development is central and where we will get the most leverage, because what matters is who is sitting around the table when the decisions are made. Until there is really more diversity in VC, we are not going to see as much diversity in the companies that get funded.*

The participants of the following conversation[§14.5] are in the same social movement as the Kapors. Charles Hudson of Silicon Valley-based Precursor Ventures;[184] Eghosa Omoigui, GP at pan-African EchoVC;[185] and Paula Groves, CIO at London-based Impact X Capital,[186] are all part of a new wave of Black-led VC funds. We talked to them about the education and careers that led them to the establishment of their funds, and how despite having decades of experience managing and growing multiple millions of dollars, they are still classed as "emerging fund managers." We also discussed the gaps in fund size for Black-led funds and they were able to provide powerful insights on what action can be taken to fix this.

In the final conversation[§14.6] about VCs doing things differently, one of the most celebrated and famous European VCs, former CMO of Spotify and partner at Atomico Sophia Bendz, talks to us about starting the Atomico Angel Programme.[187] The program gives an incredibly diverse group of people funding to invest in early-stage startups, with the aim of overcoming the barriers posed to so many by the absence of generational wealth. She shared the motivation that led to its creation:

> *The closed ecosystem presented a huge frustration for me. It was almost like a little boys' club that invested together, and while I was invited in, I felt like the only woman in the club. ... I wanted to demystify it, I wanted to tell the world this is one way of spending your time and money. I think it could lead to more people that were exposed [to investing] to potentially considering a career as a VC.*

---

184. https://precursorvc.com/

185. https://www.echovc.com/

186. https://www.impactxcapital.com/

187. https://atomico.com/insights/introducing-the-atomico-angel-programme

The next section[15] focuses on best-practice ecosystem approaches that go beyond venture capital investing. First,[15.1] we hear from Roxanne Varza, director of Station F[188] in Paris, about how at the world's biggest startup campus, there is a specific focus on underprivileged founders with their Fighters Program.[189] In the next two conversations we speak to Check Warner, GP at Ada Ventures but formerly the co-founder of Diversity VC, and Pam Kostka, former CEO of All Raise,[190] about the approaches of two of the most important diversity-focused community organizations in the tech world. We learn[15.3] about the power of community to create new role models, and about[15.2] how role certifications, like the Diversity VC Standard,[191] can formalize inclusivity in venture operations.

Next we focus[15.4] on accelerators, often a launchpad for startups at the very beginning of their growth journey. We brought together accelerator builder John Lynn with Camilla Sievers of the Female Founders[192] accelerator and Kevin Liu of Techstars[193] to discuss the role accelerators can and should play to build a different and more diverse startup ecosystem from the bottom up.

Going downstream even further, we met[15.5] Floodgate[194] GP Ann Miura-Ko and Chuck Eesley, professor at Stanford; the two teach Stanford engineering courses together. We discussed how university education needs to change to facilitate a more diverse set of students into positions where becoming a founder or VC seems realistic. Education is also the topic of conversation in the next conversation,[15.6] which features Jeff Harbach, CEO of the world's most famous VC education program, Kauffman Fellows,[195] and Lisa Shu, founder and first executive director of the Newton Venture Program[196] (a Kauffman-like program in the UK), born out of LocalGlobe VC and London Business School. Both share insights into how important it is to broaden access to education, networks, and

---

188. https://stationf.co/

189. https://stationf.co/programs#inhouse

190. https://www.allraise.org/

191. https://diversity.vc/diversity-vc-standard/

192. https://www.female-founders.org/

193. https://www.techstars.com/

194. https://www.floodgate.com/

195. https://www.kauffmanfellows.org/

196. https://newtonprogram.vc/

cultural capital in the VC industry, and their vision for the future, as Lisa summarizes:

> *To truly change what is "market" in the VC industry, you have to shift the status quo and shift that towards equality by design, and not as a mere afterthought.*

The last two conversations in this section bring in the voices of two groups often underestimated as ecosystem change makers, people who produce, work with, and report data. In the first conversation,[15.7] we speak with Tom Wehmeier, partner and head of insights at Atomico, and responsible for the State of European Tech[197] report, and Gené Teare, senior data editor at Crunchbase News[198] and the person who is single-handedly responsible for including gender (and soon ethnicity) data in one of the world's biggest startup and funding databases. In our discussion, we unearth the multiple ways in which data can be used to put pressure on decision makers as a key part of building convincing narratives. Atomico's development is a great example of this, as Tom shared with us:

> *Atomico's founding thesis back in 2006 was, "Great companies can come from anywhere." And that is what we have learned. We have spent more time understanding the industry issues around D&I, that "anywhere" really means "by anyone in any location." The more we have spent time understanding this, the more it has reinforced and strengthened our conviction in that initial thesis, specifically, our resolve to back underrepresented talent in tech.*

In the last discussion[15.8] in the ecosystem section, we are in conversation with Amy Lewin (editor of the European startup news platform *Sifted*[199]) and Steve O'Hear (formerly of *TechCrunch*[200]); together we discuss the important role that journalism should play in keeping the DEI agenda front of mind through consistent and sustained reporting.

The final section[16] is focused on potentially the most powerful change makers in the tech ecosystem, rarely seen and often presumed to be standing on the sidelines: asset owners, limited partners (LPs), and policy makers. Our first conversation[16.1] is with three LPs—from institutional

---

197. https://2021.stateofeuropeantech.com/chapter/executive-summary/

198. https://www.crunchbase.com/person/gene-teare

199. https://sifted.eu/

200. https://techcrunch.com/

investor the Mellon Foundation,[201] Monica Spencer; from US investor WeAct Ventures,[202] Darya Henig Shaked; and from European fund of funds investor Isomer Capital,[203] Savitri Tan—about both their power and responsibility to diversify their investments. While a general willingness to wire money to a more varied pool of managers surely pertains, Savitri explains how the path dependency of LPs is remarkable.

> *The decision that we make to invest, and then the long-term partnership journey that we embark on with managers to help them build their firms, have a ripple effect. Early decisions as a result of questions and challenges will become ingrained as processes in the future funds of these managers, so asking questions, monitoring over time, and working together with managers from their earliest years makes a huge difference in how they approach raising and managing their next funds.*

Our second conversation[§16.2] is with Suzanne Gauron and Anna Skoglund, the team that leads Goldman Sachs'[204]s effort to put more money into the hands of Black female founders via the One Million Black Women[205] program and more broadly diverse entrepreneurs through Launch with GS.[206] Goldman Sachs was the most high-profile financial institution to put real money to work, especially to support underrepresented VC managers—something that we hope can inspire others to follow.

Our final conversation[§16.3] in this section, is with three "lobbyists" and policy makers in Europe—representatives from startup and VC groups from the UK (Gurpreet Manku from the British Venture Capital Association[207]) and Germany (Gesa Miczaika, who is an elected representative for the German Startups Association and an investor at Auxxo,[208] a recently launched Berlin-based VC fund) as well as from the French government's

201. https://mellon.org/

202. https://www.wonderventures.com/

203. https://isomercapital.com/

204. https://www.goldmansachs.com/

205. https://www.goldmansachs.com/our-commitments/sustainability/
    one-million-black-women/

206. https://www.goldmansachs.com/our-commitments/diversity-and-inclusion/launch-with-gs/

207. https://www.bvca.co.uk/

208. https://www.auxxo.de/catalysts

startup initiative (the former head of La French Tech,[209] Kat Borlongan)—for their perspectives on what associations can do to agitate and press for reform. We were surprised that beyond gender, there was very little sense of wanting to apply any pressure from these groups.

We were happy that almost all people who were trying to push for change in the industry were willing to talk to us; however, after finishing the conversations in Part III: Best Practices, we were left with a weird feeling: Is this going to be good enough? Why, if people in positions of power are already doing things differently, are the important partner-level statistics not changing? Our frustration led us to reach out to some less obvious vectors of change, outside of the established industry players. Instead of concluding here as we planned, the final part of the book will consider how these players are looking to build off the current progress and spark further change in the industry.

---

14 Conversations: VCs Who Are Doing Things Differently

14.1 *Conwell, Messel: Raising First Funds*

Mckeever "Mac" Conwell (RareBreed Ventures)

Thea Messel (Unconventional Ventures)

Mac Conwell[210] and Thea Messel[211] have both achieved the monumental task of being able to close a first-time fund in an ecosystem that has historically said no to people from their backgrounds. Mac and Thea shared with us a little of their grit, determination, and work ethic in using everything at their disposal—including powerful tools such as data, research, and social media—to galvanize investors into their funds and begin investing in overlooked entrepreneurs.

Interviewed December 2020

RAISING FUNDS THROUGH NON-TRADITIONAL METHODS

Erika Brodnock (EB): *Mac, regarding fundraising, Twitter has been a major aid in your journey. Why have you chosen that medium? How did you make it work for you?*

Mckeever "Mac" Conwell (MC): So, historically, most funds are raised under 506(b) within the United States, which means as you raise your fund, you can't publicly disclose the bets you're raising. It enables you to take around 35 unaccredited investors, whereas the other investors traditionally have to be accredited. This is what I have always heard, that is what I have always known. I had never encountered another option. It just

---

210. https://twitter.com/MacConwell
211. https://twitter.com/TheaMessel

so happened that earlier in 2020, AngelList announced they were starting what they called "rolling funds." One of the unique things about the rolling fund was the 506(c) designation. To elaborate further, investors could be publicly solicited, but each investor must be accredited to use their platform. They already had several credit investors on their platform making investments.

This announcement came at around the same time that my Twitter following started growing. In June 2020, before I started fundraising, I had around 2,500 followers. I have been on Twitter since 2009. As of today, I have over 21K followers. As my Twitter following increased, I noticed that it was possible to raise a fund publicly. Additionally, when I decided I wanted to raise, it was really because I met a founder—somebody reached out to me on Twitter, I really liked them, and wrote them back. I tried to put a special purpose vehicle (SPV) together to make the investment. But one of my advisors said he didn't want to put money in the SPV—however, he wanted to put money behind a fund. So, I went and raised a fund. I realized very quickly, my personal network would only get me to the half a million mark, maybe a little bit more. That was a fair way off my ambition of $10M. However, simultaneously, my Twitter followers were growing, several VCs were starting to follow me. I just made it a point that if someone was in venture, and they followed me, I sent a note with a link to my calendar, saying "Hey, let's meet." Very quickly, I started to have a lot of meetings. So, between June and September, I had over 1,100 meetings, 80% of which were with other VCs. I was meeting other VCs, some were saying, "Hey, the fund you're working with sounds interesting, I'd like to be a part of it." I was already using Twitter to meet people and gain introductions. When we publicly opened the fund in early September, we informed 506(c) that we were publicly soliciting, enabling me to put a post on Twitter saying, "Hey, I have a fund, looking for LPs." I have to say at this point [at the end of 2020], I've soft circled slightly over half of $500M. Half of them are people who found us through Twitter. In the last four or five days, we have found 45 new people who are now looking at our legal documents. Whether or not any of them will ever convert into actual LPs is to be seen. However, the ability to reach an audience without having to do the multitude of in-person meetings has been phenomenal. It all happened by happenstance, I didn't go in planning, or think this is going to be the way to do it. Everything fell in my lap at the right time—good timing.

Johannes Lenhard (JL): *So instead of seeing the traditional fundraising route as the only way for you to close your fund, or thinking you were disadvantaged by the fact that you don't have the same networks as many of your counterparts, you turned an adversity into a massive advantage here.*

MC: That is essentially what happened, and I got lucky for it. I will say, though, there was not a specific or magic thing that I did here. The magic pill to solve these issues is the fact my Twitter following grew from the fact that I had been investing for seven years already. I had my own unique perspective. That is what made people gravitate to following my tweets. I was able to use that gravitation to kick off everything that has followed. Without the solid foundation of knowing what I am talking about, having the experience to speak with authority, and people finding my perspective unique, none of the rest could have been possible. My earlier work facilitated everything slotting into place, similar to the crowdfunding model—much of what transpires in public is preceded by prior hard work and grind.

EB: *Thea, what has your experience of raising been? What do you perceive to be your biggest problems?*

Thea Messel (TM): Back in 2018, when I started Unconventional, the jungle of regulatory constraints and understanding what you are and are not allowed to do still stood. However, I'm happy to hear that it's becoming easier to invest; there are some clear guidelines for when to onboard accredited investors and when not to. It is still a jungle here in Europe, particularly as there are directives coming from the EU that can have different implementations among the European countries. At Unconventional, we are based in Sweden and Denmark, and even between those two Nordic countries it has been unclear what was possible and not. When Mac speaks about publicly fundraising, here, it was quite clear that this is not allowed.

Our investment thesis is centered around investing in underrepresented founders. We could see there was huge potential in targeting these types of founders; they were outperforming, which research confirmed, as well as what we could see from the deal flow received when having this investment strategy. This is something that people would want to support if they knew it existed, but we were, and are still, constrained. We couldn't even go to newspapers and tell them we are about to set up a fund like this, because as it's in the area of impact, we wanted to be safe. We did not want to breach any of the financial authorities' rules. The first entity we set up pivoted over the first 12 months. We initially wanted to set up a small €2M–€3M as a "normal" alternative investment fund. However, we didn't manage to fundraise for that. It took a very long time because everything had to be kept under the radar, and it was just me at that point. Although I had strong first-time backers including Arlan Hamilton, and super angels from the Nordics, it all had to go through network connections, with me not being very vocal on social media. It wasn't sustainable, so we ended up creating a reverse entity. Instead of fundraising for a strategy where you don't have to identify the assets, we had eight predefined companies that we wanted to fundraise for that would be our first entity. Then we fundraised for that through our networks and onboard non-accredited investors. Those are investors who typically are underrepresented themselves, or don't have accredited/professional investor status. However, after mastering that method there was another avenue we established where we had predefined companies and pulled them into a joint entity. This presented a greater opportunity to receive funding from a more diverse pool of investors. As a result, we raised from 60 investors across ten countries over the course of two months, enabling us to put between €10K–€20K into each company.

GETTING NOS FROM INVESTORS DUE TO LIMITED TRACK RECORDS

JL: *Can you share one story with potential backers/LPs/investors that didn't go particularly well? And how did you deflect that?*

MC: I don't know if I've had any bad meetings per se yet. I haven't had as many meetings with institutions, most of my meetings have been with individuals and family offices, these are people who wanted to meet me anyway. They already had some sense of who I was. They understand my goals, what I am working towards is already there. Nonetheless, I have gotten nos. Somebody was pushing me on the thesis side of things. I have received some pushback with standard perspective, questions such as "Shouldn't you be investing in more companies?" and "Don't you think you could change the structure of your fees?" Nothing too crazy. I haven't had anybody ask me questions like, "Don't you think you should cut your hair before you do this?"

The unique thing about my fundraising is, I have some investing background, but it's limited. So, I have a limited track record. I'm a first-time fund manager. I know that if you have a standard, rigorous due diligence process to look at a fund, I am never going to pass your due diligence—ever! That is one of the reasons I have never pitched with my deck. Whenever I pitch to people, it's just me telling the story. I share the entrepreneurs that I have been privileged to help in the past, and the kind of entrepreneurs I'm looking to help in the future. If that resonates with people, then we can start having a deeper discussion from there. But if you start going through all the legal paperwork or digging into my deck, I'm not at that stage yet. Maybe when I get to fund two or fund three, I can be better equipped to prepare for that level of track record scrutiny.

When I get these nos from institutions with that focus, I am well-prepared for them. Most of the people I meet have formed an opinion on how they feel about me, or about the fund, before they ever even talked to me. It's just a matter of whether I mesh with what they thought they understood about me or the fund when we actually speak. We are lucky because during COVID-19, everybody is at home, so I could do all these meetings via videoconference. If not for that, I would be flying all over the country, and probably all over the globe to have meetings, just for people to say, "We'll get back to you in a month" and "Let's have three more meetings before I make a decision." That takes a toll. So, the idea of somebody investing an early stipend into the GP of around $250K that you could use however you need, that could change everything for underrepresented GPs. While the kickback for that early investor could be that they get to participate in management fees of all the funds you raise as the GP, and everything else going forward.

FINDING INITIAL CAPITAL AS A FIRST-TIME FUND MANAGER

EB: *What are your thoughts on whether you would have been able to do that, coming from your ethnicity, socioeconomic background, etc., if COVID-19 wasn't a factor? Is there a way that you would have been able to do this without COVID-19? Or without having some form of deep pockets (or an early investor) in the first place?*

MC: Probably not. I mean, yes, but I'll be honest, when I was thinking about doing this, I was initially trying to raise $100K–$250K for the GP, so I could have the money to go raise the fund. Raising a fund is essentially business development; using your business development skills to grow a network or have a network of people you can talk to, who could potentially be investors, is the way you go about it. I just happened to use Twitter as my tool, but it could have been LinkedIn, it could have been something else. I would have figured out a way to do it. However, some capital upfront is vital. I've been in the tech field for the last 20 years. With that being said, I have some people who I could go to, to see if I could get that money. But it would have been a lot harder for me to do it that way. To your point about people saying they don't invest in first funds, most institutions don't. Most first funds are high net worths and family offices. Those people don't talk about this stuff as much. Then for the institution side who don't say they don't invest the first funds, it's the same thing for investors today, we don't invest in pre-product or pre-revenue companies. But every now and then you meet a founder, that's pre-product and pre-revenue that you just truly have real conviction for. You take a chance on that one.

TM: Regarding COVID-19, yes, I definitely agree our operational budgets have gone down tremendously. We are affected by the fact that the investors have to accept that they cannot meet us face to face and sit down and analyze our body language. Finding other ways of connecting, especially over video call, is extremely good for the industry, in general, and particularly good for emerging managers with scrappy operational budgets.

What we tend to say is that we are a triple impact fund in the sense that we are underrepresented fund managers ourselves, in the profiles and backgrounds we represent. We channel money towards underrepresented founder segments. Then there's that meta impact in that aspect. In addition, we only invest in companies that have impact at their core. We were just about to start our fundraise in early March 2020, then COVID-19 hit and everything stalled. But after the Easter holidays, stocks rebounded and we saw a tremendous appetite for positive impact investment opportunities. At that point, we suddenly had lots of interest from institutional investors, because as I mentioned, we have several layers of impact. They were quite enthusiastic; we actually increased our fund size, I would say tenfold of what we were initially aiming for. Unfortunately, it didn't come through. In fact, what you mentioned, Mac, in terms of due diligence, well, we have the eight investments that we have, and even though they are performing well, we just do not check those boxes that the larger institutions are looking for. Even when they say they do back first-time fund managers.

Raising a fund is always hard, regardless of whether you have experience or not. What we experienced was that because we have a thesis of investing in underrepresented founders, that creates a sense of empathy in investors; it is something people like and want to be a part of. At the same time however, people were also reluctant to actually accept that the opportunity was there, because in doing so they had to accept there was a problem, and that the problem is as big as it is when it comes to the Nordics (which is known as the most equitable place in the world). What we found there was a lot of interest from outside of the Nordics, because it's easier to see both the potential and the related problem in a market that is not your own.

What was particularly hard in the beginning was deciphering whether interest came from a place of "Oh, I'm curious about this thesis" versus "I believe in this opportunity, an alpha opportunity investing in underrepresented founders, and I accept that as a white man based in the Nordics." In that process, there was a lot of talk about Unconventional. VC is a small community in the Nordics, we experienced that some investors spoke negatively about our pipeline, however that the same investors were investing in the same companies through other opportunities. This was very different when talking to investors from outside the region that found our dealflow and selected investments as high-quality dealflow. I suppose it's always like that when you try to disrupt something, you are at the risk of getting shut down based on that alone. I think it is difficult, because we really want to change something in the industry, and at the same time, there are a lot of bigger players who say they want to support that change. Yet, they want to support that change until a certain level. As an emerging fund manager, if you're going for the diversity focus, choose your battles. My advice is, be very transparent about the challenges faced by the founders you want to back and persevere. You can't really do anything about institutional investors, they have their boxes they need to check, so focus your energy where there is bigger conviction and more flexible mandates, so you can get moving and accelerate the impact.

ADVICE FOR EMERGING FUND MANAGERS

EB: *What has been your most important learning? What would your biggest piece of advice be? What would you say to emerging GPs that they should refrain from doing?*

TM: I would say, the same as we say to our founders, in order to save time and be efficient, due diligence your investors before you spend too much time on them. Spend the time on those that are more probable of actually backing you. Do they have a track record of investing in underrepresented founders or in your industry? If they say they want to invest in diverse founders, do they actually have a track record of doing that? Have they put actions behind their words when it comes to that? That will save anyone who is fundraising, whether as a startup founder or emerging fund manager, a lot of time. Then in terms of ticket sizes, if they only invest in funds that have a minimum size of 100 million, then we shouldn't spend too much time on them, even though they might like to have the conversation. When you're in the diversity industry, everybody wants to say they are a part of it, and they believe it, and they think it's important. However, very few come to the conclusion that they want to put their money behind such a strategy.

Efficient ways of deciphering who is who: do they fit your thesis in terms of putting actions behind their words? Spend time getting good legal advice from people who are progressive. It can be difficult, if you don't have a legal background, to actually decipher whether legal counsel can be effective or not. If you have the right entity, set up correctly for the type of network you have, you could open yourself to high-net-worth individuals who can quickly help you get to first close. For us, that was not the case. We knew that we would attract women and underrepresented people, those with potentially smaller funds, but who are willing to do rather than speak, and actually believe in this investment opportunity as they might have experienced biases themselves. Next was the question of how we could create a structure that could accommodate the movement we were tapping into. A combination of legal understanding and your available networks is key, even though you can build your network of professional GPs and potential limited partners going forward.

MC: Be okay breaking rules that are no longer fit for purpose. Funds have been raised in the same ways for so long that people have stopped trying to innovate and think of different ways to attack the problem of some communities being locked out, or to figure out how to fundraise differently.

I am getting a lot of praise right now. Why? Because I am doing things that others have never done before. What I am doing has in turn created a generation of GPs coming behind me who are looking to raise their funds in the exact same way. If we all collectively start to think of different ways to go about raising our funds through different structures, using the things that were historically disadvantages to our advantage (within the spirit of the rules and laws of course), we might be able to see a lot more funds being raised. We either do that, or go back to the same old, traditional patterns. Get creative!

I would also say tell good stories. Too many GPs don't tell stories when they pitch. Most have their deck and meticulously go through the numbers and what the performance is going to be, rigidly hitting the notes they know every potential LP wants to hear when they are raising a fund. Try something different. You could be really well served telling stories of founders that you have met, that you support, and speaking about how you support them. Give a real-world example or case study of a founder you supported: how you met them, how the deal came together, the things you did to support them and help them grow. Leaving those founders as references can have a strong impact on your potential LP and actually differentiates you from everybody else raising a fund with their pristine deck. Keep in mind, no matter how differentiated you think you are, you probably are not. You are all competing against others that are pretty much identical, just like companies are. There are other funds that are being raised with similar thesis, similar models. So really homing in on what makes you unique and special is key. If you can tie that into a story where you can emphasize what you do, how you do things differently, and the impact that has already created, it can be both helpful and incredibly memorable. That's just a tactical thing.

14.2 *Hsu, Villa, Jones: Investing Outside Silicon Valley*

William Hsu (Mucker Capital)

Monique Villa (Launch Tennessee, formerly Mucker Capital)

Allan Jones (Bambee)

Mucker Capital[212] has been investing outside of Silicon Valley for more than 10 years. We caught up with William Hsu,[213] one of the founders; Monique Villa,[214] one of the investors; and Allan Jones,[215] one of the investees. We sat down with all three to better understand how Mucker was founded, how it invests differently from the status quo, and the impact of this on the founders receiving funding.

Interviewed February 2021

BUILDING A VENTURE FUND LIKE ENTREPRENEURS

Erika Brodnock (EB): *William, why and how did you start Mucker Capital? Was there a specific experience that led to your decision to do so?*

William Hsu (WH): Starting Mucker Capital was part of a grand plan to conquer the world! Much earlier in my career, I had been a very young entrepreneur in my early 20s. It was the middle of the dotcom era and I had raised a ton of money, and honestly, had wasted away a lot of money for my VCs, too, and I had been fired by my board and my investors for being a terrible CEO. They were right. I was a terrible CEO. I was 22 and I knew nothing about building companies except how to throw parties and give away stuff at the office. I never had this affinity for VC because it felt to me like people who did not have a hard job. It was making bets and hoping things worked out. They do not quite understand the hard work and the travails of building a business.

---

212. https://www.mucker.com/
213. https://www.linkedin.com/in/william-hsu-032273/
214. https://twitter.com/MoniqueVilla
215. https://twitter.com/TheAllanJones

In 2011, I was working at AT&T, in a senior role managing hundreds and hundreds of people. I thought, this is it, I am in my early 30s, this is the end. Another 40 years of AT&T and what happens next? I die and go to my grave? That is not what I wanted to do. My first instinct was to quit my job and go and start a company because I like that work, and last time, I was too young and not ready. This time, I should be ready because I know how to build a business, a product, a team.

I quit my job and started looking for opportunities to start a company. I was already in Los Angeles at the time. Then my partner, Erik, who I used to work with at eBay, moved down from the Bay Area and said, "I want to start a venture fund." I thought, "No!" A) I hate VCs, and B) LA has terrible VCs. Then Erik, being the open-minded contrarian that he is, said, "Starting a venture fund is like being an entrepreneur, you are building something new from scratch. When the market is not great and competitors in the market are subpar, it is called an opportunity. Therefore, we can be entrepreneurs, and we are going to build a fund." We went from that conversation to launching in the market within 30 days. We were not incorporated. We did not have an office, much less any money. We were two regular dudes, and we did not have much money. We just launched Mucker with about $500, we spent it on buying a logo on 99 Designs and building a website on Upwork. We spent $500 to get up and running, because, on the internet, all you need is a website. We then went to a couple of friends that we knew in the press and just announced our arrival in LA as an accelerator and a fund.

Our philosophy at the time was that we are entrepreneurs, entrepreneurs build MVPs, and we want to build what the market sees and test market reality on whether our thesis is correct. If it was correct, then we go out and figure out the rest of the steps. We wanted to build a business from the market back to the product. As a venture fund, money is the last thing you need. The first thing you need is a reputation, a brand, and a way to source deals. Can we at Mucker source good deals? Within 60 days, we knew that we could. We found ten companies we loved, and we wanted to invest in them. I mortgaged the house. Erik gave up his house and moved in with his in-laws. We then put together a million dollars of our own money and started investing. It took us another three months to find an office space. Another month or so to get completely squared away on the legal side. We launched first, found companies second, found money third. Finally, we got all the legal paperwork completed around six months later. We built a venture fund the opposite way of how most people build venture funds, which is to find the money first. We built it like entrepreneurs because that is what we have done in the past.

EB: *You found product-market fit in making sure that you had the customers or the companies.*

WH: We did it like entrepreneurs do with their customers. We found product-market fit first. We decided that we needed to figure out what our product or feature set should be before we told our engineers to go build it.

TELLING A DIFFERENT STORY ABOUT VENTURE

Johannes Lenhard (JL): *Monique, a question about the thesis at Mucker. What about it made you want to join? What about it also has to do with investing outside of Silicon Valley?*

Monique Villa (MV): Venture capital is all about people. For me and Mucker, it was about the people. I had been following Mucker's trajectory in Los Angeles since they launched in 2011. I did not know them personally at the time, but if you were young and building your career in LA, you knew about Mucker. Early in my career, I bumped into Will while working for a non-profit that he was advising at the time. I remember the way he was talking about market opportunities, and the people behind those market opportunities, that made me think: this is what venture capital should be. It should be very people-driven, and people-centric. He also looked at the world through a different lens, where typically, when you meet VCs, you will hear mostly cookie-cutter responses and backgrounds. Everything in VC historically fits into what seems to be a nice, clean box.

My previous experience working in venture capital was a bit jarring because I was new to venture. I had never heard of it before, as I did not grow up around venture capital and high-growth startups. I did not know what a startup was, I did not know what any of these company logos were on venture fund websites, I had to learn it all on the fly. When you enter the workforce that way, you tend to believe what people tell you: that you must come from a certain background to be in venture, you must fit the mold, and think the same way as everyone else. When I met Will, he was telling an entirely different story about venture. I thought, I want to stay close to these people and learn from their examples.

Fast-forward, and I found myself relocating to Nashville as an LA native. I was researching around the southeast and found that there was a tremendous market opportunity in the region, and it was being overlooked by investors. I naturally brought this to Will and did not know it would turn into us working together. I was eager to get his thoughts because he always had something different to contribute to a conversation. A month later, he said, what if you join our team and open an office for us in Nashville? The rest is history. It started with the thesis that it is all about people. It is about having unique insight, and about diving in and working alongside one another and taking out the traditional hierarchy and vertical structure that has been so present in traditional venture capital for decades.

WH: We faked it until we made it.

Allan Jones (AJ): It makes me respect you guys more. As an entrepreneur, I filter a lot of the advice I get from my investors through the lens of "they have limited operating experience." The advice does not get ignored. It just gets filtered and then applied in its appropriate place. When you know that your investors have walked the operating road at a company, and then apply those operating principles of starting a business in their venture fund, it adds a different type of filter. I feel more comfortable taking the advice I get from the team and applying it in real-time.

REMOVING THE BIASED CHECKBOXES IN VC

EB: *You have just broken down how to make the impossible possible. You are not just diverse in terms of location, you are also investing in founders who have been historically overlooked for other reasons. It is super interesting that you have a Black and gay investee on the call, which is phenomenal. What is the makeup of your portfolio? What are your commitments to DEI going forward?*

WH: We do not track the outcome. I do not think it is about the outcome. Off the top of my head, about 30% to 40% of our portfolio are either a minority or a woman. My partner Erik is, on the surface, Caucasian, conservative, male, and very religious. I am an atheist immigrant from Taiwan who is very liberal. Then we have a third partner who is a Muslim American born in Cincinnati, whose parents emmigrated from Syria. The partnership we all have is very strong; we have very different views about life in general, but we are very good friends. We believe in Mucker. We found a common ground in the firm we are trying to build. Yet when you ask us anything from guns to religion to abortion, we will all have very strongly different views. That has enabled us to understand that decision-making is best made when there is some disagreement.

Independent thinking is how you get to the right outcome. The fact that we have been investing outside of the Bay Area for over ten years meant that many traditional ways that people evaluate companies do not work. In the Bay Area, you ask, "Did that person go to Stanford Business School? Was their cousin roommates with Elon Musk when they were in college? Did they work at Google for four years as a director of product?" As much as I would love to have those checkboxes checked, I do not have those checkboxes to check in LA; I did not have those checkboxes to check in Nashville.

For us, diversity is not about purposely trying to create the outcome that we want. It is more about taking away the biases of the input that creates an unfair outcome. Those biases are the checkboxes that traditional VCs use to decide whether or not to invest. Is saying that you want to invest in a Stanford graduate a bad thing? No, it is not, but if that is all you do, you will not get a truly diverse outcome. From our perspective, investing in entrepreneurs is all about the market idea, how passionate an entrepreneur is, how persistent they are, and their personal story of how they got to where they are today. Someone that had a privileged upbringing and walked ten miles might seem that they walked a long way, versus someone who does not have an Ivy League college upbringing and walked 1,000 miles; they might be at exactly the same place in life on paper, but how far they walk is very, very different. For me, it is much more about how far they walked rather than whether they got to Stanford. We are unable to, and no longer desire to, use those benchmarks to make our investment decisions. Our portfolio has been the way it has been since the very first day we started. It is highly diverse for every single metric, whether that is cultural, religion, race, or what college people went to—I do not even ask that question anymore.

EB: *What results and returns have you seen?*

WH: Mucker passed our 10th year anniversary and every fund is a top 5% fund in all of venture. We went from a million-dollar fund, about 10 years ago, and today, our latest fund is about $260M. We continue to do what we do, which is we do not invest in Bay Area founders. I do not want to get sucked into the sweet temptation of just looking at, "Did you work at Google? Did you graduate from Stanford? Great, I will give you money." That is a great shortcut, and it has hype. It is a total temptation. We do not want that. We want to train ourselves to make the hard decisions with good people rather than the easy decisions with potentially bad people.

JL: *We have spoken to a lot of people, particularly in the US, that are not like that. There is some risk assessment happening by looking at these profiles.*

NON-TRADITIONAL JOURNEYS INTO ENTREPRENEURSHIP AND HOW TO FIND THAT TALENT

JL: *Allan, tell us a little bit about your journey into the whole entrepreneur-ship game. Why did you decide not to go to Silicon Valley? How was it meeting the team at Mucker?*

AJ: I did not make a choice not to go to Silicon Valley. I come from a blue-collar family. My dad is an electrician. My mom is a nurse and grew up in a family of entrepreneurs. They ran two businesses. One of them was a pager and cell phone shop. I grew up soldering pagers back together in a small store in Long Beach, California. I had no idea what I wanted to do. I did not go to college. I went to a semester of community college, and I barely went to school. Then I met a woman at a Mariah Carey concert in 2005. We talked for two hours. She said to me, "You are smart. I am going to give you a job." I was building computers on the side. I had a technical interview for six hours for a quality assurance analyst position; I had no idea what I was talking about, bombed the interview, but got hired any-way. That was my introduction to technology, and that was sixteen years ago.

I very quickly realized I was terrible on the technical side, but I loved product. I got laid off. I read a bunch of product books, pitched myself to be a product manager. I had been in tech for seven months at a company called MyLife. I got hired by a guy named Ian Siegel, who is now the CEO of ZipRecruiter, a unicorn in Los Angeles. I realized I loved product man-agement and I wanted to be an entrepreneur. Fairly quickly, my career progressed, I was 20 at the time and I then went on to be the director of a company called Docstoc, which was acquired by Intuit when I was 21. I started my first venture-backed studio out of a technology studio called Science. They invested in Dollar Shave Club, and HelloSociety, which was acquired by the *New York Times* when I was 23. I joined ZipRecruiter as their chief marketing officer when I was 26. I was employee number 20 at that company and the operating groups, new products and services, marketing, and customer service account management functions. Coming fresh from failing my first company at 23, I was hungry to prove that I was as good as I thought I was in my head. By the time I left ZipRecruiter, there were 750 people at the company, it is now over 1,000 employees and the company is worth about $3B.

I met Erik when I was 23, pitching my first business outside of a coffee shop. He passed on the business and I went on to fund that company somewhere else. At ZipRecruiter, I proved a couple of things. One, I proved I was very good at this. Primarily, I had proven that resilience matters. From a Mariah Carey concert, I worked my way up to being at a company that was acquired by Intuit and then being the youngest CMO of a billion-dollar business by the time I was 26. Most of that was driven by the desire to prove to myself that I was as good as I thought I was. My confidence always seemed to be much bigger than the skills I actually had, and ZipRecruiter was the turning point where my skills started to exceed my confidence. After three years of being the chief marketing officer and running 50% of ZipRecruiter, with hundreds of people in my team, I realized I wanted to start another company. I realized I was not going to be the CEO of that company, and I had a different vision. I wanted to create something from scratch that I thought could be a behemoth and could create a world of difference in my lifetime.

I met up with Erik again. Will and Erik were the earliest committers to the business. From the gate, they basically said, we want to write you the biggest check our firm will allow us to do. They did. They have been deeply without doubt about my potential as an entrepreneur. They have had questions, but they have never expressed an ounce of doubt. One of the things I have learned is that the early questions an investor asks me, when I walk into the room, expose to me how high the hill is that I have to climb to let them know that I am as good as the person that they would have automatically assessed is good from Stanford. There is this list of questions that I get asked, and most of them are around proving that I even deserve to be having a meeting. The first 30 minutes is going to be me flexing my intellect, so that they can finally lean into the table, and give me the conversation I deserve. The next 30 minutes is talking about the business. I have been fortunate to say that I have moved forward enough to not have those meetings anymore. From Will and Erik, it was straight to talking about the business, speaking about the problem you are trying to solve, and the opportunity you see in the market. It was noticeably absent of the sometimes unconscious biases that are introduced in a lot of investor meetings. That has been the tone of our relationship since that first meeting.

EB: *What could other VCs do to open themselves up to talent like you? We are "underrepresented" and there is something about the under that makes it seem as though it is our fault. Instead, we are "overlooked," and putting the emphasis on the venture capitalists to make sure that they are allowing themselves to have the opportunity to invest in us is the framing that we need. What would make you want to provide that opportunity to other venture capital firms? What would they need to do to attract you?*

AJ: Diversity is not a favor to the diverse, it is a favor to the business. On the founder side, the truth of the matter is, if you are a diverse founder and you are trying to confine yourself to the parameters that investors are looking for, to decide if you are good or not, you will never be able to meet them. When I first started, I tried to talk and look like an MBA. I was spending so much time trying to look and be someone else, no one was taking my place in this God-given body. The truth is, you are perfect. The sooner you realize that the unique things about you are the things that will make you a majestically good founder, the better the likelihood that you meet investors that not only fund your business—that is only the beginning of the relationship—but also see you as you progress through your journey to help you become a good entrepreneur. The first check is the easy part, although it does not seem that way. That journey is where all the grit is necessary. The right investors to see you through that is extremely important. There are not as many of them that are looking at the right indicators, but there are the right ones. "All money ain't good money," as my Grandma Jones used to say. Partnering with people that see you for who you are, and see those measures of you as a person, being Black, being gay, being from an underprivileged background, they all makeup just your normal human element. The reason I talk the way I do, and I am brave enough to have my hair on the side and blonde at the tip is precisely because of my experiences. I just do not care; I like it. It is uniquely me. I feel free in that. Investors who see that are the investors I want. As soon as you as a founder see that as an intrinsic value, that type of intrinsic value is unavoidable for investors to see too. That is my advice to founders.

On the investor side, it is going to be harsh—spend the time asking yourself why the majority of your current portfolio is homogenous. Before you try and blame systematic failures, be accountable in realizing that you are part of that system. If you are going to look at the components of the system, point out and analyze how those components could be better, to drive more diversity, you should not do that until you analyze yourself as one of those contributing components. You are a part of the bias problem. How you make decisions about talent, though they feel intrinsically right, are intrinsically biased. Until you realize that, you will have 1% of all VC dollars going to Black founders. Until you realize that, you are going to potentially end up with a larger percentage of an investor's portfolio being African American, but not nearly the success rates that should offer, because you are investing for the wrong indicating factors, because of some skin tone checkmark versus seeing the value based on the removal of biased filters. The honesty there is what investors must confront to truly be able to find talent and unlock the market in terms of diverse value. The indicator is not about the diversity. It is about uniqueness. Unique founders are the best founders. Authentic founders are the best founders. They come in many shapes. The shade is not the metric. It is the uniqueness and authenticity that is the ultimate measuring factor.

DIVERSE INVESTMENT VOLUME AND THE RETENTION PROBLEM

JL: *Monique, do you see any early signs of positive results of what is happening? What does the future hold for you as a firm, specifically as one that is willing to invest both in terms of partners and fund managers like you, and entrepreneurs like Allan? Is there anything that you are already seeing that is going to be successful and is there anything that you already see that you want to do differently, particularly through the lens of diversity, equity, and inclusion?*

MV: When we were talking about resilience, and what founders and CEOs were up against in the middle of March 2020, and into May, our portfolio founders who went through some of the toughest moments, post COVID, had profitable businesses, and had cash in the bank and runway. Not all of them, but a good chunk of them. The companies that were excelling through some of the most incredibly difficult moments in 2020, all came from underrepresented backgrounds in the venture-backed world. That resilience, that extra 999 miles traveled, carries over into positive unit economics, which translates into cash flow management, cash in the bank, resilient teams they are managing that could think on their feet and be nimble in some of the most difficult moments that any startup has probably ever faced. This all happens behind closed doors and are not the types of things that are celebrated in news headlines. Venture capital is a long game and these companies will be the future unicorns.

To the question about the future, what we need is a volume of checks being written for founders who are closest to unique market opportunities. It cannot be about checking a box and having your one diverse investment for the year. One of my biggest bones to pick with how diversity is talked about today is looking for recognition for "diverse investments" made and leading with that when publishing your VC blog post announcement about your most recent deal. If you are trying to check that box by making one "diverse" investment for the entire year, you are putting an outsized amount of stress and set of expectations onto that single CEO and founder. We all know this is a numbers business, this is a volume business, you have to have volume, and writing that one check a year is not going to do it.

We need to focus on fixing the retention problem. From the venture capital side there are multiple times when I could have left this industry and said this is not for me as a half-Mexican, female, non-pedigreed, aspiring VC. Post-Mucker, I am so glad that I stuck it out, because we have so much work to do. I wrote about diversity recently in a *TechCrunch* op-ed. There are lots of VCs that are talking about diversity now, talking about investing outside of Silicon Valley. Over Christmas, I kept getting calls from people saying, "We want to pick your brain on the Southeast, or Nashville, or Latinx founders." Apparently, I know all of them, but I do not.

When we are talking about investing outside of Silicon Valley, we are talking about America, and America is this bigger idea that is known around the world as being a place for everybody. Why are we so set on investing in this seven-by-seven-mile footprint of San Francisco, when you have the entire United States? There are also obviously lots of opportunities around the globe, but what if we just started there: instead of fixating on this concept of "outside of Silicon Valley," outside of purely Stanford and Harvard grads, instead of finding yet another way we can make life more convenient for everybody who already has money, maybe there are market opportunities outside of that. This is why I show up every day. This is why I did not give up. I want to solve the retention problem. It is not a pipeline problem. It is the retention problem of scaring people away who have been told that they do not belong, and also recognizing there is a whole world out there to invest in. It is our job to go and invest in that world. Let us stop talking about one diverse investment for the year. Stop patting yourselves on the back and get to work.

14.3 *Yin: Hustle Fund*

Elizabeth Yin (Hustle Fund)

We caught up with Elizabeth Yin,[216] *co-founder and GP at Hustle Fund,*[217] *about her experiences growing up in Silicon Valley. From working in big tech and starting her own company, to becoming a partner at 500 Startups and raising her own fund, Elizabeth has really seen it all. With Hustle Fund, she's now on a mission to democratize wealth by investing differently (earlier, quicker, and to a wider pool of people). Together we explored how, as an Asian woman, she has been able to navigate the culture in Silicon Valley and, in spite of all the assumptions and stereotypes she regularly comes up against, she has attained investor positions where she can "try to change the system."*

Interviewed November 2020

GETTING STARTED IN SILICON VALLEY

Johannes Lenhard (JL): *Let's start with the very beginning, when you started in tech in the mid 2000s. What was the tech world like then? How bro-y was it back then in San Francisco?*

Elizabeth Yin (EY): Wow, what a question to start out with. So I've grown up in the San Francisco Bay Area and in what they call Silicon Valley; I'm from Mountain View, California, which is the heart of it. So, I've been in tech in many different ways, for a very long time, even before my professional career through a variety of internships, even before college. Even from that time, the stereotype of white and Asian men with geekier tendencies very much resonates, and I think that that's the foot that the industry got started off on. From there, it just flywheeled into many other ways.

---

216. https://twitter.com/dunkhippo33
217. https://www.hustlefund.vc/

I do think, just intuitively, there is something to the fact that people tend to hire people who are their friends and their friends tend to be people who are like them, which certainly extends into race and gender. So that is also where I got started, even way back when I was a child in the 90s. It has just bloomed into what we see today. Where we are today, we are playing defense or catch up [to the people the industry started with]. The way out is to get other flywheels going and to get them going fast and to the same scale. That's just a very challenging problem.

COMBATTING ASSUMPTIONS AND STEREOTYPES

Erika Brodnock (EB): *How does this relate and work with the idea of meritocracy? For instance, you started your own company quite early, Launch-Bit, where you were the CEO; you managed to exit that in 2014. How was it being an American-Asian female entrepreneur and founder of a tech company, and what was your experience raising capital?*

EY: So sometimes, one of the challenges is that you don't know if people are responding positively or negatively to something about your company or because of who you are, your race or gender; it's really hard to separate that. In other words, if an investor passes, you don't really know why it is. And I would even go as far as to say that sometimes the investor may not know because unconscious biases are a real thing.

That being said, on occasion, you are given a little bit more. I'll tell you a story about how I pitched an angel investor for my company Launch-Bit. At the end of the pitch, I asked him, so what do you think? And I'll never forget his response. He said, "I don't want to say the wrong thing and call you a meek Asian woman, but I question how you'll lead a company of 100 people." And at that very moment, just all kinds of thoughts were going through my head. I studied engineering, I went to work at big tech companies, including Google, all of those places are very skewed in demographics. In many of my classes, I was the only woman, and even at Google, there were not that many women. I just actually had never heard anything like that before. Nobody ever said anything like that to me, even if people felt like, "oh, she's incompetent," or even if people felt like "she's just here because she's the token woman." So that was the first time I had ever heard anything questioning my competency because of both race and gender.

After that experience, I really thought very deeply about it. I actually walked away from it rather positively, as weird as that sounds, because it made me think: if this person is thinking that, then perhaps a lot of people are thinking that, either consciously or unconsciously. Maybe everyone out there thinks I really am a meek Asian woman and am unfit to lead a company. Therefore, if I want to do this, I must do everything I can to combat that stereotypical impression. After that, actually, I started focusing on my posture, sitting up in my chair, speaking even louder, even though often I felt like I was shouting, just bringing extra energy to the table—all this stuff that is stereotypically associated with being a good leader. It actually worked out a lot better; I started closing checks. I don't think he should have said that; it was very inappropriate. But it actually was a gift in a weird way.

CAN FITTING IN AS A LEADER MEAN BEHAVING "LIKE A MAN"?

JL: *So, the takeaway is that you have to behave like a man, stereotypically speaking, in order to be successful in this world.*

EY: Oh, 100%. And, to be clear, I'm not saying that either his behavior was right, or that the stereotypes people have around what is a good leader are right. I'm just saying that from that particular situation, for the situation I was in, I was able to take something away from that, and apply it to that at hand.

At Hustle Fund, we are trying to change how people think about what a good leader is. A good leader, almost by definition, is somebody who can lead a group of people to execute well, right? That says nothing about what you look like, or how you talk or how loud you are. And I know plenty of CEOs who are not charismatic people, but have led very effectively. But people do have all these stereotypes, and that was one of the first times somebody explicitly said that to me. I had heard all these murmurings of how people think about things, but that was an experience where somebody explicitly just laid it out.

A second example, where I left actually dejected, also involved in fundraising for LaunchBit. I was pitching a VC and my contact at the VC firm was very excited. He took me to the all partner meeting. The firm is big—they had seven partners, two of whom were remote, five were in the room. And you can imagine video conferencing back then was not that great. So things kept on dropping all the time. All the partners were also men, and the reason I bring that up is, I think, from a physiological perspective, it turned into a big shouting match. You have seven men yelling, two on video conference yelling, and I'm trying to get a word in edgewise and yell over them, which is entirely impossible. I knew leaving that meeting, I did not get the money, because I just could not even be heard. I felt like, "Okay, this is an example of where gender does not help me, for sure. The whole setup of that meeting did not work in my favor, already I was going in at a disadvantage."

SEEING FUNDING FROM THE OTHER SIDE OF THE TABLE

JL: *After LaunchBit's exit, you switched camp in 2014 and became a partner at 500 Startups. How was it to look at it from that side of the table, from the perspective of an accelerator?*

EY: It gave me a lens that I think a lot of people don't have, because 500 Startups has invested in so many companies over the years—at this point, it's well over 2,500 companies. They invest all over the world, all across demographics such as race, gender, age, types of people, just everything. So basically, I got a snapshot into a lot of different teams. That was very informative for me, because as I mentioned before, when it's just you, and you're pitching your startup, you're a data point of one. But when you see larger sets of data, then you can start to see very interesting patterns. One of the interesting patterns that got confirmed for me was the following: if you're a white male who worked at Facebook and went to MIT, it almost doesn't matter what you're working on, it will be really easy for you to get funded.

The other interesting thing about working at an accelerator is that we would fund all these companies, and then they would come into my office to work. So I had information that many other investors didn't have. How did these teams actually work? Do they get along? Do they actually work hard? Are they focused? Are they executing with speed? You see the day-to-day, the week-to-week; that granular level of information that investors don't see is very telling. After every batch for me, I could pick a subset that were really interesting. And time and again, the companies that I thought were the best did not necessarily overlap with the companies that other investors thought were the most interesting, because they were making decisions based on very different methods.

DIFFERENT FOUNDERS AND COMPANIES DON'T GET THE SAME

SHOT

EB: *The companies you chose from the batch looked different—can you give us any example of what one of them look like?*

EY: Yeah, so actually one of my best companies from 500 Startups was passed on many times. In fact, she basically couldn't raise any money, but now is doing incredibly well. She owns most of the company, she raised a large Series B from NEA, which is a big VC firm here. She raised on her strong traction at this point, rather than based on a pitch deck. The company's called Mejuri; they make custom jewelry. The founder is a kick-ass female, originally from the Middle East, but she has made her home in Canada.

Why was she not able to raise money for a long time? A lot of VCs just don't understand jewelry, or women's products; certainly direct-to-consumer is not a big thing for them, just in general. Female founder, more or less solo founder, not from Silicon Valley; she didn't really fit the mold.

But now, I think in retrospect, after she's grinded this out for many years and eaten glass to get to where she is, things are wonderful for her because she now owns most of this wonderful business. It's a good example of somebody who was able to do it partly because of a specific trick in her business; she didn't get VC funding, but she did get debt funding. What underwrites the debt funding is the jewelry. She was able to stay on for that long because of receiving financing to get to that stage, even if it wasn't VC financing. Think about all the other entrepreneurs who, like her, don't check a number of those boxes, but just cannot get any financing. They just don't even have a shot on goal.

CHANGE IS STARTING, BUT IT WILL BE LONG TERM

EB: *Since you joined 500 Startups, has the number of investments in companies led by diverse founders increased?*

EY: Intuitively and knowing some of the data, it feels like there are just more founders in general, including more overlooked founders. So I think numerically, I do want to believe that more people are getting funded that come from diverse backgrounds and don't tick all the boxes, but not relatively speaking.

Now, that being said, it takes like seven to ten companies to build a big company. So when we go back to this concept of flywheel, I know a lot of people are really frustrated. Not a lot of funding is going into overlooked founders, and not a lot of overlooked founders are building big businesses yet, but I think it just takes time. You start the flywheel now, you find some people, a percentage of those people will build big businesses, and then will become funders, and then they're starting another cycle in another ten years. You cannot get this flywheel going in this manner fast enough. There need to be other solutions here. I do think that flywheel is starting, but you're talking about like a 30-year process or more.

ADVICE FOR THE NEXT GENERATION OF DIVERSE ENTREPRENEURS

JL: *Looking back at what you've gone through and knowing the world as it is now, if you were asked for advice from your own 18-year-old self about going into entrepreneurship and venture capital, what would you say they should do?*

EY: One person said it very elegantly to me recently; he said, "My melanin does not work for me." Other people in my portfolio have been very blunt like, "They're not going to fund me, if only if I were a man." I've heard a spectrum of comments now from my own portfolio. The data is maybe not in their favor, statistically, but the problem is, you cannot go in psyching yourself out. Statistically speaking, you should not be building a business if you're looking for your optimal chance of, for instance, making a lot of money. There are much better ways to make a lot of money. You go into entrepreneurship to play your own game—maybe you're going into it to solve a particular problem you're really passionate about. Along the way, you just get inundated by all these other people, rightly or wrongly, and mostly naysayers. The way to play the game is to mostly ignore them and take in some tidbits of feedback here and there. Too many people, especially overlooked founders, end up getting into this weird mind trap of what all these other people are saying to them. That's a problem, because most of the battle with entrepreneurship is with yourself. You are just psyching yourself out. But the way to succeed is to just focus on what you need to do and ignore everything else.

I completely agree that the landscape is unfair, everything from the pattern matching to even the setups of how investment meetings work. But that being said, that isn't the thing that a founder should be trying to address right now or even necessarily be worried about. It's probably because I have gone through this myself, where I know that the best path forward is you have to just work with the system and just plow through it for now. Once you have been successful, maybe you can come back and we can work together and try to change the system.

14.4 *Kapor, Kapor Klein: Equitable Access*

Mitch Kapor (Kapor Capital, Kapor Center)

Freada Kapor Klein (Level Playing Field Institute)

This conversation features a power couple that truly deserves the name: Mitch Kapor[218] and Freada Kapor Klein[219] have been leading the charge of VCs investing in companies that close the gap to access in low-income communities and communities of color for several decades. Mitch tells us how after founding and leaving Lotus—the Microsoft of its day—and meeting Freada, the two decided to dedicate their time, influence, and money to funding people and startups for underrepresented groups. Kapor Capital[220] has done so, and has not only been incredibly financially successful, but has also inspired a whole social movement.

Interviewed February 2021

THE ORIGINS OF KAPOR CAPITAL

Erika Brodnock (EB): *Tell us about the thesis at Kapor Capital. How did it originate?*

Mitch Kapor (MK): I was a tech entrepreneur from the '80s who built a very high growth company, Lotus; Freada was hired to make Lotus the most progressive employer in the US. We did a lot of things back then that people still are not doing in terms of diversity and having an inclusive culture, while being a responsible corporate citizen in a very affirmative way. For instance, we were the first tech company to adopt the Sullivan prin-

218. https://twitter.com/mkapor
219. https://twitter.com/TheRealFreada
220. https://www.kaporcapital.com/

ciples, which were the principles by which a company refused to do business with South Africa during apartheid.

I have a long history of angel investing. Freada and I worked together in the '80s and got together as a couple in the mid '90s. She had been doing independent consulting. As I ramped up angel investing activities in 2008–2009, we began to have a dialogue, and she urged me to think about the social impact of the companies that I was investing in. I was initially skeptical, because I was concerned that we would be missing out on the good deals, but Freada could be very persistent. We conducted a set of experiments and I actually found that there was a different and better way to look at it, which was that all companies have impact, some positive, some negative. There is no such thing as neutral. There was a class of companies with their founders who simultaneously created value that had an economic dimension and a social dimension.

Over a period of a couple of years, in the early 2010s, we brought some other people in to help with the investing, and we began to put it into an investment thesis with the idea of selecting companies that closed gaps of access or opportunity or outcome for underserved communities.

Freada Kapor Klein (FKK): A very important dimension of how this evolved was rather organic. Our San Francisco office brought together and housed a non-profit that I started called the Level Playing Field Institute, which sponsored the IDEAL Scholars Program at UC Berkeley. This was explicitly started to counteract Proposition 209, which, in California, ended affirmative action in public institutions. We started a scholarship program for underrepresented students of color who were admitted to UC Berkeley race blind, and then we created a race-conscious scholarship program for them. That is important for a few reasons. Our Kapor Capital partner, Ulili Onovakpuri, was in that program and we met her as a high school senior.

Level Playing Field Institute was a non-profit that I had started in 2000–2001 as a research organization to investigate why diversity in corporate America had failed so miserably. That was now 20 years ago. I had come to that conclusion after leaving Lotus in 1987. I then started my own consulting firm on issues of bias, harassment, and discrimination. It was global. I had as clients the UN, World Bank, Goldman Sachs, McKinsey, Harvard Business School, and Sanwa Bank. I did proprietary surveys and customized training. In that context, I said, "If it is serious, corporate

America gets done what it wants to get done." Obviously, it did not want to get it done. That was the purpose of starting that.

One of our first major research studies was the Corporate Leavers study in 2007. It was part of my book *Giving Notice*. Ten years later, we did it for the tech sector as the Tech Leavers Study, which is on the Kapor Center website. Housing together Mitch's foundation, Level Playing Field Institute, and Kapor Capital meant that ideas already started cross-pollinating. For instance, I met a woman through my consulting practice named Sherita Ceasar who was the highest-ranking Black woman in cable. She had grown up in the Chicago housing projects, and was in a program for underrepresented high school students of color. She credits her trajectory change to it. Sherita and her brother came in to pitch a math app for kids, and we knew that Ulili had been talking about how to keep her little brothers engaged in math. Ulili was working on the Corporate Leavers study. She had a full-time job at Level Playing Field Institute. She had no idea what venture capital was, but all of us hung out at lunch together and Ulili would always go hang out with the geeks. She was a natural and loves tech. She designed her own major on international healthcare and leads our healthcare investing. Mitch invited her into this pitch of the math app.

MK: I could see she had an instinctive feel for what would make a good app. She had the basic perspective and skill set, and I was impressed. I went to Freada after the meeting and said, "Can I get 50% of your time to work on deals?" If we had not had the cross-pollination, this never would have happened. Ulili was not looking for this kind of job, but she fell in love with it. She was good at it. She wound up working as an analyst for Kapor Capital, going to business school, working for a couple of other venture firms, and then coming back to Kapor Capital and becoming a partner. We look for talent in places that people do not otherwise do, in terms of our own team and the founders we support.

FKK: The other thing is the melding of philosophies and programs. What Ulili did first as an analyst at Kapor Capital is start a summer associate program. A traditional analyst, "pre-MBA, I want to be a VC," it just would not have occurred to them.

MK: Even if it had occurred, they never would have gotten permission to start that kind of program.

FKK: She got the financial support, the readjustment of her job responsibilities, and she did it. Our first summer associate in 2011 was Brian Dixon, who is our other partner now.

HOW TO MOVE TALENT UP THE CHAIN

EB: *You seem to have a great way of inclusively moving people through the ranks. One of the things that we have seen from research is that people make diversity hires, but they do so at an intern level and scout level, and then they stay there. What would your advice be to anyone who wanted to actually actively start to see more diversity at the top of the chain?*

FKK: Homegrown talent is really important. While it is usually used as a way to exclude people, there is a kernel of truth about culture fit. You are much more likely to get culture fit if you have homegrown talent, as opposed to bringing someone in who was at Goldman Sachs for many years, for instance, where you have to undo that culture and redo your own. After the George Floyd murder in the US, many VCs reached out to us for help—both for help hiring their internal teams and help with deal flow. We had a call recently with a whole group of Seattle and Washington VCs about how to run a summer associates program. The problem that they have is they do not have underrepresented talent on their team to be mentors or to guide the program. For a summer associate program to be successful, not only do you have to commit the time and money, but somebody must shepherd them through. Ulili said we are getting 700–900 applications for our summer associates program and we take seven. We do not want them to go into a firm with no diversity, because that is not going to succeed. If that firm does not have diversity, how do they start? One thing we are doing is saying, "Only take a pod, never take an only." They also need to leave their Fridays open. Every Friday, we bring all the summer associates together under our leadership for training and support, like an employee resource group.

EB: *So, it is a hybrid model that gives them experience of working in a firm, but then also keeps them in a supportive network where they can be nurtured and shielded from some of the lack of inclusivity that is out there at the moment.*

INCLUSIVITY IS AN ASSET, NOT A RISK

Johannes Lenhard (JL): *There was this fear in the beginning that you had to trade off being an inclusive fund and being diverse in your investment decisions in your team and hiring decisions, vis-à-vis make money. You have proven that it is not a tradeoff. You are showing you out-perform most other funds by far.*[221] *What are the most important attributes to that success?*

MK: It is a combination of things. It is the mindset and the understanding of how you create value. I have come to the conclusion that conventional wisdom is just wrong. Conventional wisdom says that if you think about anything else, besides making money, it is going to be a diversion. You will introduce risks, and you should not take risks. We just happened to be in a period of time where there is widespread ignorance about that. We have been very rigorous in learning from our mistakes when we analyze investment opportunities. We think about the things that other VCs think about—such as total addressable market, how strong is the team—but we also really ask ourselves, if this business succeeds, who will be better off and who will not? Will it increase the gaps between the haves and have-nots between the people at the top or bottom? Or will it narrow them in some fashion? Which specific demographics will get served and how will we measure that? We have these dialogues with our founders before we make the investment commitment to see what the quality and depth of their thinking is and what their quality of their commitment to their mission and strategy is. We have such a different process because of that. It differentiates us and it has helped us create a brand by which we have enormous amounts of inbound deal flow. Conventional wisdom puts tremendous latent demand among founders for value-aligned investors. Conventional wisdom says take out any mention of diversity impact from your deck, because it is not going to help you get funded. We say, "Bring it on!"

It gives us an enormous competitive advantage. We are about to get into a deal where we wound up beating five other firms to the deal. It was highly competitive, oversubscribed, with multiple term sheets. We established a relationship with the founders, and they know what we stand for. They understand what help we can provide.

---

221. https://www.axios.com/2019/05/10/
    kapor-capital-wants-to-dispel-myths-about-do-good-investing

FKK: If everybody is hiding, we cannot find each other. They did their due diligence and talked to other founders in our portfolio. It is a company with two Black women co-founders. For many years now, an Atlanta-based group has put out the Project Diane report[222] on who funds Black women entrepreneurs. The first couple of reports were done two or three years apart, but the first one was eight years ago. We were always at the top of the list, which is appalling when you think that a billion-dollar fund does not invest in as many Black women as we did when we were a $50M fund. This company just won a challenge sponsored by a couple of foundations at MIT, and they made their decision after talking to everybody about who they wanted in their round. We got into a company late last year called Welcome. It is a next-generation virtual events platform, which is far superior to doing a big event on Zoom. The Latino CEO and co-founder is Puerto Rican and grew up with a single mom in a low-income neighborhood in Philadelphia. A program in high school got him on his trajectory. He has done a couple of startups, one of which was bought by Yahoo. Ten years ago, he moved through the ranks, managing all of mobile for Yahoo. He came and spoke to our SMASH scholars, which is the STEM college access program I started almost 19 years ago, for low-income, underrepresented high school students of color—half of them girls. We got in and beat out Sand Hill Road firms because he knew who we were and what we stood for.

MK: In this business, success begets success. You develop momentum and your networks get better. Your brand gets better and your deal flow gets better. While there is never an excuse for complacency, at this point, as a firm, we built an array of intangible assets that give us an ongoing competitive advantage.

LESSONS FROM RESEARCH AT THE KAPOR CENTER

EB: *Tell me a bit about the Kapor Center and what you would define as some of the most compelling research to emerge from the center thus far?*

MK: There are a lot of different organizations with different names, because we have been at this for a long time. Level Playing Field was renamed to SMASH. The Mitchell Kapor Foundation is also the same thing as the Kapor Center. It is the home of the research.

---

222. https://www.projectdiane.com

FKK: The research group started at Level Playing Field Institute and migrated over to be with the foundation in Kapor Center. The way to think about it now is that we are all co-housed; SMASH, Kapor Capital, and Kapor Center are in the same building. We collaborate on several activities. In 2019, the last full year we were in the building, we sponsored 185 events in the building. We have an auditorium that seats 125 with a roof deck that we can pack about 200 on. There is wonderful weather in Oakland and you can have evening outdoor events at least six months of the year. We have a wonderful Oaxacan walk-in restaurant on the ground floor, and an elevator between the restaurant and our rooftop.

Kapor Center was doing First Fridays, which was an open meeting that was always oversubscribed, primarily for first-time Black and Brown entrepreneurs. We bring Black and Brown successful entrepreneurs, VCs, and others to this, with a program and we implement an "ask me anything" format. We have invested in companies that came through that network. Level Playing Field Institute is where the research started. As research moved over into the Kapor Center, all of the publications are actually on kaporcenter.org.[223] We have a website, leakytech-pipeline.com,[224] where we put all of the rigorous peer-reviewed research on leaks in the pipeline to tech and VC, starting at pre-school. A study done at Yale, for instance, found that preschool Black boys were labeled completely differently than preschool white boys engaging in identical behavior.

There is this huge debate often going on Twitter: "There is a pipeline problem" or "No, it is a racism problem, it is a bias problem." That is the wrong question, because there are biases and barriers that underlie both. One of the studies that the Kapor Center did is about access to computer science education in California. When you see the number of Black or Brown kids that have access to computer science in public education, it is minuscule. By definition, that is a pipeline problem. The bias problem comes in when tech companies only hire from Stanford or MIT, and when a third of those students are legacy admits. The Leaky Tech Pipeline framework and the Tech Leavers study look at who leaves tech and why, with an intersectional lens. It analyzes the single greatest reason that Black women leave tech is being passed over for promotion. That is a dif-

223. https://www.kaporcenter.org/
224. https://leakytechpipeline.com/

ferent reason than why LGBTQ talent leaves tech or why white men leave tech. Unless you have taken an intersectional view and put in intersectional solutions, nothing is going to change.

I often talk about tech approaching diversity as though filling a bathtub with the drain open. There is a study that won Best Paper at the International Computer Science Education Conference in Bologna a few years ago that looked at barriers to pursuing STEM for girls of color. Mitch used to call us the home for wayward PhDs as we have a lot of PhDs hanging around. We believe in rigorous research that answers very practical questions.

WHAT'S NEXT FOR KAPOR?

JL: *In terms of Kapor Capital and the Kapor Center, how do you intend on moving the needle in terms of DEI when it comes to tech and investing? Can you share some ideas for the future?*

MK: Talent development is central and where we will get the most leverage, because what matters is who is sitting around the table when the decisions are made. Until there is really more diversity in VC, we are not going to see as much diversity in the companies that get funded. Our summer associate program, which we are now trying to make industry-wide to allow other firms to participate, could have the effect of giving many more underrepresented folks a foot in the door and into VC as a first step. If that is done well, and there is the right follow-on over time, it can have a big impact. The industry has to hold up a mirror and look at itself. The successful white male VCs have to do this. Getting more diversity in your firm is not going to a big store, heading to Aisle 12, and picking a diverse founder up off the shelf. You have to be willing to look at the ways your firm has actually perpetuated the lack of diversity and how it continues to do that. Holding up a mirror is a hard process. It is a journey, and it does not happen all at once. If we can find better tactics to encourage self-examination, people can begin to understand that power can act differently to produce different outcomes.

FKK: There are external forces that play to our strengths. An emphasis on stakeholder capitalism[225] in the mainstream financial services world is helping because you cannot engage in stakeholder capitalism without

---

225. Stakeholders as opposed to shareholders, considering groups such as employees/ workers, suppliers and the local and natural environment among others.

looking at employees and impact on the community. The tendency towards looking at [Environmental, Social, and Governance] (ESG) factors in investing also helps us. The changing demographics also help. This suggests who is going to be your customers and employees. Your ability to attract and retain them, as customers and as employees, is critically important. Brian and Ulili are our two partners of homegrown talent. Brian was promoted to partner in 2015 and one of the youngest VC partners ever. It took him four years from summer associate to partner. Ulili was made partner in 2018. She hired Brian as a summer associate, but she had not yet gone to business school. They are our two partners, and Kapor Capital is for the first time raising outside funds. Brian and Ulili, two Black GPs will be the co-managing partners, and Mitch and I are stepping back to be the anchor LPs.

We still have 178 companies that have not grown up yet that we will still help tend, but we are not going to be making the new investment decisions. That is part of how we are going to continue to grow and evolve. As the summer associates program grows from a Kapor Capital program to an ecosystem program, it is going to move over to the Kapor Center. This way it can have more philanthropic support. We test all kinds of ideas and we move the ones that stick over to the foundation or elsewhere. We have done some pioneering pitch competitions, which will be taken over. One was our People Ops tech that I started six years ago. People thought it was nuts that we were going to fund seed-stage tech companies whose purpose was mitigating bias in any stage of employment or education. In 2019, you had to have a product in market. It could not just be an idea. You could not have raised more than $2M. In two weeks, we had 150 applicants. We would like to pioneer things of this nature, and then let other people work with us or just take them and run with them.

REFLECTING ON SOCIAL SHIFTS IN THE INDUSTRY

MK: Let me amplify one thing. I would identify an area that is ready for some intentional experiment on our part. We have not done this yet, but we want to think it through. There is so much interest among allocators of capital for ESG investments. I would not say that their understanding of what that means is in depth, but there is an opening. They are coming to the funds that they usually invest in the big PE growth firms saying, "What have you got?" There is a scramble going on. Everybody now has an "impact" fund, but I do not think it is meeting the underlying need.

There is an opportunity now to do something, given a social shift in desire among the capital allocators.

FKK: We work closely with London-based Generation Investment Management. They have 25 billion under management.

MK: It was a firm started by Al Gore and David Blood.

FKK: We have worked with them since the beginning. We were their second client in terms of investing foundation assets. We have a survey in the field which we are closing up in a week. I have done every employee survey Generation has ever had done in seventeen years. We work with them on human capital issues, but they have a very rigorous view of sustainable capitalism. Although their primary focus is environmental, one of the first things I worked with them on 16 years ago is for their public equities investing. When they go to a public company, they are trying to figure out how to measure a sustainable approach. They know how to measure a sustainable approach to carbon, but now how to measure a sustainable approach to employees. I gave them a series of questions and issues that they have updated and iterated on over time. When they are doing their diligence, and they ask to speak to the Human Resources person or the chief people officer, people get really nervous. No one ever asks in diligence to speak to the chief people officer. If everyone agrees that we are in a knowledge-based economy, and people are the greatest asset of nearly every firm, the fact that nobody ever talks to the head of people in their diligence is all by itself remarkable. Generation did not release their returns for the first ten years, because they are against short-termism. When they did, they were the third-highest in terms of financial returns fund in the world of all categories. They have maintained being in the top five for their existence.

FKK: The focus on people. Lila Preston is a white woman who heads their private equity. They do growth and they do not do seed stage. They are a billion-dollar fund, and they led the Series C in Asana, where we were the seed stage. They led the Series B in Nest where we were an investor. They now ask to meet all of our companies at the seed stage and follow them. They think we are a great feeder of talent. They have asked me for help on racial equity. There is a group of impact private equity investors with about a dozen people. Lila sponsored a meeting in December where I did the opening framework on how impact investors are all billion-dollar-plus funds and ought to be thinking about racial equity.

MK: That is a new conversation.

EB: *It is a new conversation, although it should not be. In 2020, we saw that investments in women went down. Is that alarming? Is there a problem for diversity? Are we going in the wrong direction as a group or as an ecosystem? What are your predictions for where we are at the moment, what we need to do next to make sure that we continue the upward trajectory and get issues such as ethnicity to the table?*

FKK: Despite being a white woman myself, I am very critical of white women and white women in the investment space. I am the only one who spoke out critically on record[226] when All Raise formed a few years ago. There is a fundamental issue. In the US context, the majority of white women voted for Trump in 2016, and a greater number of white women voted for Trump in 2020. Until you talk about all the white women who tried to overthrow the US government at the Capitol in January 2021, we cannot have a gender lens conversation that makes sense to me, unless we have an intersectional lens. The gap-closing framework makes much more sense than a demographic framework. We should look at the impact on communities if a business succeeds. Kapor Capital implemented a founder's commitment in January of 2016. For five years, we do not write a check, unless the founders commit to hiring a diverse team and building an inclusive culture. This is not a check-the-box, and it is not a test. We want to help them. We emphasize that there is not a one-size-fits-all. We look at the demographics of the team, we help them set goals. We will help them hire, as we have a full-time talent person who helps our companies hire. The goal should be to have the employees look like the customers. If somebody does not have that goal, I would question their ability to design the best products and services. Some people think we are just about political correctness, but we see it as the best possible business strategy. We see it in our returns as well. The majority of kids in kindergarten through 12th grade education are kids of color in the United States. If you are an EdTech company, the majority of your employees ought to be kids of color, because they are going to design the most effective educational materials.

---

226. https://www.mercurynews.com/2014/12/18/
        freada-kapor-klein-diversity-isnt-just-gender-women-arent-just-white/

14.5 *Hudson, Omoigui, Groves: Black Fund Leaders*

Charles Hudson (Precursor Ventures)

Eghosa Omoigui (EchoVC Partners)

Paula Groves (Impact X Capital)

Charles Hudson,[227] Eghosa Omoigui,[228] and Paula Groves,[229] are venture capital titans. With careers spanning multiple decades, each of them has cut their teeth in traditional venture capital, both managing and amassing multiple millions for their respective funds, before venturing out to create their own. We talked to them about their experiences in the venture ecosystem, the perils of raising funds while Black (despite their qualifications, credentials, and experience), and their desires to see peers invest in the best founders—irrespective of background—alongside them.

Interviewed January 2021

CAREER JOURNEYS FOR THREE BLACK VCS

Erika Brodnock (EB): *To start with, we would love to hear about your journey to becoming a venture capital investor. Tell us about your pathway and whether there have been any roadblocks or headwinds to overcome.*

Paula Groves (PG): I began my career at Stanford University, where I received my undergraduate degree. I then moved to New York City to work for Credit Suisse First Boston on Wall Street. I loved being in New York, by the way, and afterwards went to graduate school to get my MBA at Harvard. One day, I received a call from one of my former bosses at First Boston, who said that he was starting a venture capital firm in Boston and asked if I would like to join. I said, "Sure." It was a double bottom line fund that we started back in 1992. It was probably one of the first of its kind. Social impact investing and double bottom line investing are

227. https://twitter.com/chudson

228. https://twitter.com/EghosaO

229. https://www.linkedin.com/in/paula-groves-a079023/

more mainstream today. Back then it was quite novel. The State of Connecticut pension fund wanted us to focus on both job creation as well as financial returns, and that was the mission of the fund. We then secured a second mandate from CalPERS [California Public Employees' Retirement System], and ultimately grew the fund to about $800M of assets under management. I then spun out and launched Axxon Capital, which was focused on women and minority-led businesses, in 2000. What is most interesting is that, in 2000, less than 1% of venture capital dollars went to African Americans and less than 4% went to women-led businesses. Unfortunately, that data has not changed. Even today, those numbers are still the same. The question is, what can we do to make a difference, to raise the bar with regards to getting access to capital for women- and minority-led businesses? That has been the essence of my career.

A partner and I ran Axxon Capital for a number of years. Unfortunately, the dotcom crash happened, and we shut the fund down in 2004. Then I moved out to Oakland, California, and ultimately ran a US Small Business Development Center, set up by the US Small Business Administration. Over time, a team of us secured a contract with the City of Oakland to provide capital to minority-led businesses in the most marginalized part of Oakland society. These were entrepreneurs who had been formerly incarcerated. They were entrepreneurs who had 80% of the median income in Oakland. It was really focused on trying to provide access to capital for those who do not find capital in any other places to launch their business. I did that for a number of years before I received a call from my partner, Eric Collins, who is the CEO of Impact X Capital, who said he was launching a venture capital fund in London to provide capital to underrepresented entrepreneurs. We launched Impact X in December of 2019, and I have been working in the London space since then.

Charles Hudson (CH): I grew up in Michigan and moved to California for college. Like Paula, I went to Stanford, and I studied economics and Spanish and thought I was going to go into international development work and get a PhD in economics. I decided not to do that because in the late 90s, being at Stanford, the internet was all around you. Startups and tech companies were being started on campus all around us. I did not know anything about technology or startups until I took an internship at a company called Excite, which later merged with a cable broadband company called @Home. I worked there for the summer between my senior and junior year and decided that instead of going into development work or public equities, I was going to focus more on tech because I thought it was a really interesting space. I thought that the internet was going to be this huge economic force. It was going to radically change markets, and I decided that was going to be what I focused on.

While I was at Excite, I worked for a woman whose husband, it turned out, was running the CIA's venture capital fund. When I told her about my interest in going into investing, she said, "Hey, you should really talk to my husband. He has this fledgling venture capital fund, and he could really use some help. In terms of resources, you could do some great work for him." Instead of taking a more traditional job on Wall Street or consulting, I ended up working for In-Q-Tel, the CIA's venture capital group, for three and a half years. It was a lot of fun and I invested in a ton of really interesting companies, including companies like Keyhole, which is the team behind Google Earth, Palantir, and a number of other really interesting companies, some of which are still going to this day. That exposed me to venture capital and made me interested in learning more. As a newly minted undergraduate, I did not have all the work experience or business experience I wanted to bring to the table. I went back to business school at Stanford, came out and worked for a number of startups, some on the enterprise side and some of the consumer side. In 2010, I started angel investing on my own and made a couple of investments that worked out well, and quickly realized that after about eight years away from investing, I was ready to get back into the business.

I joined a firm called SoftTech VC, which is now Uncork Capital. At the time, my business partner Jeff had raised $15M for his first institutional fund and was looking to scale up that enterprise. It is pretty crazy that back then, they had $15M under management, and just 10 years later, they have half a billion dollars under management. The firm has really grown—we went from Jeff, to me and Jeff, to now they have three or four partners over there and have completely built out staff and have raised much more funds. While I was there, I noticed that early-stage investing was changing. When I first joined Uncork, we routinely wrote small checks—a couple $100K, to $1M or less—and that got us into companies like Postmates, Eventbrite, Fitbit, and Postmark. As our fund got bigger, it was harder to write those smaller checks. We needed to write bigger checks to make the math work for our fund. The thing that went away as we increased our check size was our appetite for writing small checks to people that were out of our network, or we did not know so well. Those were mostly first-time entrepreneurs. I felt that all of the early seed funds that had been successful were going through the same process of growing up, raising larger funds, and moving away from that early first check investing. That was the work I wanted to do.

Five years ago, I left and started Precursor Ventures and we have raised three funds plus a little sidecar vehicle of about $100M under management. In total, we really focus on finding early-stage entrepreneurs that are oftentimes pre-launch and pre-traction but are also outside of our network, or not coming out of Pinterest, Square, Stripe, some really obvious company where they get the benefit of the doubt. When you have that strategy, you end up backing a lot more women and people of color because many of them as entrepreneurs fall in that bucket.

Eghosa Omoigui (EO): My path to where I am today was a non-traditional one. I went to law school in Nigeria and then worked as a lawyer at a corporate oil and gas and general corporate for two years. I then decided to go to graduate school to pick up exposure to cross-border work. I left Nigeria and went to the University of Pennsylvania, and I was able to craft a degree that was mostly corporate law and quite a bit of corporate finance. This was on the East Coast and I was not steeped in the Stanford startup world. I was lucky, as I had a professor at Wharton [the University of Pennsylvania's business school], who talked quite a bit about the startup world because his wife was on the West Coast. That exposure got me thinking. It was intriguing, but I did not think I would focus on it. When I finished studying, I had two options to go down the traditional path: work at a New York law firm or Jersey Big Four firm.

There was a small company out in California that wanted a business development corporate lawyer, and I said, "I am going to try that for a year. See if that works." It made absolutely no sense to my parents in those early days. I went there for about a year and the company ended up being acquired. At that point in time, I said, "This is super interesting. What should I do next?" I was in LA; I was still not in San Francisco or Palo Alto. I was then recruited to join a corporate law department, and they were doing a lot of very interesting transactions and securities. I said, "Let me go beef that up." I do not think I was designing a career path at that point, not as much as I was just trying to increase my surface area of exposure to different things. It turned out that just because I left the next gig, I was hired by a law firm to do more venture work. I became really interested in venture and decided that I wanted to create my own startup. This was in 1999, 2000. Weirdly, I left the firm around five days before the NASDAQ crash. I am always saying that timing is everything.

I ran the startup until around November, but it was obvious that we could not get anywhere or secure financing. At this point, Intel Capital called and said, "We would love to have you join us on the Intel Capital legal side." I said, "Great, I would be able to get a salary again." I started off with Intel in the portfolio management group, which is the group tasked with managing the post-close portfolio. From there, because of the timing, I started realizing that there were other things we could be doing. I started a patent purchase group, where we were essentially buying intellectual property from companies that were failing. I also restarted a bankruptcy and restructuring group for the startups that we managed. I was in the Bay Area at this point in time and realized that it was going to be almost impossible for me to break in, with a non-traditional background, without a strong signal of belonging to the tribe, which would be an MBA. I could not figure out for the life of me how to do an MBA—the opportunity cost was very high, as I had a family. I decided to do a fully employed, full-time MBA. I did that over a two-year period, flying back and forth between the Bay Area and Boston. It was a really hard trade, because it cost me my marriage, even though I still have my kids. I realized that I had to pay those dues to be able to break in. Fortunately, one of my bosses at Intel Capital decided to offer me a job to become Chief of Staff for Intel Treasury Global. I did not have my MBA at that time. I did not have anything. There was a lot of internal resentment that I suddenly fell into, where people were saying, "He does not have a CFA. Does he have an MBA? Why did you pick him?" It was interesting, because he had me on this interview process for three years, that I had no idea was going on. From there, I blossomed.

I hit escape velocity when I wrote a thesis for Intel, "Investing in the Next Generation Internet," and I was told, "You can do this, go and find some good companies." Over the course of a four-year period, I was able to bring in many interesting companies, but the big ones were Facebook, LinkedIn, Pandora, and AdMob. Intel did not invest in any of them, so I left in 2010 out of frustration. I made my reputation at Intel for being able to craft the pieces for doing those deals, and it turned out to all be great. I left in 2010 and my thesis was that investing in underserved economies and emerging markets was going to be the next big thing. Africa and

Southeast Asia were going to be highly correlated and will be interesting, but no one believed it. I formed EchoVC and went to Africa first in 2014. In 2016, we formed a strategic partnership with TPG Growth. We have been running for six years and it has turned out to be incredibly successful.

THE BARRIERS HOLDING BACK BLACK VENTURE FUNDS

Johannes Lenhard (JL): *Charles, you began this whole journey at Stanford, and have scaled to all kinds of heights, but how do these early networks play into the ecosystem as it stands, and the reproduction of the status quo? How did you raise your first fund and your own capital? Did you find that the connections that you made at school or in the early years in software help with that? If you had not gone to Stanford or Oxbridge or the Ivy League, how could you do the same thing? How important is networking? How do you get that network together?*

CH: Network work is really important. Richard Kerby's last survey said around 40% of all VCs went to Harvard and or Stanford,[230] and my guess is 30% went to both. For a long time in venture, there was more of a focus on insularity as a benefit. It meant everybody knew everybody. That was considered a good thing, not a bad thing. It was high trust and comfort. People did not think as much about, who are we keeping out by having these barriers?

When I left Uncork, I thought I would have a reasonably straightforward time raising my first fund. I had been a partner at the firm for five years and I had done some good deals. I knew our LPs. It was the opposite of what I thought it would be. I thought it would take a year or a year and a half to raise. It was not at all what happened. Most of our existing LPs from my old fund were just not first fund LPs. They are the folks who want to see some track record and see some cards get turned over.

The main reason I was able to raise the fund is because I was already part of the network of other VCs. I had other people from other firms who connected me with their limited partners and investors who helped me refine my pitch. They did it because they knew me, I do not think they did because they just generally want to help the world. They helped me because they knew me. When I think about the barriers that keep other Black venture funds from getting started, network is the big one. Without connections to other VCs or limited partners, it is very hard to raise the

---

230. https://medium.com/@kerby/where-did-you-go-to-school-bde54d846188

funds. The other thing I have been fortunate in is that some of my angel investments had worked. I had enough of my own capital to be able to float myself for the two years it took to get our first fund closed, and then to continue to absorb the well-below-market pay that you make as a new fund manager on your first fund.

I tell people it takes about a million bucks to start your own fund, and that those are hard dollars that you will need to part with. If you just look at the wealth creation statistics by race, there are not a lot of Black people that are going to clear that bar. There are just so many structural barriers that get in the way for people starting new funds. People are beginning to recognize that when I got into venture, it was okay to just say I can only go to invest in people I know. That was an accepted wisdom and best practice, and investing in people outside of your network was considered borderline negligent. That is changing, but it is changing slowly. It is changing probably faster for VCs than it is for LPs.

The other thing people said is, "I want to invest in companies that are close enough that I can ride my bicycle to go visit them." If you think about that, where does venture capital happen? For the most part, it happens in Silicon Valley, one of the most expensive and least racially diverse—in terms of Black people—places in the United States, and New York City, which is more diverse, but also expensive. For a long time, I would say venture capital was geographically isolated from communities of color. I would also say the barriers of getting into the business were financial and just did not allow for much entry.

The third thing is the easiest way to become an independent venture capitalist is to be a venture capitalist at someone else's firm first. If you look at the statistics of our industry, putting aside partners, there are not that many analyst and associate principal Black investors. All of the places, the mechanics for the pipeline, front doors, all the things that work, none of them really include us right now.

EB: *There are not many Black investors that have the credentials and qualifications that you have. If you find it hard, it makes me wonder what hope there is for the people who have not had that educational background or have not had the doors opened by Index, and the various funds that you each worked at before you started out on your own.*

LEVELING THE PLAYING FIELD FOR DIVERSE ENTREPRENEURS

EB: *Paula, you have previously given me an example of when a state-led intervention positively impacted access to diverse entrepreneurs, and particularly those of Black and mixed heritage. Could you tell us a little bit about the Equal Opportunity loan program and what you think that might look like today, if it was going to be recreated to level some of the playing field?*

PG: This goes back to the civil unrest that occurred in the 1960s, just as the civil rights movement was starting in the United States. One of the insights that the federal government had was that the key to solving the problem of civil unrest was providing economic opportunity. They decided to establish what would ultimately become the US Small Business Administration, where they provided loans to underserved communities and underrepresented entrepreneurs. Access to capital creates opportunity, and with opportunity, there is hope. With opportunity, access to capital, and hope, you can spur entrepreneurship, which allows people to provide for themselves and their own communities.

There was a study that I did working with the City of San Francisco back in mid-2015. I wanted to understand why the percentages of African Americans living in San Francisco had declined. It had become fairly expensive to live in San Francisco, and people had to move out to the suburbs to find their own economic opportunity. Most interesting was that there was a high correlation between the repeal of Proposition 209 and the decline in African American population in the city. Proposition 209 said that San Francisco was no longer allowed to consider race when allocating government contracts to businesses. Historically, a lot of government contracts had been allocated to underrepresented entrepreneurs, and when the city was no longer allowed to consider race as a factor in allocating contracts to diversify their supplier base, those contracts went away. Many of these contracts had been awarded to entrepreneurs who had in turn become pillars of their community. They had contracts with the airports, for example. These successful entrepreneurs were then able to employ people that look like them, which is an important factor when you consider diversity and entrepreneurship. Diverse entrepreneurs tend to employ diverse employees. When these contracts went away, these companies declined and were no longer pillars of their community, which had led to the barbershops, restaurants, and the thriving economic environment. Those companies went away, and those communities ultimately went away. There was a high correlation and evidence in the US that says that when you focus on diversity and entrepreneurship, backed by the federal government, that can indeed lead to diverse communities and higher economic growth within those communities.

EB: *If we were to recreate that today, how would you feel about overlooked founders being provided with interest-bearing loans, when compared to their counterparts who are being provided with equity financing that is non-interest-bearing and they do not need to pay back straightaway?*

PG: Access to capital is access to capital. If we provide interest-bearing loans as a means of helping companies get started, that type of access to capital can be a lever that can be very effective. That is one of the other tenants of the US Small Business Administration in the United States. I used to run one of the business practices for the US Small Business Administration in Oakland, California, where we served over 4,000 entrepreneurs. One of the tools that the US Small Business Administration uses is low-interest loans, specifically for young entrepreneurs and startup entrepreneurs. It is a tool that has been used very effectively in the US. Now, loans versus equity, that is an important consideration, in that equity tends to be risk capital, and we absolutely need risk capital to help underserved communities and underrepresented entrepreneurs. If the choice is low-interest loans versus nothing, then I would take the low-interest loans, but we need both. You need loans as well as risk capital to get the economic engine going and empower our communities, but low interest is better than nothing.

CHANGE HAS TO GO FURTHER THAN FIRST-TIME FUNDS

JL: *You often hear that 90% of funds are invested in white, all-male teams, and that is true across the board in the European landscape. Eghosa, what steps have you particularly taken at EchoVC to change this? What are you already seeing and having early success with, in your strategy?*

EO: There are so many things that get conflated when we talk about the statistics. When we speak to LPs and other participants in the ecosystem, there seems to be confusion as to what to do and how to do it. There is activity now, where more diverse first-time fund managers are emerging. These are very small teams to begin with. A lot of folks say, "Okay, let us invest in these new managers." Venture is a statistics marketplace, in the sense that nearly 99% of these companies will need further, larger financing. As a new seed manager, if you do not have a network that allows you to push the companies you invest in at the pre-seed stage, downstream to later stage investors, you then do not get the track record that LPs like to use to measure success. Investors are much more interested in things such as, who could invest with me in this deal? Who invested later? The key is, they want to see brands that they like. An LP who does a little bit more work may dig into the portfolio companies themselves and say, "That is an interesting company, let us invest in it." A lot of them do not do that work and they are looking for very high-level superficial signals. It is all pattern matching, all along the way. The VCs pattern match the founders they bet on. The LPs pattern match the funds they bet on. You see this all the time. If you decide to be non-consensus, you might be out in the cold for a long time, until you have enough of a track record.

I have a friend who started seven years ago. He is not white, and it has been interesting to talk to him about his fundraising dilemma, and how six unicorns into the portfolio, LPs are still telling him that maybe he is just lucky! This kind of feedback is all too common. How do you change this? It is something that I try to figure out, because as a Black fund manager, you carry a lot more weight on your shoulders. In many cases it is invisible, but everyone is looking to you to be solely investing in diverse founders—Black, Brown, women. The truth is, you actually want to be able to have some flexibility in the types of companies you invest in, because of specific interests. If you have an interest or expertise, and you see a company that could really drive impact, how do you balance that out? Are you better off trying to improve that company's management team from the inside by becoming an investor and bringing diverse talent to the attention of the founder? That is one way to do it. The other way to do it is to figure out how to encourage these founders that are sitting inside other companies that do not have the confidence to come out, because they do not think there is anybody out there who will fund them. Being unapologetically diverse in the approach to investing takes a long track record. You have to not care. You just have to do what you want to do. You have to have enough of a return, or the kind of track record where people say, "I get why he or she does that, and they have shown an ability to do it consistently." There are interesting interplays here and being able to have more managers in the ecosystem, more emerging managers, that is great, but we need more managers at every tier. We need more managers at seed, at A, and at B. Here is the funny thing, as you start going downstream: it is a smaller and smaller group of GPs that know how to do those deals. I like to ask people: how many Black GPs can do Series B or Series C? It is probably less than 50. It might be less than 30 in the total of the entire US.

JL: *The NVCA [National Venture Capital Association] put out a report[231] with Deloitte, called the VC Human Capital Survey, and the first version that they put out in 2019 had zero Black VCs in it. They went away, found some, and put them in there. The second version looks a bit more polished now and has a percent or so. That is how bad the numbers are. You are absolutely right, if you are going downstream, it becomes even thinner.*

EO: The answer has been there. When people say, "what should we do?" There are interesting things. One is, for some of the bigger firms that will do the later stages, how do we impanel diverse investors in those funds? The weird thing about those funds is that the few folks who are in these funds, that I mentor, keep running into the same problem, which is: what is the quota of diverse founders you can bring in before people start to wonder whether that is all you came into the fund to do? You run into this, "I do not want to get pigeonholed, because that means that I do not get advanced. I want to bring the deals that I think I can sell to the IC [investment committee]." You then find that they do fewer and fewer of these diverse founder deals because the fund does not invest in them. There was a fund; their actual coverage in their entire portfolio for Black founders is less than 1%, but they are one of the most active on LinkedIn and Twitter about BLM matters. You would not believe that they are less than 1%, if you correlated it to how much noise they make.

For us, it is getting the LPs to say, "How do we get more of these investors to 'invest' rather than talking about investing in diverse founders?" The truth is, as Paula says, until you invest in people who look like them, you are never really going to see any traction. We have about 30–40% women in my firm, and we have had interesting pieces of feedback from women founders who say, "The most interesting thing interacting with your firm was seeing women on the other side of the table." These are soft elements that do not show up in slides, data, or graphs, but matter in terms of how accessible you are and how amenable you are to listen to experiences, and not punish them because they do not match patterns. That is a real issue.

Until LPs essentially make it a mandatory KPI that funds invest in diversity, things will not change. LPs need to build a process or a pipeline where they are looking at the deals and the funds they are investing in. The money needs to start to talk. That is going to be important. A lot of LPs in some of the very best funds are afraid to say anything, because they do not want to get kicked out. The truth is, there will always be big wins that these funds miss. If diverse fund managers are able to pick up the wins, incumbent funds completely missed or discounted, then they begin to trust diverse judgments. In the end, that is what venture is about: trust in judgment, whether it is on the investor side or on the founder side.

Stanford released a study[232] about how difficult it was for diverse fund managers who were on their second and third funds to raise money, and it is absolutely correct. Even when LPs tell you, "Come back in fund two, with your track record." You go back with fund two and the track record, and then they will have you come back for fund three. The goal posts just keep moving. In reality, they are much more willing to invest in first-time managers because losses can be subsumed under a "special program." However, once you look for fund two, fund three, then it means that you are now saying, "I really actually want to do something here and I am going to match the record." It is not some unique giveaway program.

Charles is probably one of the most experienced VCs. He deserves to manage a bigger fund. LPs are giving money to mediocre managers, and I do not understand it. Charles has paid his dues over and over and over again and is an outstanding investor, and he is still struggling to get support. The system is broken. We keep pushing, and we keep talking, but it won't change until there is some externality that makes one or two or three LPs say, "I am going to deploy money fairly. I am going to give it to folks who are willing and able to invest in diverse founders without apology." The unapologetic investor.

WILL INVESTING IN BLACK VCS DIVERSIFY THE FUNDING PIPELINE?

EB: *I 100% believe that, if you are the only person in a room of your hue or of your gender, survival instinct kicks in and will force us to try to conform, so that we fit in and do not lose the food out of our own mouths in order to put*

---

232. https://sparq.stanford.edu/racial-disparities-investing-are-more-pipeline-problem

it into someone else's. That is a well-known phenomenon. Does LPs investing in Black GPs en masse and investing it in Black funds actually work? Is the pipeline broken in various different places? Or is it just that if LPs gave more Black GPs money, then the Black GPs would then give it out to more diverse entrepreneurs? What is the broad thesis of your funds and how does this set you apart from other funds in the market?

PG: Yes, absolutely. The more money you give to Black GPs, the more Black entrepreneurs that would be funded. If you look at the Silicon Valley model, GPs tend to invest in people that they know and people that they are comfortable with, rowed crew with, or have attended their son's wedding with. Getting to know you is one way in which people gain comfort. Venture capital investing is a high-risk business. At the end of the day, despite all the spreadsheets, reference calls, and Google research that you can do, you must still come to that final gut decision to make an investment in an entrepreneur. If you know them and if they are known to you, then making that gut decision adds a level of comfort and makes the decision a bit easier. If you are not in those networks, then it is hard to be known and hard to get through that subjective evaluation process. If you are Black, you tend to have Black networks. I am stating the obvious. It is easier for you to do the reference checking, because if you do not know the entrepreneur directly, you certainly know someone who does know them. If your venture capital investing model is based upon investing in people that you know, then if you are Black, you have the Black network, and therefore, you have access to the Black entrepreneurs who you can gain comfort with to make the investment decision. That makes the subjective decision easier. Intuitively, it just makes sense that if you give more money to Black general partners, then more Black entrepreneurs will have access to capital.

DIVERSE FUNDING SHOULDN'T FALL ON BLACK VCS

CH: The expectation right now is that Black VCs are going to fix the Black founder funding problem, and it does not look like that is actually going to work because Black VCs are not large, and they are not given nearly enough capital relative to the opportunity. I want to pick up on two things that Eghosa said that are really important to understand. There are not that many Black VCs at the later stage, which means all of the activity ends up happening at the early stage, such as with what I am doing. The problem with that is, it takes five to seven years for an early-stage fund, generally speaking, to start to bear fruit, which means you probably have to be good enough at the job to get two and maybe even a third fund done on very limited realized performance. There are a lot of LPs who will back you on that first fund as Eghosa said, "Oh, we have a mandate, an allocation, a thing to do." When it comes to that second and third fund, you are swimming in a different pool. My fear is that there are a lot of first-time funds being created that are subscale, that by the time those people go back to raise that second fund, that the people who were enthusiastic about that first fund will have moved on to something else, because they are not really long-term backers in venture. Those funds will not have enough realized performance to make it a no-brainer for new money, and they might just die on the vine.

It is also worth saying that not every Black VC wants to invest in Black people. I do not think they should have to, honestly. There are some Black-led funds that have almost no Black founders in their portfolio, and it is because eventually the market needs to mature to this place where all Black VCs can be diverse within the Black VC tier, and you will have some people that are impact oriented and very focused on funding Black founders, because the strategy they have either yields a lot of those or explicitly focuses on those. You will have Black-led venture funds whose portfolios look, maybe embarrassingly, not diverse. We need to separate having Black venture capitalists and leadership positions at firms from the responsibility of Black VCs to fund black founders, because we cannot give the rest of the venture industry a pass and say, "The funding of Black founders, that is the Black VCs' problem. We can outsource that to them, they are responsible for it." That is a cop-out approach. I just bring it up, because I do think when you walk in the room as a Black fund manager, people's default assumption is you are running a diversity impact fund, no matter what is in the deck. I know this to be the case, because it happens to me all the time. The irony is we do not have an explicit focus on diversity, we have a focus on finding people that are out of network that the market does not know how to underwrite, because in a world of a thousand early-stage venture funds, the only way you can make money is either be first round capital, top skim the best repeat founders, or you have to have confidence in your judgment that you can pick people that other people either do not see or do not value, and to be right. Anything else, it is a hard way to make money in this business. We are at the first inning of this conversation around Black venture capital. Right now, it is a bit of a strait-jacket. The LP expectation is that if you are a Black fund manager, you are going to invest disproportionately in Black entrepreneurs, and not everybody that I know has that as an important and core piece of their strategy. Even if just by their lived experience, they are going to end up doing better than our industry, which basically is 0%.

FOR US, BY US—BUILDING THE MISSING ECOSYSTEM

EB: *The follow on is that people who do invest in Black founders end up putting those founders back out into a "toxic" market, and some will fail simply because they cannot secure the next round of funding they need to be able to survive, rather than because the VCs made the wrong decision in the first place. What can be done about that? Further, what needs to be done to keep the momentum?*

CH: We do not have a vertical Black venture capital ecosystem where I can do the pre-seed, and then I can hand it to Richard Kerby at Equal Ventures, and then he can hand it to someone else. I would argue that on the gender lens, you could probably go full-stack female, female GP, from VC to IPO. That ecosystem is developed enough that it can be totally self-served. Black venture capital is not there yet, which means at some point, these companies are going to have to either get profitable or grow like a Calendly. Or they are going to have to be able to bridge back into mainstream venture capital firms, and that happens with relationships. Yes, company performance matters, but right now everybody is drowning in deals and drowning in things to look at. A lot of people are saying, "I am going to pay attention to stuff that Paula and Egohsa send me, because I know them. The person I do not know who sends me something could be a great company, but I do not have time for it." Without those bridges back, particularly at the Series A or B, which are really the choke points in the system ... And, of course, the question is where do those relationships come from? The circles and relationships come from being in the business and getting to know people. If you cannot get in the business and get to know people, you cannot build those relationships.

My hope is that this new generation of Black managers that we are launching into business, that they are able to build those relationships with people fast enough to help their portfolio companies when they need them. Otherwise, I do think it will be difficult. Unless you have outstanding, out-of-this-world performance, then you can probably still get financed even with the weak network. That is not most companies, most companies do need help. They need help from their investors to grease the skids with these other conversations. You also need an investor who knows what a Series-A-ready company looks like. You only know that by getting Series As done and working with good investors. Everything in this business is this really unfair, brutal information feedback loop, and the real question is, will this new generation of Black investors who are finally getting the opportunity to show that they are good, will they get enough time to run that loop, before investors make a decision about their next fund?

PG: We as Black investors have a real opportunity here to create the ecosystem that Charles has identified as missing. If we can develop it ourselves, build it ourselves, and prove the model, that would go a long way towards validating the marketplace. I resist the notion that the only way for Black entrepreneurs to make it to the IPO is a model that is reliant upon mainstream VCs. I want to do the "For Us, By Us," the FUBU approach, and work really hard to get there on our own, and to get the exits and generate money for LPs. If our model is reliant upon Silicon Valley for success—Charles is absolutely right—we are never going to get there. I look for the opportunity to do the "For Us, By Us" approach and do it full stack. If we do not know how to do it yet, we are smart enough to figure it out. That is my belief. If we do the full stack from launch to IPO, and do the hard work—so that we are not dependent upon Silicon Valley—that could go a long way towards providing access to capital and attracting more capital to the space of underrepresented entrepreneurs.

14.6 *Bendz: Atomico's Angels*

Sophia Bendz (Cherry Ventures, formerly Atomico)

Sophia Bendz[233] already became famous as the chief marketing officer at Spotify and one of tech's first female big-name executives; she started using her power at the latest since joining Atomico as a partner in 2018. It was at Atomico where she rolled out the Angel Programme,[234] which is the focus of the conversation here and also something she is looking at repeating at her new fund, Cherry Ventures, where she joined as GP in 2020.

Interviewed November 2020

FROM SPOTIFY C-SUITE TO ATOMICO'S ANGELS

Erika Brodnock (EB): *Sophia, please tell us a bit about your background.*

SB: I'm a storyteller and marketer at heart and by trade, and was lucky enough to join Spotify early on. We were just eight people in a tiny flat in Stockholm and I learned a lot. That was my segway into the startup world. I spent seven years as the global marketing director. There was lots of blood, sweat, and tears—it's hard to start a company and grow it from zero users to 100 million users. I helped launch the service in 56 markets. During my last five years with the company, I lived in New York City. When my firstborn arrived I decided to move back to Sweden and started angel investing, bumped into Niklas Zennström, joined Atomico, was promoted to partner looking after the Nordic Region, and was fortunate enough to also head up their angel program and be part of their Diversity and Inclusion Task Force. That is one of the best things about big funds: they have resources.

I ended up coming back to the early-stage investment landscape because I am an operator and not a traditional banker per se. That is why

---

233. https://twitter.com/sophiabendz
234. https://atomico.com/insights/introducing-the-atomico-angel-programme

I joined Cherry Ventures. I have been with them since September 2020, based in Stockholm. I am still interested and very much involved in the angel landscape, as well as being an advisor to Atomico.

EB: *How did you come up with the idea for the original Atomico Angels program, and what were your motivations?*

SB: It stemmed from frustration in me. When I met Niklas Zennström, I was proud to show him my track record and that was my ticket into the VC world. I was on the ground in Sweden, good at sourcing deals. I said to him, I think Atomico needs to be closer to the angel community. From a personal perspective, I was frustrated because there were so few women on company cap tables. Normally when you do a deal, you share it with other investors who could be interested in it and that could potentially help from a strategic point of view. So, as an angel, I grew my network and actually expanded my contacts. However, many of them were men and I wanted to see more women on cap tables. I wanted more people like me and my friends to be able to invest. The closed ecosystem presented a huge frustration for me. It was almost like a little boys' club that invested together, and while I was invited in, I felt like the only woman in the club. I wanted to open the doors, and I wanted to talk about it, because it's not rocket science. And if you have money to spare that you can live without, I think it's an interesting investment class. I wanted to demystify it, I wanted to tell the world this is one way of spending your time and money. I think it could lead to more people that were exposed to potentially considering a career as a VC. That was my long-term goal. But if we open up an angel program for more people, my dream was that some of them would continue to invest, as we move along and after that year is done.

SUCCESS THROUGH OPENING UP DEAL FLOW

JL: *Can you go a little deeper on how you designed the program? What principles were in mind? And what do you think now, having done two batches, what is most crucial for the success?*

SB: My colleague Will Dufton is an absolute star and is equally passionate about this area. He and I created the Atomico angels' program together. The aim is that angels connect, share experiences, and do deals together. Niklas thought it was a great idea and asked us to come up with a proposal. Will and I created the proposal together. Our main aim was to avoid repeating what the Silicon Valley VCs were doing, because it seemed to me, and maybe some say different, but in my view, they were reinforcing a closed boys' club atmosphere. They were not transparent about where money is coming from, and for me, it is all about trust. If you cannot be honest with where the money is coming from, that really isn't a great way to build a relationship. Transparency is key.

Moreover, they were backing founders within the exact same circles they were in and giving money to many who had already achieved a liquidity event, most of the time. A great number of deals happen at barbecue parties in the local neighborhood, many of the founders and investors live on the same street and are already friends. I think that is just a way of putting more money into an already closed system. I wanted to create and put money into a new system, or a new group of people, or new individuals. I wanted a rotating program so that we would not ever stagnate or become an elite club. I wanted it to be open. We wanted to reach and engage people and talents that we normally would not have met—people we suspected had access to good talent and lots of entrepreneurs, what we refer to as "good deal flow." So many of these people are company builders, sector experts, or community builders. The common theme among them is passion for what they're doing. Normally they're helpful and good at connecting with people, they have an excellent network. So, we decided to create a rolling schedule with a new class each year. We also wanted to provide training so our angels felt supported. Finally, we wanted to create network and mentoring opportunities that paired new angels with an alumnus and encouraged them to do deals together.

EB: *On the second program, was there a wide array of people from all sorts of cultures and backgrounds as well as gender?*

SB: This was super important for me, because I realized that's essentially untapped business. If we, as investors, normally invest 98% of the capital into the same type of profile, we understand that there are so many other interesting businesses out there that we are not getting access to. We wanted to get access to pockets of talent that we normally wouldn't meet. Normally we go and source deals at conferences, and incubators and accelerators, and many times, you see the same type of CEO or founder profile. We wanted to broaden that perspective and put a bigger network in play that could help us access a more diverse and interesting set of talent.

MEASURING SUCCESS AND CHERRY'S NEXT STEPS

EB: *How would you judge its success so far? Did it fall short? Did it meet your expectations? What do you think the reasons are for either the success or not? And what's next with Cherry?*

SB: I would definitely call it a success. One proof point is that it still lives on, even though I left Atomico. And now we're preparing for next year's batch. It's hard to determine if a company is going to be a big success, because it takes time and you start investing early on. The biggest milestone is seeing if they get good follow-on investments from top-tier seed or Series A investors. So far, the stats we've seen have been really good. That's why I would say it has been a success. Also, from my personal view, it has been successful in getting new people to find VC interesting. Seeing that someone like Roxanne Varza,[S15.1] for instance, is now a scout for Sequoia. I got a message from one of this year's angels and she wanted to share some news ... I'm expecting that it's an offer that she wants to brief me about. So that also feels like it has sparked something in more people. I really take great joy in seeing that.

I have not defined what we're going to do at Cherry yet. It's something that I'm working on now. The relationships that I have gathered from the angel program are incredible, they helped me with sourcing across core geographies in Europe. I think that it makes more sense to run an angels program when you are a seed fund, because then you can invest in the follow-on round. The deal flow that I have from angels was harder for me to harness when I was at Atomico, because they needed to grow through a pre-seed, seed, and then Series A. The investments of the angels can quickly turn into pre-seed or seed, and that makes perfect sense for Cherry to do.

WHAT FUNDS CAN DO TO IMPROVE THEIR DEAL FLOW AND D&I

JL: *Would you say other funds can put similar things in place? Where would that be most needed? With what focus? Let's talk angel first, and finally, what other initiatives do we actually need?*

SB: When it comes to angel initiatives, it's an easy way to engage in the community. If I was starting my own VC fund today, I would definitely do it. You want to have good relationships, so that your companies can get funding from the best follow-on investors in the next round. On the other hand, you also want to have good relationships with the people investing earlier than you, because you want to get the best deal flow. It's very much a system where everyone is interlinked and exchanging information and deal flow. I think finding a way to connect with angels is crucial. Rounds are getting much more competitive. The earlier you build a relationship, the better chance you have at investing in the very best companies.

EB: *Knowing what you know now, how would you go about creating a new D&I initiative? What would be the steps to setting it up? Is there anything specifically around how much you give the angels?*

SB: I think it depends on what type of fund you're working at and the size of the fund. If I think specifically about diversity and inclusion initiatives, I would go about it the same way, but maybe be more confident this time around. Setting up the D&I Task Force internally, have the right stakeholders at the table. It is not a women's issue that should be run by women, it should be coming from the top—everyone needs to walk the talk. It needs to be something that is interlinked with the company's overall objectives. It helps a lot that here in the Nordic countries, we have a lot of LPs who are very good at driving the diversity question. This forces most VCs to have a strategy for it. Once you have that group set up internally, it's good to have bi-weekly meetings. Listen to others who have already done it well, to learn. List the activities that could be done, then decide what can realistically be done from that list. There are a few essential areas: you need to ensure a pipeline of diverse founders, and set targets for how many female founders or how many diverse founders should be in your pipeline.

Then you can also begin to support your existing portfolios with their diversity work. That is the role that VCs can play if they take responsibility. If we back an all-male team, for instance, I think it's my job to ensure they think about how to fix that and implement a diversity plan before growing the team. I know one VC firm here in Sweden called Kinnevik, they have linked diversity to financial targets, stipulating that there will be no follow-on investments unless diversity goals are achieved. It is the best example of putting money where your mouth is. At Cherry, we have specified in the term sheet that our investees must have a diversity plan in place. This is proving to be a strong way of ensuring diversity is on the agenda, talked about, and prioritized.

Funds can impact diversity in three key ways:

1. **Portfolio companies:** How you influence and support them.
2. **Pipeline:** See all good deals rather than hiding behind the fact there were too many companies to look at. Then,
3. **Internal team setup:** Female investment partners lead to more female founders. The same can be applied to other forms of diversity too.

Tech plays such an important part in how we build society moving forward. If we only allow one portion of society to build that tech, then it's going to be a really weird world that we build. I feel like we need to back men and women equally when thinking about the future, and we are not today. So, shame on us. We need to do better.

15 Conversations: Rethinking the Ecosystem

15.1 *Varza: Station F*

Roxanne Varza (Station F, Sequoia Capital)

Roxanne Varza[235] is the director of Station F,[236] the world's largest startup campus, which gathers more than 30 incubators in one campus in Paris. Based in the 13th arrondissement of the city, it opened its doors in 2017. One of her core goals with Station F is to make the startup world a more inclusive space. We talked to her about Station F's Fighters Program for underprivileged founders and were lucky enough to include two of the Fighters—Dinal Kurukulasooriya (founder of Autochatic) and Brian Thielly (founder of LinesDude)—in the conversation.

Interviewed November 2020

THE ORIGINS OF STATION F

Johannes Lenhard (JL): *We really want to talk about how you make space for underprivileged founders at Station F with the Fighters Program. What is this program? Why did you start it? What are the features of it?*

Roxanne Varza (RV): The Fighters Program is our program for underprivileged entrepreneurs. At Station F, to be completely inclusive, we do not specify what it means to be underprivileged. Our assumption is that we cannot even begin to imagine all of the different situations that people may have found themselves in. We provide some examples for guidance, but we are open to people from all contexts and walks of life.

Fighters could be refugees, or anyone who has lived through a difficult situation. Examples of people who have previously gone through the pro-

---

235. https://twitter.com/roxannevarza
236. https://stationf.co/

gram include a former prisoner and somebody who has been homeless. We have also worked with entrepreneurs without formal higher education who are from particularly difficult regions and ecosystems where they couldn't implement their project locally for political or other reasons. We are open to everyone who has faced adversity.

Once someone has been taken onto the Fighters Program, we provide them access to the formal Station F program free of charge for one year. This means they are integrated into our Founders Program—our main program that welcomes 200+ early-stage companies—and ensures that the bar and expectations for our Fighters is the same as for other entrepreneurs, but we support Fighters with additional resources and an extended time frame to reach their entrepreneurial goals if they need it. That is essentially the mindset behind the program.

You asked, why are we doing this? The answer is simple, diversity is incredibly important to Station F for a number of reasons. What is interesting about the Fighters Program is that it was actually one of the core reasons that our founder, Xavier Niel, wanted to create Station F. Besides filling a big building with entrepreneurs and creating an ecosystem, he also really wanted to prove that anyone can be an entrepreneur. This is a very important message, especially in France, where there is an elitist entrepreneurial mindset, built upon an elitist educational system. Often, even in the Station F ecosystem, we see that there are subsets of people who are on a path to succeed: those with a specific educational background or who are from a higher socioeconomic background. Our founder really wanted to prove that this is not the only background with which entrepreneurs can be successful. Hopefully, we're contributing positively to that narrative with the Fighters Program.

HOW THE FIGHTERS PROGRAM SUPPORTS FOUNDERS

JL: *Can you share a little bit about what the Fighters Program entails? How many people do you take? What do Fighters receive in terms of benefits? Is there an education element to the program? Is there a stipend? I can imagine moving to Paris in normal circumstances is expensive. Where do Fighters live?*

RV: Firstly, I must put this into context and comparison with the other programs on the Station F campus, which are very hands off. Entrepreneurs are usually provided with workshops and access to support and it is largely up to them to make use of the provisions, or not. A lot of the startups on campus—because they are part of a dedicated partner program with a dedicated team—won't necessarily have contact with the Station F team, unless in a specific context of specific groups, events, or meetings. For the Fighters, we have a very different approach; we started small, because we thought we really needed to get to know each of the Fighters, see them regularly, work with them very closely. It's a much more hands-on approach. Our first batch was three years ago, and we are, for the first time, increasing the number of startups we take this year from 15 to 30.

The real challenge is often just getting them up to speed on the basics, things like how to incorporate a company and how to find and file all the paperwork. They have all heard the jargon, "I need to fundraise." And we're like, no, we need to build a product and to get a team first. We have to walk them through the steps. To do this effectively, we see them on a monthly basis. We also organize additional workshops for Fighters that we wouldn't necessarily host for the rest of the campus, because lots of our entrepreneurs come to us with an entity already created, an existing team and a product. The Fighters tend to be one step earlier. And then to your question about stipend, we're looking at reinforcing some of the financial elements in the next edition of the program. The Fighters Program is free for all entrepreneurs for one year. Meaning there is no cost to be at Station F and participate. Then there is the housing we offer. Our housing is very low cost at €400 per month per room. We don't provide any additional discount for Fighters at this stage, because we would lose money. But we are looking at how we can provide a stipend in the future.

Erika Brodnock (EB): *I am intrigued. How does someone who has previously been imprisoned or homeless afford to do the program? Do you allow mixed teams—can there be just one Fighter in a team if it's a team of two, or do both team members have to be Fighters?*

RV: Yes, we do have mixed teams. I think what we are looking for is a mixed team that is somewhat balanced. We don't want somebody who has a big-name MBA and has built their business and then they find a Fighter to add to their team as an easy way to get a free year at Station F.

However, we don't usually see that. What we do see is Fighters doing the searching. One of our Fighters had to search long and hard to find a CTO for his business. It has been very challenging for him, but he's done an excellent job.

We have only ever had one team that couldn't stay in the program for financial reasons. This was before we had housing available, and they really struggled to pay rent in Paris and to find a place that they could live in. As a result of this, when we launched our housing units, we did so ensuring that a lot of the criteria needed for an apartment in Paris don't apply to our housing. Rent is affordable and entrepreneurs do not need a guarantor. As a result, a lot of our Fighters live in our housing units. Other than that, the program doesn't require full-time attendance on campus. Entrepreneurs can therefore do consulting, and other things to make ends meet outside of launching their business. We also have people who have saved some money or who are scraping by while bootstrapping, crowd-funding, and finding different ways to make it work financially. Because the program is free, they are not actually paying to be at Station F, so all the money generated goes back into their businesses.

HOW STATION F BUILDS A COHORT

EB: *How do you find the right people to support? How do you encourage them to apply? And how do you look beyond your existing network that may indeed be privileged, in some respects, to find the right people for the program?*

RV: There are two things. One is we have actually changed the application criteria for Fighters who are applying. For all of the other Station F programs on campus, we use a lot of startup lingo, we require that you apply in English, we say you need to show us a working MVP, and that you need to have traction. These are things that I think people who are less familiar with the startup ecosystem would not be able to provide. So, for the Fighters Program, we opened up the criteria by saying applicants just need to show us that they have an idea and have done something with it. Some entrepreneurs applied with a Facebook page and a multitude of subscribers, while others had launched a series of YouTube videos they were struggling to monetize. We take the fact our Fighters had an idea but didn't just sit there with it as a proxy for having the hustle they need to succeed. The second element is that it is the only program on campus that can be applied for in French. Both English and French applications are accepted to enable Fighters to apply in the language that is most comfortable to them.

In terms of how we find Fighters, that is a really good question. In France we have a very solid network of partners that help us. We work with a number of different networks and organizations doing outreach in primarily suburban and rural areas in France. On a global level, I think we could do more to generate greater visibility for the program. We don't have any global partners, so all of the incoming applications have been organic. We have noticed that global applicants have a very similar profile to the Fighters we get in France: we have received applications from people who have been persecuted for political reasons and people from very difficult educational backgrounds.

TRANSLATING LIFE EXPERIENCE TO ENTREPRENEURIAL SUCCESS

JL: *Perhaps one more question before we move to questions for the Fighters: from your perspective, what is the biggest success story you have seen from the Fighter Program so far?*

RV: It takes longer for the Fighters to mature their companies for two reasons. One is they're coming to us at a much earlier stage, a lot of them are coming pre-product, pre-team, pre-everything, and in a lot of our other programs, they already have some kind of metrics and traction and revenue when they come. The second reason is simply because Fighters face a lot more barriers and challenges. The biggest success we've seen so far is Tally. He is a former prisoner and the founder of DigiTall Paris. His story is incredible. He was initially arrested for car theft and went on to create an anti-theft device for cars.

He brought this prototype. And there were so many wires. And I was like, "Tally, what are you showing me?" But he knows exactly what he is doing, and it is fantastic. Yet, he had a very difficult time finding cofounders, he had a very difficult time getting funding, because obviously all the investors didn't want to fund him given the fact that he had a prison sentence that was pending. Despite all this, he didn't give up. He was just like, "I'm going to build this and we're going to see what happens." But now that's all behind him, he actually managed to sign a partnership with Sigfox, which is a French unicorn company. They are helping him with the industrialization of his prototypes. They are co-building them together. He has also managed to secure a couple of investors. He also managed to finally secure a CTO after two years.

TWO FIGHTERS TELL THEIR STORIES

JL: *Let's also hear from two of your current Fighters—welcome Dinal and Brian. You are both Fighters from Season 2, so are still at Station F as we speak. How has the program helped you so far?*

Dinal Kurukulasooriya (DK): As a foreigner coming from a low-income country, Sri Lanka, it gave me time to settle in since I had no office space cost. I have made a few friends at Station F, too. But a big part of the benefits are financial: I was able to get perks for cloud space and for technologies such as Stripe, which we wouldn't have had access to in Sri Lanka. What Station F also really helped us with is to see the market we are in with Autochatic from a European or Western perspective; the viewpoint helped us to understand aspects such as pricing, product development, value propositions, and especially sales, better.

Brian Thielly: For me, the Fighters Program helped me so much with visibility for LinesDude in the press. I'm frequently contacted by journalists who heard of me thanks to the Fighters Program and it enables me to grow my business network, which is really powerful in this early phase.

EB: *What advice would you give to others in your previous situation wanting to start a business?*

DK: First, you need a kind of emergency checklist: always make sure you have enough money in hand. Ask yourself: are you ready to go through a stressful and an anxious period with a lot of ups and downs? Also, make sure there is someone to start the business with—being a solo founder is really hard. To find the right person: make sure the business idea you're willing to pursue is in your (or co-founders) core competencies. Once you are on it: move fast, validate fast, iterate fast, and fail fast (something we took time to learn). And back to my first point: money. Ideally, you can make sure the business can stay alive on its own for a long enough period of time without external funding.

WHAT'S NEXT FOR STATION F

EB: *To wrap us up, Roxanne, I am keen to hear about the next steps you are taking to help overlooked founders at Station F. You mentioned before that you may be able to offer stipends, is there anything else? And what other aspects of the ecosystem are you working on?*

RV: Today the Fighters Program has been largely the Station F team meeting with the Fighters companies, organizing workshops, and offering support. We think that we can do more. Everyone is talking about diversity, but people aren't actually doing so much. We're looking at strengthening the program one step at a time. We have doubled the program in size. Next year, we also want to find a number of partners and financial supporters so we can provide Fighters with financial aid, but also, we're realizing that many of the big companies, the Googles, the Facebooks, and Microsofts, they all want to make a difference, but they are not currently doing very much. We are looking at how we can work with them to better support the Fighters Program. Can they mentor the Fighters? Can they provide more tools for free? Do they have content they are not making as available as it should be? We are speaking to a number of different potential partners right now to really reinforce this.

We have also asked all of the Station F partners who are on campus to somehow contribute to the Fighters Program. They are on campus, so they are accessible, but the Fighters probably don't dare to go and speak to them unless they really see an opportunity that they want to take advantage of. We want to reinforce the whole experience and offering by ensuring the Fighters have greater access to all of our partners. In terms of a stipend, we have a deal in place for the upcoming year with La French Tech for all of our Fighters to access a grant of up to €12K.

15.2 *Warner: Diversity VC*

Check Warner (Ada Ventures, formerly Diversity VC)

Check Warner[237] is one of the co-founders of Diversity VC, an organization that was started in late 2015. Check raised a fund in 2020, as general partner at Ada Ventures, focused on overlooked founders and markets. In this conversation with her, we talk about organizational and structural efforts, with a particular focus on the venture ecosystem in Europe, to change the lack of diversity and inclusion, including the power of statistics, internships programs (such as Future VC[238]), and Diversity VC's new Diversity Standard.[239]

Interviewed October 2020

THE ORIGINS OF DIVERSITY VC

Johannes Lenhard (JL): *Tell us the origin story of Diversity VC. How did it all begin?*

Check Warner (CW): I had come into VC from a very unusual background for most associates in the industry. I started out in advertising and I studied English literature. When I got my first job in venture capital, it was through a series of fortunate events and some nepotism and introductions. After my first few months in the industry, I was really shocked looking around at all the founders we were meeting, everyone who worked in the investment teams, everybody who worked in the industry at large, when I went to networking events, and all the conferences: it just seemed like everyone was pretty much coming from the same background, which was either accountancy or finance or consulting, from the same handful

---

237. https://twitter.com/checkwarner

238. https://futurevc.com

239. https://diversity.vc/diversity-vc-standard/

of universities, from the same private schools before that. And they were all white, and they were all male.

At that time, I assumed there was someone who was already doing something like Diversity VC. And it turned out there was nothing. I joined up with Lillian Li,[240] who was running a series of dinners for women in VC. We talked about the fact that something much bigger, something more structural needed to exist, that was actually going to address the root causes of this. It was all very well to have a couple of dinners getting together with the few females who already worked in the industry, but what Diversity VC was intended to be, and is, is a body that is created for the industry, run by people in the industry. Diversity VC is actually empathetic to the context of venture capital, while helping VC funds to be more inclusive in how they operate, and addresses the root causes of the lack of diversity and inclusion in the industry, both in terms of the industry itself, but also the founders who get funded.

BEST PRACTICES FROM FIVE YEARS OF INVESTIGATION

Erika Brodnock (EB): *Over the last five years, what best practices have emerged to really shift diversity and inclusion for VCs?*

CW: The first one, and what we started with, is actually understanding the state of play as it is today. We were quite horrified to find out when we went to talk to the industry body, which is the BVCA (British Venture Capital Association), that there was no data on, for example, how many women worked in the industry. That was our first port of call. We needed to actually understand what was going on in order to try to design good interventions that would drive change. We've done quite a lot of research since then, also in much broader areas than just gender. But in terms of best practices for VCs, actually understanding where they are at within their firms in terms of both who's working in their firms, and do people in their firms feel included? Do they feel like they have a voice? Do they feel like they can bring their whole selves to work? And on the flip side, who are they investing in? Who are they seeing at the pipeline stage? And how is that translating into invested capital? Collecting and understanding data is a really important and fundamental best practice.

The second piece is thinking about the pathways into VC firms. We decided to set something up called Future VC, an internship program. It

---

is a first of its kind program, whereby we take all of the difficult parts of actually running an internship program in terms of recruiting the talent, assessing the talent, teaching the talent, and building a network between them, away from the VC firms. And we have now had at least 16 people who've now got jobs in the industry and another nine on internships who've come through the Future VC program. Future VC is still in its infancy, not even four years in. But we want it to be a program that enables people to come in at all levels. Partner level, principal level, and associate level, as well as intern. I think that we have been facing the perception of a cold start problem. VCs are currently saying, "We need you to have experience, otherwise, we can't hire you". And with Future VC, we're giving candidates a foot in the door to get two months experience under their belts. Often that then becomes a six-month internship. It's often also turned into an associate position that's full time. And then what we want to do in the future is help operators to understand investing. So actually getting them up the curve of becoming a VC. Eliminating some of the basic blocks and tackling issues such as: What is a cap table? How do you assess financial models? If you're looking at it from a VC's perspective, how do you structure investments? That's the kind of thing we want to do with Future VC to create a more senior pipeline going forward.

And then the third piece is about best practices and concerns on the inclusion side, within the firm. It's all very well to recruit diverse talent, but actually, unless you change your organization to make sure that they are heard and included, and they feel seen, and they feel supported, then they're not going to stay in your organization and thrive. So we've focused in a couple of ways on that, both in terms of a toolkit, and also in terms of the Diversity VC Standard, which we recently launched.

GUIDANCE FROM THE DIVERSITY VC STANDARD

JL: *The Diversity VC Standard is a set of practices for everyone who wants to change something but doesn't know what, right? So, what does the Standard's toolkit look like?*

CW: The first thing we did was training and, again, helping VCs to understand the nuance and complexities of these issues. Because I think a lot of the time I hear people saying, "I want to do something about it," but they haven't actually taken the time to even really understand what's going on, and what's driving the issues. And you do need to engage with that if you're going to be successful in helping people feel included within your organization. So we actually ran a training session where we had 16 European VC partners with a group called Fearless Futures. That would be the first really concrete thing I'd suggest people do: D&I training, including at partner level.

And then there are a huge number of evidence-based interventions that you can make, that ensure that you are being inclusive in how you operate. So what we've done with the Diversity Standard is actually just distilled those into an assessment and certification process with the funds. For example, when looking at your shortlist for the people that you intend to interview, have you got a 50/50 shortlist? Have you got a diverse shortlist of people to interview when you're hiring for the new candidates into your fund? And many of them say, "Oh, no, we've never thought of that." So that's something that we know works to create a more diverse employee base and recruitment. And that's just one example. There are 30 different policies across recruitment, pipeline, internal policy and culture, deal flow, and portfolio support.

This Standard was really an evolution of what we started out doing, which was the toolkit, but we found that people just weren't using or implementing it. We did a study about a year after we had published the toolkit and over half of the funds that we surveyed, which already were a self-selected group of people who were quite interested, had no D&I representative, no one in the organization was responsible. They didn't have parental leave policies, they hadn't done the basic stuff. And so we thought, we have got to go much further than just creating a toolkit, which is a PDF that they can download from our website. We decided to look at, how can we use behavioral science to drive FOMO, fear of missing out, or the competitive spirit of the funds? So the Standard is about trying to bring the whole industry up to a better level of compliance and implementing a lot of the things that we know work to increase diversity.

Concretely, we decided to work with a group called Diversio, which is an organization based in Canada. They've done a lot of work for big asset managers, and thought leadership work with groups like McKinsey. And with them we have designed this set of best practice guidelines that is based on existing research and evidence. We take the VC funds through the assessment, and we ask them to provide evidence of what they're doing. And we look at all of that evidence, and then we can then show them, in terms of their industry, how well they're doing in relation to other funds. We can benchmark them and they get a kind of industry average score, including a breakdown based on deal flow, internal policy, culture, recruitment, and portfolio support.

The benchmarking has already started to create so much more action on the part of the funds that we are trying to get to move. One particular fund, for instance, said, "We had D&I kind of on our roadmap, but there was no real forcing function to put any of it in place. So actually being part of the Diversity VC standard has accelerated all of it, internally." For the launch, we had 16 funds, five in Canada and the rest in the UK. Since then, we have had funds in the US, in France, in the Nordics, across Europe, already taking part in being assessed. Eventually, we want this to become a kind of global benchmark, which over time will move; we can make it harder to achieve level one and level two at the Standard.

THE OUTSTANDING NEED FOR TRANSPARENCY AND CLARITY

EB: *What are some of the big issues outstanding in the UK and EU ecosystem? And what are the next steps that you intend to take with Diversity VC to tackle them, and indeed the data?*

CW: I think we need to make progress across the board, we are right at the very start. And I wouldn't want to let any of the issues off the hook by talking about things we need to move onto because actually, we need to do all of it. But what has come through the work with the Standard is that, on two fronts, funds are doing badly. One is actually investing the capital. We've seen during COVID-19 that funding going to diverse founders who come from different backgrounds has actually gone down and has gone down quite dramatically. And this is at a time when, generally, venture capital funding has been going really well. And so I think a lot more progress needs to be made in terms of the mechanism of access, in terms of transparency, in terms of mentoring founders in what they need to look like, and what the business needs to look like.

So far, we're trying to help where we feel we can, and I think there are elements of this that are beyond our reach. Unfortunately, and it makes me really sad to say this, but the stories I hear, day after day on the ground, in terms of the feedback the founders that I work with get from the market, it's just incredibly bleak and incredibly depressing. So I think a lot more work needs to be done there.

EB: *Is the answer then to give the founders more mentoring and to shape their propositions better? That kind of buys into the notion that there is a pipeline problem, that the founders aren't educated enough or competent enough or running good enough businesses, right? As opposed to, there's an issue on the other side.*

CW: Definitely. It is always a bit of both. But I'm not advocating for more mentoring, more mentoring, because the crucial change will come from sending the wire and making the hire. It's not mentoring so much as transparency and clarity. Let me give you an example: I heard a stat this morning, from a pitch event I was at, which is that 80% of the female founders that were at this pitch event didn't know the difference between angels and VCs.

I was surprised by that. But the industry is still a bit of a black box in lots of ways—funds don't publish things like their average check size, what they are concretely looking for, what kind of sectors they invest in. None of that is visible on VCs' websites. Also, very basic things like: how do you contact us? The other piece is VC funds that have portfolio companies already, pumping capital into those portfolio companies. They need to do a lot more to support, challenge, and ultimately restrict funding to companies that are not taking this issue seriously, or not doing the right things. And I think currently, because the VC funds themselves don't feel that they're there in terms of their own work, they're not doing it. And that's a big gap.

15.3 *Kostka: All Raise*

Pam Kostka (formerly All Raise)

We caught up with Pam Kostka[241] while she was CEO of US venture diversifier All Raise[242] for her take on how and why All Raise came about, and how to build a more prosperous, equitable, and sustainable future for all.

Interviewed October 2020

THE ORIGINS OF ALL RAISE

Erika Brodnock (EB): *Tell us a little bit about the history of All Raise. And when did it start and why? What are the goals for the organization?*

Pam Kostka (PK): All Raise started as a grassroots effort. The #MeToo movement in Silicon Valley served as an external impetus. Susan Fowler's blog post about her experiences at Uber was followed by Justin Caldbeck in the headlines[243] and it just struck a nerve. It was the right time, the right place, and every woman in tech resoundingly said, "Yes, that! I've been there, experienced that." What was impressive is that Aileen Lee went on to become an organizing force. She sent out an email to the community. Thirty-six or so women responded immediately to say, "Yes, this is a time, this is a moment when we can do something."

I think it's emblematic of a couple of things. One, the need for it in the industry: things had been bubbling up in the community and the ecosystem, not just for years, but for hundreds of years! It was incredibly important that these were women of power and influence who came together and said, "We have a platform, we have power and influence, and we can share that to actually drive change." Thus, All Raise was born, first

---

241. https://twitter.com/PamKostka

242. https://www.allraise.org/

243. https://eu.usatoday.com/story/tech/news/2017/06/24/
women-speak-up-about-silicon-valley-sexism/103169902/

as an all-volunteer effort, then we actually "incorporated ourselves" as a 501(c)(3). We started that process in 2018 and finalized it in 2019. We then brought in myself and some other staff to professionalize the organization and make it operational so that we could expand.

EB: *Can you clarify what a 501(c) is? Is it a B Corp?*

PK: It's non-profit status in the United States. We call ourselves a startup non-profit, because we take the ethos of how to build and scale a startup, how to be a disruptor in the industry, and apply it to our mission. We just happen to do that via a non-profit structure. It's interesting that in our financing structure, part of the uniqueness of who we are is the magnitude of power and influence in the community that we've brought to the table. It's traditional philanthropic organizations, and corporations that support the tech ecosystem here in the United States, such as Silicon Valley Bank, J.P. Morgan, UBS, Bank of America, EY. In our recent fundraising initiative, the venture capital firms and high-net-worth individuals in tech themselves are coming together to fuel our mission. We see that as an interesting investment model, where we have this large investment base coming to us and funding the disruption of the industry. That aligns with our mission, which is to accelerate the success of female founders and funders for a more prosperous and equitable future. That mission drives everything that we do and now we're getting the power and influence curve to say, this is something that matters to us and to women throughout the industry.

Moreover, everybody who contributes philanthropically to the organization is also put to work in our community in service of the mission. We have a bias toward action, so it's not enough to just write a check and let us do the work, our donors also need to be part of the change that we want to see. So every conversation we have with Reid Hoffman, with Sequoia Capital, with the long list of individuals who support us, is centered around engaging them to join in and be an advocate—not just a voice, but an advocate for change.

HOW TO BUILD A MORE PROSPEROUS AND EQUITABLE FUTURE

Johannes Lenhard (JL): *Picking up from this mission that you talked about, what are your high-level goals? And how have you been working towards these over the years?*

PK: As I mentioned earlier, our mission is to accelerate the success of female founders and funders to build a more prosperous and equitable future. We fundamentally know that diversity generates better results. It's not just about the redistribution of power and influence in the industry, but the wealth creation that is generated when you do that. Morgan Stanley estimates that we have the opportunity for net new wealth creation of up to $4.4 trillion. In the industry, that's huge! Investing in diversity, equity, and inclusion (DEI) is a massive opportunity on par with the moonshot investments that the venture community likes to invest in.

At All Raise, we call this the guaranteed moonshot: if you invest in this, benefit will come from all avenues. If you're an investor, it's to your portfolio. If you're a founder, it's to the effectiveness of your company. There is a wealth of power and momentum at stake. We hold ourselves and the industry accountable to two North Star goals. One is to move the needle on the number of women, including women of color, who are check writers at partner level within a venture firm. It was 9%, when we started. By 2028, we're looking to move that number to 18%. We're still doing the crunching for what happened in 2020, but as of 2019, we know that number was at 12%. That's great progress, yet 68% of venture firms still don't have a single female partner. And the numbers for women of color in the industry are abysmally worse, in the low single (like 1%) digit range. We recognize that we have a lot more work to do there as we continue to move the needle.

Our second goal is to accelerate the percentage of funding going to female founders, and we've changed this goal since we started. Originally, we were looking holistically at the system, then we began to use data to make ourselves smarter. In that process we learned that, when a woman raises her Series C she has an equal likelihood of raising as her male counterpart. I'm not saying it's easy for her as she still faces obstacles and hurdles, but the raise is equally likely. So we shifted our focus to hone in on seed, Series A, and Series B, because that's where women are at a significant disadvantage—by as much as 35%—relative to the male cohort at a similar stage. Our 2030 goal is to move from 11% last year to 23% of funding going to female founders in 10 years. We also look at top of funnel, early stage rounds to make sure that we're empowering a lot more women and women of color to get funding and drive that change through the ecosystem, so that in 10 years we can see women we supported in the early stages becoming unicorns.

Our vision for how we get there is twofold.

From a top-down approach, we aim to reshape culture to move beyond DEI being a checkbox activity towards making it synonymous with success. We call that moving from FOMO to DOMO: we're moving from the "fear of missing out" to the "danger of missing out." If you are not diverse and inclusive, your business will not succeed. That may mean, as a venture capitalist, you're not attracting the best talent. As a founder, you're also not attracting the best talent, you're not building the best products, and therefore you're missing out on the economic opportunity available to whichever side of the equation you're on.

A lot of that for us rhymes with creating a megaphone: DEI is this unstoppable force that is coming in the industry, for women, for underrepresented individuals. It's like a freight train coming down the tracks. We do this by leveraging our 20,000-strong community and thousands of the most powerful male and female venture capitalists we have attracted to our table. We're working with around 1,500 of the most iconic founders, funders, and unicorns—people who have succeeded, as well as those who are up and coming—to understand how we can leverage their voices to enact the change we want to see. Our ethos of enabling important people with power and influence to take ownership, to make the change, and to be the drivers of the change is again clear to see.

An example of reshaping culture is the All Raise Visionary Voices speakers bureau. Women's voices, especially underrepresented women's voices, are not widely recognized in the tech ecosystem in conferences, panels, and media coverage. We wanted to address the red herring issue of, "I couldn't find anybody." This is not a pipeline problem. This is an access problem. To that end, we've made 1,000 women available through Visionary Voices, a database of vetted speakers who have great talent. Their expertise and area of knowledge is made clear and anyone can tap into it. The list is growing every quarter, and we have worked with prominent media and conferences to make sure that they are being diverse in their panelists and in their coverage. Of course, we also use the list ourselves when sourcing speakers!

After the top-down reshaping of culture, we look at what we can do from a bottom-up perspective to achieve those two North Star measures. We focus on rewiring the industry from the inside. The flywheel we have today is a continuous cycle in which white men fund white men, they become very wealthy founders, they exit, and they make investments in people that they know within their network. This is not necessarily intentional, it's about networks. Who do they know? Therefore, who do they invest in again? This results in a very powerful flywheel that has been perpetuated and strengthened over time. When we look at the statistics in 2020, 68% of firms don't have a single female partner and, amidst COVID-19, the amount of funding to women is actually falling this year.[244] That is statistically improbable, therefore there has to be some kind of an intentionality behind the decision not to fund women this year.

THE ROLE OF RESEARCH AND ALL RAISE'S THEORY OF CHANGE

EB: *Data shows the raw amounts being invested are going up, while the numbers invested in females are going down. As you said, this is statistically improbable, therefore, it appears there is intentionality behind underinvesting in women. There are a couple of things here, because one, how has research shaped your approach? And two, now that we have data like this, what do we need to do to change this?*

PK: We're big believers in data, because what doesn't get measured doesn't get fixed. That's true in life in general: If you want to run a marathon, you've got to put yourself on a schedule and know what your mileage is in order to know you can finish the race. Every day, you've got to mea-

---

244. https://www.bloomberg.com/news/articles/2022-01-11/
women-founders-raised-just-2-of-venture-capital-money-last-year

sure yourself. If you do the work, you will complete your marathon, if you don't do the work, you're not going to complete the marathon. Simple. At All Raise, we believe data is core to our understanding. We are constantly reporting on our two North Star objectives, as well as on the obstacles that are behind the numbers.

Based on our research, our theory of change is access, guidance, and support. Access is crystallizing the point that this isn't about capability. This is about networks. If you don't know a female entrepreneur, or you don't know a Black or Latinx entrepreneur, then it is much more difficult for you to connect, and for them to break into, for example, the circle in venture. We want to make sure that from an access perspective, we're blowing that up and creating intersecting networks and creating moments when connection can happen. We are facilitating access to opportunity, mentors, money, talent, people, and experts. If entrepreneurs have a question about doing something, they usually have to Google it and try to figure it out, or they tap a network that can help.

Access guides a lot of our programming. For example, When Founder Met Funder[245] is a very dedicated program that recognizes the unique lived experience of Black women, and we're going to be extending it to Latinx women next year. We've run this program for two years and the purpose is to give some guidance, but also to bring venture capitalists and these amazing Black entrepreneurs together so that they meet each other and can develop a relationship before there is the need for a transaction or an ask for money. Bringing those networks together is important because it invariably leads to the scientific phenomenon in nature called the edge effect, which is when two different ecosystems brush up against each other. An example of this is where the savanna meets the desert. The most biodiversity is found right where they connect together. As we bring these two communities together, we create those edge effects where we can see the amplification of money and power between them. We have been privileged to see creation and creativity blossom in that area. The benefits of this are extended to both the entrepreneurs and the venture capitalists who get together and meet one another.

Guidance is the second pillar in our theory of change. There is a language of venture, the venture-backed ecosystem and venture scale companies, and while we're not trying to teach women to become men, we

---

245. https://www.allraise.org/events/all-events/when-founder-met-funder-1

are trying to teach them the rules of this particular game. What is the language? What are the expectations? Making sure women are getting that inside knowledge so that as we rewire the industry and seed that new flywheel, it is successful. We want to pass on insider information, the things that people aren't going to tell you, that you can't Google. An interpretation and explanation of when they say "x," it really means this. Many of our bootcamps and digital programs do that for women. Our VC summit is one of our biggest programs of the year, taking place every fall. We regularly convene over 800 women in venture. It is the largest convening of anybody in venture and brings women together for a day of inspiration, but also guidance, across areas including career, negotiation, how to be a good board member, how to improve your investment thesis in a particular area, and more.

Finally, the last pillar is support. All Raise offers support through cohorts. Being an investor or founder in tech is a lonely journey for women. We use a cohort-based model both on the venture side and on the founder side to make sure that women get the support they need. Ten to 12 entrepreneurs develop deep relationships with people whom they can ask the awkward questions they can't ask in their own companies. Real business gets done. It's not just emotional support, it is also deep, impactful business. In the venture circles, we see deals being shared and won competitively against incumbents in the industry. In the founder realm, we see people being able to materially accelerate their business forward through connections, introductions, knowledge-sharing, and access to something they need.

EB: *You've given us tangible examples detailing how All Raise could be recreated by others in their local tech ecosystems. A cookie-cutter approach that could be adopted and adapted seems to be emerging, which is fantastic.*

PK: We have a bias towards action and hope we are creating a platform that other businesses can replicate and leverage.

PERSPECTIVE ON KEY PLAYERS IN THE FIELD

JL: *Looking at this from a systemic perspective, who do you think are the key players that have to move now? What do you think about the role of LPs? Do they form part of the structures you are addressing? And if so, how?*

PK: The first part of your question was, who needs to be engaged in this movement, right? And the answer is everyone needs to be engaged in the movement. But there are two levels. One, people with power and influence, absolutely need to be willing to accept the responsibility of sharing their power and influence. We believe that the way to get somebody to do that is not just to appeal to the moral rightness of this movement. Because we are a venture-capital-backed ecosystem, we look at capital gains and benefits as the main driver. Increased DEI yields better results. People at the power and influence curve in the venture industry are always looking ahead at who's seeing around the corner and what the next trend is ... The next trend is DEI. Two key events have occurred. The first back in 2017, which sparked All Raise, then in 2020, George Floyd and Breonna Taylor were murdered, and that opened up another aperture around social justice. These are moments in history that we're not going to move back from. There is a change afoot. The tech and venture industry can either acknowledge and embrace that and be drivers of that change, or be left behind. That serves as one of the key motivators for the industry. The way All Raise started was with 36 amazingly powerful women who had succeeded, and recognized they had a chance to accelerate the pace at which change could happen, and engage their male peers in that conversation too.

We see examples everywhere of those with power and influence taking responsibility to be the change. David Swensen, the head of the Yale endowment, which is one of the largest endowments in the United States, has come forth from the LP perspective to say, "We invest in you, so you can invest our money. If you do not diversify, I'm going to pull our money from you." That is a powerful move from somebody who has their hands on the reins of substantial amounts of money. He's doing that because it is both the right thing to do and it is the economically prudent thing to do. This serves as a clear economic incentive to venture firms to make change. It's a great example. Goldman Sachs coming out and saying, "We won't take somebody public unless you have one diverse board member by the end of 2021. And two by the end of 2022." NASDAQ, coming out and saying, "We'll delist you if you are not diverse." These are powerful motivators for people that it is time to move. As I mentioned earlier, what gets measured, gets done! We're all good at setting OKRs for key results and measuring ourselves on them. It is hard work, but if we measure, put incentives in place, and those incentives are appropriate, we will see change. It is about power and influence, and the truth is everybody has power and influence.

As part of our community culture, everyone who has been to a program at All Raise has a responsibility to pay it forward. All Raise participants get access, guidance, and support, thus, are more empowered on the flip side than when they started. So, when the next woman, Black person, or Latinx person reaches out, it's an obligation to share what has been learned to create an opportunity for that individual. It's not just the top of the pyramid. It's everybody in the ecosystem, driving macro and micro changes.

SUCCESS STORIES FROM ALL RAISE

EB: *What are the biggest success stories that you think All Raise has contributed to, or indeed, instigated and written?*

PK: We have a couple of success stories; one is at a campaign level. Founders for Change[246] was the recognition that there was an increasing generation of founders who care deeply about diversity, equity, and inclusion in their teams, on their boards, and, when possible, in their choice of investors. We rally these founders together, not only to give them a support framework of others who share this ethos, but also as a communication to, for example, the venture community, that we are your lifeblood. If I walk into your organization, or go to your web page, and see that you're all white men, I could make the choice not to work with you because I don't think I'm going to get the benefit from working with a monoculture and I want something that's more diverse. Founders for Change was very much a social campaign, and we continue to work with it. It served as a wake-up call and that is where we started to see a change from that 9% [of check writers at partner level within a venture firm being women] moving to 12% [in 2019].

I would say every woman that we engage has such a powerful, amazing story. There are many throughout the ecosystem, but Tiffany Dufu stands out. We connected at a party for the Alpha Girls book, a book about the four female pioneers in venture, on whose shoulders we stand today. When I met Tiffany, she said, "I'm looking for funding and somebody said I should talk with you." We started to network, and I plugged her into the All Raise network. We always call ourselves the rocket fuel accelerating powerful women founders. Tiffany is amazingly charismatic. She has a

---

246. https://www.foundersforchange.org/

business called the Cru and she is one of the few Black female entrepreneurs [as of 2020] who's recently raised over a million dollars. She's amazing. I never want to take credit for her success. She did that. Yet, we had an influence there. Tiffany went through some of our boot camps and we were able to plug her in and make introductions. Even though she has now raised, Tiffany has joined our next boot camp. We want to continually support a female entrepreneur throughout her journey. She's a great success story.

We can see this new flywheel turning now. Is it turning as quickly as the established, white male flywheel? No, but we're beginning to slow that one down as we're ramping up this new flywheel with funders, founders, and operators, so that women and underrepresented individuals can participate in the funding, founding, and scaling of companies.

JL: *We're actually going to interview two of the Alpha Girls, Sonja and Theresia,[§9.4] for the history section.*

PK: Sonja is amazing, as is Theresia. They're both part of the All Raise network. The work that we do is cumulative. We're standing on their shoulders. The generations that will come will stand on our shoulders. And that's the whole point.

HOW QUOTAS FIT INTO THE CHANGING ECOSYSTEM

JL: *Do you think quotas are going to play a role in changing the ecosystem? If so, for whom? On what level? Or is there something else that you think we need to bring onto the agenda?*

PK: I don't think quotas are inherently good or bad. They're neutral. We talked about the importance of measurement, right? Quotas, in some ways, are just measurement tools. What gets measured gets fixed. Quotas can have a negative side, of course, if people are using them for checkbox reasons. Where I see quotas being effective, and quotas mean something different to everybody, is when you're tying the quota to an economic imperative. It is NASDAQ saying, "I'm not going to tell you how many people per se you need to diversify your board, but here's the de minimis that you need to do. If you don't, you can be delisted." Is that a quota? Yes. Is it a quota tied to a relevant economic incentive for the organization? Absolutely.

Conversely, "you just need to hire two people" doesn't work so well. The problem with some quotas is that you don't get inclusivity. You can end up seeing a revolving door where individuals are brought in, but then there's no inclusivity, they don't feel welcome, they don't feel effective, and they leave the organization as quickly as they came.

What I think is interesting about board-level initiatives is that now you have board members helping to drive diversity, equity, and inclusion down through the entire organization. One of the things we focus on a lot is how to encourage boards to focus on all facets of DEI, including, what are the numbers of people, but also on questions such as: Who is leaving the company? Why are they leaving the company? What is being done to create inclusivity? And to look at that, not just in your employee base, but in your product operations and your supply chain. Measuring and treating DEI as a core strategic value for the organization and as important of a board topic as the sales pipeline.

I think many industries are getting more sophisticated in the way we think about and measure quotas, not just at a moment in time, but for long-term success. Tying a metric to an economic outcome and measuring impact is an important trend of the future and will lead to a tipping point, the beginnings of which we are seeing now. I think one of the reasons we're seeing this in the boardroom is board members can impact what the company does and hold the company accountable.

TECH'S ROLE IN MEASURING DEI MORE CONSISTENTLY

EB: *Finally, do you think that tech has a role to play in terms of real-time measurement? It's almost as though diversity, equity, and inclusion tend to be surveyed once a year, and not focused on much for the rest of the year. There isn't an All Raise in every single country where there is venture and tech. So how do we keep this current at the front of mind, all the time, rather than just some of the time?*

PK: I think tech absolutely has a role to play in how we approach diversity, equity, and inclusion going forward. And where we focus, I think there's been a lot of focus on the "D" in DEI. And that's measuring the inflows, but not a lot of measurement on the equity and inclusion piece. Tech runs on data, we have a lot of data, but we still need to add data! So we're talking to, for example, Crunchbase and PitchBook about how they, as trackers who have data on the industry, add data on race and gender, and do that in the right way for self-identification. They do a good job of producing quarterly reports, but how can they start to report on a regular basis and allow people to make informed choices, while making the state of the industry transparent? I don't think you can measure this in days. This is not real-time trends. But when we look at moving the numbers and measuring the industry, we look on a quarterly basis, and by doing that, then you avoid that end-of-year shock. DEI needs to be woven into the fabric of organizations. It's also why we say that at the board level, it's a strategic imperative to measure. The board's going to meet at least quarterly and if your obligation is to report to the board and have a strategic conversation about DEI—where you're succeeding, where there's room for improvement—you're measuring, again, what's happening on the back end, who's leaving the company and who's not, as well as issues like pay equity.

I'm excited to see what this next generation of companies will do, when they're looking at whatever space they're looking at and incorporating more real-time information, whether it's around how they build their product and who they target. There are so many products, and thus companies, that could be so much bigger if they were thinking more broadly about who their customer base is and really infusing DEI throughout every element of the company. It's not just an HR problem. It's not just a team-building problem. There are a lot of things that companies can and should be doing, and tech is going to play a role in that.

15.4 *Lynn, Sievers, Liu: Accelerators*

John Lynn (Cela)

Camilla Sievers (Qi Health, Female Founders)

Kevin Liu (Techstars)

More and more startups go through their phase of initiation with accelerators and incubators; dozens of these institutions are appearing each year, many with a specific focus on an industry, a particular group of founders, or a geography. We spoke with three accelerator experts: John Lynn,[247] who has built many accelerators over the years with Cela[248] out of New York; Camilla Sievers[249] from Female Founders[250] in Austria; and Kevin Liu,[251] investor in San Francisco for Techstars.[252] We asked them about the role and responsibility of accelerators in considering DEI. We also discuss unconscious bias, opening up the funnel, and the importance of fostering not only diverse hiring and accelerator intake, but also inclusive practices within the accelerators and portfolio companies.

Interviewed December 2020

BUILDING COMMUNITY FOR WOMEN AND SUPPORT FOR DIVERSE FOUNDING TEAMS

Erika Brodnock (EB): *Camilla, you're a part of the Female Founders accelerator in Austria. What motivated you to start at FF and what are the aims of the program?*

247. https://twitter.com/jmlynn7

248. https://celainnovation.com/

249. https://twitter.com/CamillaSievers

250. https://www.female-founders.org/

251. https://twitter.com/ckevinliu

252. https://www.techstars.com/

Camilla Sievers (CS): I became part of the startup world from early 2013. At that time, while there was only a small ecosystem in general, there was for sure no visibility for women at all, no female role models, no network, no female investors—none of that. As these things go, the couple of females that were in the space in continental Europe found each other very quickly. We immediately saw that there's huge potential in this market because people don't know that they have a place to come to, where they will be understood and welcome. So we want to encourage women to become part of the industry, to have role models and mentors and people they can talk to about ideas and about problems that they're facing. We started by building a community for women to meet each other.

Now the core of our program, the mission of our accelerator, is, obviously, to foster diverse teams across Europe. We all know female-led startups or even diverse teams aren't funded. They, at the moment [in 2020], get between 2% and 3% of all VC money.[253] This is crazy when we also know that they tend to outperform male-led startups by two to three times.[254] We don't just focus on female-led teams but diverse teams more broadly, and then the potential within the marketplace becomes even bigger.

We believe that biased investors or investor networks, where women are not represented as much, are a core reason why women are not put in positions where they are actually visible. So diverse and female-led teams have a much harder time to raise capital to get into this network that is very much male-driven, and find the resources that they need. That's where we come in: we help them build the network, and meet role models and mentors. We help them become investment ready, which is at the core of our program, and then help them with the fundraising process.

THE ROLE OF DEI IN SETTING UP NEW ACCELERATORS

Johannes Lenhard (JFL): *John, you've helped quite a few accelerators over the last five years get off the ground. How important are different principles of diversity, equity, and inclusion when you set up a new program, and why is that something that you care about?*

---

253. https://hbr.org/2021/02/women-led-startups-received-just-2-3-of-vc-funding-in-2020

254. https://www.forbes.com/sites/falonfatemi/2019/03/29/
the-value-of-investing-in-female-founders/

John Lynn (JL): We believe that the essential function of an accelerator is to systematize access. So it's inherently a tool that can be a vehicle for inclusion and diversity. Installing an accelerator system that can be applied to address the problem of inclusion and set up in the right way is essential to a good accelerator, even if it's for a homogenous group. I think from the perspective of what makes an accelerator work, being able to understand what kinds of access someone needs and prepare their contact with your network to achieve that need—that should be at the core of an accelerator. But from the other side of things, it's also what makes accelerators a really good tool for solving the problems of diversity to some extent. So not only is it something that makes an accelerator work, but it's also a resource that's only beginning to be tapped in the right way to solve this greater problem.

STRATEGIC COMMITMENTS AND WORKING WITH DEI DATA

EB: *Kevin, you've been with Techstars for more than two years and you mentioned before that you're doing some interesting things around DEI. How important is it to you, and can you go into the specifics of what you're doing to increase DEI in your programs and investments?*

Kevin Liu (KL): At Techstars, DEI is very important to us. Over the last few years, we've done various efforts at the strategic level. For example, we kicked off our 1,000 diverse CEOs initiative.[255] The goal is to invest in 1,000 diverse CEOs through our accelerators by 2026. This has been primarily led by our head of D&I, Andrea Perdomo, and she's done a fantastic job to push that create a culture of awareness for D&I within Techstars.

From the investing side of things at Techstars, we do want to have high percentages of companies that do well financially. So at the end of the day, we as investors push DEI because it has been proven to be good for startup businesses,[256] too. That is an opportunity point that we do want to push on. That is also very much in line with our overall philosophy and vision. When we began Techstars in 2007–2008, the goal was to go into a market and help entrepreneurs and places that historically were not seen or sup-

255. https://www.techstars.com/the-line/pov/
      our-commitment-to-diversity-equity-and-inclusion-entrepreneurship
256. https://hbr.org/2017/09/
      the-comprehensive-case-for-investing-more-vc-money-in-women-led-startups

ported; our founders did not focus on the coastal cities. Most of our programs are in the Midwest here in the United States.

One other observation I want to bring up is this: if you're not tracking it, you're not going to improve it, right? So, DEI is something that we do track. So, you know, looking at my dashboard right now, and some high level stats, I can present here, about the kind of companies that apply and are accepted, the makeup of teams. And we have good news there: close to 30–35% of teams that are accepted into our programs have one or more female founders in that mix. Another interesting stat: about 40% of the companies that are accepted have one or more underrepresented founders from the race and ethnicity side.

Now that we know that, what do we do with this data? How do we increase the numbers? I'm looking at the questions right now. The problem of increasing a number and widening a pipeline is not just about the portfolio and the companies in our program; it is also about the decision makers. We are always actively trying to increase the number of manager directors that we have in our pool that are female or come from underrepresented backgrounds.

One final thing I want to mention is the work we do with portfolio support. A lot of the work we do is post-program support work. How do we help companies when they graduate, go out, and find capital? We do have active programming, where we help connect founders to the right investors. One of the parameters that we recently introduced is, for instance, if you're a female founder and a female-focused fund, we will make that connection more systematically than we have done in the past.

TACKLING AND REVEALING UNCONSCIOUS BIAS

JFL: *Camilla, you have already built in a certain bias in your accelerator given your specific focus. And Kevin, you just talked quite a bit about how you're trying to widen your lens as much as possible. But do you believe that you have had unconscious bias in your programs before and that you have been able to eliminate it?*

CS: We explicitly talked about certain biases we needed to avoid and eliminate. We also went the other way and tried to not completely overcompensate; we decided that we didn't want to have a female-only funnel, a female-only investors network, a female-only venture partner network, ambassador network, etc. It needed to be diverse, as we can only achieve our goals in equality if every stakeholder (and sex) gets involved and contributes to the conversation. We believe that in terms of age of gender, ethnicity, and probably also life experience, we need to be diverse in order to build the best product and I think we are on a good way to raise awareness about bias and be mindful in our day-to-day operations to foster an unbiased environment.

JL: In the overall ecosystem, we see the element of unconscious bias permeating many business relationships. It is especially hidden in language—the culture of emailing and calls (VCs are known for using subject-only messages, or messages in the body of an email that have no capitalization, punctuation, greeting, etc.), entrenched terminology (almost any startup term: hustle, scalable, innovative, disruptive, etc.).

We've seen coordinating direct interactions between diverse entrepreneurs and key stakeholders like investors or customers has been a high-cost but impactful solution—and is ever-present in accelerator program experiences. Our own Cela Office Hours series focuses on producing direct interactions between diverse founders and mentors that identify the same way as the founder. Finding mentorship that identifies the same way as the founder is the top problem of diverse entrepreneurs (next to capital), so we're able to address it by isolating this key connection activity in accelerator programs. This is a crucial part of what has made the access elements of acceleration central to our belief that accelerators offer a missing piece to education, generally.

BEST PRACTICES FOR WIDENING AND FILTERING THE FUNNEL

EB: *In the interest of sharing good practice, what are some of the key processes that you are using in your respective programs to widen participation and filter applications?*

KL: As Techstars evolves, we've played around with many different methods around sourcing companies into the accelerator programs. Historically, sourcing was done very locally, the managing directors would go out sourcing companies; these days, we have a central sourcing function with a team of people who do sourcing very broadly. What we are trying to do is engage in a more systematic discovery process of what opportunities are out there; we believe that doing this centrally can help with eliminating some of the more local biases. So the sourcing effort now involved a lot of different puzzle pieces (in addition to MD-led sourcing efforts) to achieve this goal: it is everything from having associates go through conference schedules, looking at relevant companies in Pitchbook (and Crunchbase), and plugging into special interest forums—for example, Techstars worked with Barclays to run their Female Founders First program.[257] The global pipeline team aggregates those leads and then distributes them to the MDs, making sure they're a fit for specific programs, corporate partners, and themes that the programs are focused on. So that's a big piece we've done in the last year or two to invest in some central resources that we hope will yield a lot of longer term benefit in terms of increasing the diversity of our sourcing channel.

JL: A concrete step for every accelerator is to have a systematic process for applications, and to minimize warm introductions. What you see happening a lot is that a system or process is lacking completely; the investors see a startup out on a platform or an article and they hunt them down. The number of startups that are applying and getting in is often quite small, there are accelerators that get thousands of applications and half of the 50-company cohort that gets into the program has been found in other ways, based on the personal preference of individuals. So there should be an institutionalized application process that every company has to go through and that is influenced by a large group of people. The diversity of decision makers in that process can again eliminate a lot of bias.

ENCOURAGING DEI IN PORTFOLIO COMPANIES

JFL: *For portfolio companies, or the companies in the accelerator, how do you think about D&I and address it there? What are tangible actions when it comes to increasing DEI in the companies?*

JL: This is right—while accelerators can help produce progress on DEI, the ultimate outcome for the ecosystem is that companies themselves can bring on more diverse leaders and team members. One of the key struggles of entrepreneurs is that they are looking to move too fast—helping them realize that they themselves are investors of time, energy, skills, recruitment, and that they should take time and care in making those investments, is a fundamental concept that can help them build more diverse teams early on. Accelerators are in a key position to make this case, and to start making it a part of the startup's DNA by including it in the curricu-

---

257. https://rise.barclays/female-founders/programmes/
    female-founders-first-by-barclays-and-techstars/

lum or other program activities. Next, attaching key outcomes to greater diversity can work as well: diversity can help attract better talent, capital, and overall make for a more comprehensively creative and productive environment.

CS: It starts with the startup team itself; we need to foster the mindset in them that it is in their biggest interest to increase diversity. At the end of the day, they will make the decision on who to employ. Again, role modeling can play a big role here, we need to show them what works and connect them with the right people to implement change if need be. At Female Founders, we have a job platform, where they can put up job posts, for instance. We actively share best practices on how you can diversify your funnel. We give them some input on how to win female talent, for instance, because women have to be addressed differently.

And once you manage to recruit, for instance, women, you have to be aware that this talent needs to be supported so that these people stay on. One way of encouraging thinking through the whole process from diversity to inclusion is to suggest to companies to nominate a diversity and inclusion officer. They are responsible for diversifying the recruiting but also the development of the team; it is important to grow a feeling of belonging and openness. Diversity needs to be fostered every day and lived every day. That is why we also focus on personal development topics within the accelerator to address these unconscious biases that one might have, and how to be more aware of them.

15.5 *Miura-Ko, Eesley: Universities and DEI*

Ann Miura-Ko (Floodgate)

Chuck Eesley (Stanford University)

We chatted with Chuck Eesley[258] (professor in engineering at Stanford) and Ann Miura-Ko[259] (GP at Floodgate[260] but also a teacher at her alma mater, Stanford, in Chuck's department) about the role of education for DEI in tech. We touch on issues such as how to achieve fair representation both for faculty and students, the right teaching materials, and diversifying the educational experience as such. The bottom line: schools like Stanford absolutely have a responsibility to drive this effort—and they are standing up for it; the difference they are pushing for now will take a while to pay out in tech, but then will hopefully help us achieve a sea-change that does away with the often cited "pipeline problem."

Interviewed January 2021

EDUCATION'S FORMATIVE ROLE IN DEI

Johannes Lenhard (JL): *We are talking about diversity, equity, and inclusion, and we are thinking about what the role of educational institutions can be when it comes to driving change on this front in tech and venture capital. What do you think the responsibility and the opportunities are for places like Stanford when it comes to producing a more diverse tech and VC ecosystem?*

Ann Miura-Ko (AM-K): I believe the years of schooling, of university, are such formative years. How you think about yourself and how you relate to other people are formed in high school and college. I reflect back on

258. https://www.linkedin.com/in/eesley/
259. https://twitter.com/annimaniac
260. https://www.floodgate.com/

my own days as a student; one of the magical pieces of being an engineer, and being at PhD programs in quantitative sciences, was that I had this opportunity to meet very diverse groups of people that I normally would not be friends with. This is really important as an experience. In college, I remember complaining to my mom that I was the only woman in most of my classes. My mom said to me, "Why does that even matter? Are you looking for friendship in your classes?" That was a turning point for me about the way I thought about this; I can form different kinds of relationships in different kinds of contexts. It turns out, I made great friends in undergrad with people who were very different for me. That became a skill set that I learned in college to forge those relationships.

The second thing is something that my husband taught me. He was in law school and, I remember, he realized he could not read all these things that he needed to read, so he had to create a study group really quickly. When he looked for his study group, he did not look for just people who he could be friends with, he looked for the smartest people in the room. When I looked at his group, it was an incredibly diverse group of individuals. It was the nicest guy in the room who was from Canada. It was another kid from Indiana who grew up on a farm. It was an Indian woman from Chicago. It was another woman whose lifelong desire was to become an activist for Latinx people. It was really interesting to see the diversity, but he was just picking off who he thought were the smartest people in the room. It taught me to learn how to work with other people, to recognize really incredible talent. That is a skill set. You should start to learn and exercise it when you are in college and are being encouraged to get out of your comfort zone.

The last piece that I would say is the reason why it is important as an educator to give students those experiences and to coach them into those experiences: it teaches students to think about the network effects of the actions that they take. I have always said, in hiring, you want to have these network effects. That is why you want to access these diverse talent pools, because if you only stay within your own talent pool, you are limiting the network effects that you have. Those are the exposures that you want to give to students, and I am excited by having those conversations with our students early on in their careers.

Chuck Eesley (CE): There are so many opportunities, but there are also so many challenges for universities indeed. I often think both about the teaching side and the research side slightly separate. On the research side, we have increasingly strong evidence, larger data sets, and more context that there are real benefits to diversity, but also more research about how homogenous both venture capital firms and startup teams tend to be. Due to both systemic racism and unconscious bias, we are really innovating with one hand tied behind our backs. If you look at engineering schools, the faculty and the students are not particularly diverse. There are real challenges to changing that. Business schools have this problem, as well as the university as a whole. There is a disconnect there, between what we see in the teams, faculty, and students, and what we know is more beneficial for innovation.

On the teaching side, there are three aspects. As the head of the committee that is working on this for our department, we think in terms of diversity, equity, and inclusion. Diversity, meaning, how representative are the people that we are putting up in front of the classroom as role models, and how representative of the country or the world are the students that are sitting there in the classroom. We have a bunch of initiatives [one example is SERGE[261]] that are trying to make a dent on that side of it. Inclusion means that everyone feels equally part of the community, that is, they feel included. Even if we make great progress on diversity and bring a more representative set of students and faculty to the university, if they are not happy and not having a good experience while they are here, then that is not going to last for very long. That is the inclusion and belonging piece of it. Then, the equity piece, making sure that those students all have equal access to the same opportunities, regardless of their background or their financial situation.

TACKLING THE FEAR OF ENTREPRENEURSHIP IN UNDERREPRESENTED COMMUNITIES

AM-K: When it comes to diversity, I am a co-director of a program called the Mayfield Fellows Program,[262] which is for 12 undergraduate students to get exposed to entrepreneurship and leadership. We are making a really big push this year to get many more students just to apply to the program from a diverse set of backgrounds. We have specifically targeted Black, Latinx, and low-income students. What has been interesting for me is that

261. https://engineering.stanford.edu/students-academics/equity-and-inclusion-initiatives/prospective-graduate-programs/stanford-exposure
262. https://stvp.stanford.edu/mayfield-fellows-program

there is not only a lack of awareness about the program, but also fear of entrepreneurship in many of those communities. Many believe that the lack of stability in entrepreneurship may be a risk that they cannot take. A lot of [the push] has been real targeted outreach to talk about the fact that, if you work at a startup, your salary is just as good as many of the other large companies. You just get the upside of equity, and if the company does not do well, that is actually okay. From a venture capitalist perspective, or a hiring manager's perspective, that is not seen as a blight on your resume.

That outreach, the inclusion, but also the knowledge sharing, are important, because as students go from being a student within Stanford, or any of these other universities, out into the real world, understanding what opportunities sit in front of them is hard to untangle. I take that really seriously as an educator; not just for the students who enter into the program, but that educational outreach into these communities to say, you actually belong here, we want your thoughts and your opinions. Your experiences are very relevant to entrepreneurship, to leadership. But more importantly, even if you are not part of this program, when you go out into the real world, you should know that these opportunities are not out of reach, they are not high risk, and that you should take them.

STANFORD'S RESPONSIBILITIES TOWARD DIVERSITY

EB: *Chuck, you are faculty in one of the programs that produces quite a few of the Silicon Valley engineers and entrepreneurs, the STVP program.*[263] *What kinds of responsibility do you, your department, and the university have to actively increase DEI? What specific measures are you taking at the moment to make sure that happens?*

CE: First of all, it is good to also take a step back and take a look at the big picture of the university system, and to put into perspective Stanford's specific responsibility. We have an important leadership role to play, as the major university in Silicon Valley. A lot of people look to us for best practices, for how to do entrepreneurship education. We set an important example in that role. That said, I am actually a lot more optimistic about the HBCUs, and Latinx serving institutions, and the community colleges that MacKenzie Scott, formerly Bezos is funding right now. I have a friend, Hadiyah Mujhid[§19.3] from HBCUvc, who is basically saying, "All this stuff

---

263. https://stvp.stanford.edu/

is perpetuated via networks. Those networks right now tend to be white male. We are just going to do a parallel thing to what Stanford has done for those rich white male students with HBCU universities, where we are not starting from such a low percentage of diversity in the first place."

When I look at the numbers, especially Black, Latinx, and low-income students that we are admitting into Stanford, we have got a long way to go to have appreciable numbers where we can really make a dent in Silicon Valley. Even if we can get them admitted into the university, funded, and into the classes that we teach, then getting them access to funding from VCs (who are over 90% white male) or from angel investors is a further challenge.

Stanford is also in a unique position in having such a big endowment and being one of the universities that allocates a fairly high percentage of that endowment to invest in venture capital firms. This is in fact another starting point: one of the things that I started working on earlier this year was, why does the endowment management company at Stanford have so many white males making the investment decisions, and why can they not invest in more diverse VC funds? I had a number of conversations with former members of the Board of Trustees, others that advocate for more diversity, and asset allocators. They say, "These funds are too new; they are too small for us to allocate significant capital to." These are all excuses. There are multiple levels to this, and that is why it is systemic. At one level, it's getting those endowments invested in a more diverse set of VCs, getting a more diverse population of angel investors that have experience to become those VCs, getting more diverse students admitted to the programs in the first place, raising more funding to provide financial scholarships to low-income communities.

The other big responsibility is teaching the content in such a way that it connects with diverse communities. That is along the lines of what Ann was referring to there, that it is not, you raise $50K from friends and family, and then you do not take a paycheck for a year and it's no problem. Then you reach out to all your wealthy angel investors in your network, and then you raise venture capital. Presenting the content with diverse perspectives, diverse role models, diverse mentors and judges up in front of the class, that is the other key responsibility. That is why we are excited to have folks like Ann as adjuncts and lecturers, as part of the program, and we need to further double down on those efforts to diversify the staff and the faculty.

THE INDIVIDUAL INSTRUCTOR'S ROLE IN DIVERSIFYING LEARNING

JL: *Looking back at what you have done so far, and forward to what you want to do, can each of you share a best practice when it comes to teaching and increasing D&I in the classroom and bringing people in? What should every instructor and teacher do differently?*

AM-K: This is a really critical question. One point that I wanted to make that Chuck was talking about: the change that you were mentioning that is needed is coming. You start to see it already, even with the Yale endowment, which sent out a letter to all of their managers asking for diversity numbers, driven by David Swensen, their CIO. He wanted those numbers. He has had those conversations with managers, and he is pushing them to make these hires. When a Yale endowment does that, because they are one of the leaders, you will see that actually reflected in the numbers. You will start to see more diversity.

The second other point was that in tech, it is not just at the pipeline issue, because I see this as an Asian woman. When you look at the senior levels of executives and board members, you do not see that many Asians at that level. That is not a pipeline issue, and I have talked about this to multiple people to just try to understand what is happening. If we say we are just going to solve it at one level and ignore the rest, we are not going to be able to get there. This comes back to your question of, what are tactics that we can do at the educational level in colleges?

First of all, in the classes that I teach, I am actually constantly revisiting the topics that I am uncovering. I am looking at the case studies that we use. I am looking at the guest speakers that we have. I am looking at the students that are represented in the class. I am looking at how we recruit the students. It is comprehensive in terms of looking at the class from various angles, and it is not just my own eyes, I am sending this out to other students that represent different pockets to say, "How does this look to you? Who else would you want to hear from?" I may not be able to incorporate it this year, but I am going to incorporate it in the future, and I am just trying to keep a living list of what I should be doing better. Not thinking about my course as a static thing that is optimal already, but that it needs to always be changing.

The second thing that I do think about from a venture capitalist perspective, and taking off my educator hat, is we actually run programs for different types of students. Most recently, one of my partners ran a building breakthroughs class that ran for ten weeks. It was what we taught at Stanford,[264] but we opened it up to Black entrepreneurs and Black students. We had fifty underrepresented minorities within this program. We could tell it was just the start. The quality of the applications that we were getting were mind boggling. Some of it is, what do we do within the confines of our university? There is a second order question: what can you do outside it? How can you use your megaphone to then bring others into the fold in ways that are now possible, because we have things like Zoom, and we are all sitting at home being able to educate others?

DIVERSITY INITIATIVES START WITH UNIVERSITY LEADERSHIP

CE: Bottom-up initiatives are always helpful, but the most important thing is people in leadership positions in the university have to talk about this, as a critical challenge and mission for the university to diversify in general, and diversified entrepreneurship programs in particular. If those university leaders, deans, and department chairs do not speak up about it and do not change the way that resources are allocated for new faculty hires or for adjunct lecturers or for funding students, then it is very difficult for those of us that are trying to do stuff from the bottom up to make a lot of progress. That is the most critical thing.

GETTING HELP FROM STUDENTS (AND COMPENSATING THEM)

CE: Tactically, we have hired a couple of RA [research assistant] students. Not asking for free labor, especially on the part of the affected communities, is really important. We hired a couple of master's students and they have helped us to make a ton of progress. They've helped with recruiting, such as running the MS&E [management science and engineering] department version of our SERGE graduate recruiting program. They've also been meeting with faculty to help diversify the syllabus readings and guest speakers. Recently, they've helped us to coordinate an undergraduate diversity in research program. Finally, they are helping with some literature reviews in this area of what works and what doesn't.

Relatively inexpensive RA positions have really infused us with a lot of energy in the department. They have been going around and setting up guides for faculty about how to diversify your syllabus, setting up networks of contacts for more diverse speakers, pestering faculty to meet with them to sit down for a half an hour and go through the syllabus, class session by class session. We have hit some resistance on that along the way. Faculty are very hesitant to have other people meddling with their course syllabi, but done in a sensitive, thoughtful way, we have gotten people to realize, "This is fairly painless, and nobody is going to yell at me, and I can make a few small tweaks and make some improvement in the experience for students."

JL: *Chuck, a last question for you: what do you think is a concrete next step you want to take to make your bit of entrepreneurship education more diverse and inclusive? What are your plans for the coming two years?*

CE: One concrete step is in hiring more diverse students as teaching assistants in our classes. In terms of plans for the coming two years, it's really focused on recruiting more diverse students and faculty to apply to the department.

15.6 *Harbach, Shu: Investor Education*

Jeff Harbach (Kauffmann Fellows)

Lisa Shu (formerly Newton Venture Program)

The default pattern-matching that skews the venture capital industry in favor of elite, white, male founders can as easily be ascribed to a lack of investor education, acumen, and skill as it can a lack of worthy pipeline or ability to source diverse deals. The apparent issue the industry has with the former is that it places the buck in the court of the LPs and GPs who are overlooking diverse talent, rather than on the diverse talent themselves, as has historically been the case. We were delighted to sit down with Jeff Harbach[265] and Lisa Shu[266] to learn how the Kauffman Fellows[267] and New-

---

265. https://twitter.com/jeffharbach
266. https://twitter.com/ProfLisaShu
267. https://www.kauffmanfellows.org/

ton Venture Program[268] *plan to disrupt the venture capital ecosystem by training the next wave of GPs to be more inclusive than those who have gone before them.*

Interviewed February 2021

CHANGING VC IS NOT ABOUT QUOTAS

Johannes Lenhard (JL): *VCs happen to be mostly white men with Stanford, Harvard, and Oxford degrees. Is that something you want to change with your respective organizations?*

Jeff Harbach (JH): At the Kauffman Foundation, the way that we think about diversity in venture is not about quotas. It's important to remember why the organization came about: we have long believed that in order to best understand the world's greatest challenges, the future of the VC industry must be diverse and more reflective of society as a whole. The Kauffman Fellows Program originated as an endeavor of the Kauffman Foundation, from which it was spun out in 2000. The Kauffman Foundation was started by Ewing Marion Kauffman, who cared a lot about two things: entrepreneurship and education. Since the early 1990s, the Kauffman Fellows have pushed to build a global fabric of smart, connected capital that will fuel entrepreneurs everywhere and support entrepreneurship as a catalyst for economic growth and social change.

We recognize that many people do come from Ivy League institutions, however we think about it in terms of how do we continue to be a catalyst in making sure the venture ecosystem is more inclusive, equitable, and reflective of society as a whole? Over the next 25 years, we think that the venture ecosystem will continue to be a catalyst in supporting high-growth entrepreneurship. One of the key ways we think that venture is going to evolve and continue to change is that venture as a vehicle for supporting entrepreneurs is going to be more easily adaptable to businesses that are solving the world's biggest problems in areas such as healthcare, education, food, water mobility, and energy, for example.

Due to Moore's law and Metcalfe's law, with technology getting faster and cheaper and people being more connected through technology than ever before, we will now be able to develop companies that are actually addressing some of the world's biggest problems that we have not been

---

268. https://newtonprogram.vc/

able to do in the past because of some of these limitations. If that is true, and we believe it is true, then we believe the entrepreneurs that are going to be launching companies that are solving those problems are going to be individuals that have experienced those problems. Those individuals are going to be more reflective of society as a whole. If we are not as a venture ecosystem also more reflective of society and [with experience in] those same issues, we will miss those opportunities, some of those category-defining, and frankly, world-defining companies that will be built over the next five, ten, twenty years.

For us, this is not about quotas—it is about making the venture ecosystem more reflective of society as a whole, because it cheapens the conversation when we talk about quotas. It enhances the conversation when we are truly talking about economic development, in terms of building companies.

Lisa Shu (LS): I have to echo Jeff in the notion that decisions made by VCs trickle down throughout society and who gets funding determines which of society's problems get solved. In its current form, venture excludes too many, and it serves too few. Newton has the explicit mission to make the venture landscape fairer, more inclusive, more representative of the population it serves. While we all agree that no one group has the monopoly on talent, overwhelmingly one group does seem to have a monopoly on power in the venture ecosystem. We take a quantitative approach with the Newton Venture Program in terms of looking at the investment landscape.

At the very top, we need to ask ourselves: who is in the rooms where decisions are being made, and who is left out of those rooms where decisions are made? We share the same ethos with Extend Ventures.[269] Through this quantitative approach, we measure who is not in the room, and we ask: how do we get those individuals into these rooms in order for more of society to be served? It is the representation that is so important to capture among the decision-makers at the very top of that ecosystem.

BEST PRACTICES FOR DEI IN VC EDUCATION

Erika Brodnock (EB): *How exactly are you tackling diversity, inclusion, and equity in your educational programs? Are you able to share a few of your best practices and initiatives?*

---

269. https://www.extend.vc/

LS: We set a very clear mission from the outset. Newton was incorporated in September 2020. Kaufman has 25 years of history ahead of us. Our vision is that by 2030, venture investors will be 50% people from currently underestimated and overlooked groups. Working backwards, what do we need to do to get there? In every cohort of Newton learners, we ensure that at least 50% of our learners are female, and at least 50% of our learners come from Black, minority ethnic, and other underrepresented backgrounds. We also focus at the top of the funnel to ensure we attract candidates who might not otherwise naturally see themselves as a venture investor. Most of us do not naturally see ourselves as a venture investor.

We were very specific in planning our content, in partnership with like-minded partners such as Colorintech and Black Tech Fest, to make sure that we build content on how to build a more inclusive venture ecosystem for investment. We communicate that this is for everyone; venture is for everyone—it should be for everyone. We also have to acknowledge our own decision-making biases. I have a background in behavioral science, with a PhD in judgment and decision making. We have to acknowledge that we all bring our biases to the table. We have to guardrail against that in our selection process. This is where the beauty of technology comes in to help us with this.

At Newton, we use Applied, which is a blind recruitment platform. We rate our applicants through a blind selection process—no CVs, no names, and no demographics are attached to any individual's application. We know the group demographics in terms of how they self-report—but we have no idea who's who, where they went to school, where they are employed, if they are employed, etc.—when we admit our applicants. We are radically transparent about how we do our selection. The radical transparency involves blinding ourselves from who we are actually admitting to our classes.

EB: *Will the use of Applied extend to how venture capital investments are made via the fund?*

LS: There has been some traction in that direction. I know the fund Blackbird VC (based in Sydney, Australia) selects founders to meet with based on this blind process. There are some indicators that more and more firms will use this blind selection process—either for their own hiring needs, the hiring needs of their portfolio companies, or deal sourcing.

JH: We have two things that we focus on with Kauffman Fellows, and we are developing more. The first is our core program. It does not necessarily focus on the top of the funnel, but it rather focuses on individuals that are in venture right now. The median fellow is a junior partner in their firm. Some are more senior partners, some will go down to maybe principal, but the average investing experience is five plus years. The average operating experience is more like ten plus.

Each year, Kauffman Fellows identifies and develops a new cohort of accomplished investors who attend the two-year program part-time while they are investing full-time. The Kauffman Fellows Network spans six continents, representing over 50 countries globally—and is nine times more diverse than the industry average. Each year, we intentionally recruit, build, and design the incoming cohort with diversity as our north star and driving force. We focus very much on who we select, and we want to involve ourselves with all the different communities of individuals that are not our standard, typical communities that are, for instance, my network as a white man. We focus on talking to all the different groups that are working on diversity and getting individuals that are working in the business.

One of the core beliefs that we have is that it is actually easier now than ever to get into venture. It is hard to stay in the industry beyond five years, and it can feel darn near impossible to stay in VC beyond ten years. The reason why is because to stay in the industry beyond ten years, you have to start returning capital to LPs. I hate to say it but your tenure in venture is not measured by how many blog posts you write or how many speaking gigs you do or any podcast you launch. It is measured on a spreadsheet and on how much capital you returned to your LPs.

Our goal is to ensure that we surround these individuals once they are already in venture, to help them succeed. One of the ways we help them succeed is to learn beyond the rate of their own experience. We do that in two ways. One is we understand that networks in venture matter. With the Kauffman Fellows Research Center, we did some analysis using a network betweenness algorithm that actually put numbers to strengths of networks. We did this not by using weak social media data, but rather, taking how closely people are connected with individuals that have worked together multiple times either on boards, executive teams, at venture firms, etc. If they have worked together multiple times, the strength of that connection becomes that much stronger.

If you have a top 1% network in venture, your average realized multiple is over 10X, if you drop down to a top 10% network, your average multiple drops down to a 6X, which is still great. If you drop down to a top 25% network, which is top quartile, your average realized multiple drops down to about a 2X, which is under the industry average realized multiple. What we do with Kaufman Fellows is we try to make sure that we surround these individuals with a diverse, trusted network of individuals that are going to help them succeed. What I mean by helping them succeed is helping them with due diligence, helping them think about their next LP conversation, or helping them with situations like bringing on a new partner to the firm. It is having that trusted expert network around them that will help accelerate their learning and growth. These pieces are critical to helping these individuals learn and grow faster than they would on their own.

The second at the top of the funnel is we have a program called Venture Deals. It is a free program that we have been offering for seven years now, most recently in partnership with Techstars. We run it in partnership with Brad Feld and Jason Mendelson from Foundry Group, and it is open to everyone. That is our way of saying, "If you are interested in venture, and want to learn more about the industry, either from the perspective of an entrepreneur, aspiring venture manager, or established manager, you can learn this through the Venture Deals course. It helps you shore up your knowledge about term sheets, diligence, and all the pieces around venture." That is how we think about it programmatically and it is the way that we approach DEI in the business.

The magic around any kind of conversation around DEI goes to getting a group of individuals together and creating what we call a brave space. It is not good enough just to have a safe place, but rather a brave space, where we are able to share all the messiness around this conversation. Having DEI conversations are uncomfortable, and they are hard. We all use different language. As a white man, am I supposed to say this? How do I recognize blind spots? How do I improve my knowledge and broaden my perspective on the things that I do not know? Those discussions are where we really think the magic happens. It is a best practice that anybody can do.

CONSIDERING CLASS AND SOCIAL MOBILITY IN VC

JL: *Let us address one specific area that is not talked about much in this space, which is class and social mobility. Supposedly, one even more so than* *the other is very expensive. Is that something that you think about, because it makes it harder for certain groups to participate?*

LS: Our programs are at different price points, but they are expensive for some. It starts at £2,000 for the digital program and up to £20,000 for the on-campus at London Business School program. In creating these programs, we wanted to ensure that inability to pay does not pose a barrier to entry, because there are already too many barriers to entry into the venture ecosystem. We are very lucky to have partnered for our initial cohort with founding sponsors who have underwritten 30 of the 60 spots for our first cohort, and we have lined that up for the next ten cohorts. It does not matter what the amount is; we do not want to add to the barriers into the venture ecosystem. We are explicitly eliminating it by partnering with like-minded partners, and the beauty of partnering with multiple sponsors is that you form this collective action. We have many different parts of the ecosystem engaged from all different fields, whether it is law or finance or government. It is really wonderful to see the collective movement building within the venture ecosystem. The more inbound requests I receive to sponsor a spot, the happier I am. It is about the number of firms, organizations, and individuals that we can mobilize towards collective action—even more so than the actual number of scholarships that we can deliver.

JH: Venture Deals is a free course for anybody that wants to take it. The core program that we have, which is a two-year program that is measured by nine different experiences or events, is $80K. Number one, we do not want this to be cost-prohibitive for individuals, especially those that are launching their first-time funds. When you are a first-time manager, and you are launching a $10M–$15M fund, and you have your GP commitment that you have to do as part of launching your fund, you do not have management fees and other cash flow to be able to pay for an $80K program. We understand that. We are aggressive in the way that we focus on scholarships.

The Kauffman Fellows Program is a non-profit with a tuition-based business model. Historically, we have granted scholarships almost entirely off of our own balance sheet. Over the last couple years, as we have increased the number of scholarships that we are giving, we have been grateful to individuals and organizations that have sponsored scholarships alongside us, allowing us to further increase access to our program.

This year, between KF-sponsored scholarships and partner-sponsored scholarships, we were able to provide almost $1M total in scholarship funds.

What we want to focus on is merit. We look for candidates with an entrepreneurial spirit, deep domain expertise, leadership potential, and an appetite for risk, ambiguity, and the unstructured environments that the innovation ecosystem requires. More important than these traits, however, are core value traits like integrity, humility, empathy, service orientation, and a deep sense of gratitude. All of these "behavioral fitness" components distinguish outstanding finalists from the pool of extremely capable nominees. We want people that we believe are going to have a long-term impact on this business. If the cost of the program is the only thing that is holding them back, we won't let this be a determining factor. We care a lot about there being access for all that are really on the path to making a long-term dent in venture.

HELPING UNDERREPRESENTED PEOPLE MAKE IT TO THE TOP

EB: *Are there any plans to create an emerging fund manager program that is specifically catered towards combating the issues where people from overlooked backgrounds tend to fail to progress to partner stage?*

JH: Yes. We are always looking for what we should be doing to support our mission of helping the venture ecosystem look more like society as a whole. If you just have an emerging manager program, then you're going to miss out on the important discussions that you get from having emerging managers, established managers, geographic diverse managers, and new managers all in the same room. We define diversity not just on the basis of gender and ethnicity, although those are two very important characteristics of diversity. We try to take a more inclusive position on diversity and view it through the lens of characteristics like gender, ethnicity, sector, stage, geography, and age to name a few. We want there to be an inclusive nature around all these discussions so that we are getting the value from seeing how different people are viewing this from different stages and different perspectives. I understand the purpose of an exclusive emerging manager program is to really make sure that we are focusing on the fact that oftentimes emerging managers or overlooked managers are not making it through that glass ceiling or making it to the partner level. We think that we are meeting that by seeing many of these new managers—especially over the last two, three years, and even at an accelerating rate over the last six months, based on what is going on in the US—becoming first-time managers, launching their own funds, getting to partner.

Our job is to make sure that they stay there. They are successful in that role, because that is ultimately the long-term vision for us. As of right now, while we are always open to new ideas, we are never going to get so set that we say no to something. As we measure this, and we think that we are not meeting the demand for the emerging managers that we think are out there, then we would either look at expanding the size of the class or starting a new emerging managers program. We have to balance that with our deep belief that it is not good enough to just have an emerging manager program, a Black VC program, or a women's only program. We need them to be part of the entire conversation, because that is the way that we are truly going to advance this.

LS: I agree. I have been heartened to see programs such as VC Include develop a BIPOC fellowship, specifically to target these overlooked groups. As we build out Newton's learning ecosystem, we have thought about what kind of custom programming we could develop for emerging fund managers. When you look at a cohort size of 60 individuals, and you look at the number of one-to-one relationships, that is 1,770 relationships. Take the perspective of a learner: who else is in the room with me? There's 60 people but 1,770 relationships; 1770 is the real denominator, because venture is not done in a vacuum. Who raises from whom, who co-invests with whom, who sources from whom—all involve multiple parties; there is no individual contributor in VC. If our mission is inclusive representation, I do not think that we can limit it to just specific groups.

GOALS AND CHALLENGES FOR THE FUTURE OF VC

JL: *What is your specific vision for the VC industry in five to ten years, and what do you think is the biggest challenge to get there?*

LS: We have a very specific vision that by 2030, venture investors will be 50% people from currently overlooked and underestimated groups. The biggest challenge that I see right now is: we can create the best investor training programs that £2,000 or £20K or $80K can buy, we can provide the supply of the most talented diverse pipeline into the venture ecosystem, but what we cannot control is the demand for this talent. The rate at which firms hire is very slow. That is changing and there is an unprecedented amount of capital in both private and public markets. There is a macro shift from public equity into private equity.

To truly change what is "market" in the VC industry, you have to shift the status quo and shift that towards equality by design, and not as a mere afterthought. It is not enough to just create this brilliant pipeline; they have to have somewhere to go. There are more stages than just attraction and selection of diverse talent; there is also retention, belonging, and promotion. It is that ten-plus year journey after your first fund, whether or not you can raise your second, whether your LPs commit to this vision, that is the piece that poses one of the biggest challenges.

JH: One of the major challenges that we face in venture is the reality that less than 5% of the industry ever cashes a carry check and that most venture managers are going to fail because most startups fail. Going from fund one to fund four and beyond is really hard. It does not matter what background or stage or anything else you come from. It is making sure all the energy that we have around wanting to see the venture ecosystem look more like society as a whole, sticks to signal and turns into a signal, and it stays. The staying power means we must help more of these emerging managers.

We have to spread the success beyond just the relative few. That is not democratizing returns, it is instead making sure that we are looking in places that typically have not been looked at and that the venture managers are looking at those types of companies, because they recognize them, because they also come from those backgrounds. The biggest tragedy that we would see is if all this energy put around supporting diverse and emerging managers ends up seeing little success coming out of there in five to ten years and ends up reverting back to the mean or where we have already been. It is hard because the people that are realizing success have been doing this for 20–40 years.

Another worry is anybody out there who views venture as the cool job or easy way to make money or trendy cool thing is kidding themselves. One of the very first questions that I ask any manager that wants to be in venture is, "Why do you want to do this?" What is driving you to want to be in venture capital when the trends would say that you are better off learning something about another industry before coming into making investment decisions, and then ultimately mentoring and coaching decisions for the people that are building companies in that industry? It isn't about where you get your experience, but it is about some sort of experience. It tends to mean that the more that you bring to the table, the more you are going to be able to both help evaluate and help those companies grow. That is tricky because we do not want to select only on education or experience. If we do that, then we end up reinforcing the biases that have been there in the first place. How do we make sure that we are supporting the individuals that are going to continue to drive more diverse outcomes, as opposed to just people getting in the business? How do we ensure we sustain this long term?

WHAT BUSINESSES NEED TO REACH ESCAPE VELOCITY

EB: *I have this analogy that if there is a fish and the fish is sick, if you do not change the water, the fish continues to be sick. This is the venture partners or emerging fund managers that are setting up new funds that are going to invest in new businesses, if we do not ensure that those businesses have a way of being successful, by potentially ensuring things like supply chain practices are changing. I have spent a lot of time thinking about what is needed to ensure that some businesses can reach escape velocity because once they do, the founders can become the LPs and even the GPs that are creating that cycle. We need to create one full cycle to do that. How would you say we need to go about ensuring that other pieces of the puzzle are in place so that it does not result in the failure that you just described?*

JH: I am not going to pretend like I have the answer to this. My initial reaction is that I get antsy around everybody thinking that venture is the most important piece of this puzzle. It is not the venture layer; it is a service layer. Let us just put things in perspective, venture managers come and go, the true heroes in our story are the entrepreneurs. They are the ones who are solving the world's greatest problems. They are the ones that are creating economic independence for many and are going to help solve these things from the supply chain all the way up and down, where we need systemic change.

From a venture perspective, we can help change that by overshooting the influence that venture has. I do recognize that there are power dynamics in all forms of life. That is where the power dynamic exists in venture is that between the entrepreneur relationship and the venture relationship, oftentimes the venture manager has more capital and they are perceived to have more power, because they have that checkbook. Any entrepreneur that has ever had a hot round or had their choice of venture managers would tell you that they really did possess the power in that dynamic. That power dynamic is only perception. It is not reality.

To think that venture can change all the systemic areas where we need change is overselling the impact of venture can have, and underselling the impact that the entrepreneurs can have. Do we play a role? Absolutely, but this is going to take all of us working and rowing in the same direction to ensure we are focusing on how things can change from the past, in order to succeed in the future.

You could not have imagined even ten years ago that Zoom would have the kind of impact that it has today, because of what we have seen in the democratization of technology. What do 2025, 2030 look like? Whether you are in NYC, Austin, or Johannesburg, it is going to look like having the same access to products and services because of this democratization through technology. We have to ensure our supply chains and everything up and down the stack are also representative of society as a whole. We all play a role in making sure that every part of this ecosystem is more reflective of society as a whole.

LS: I love the notion of the full-stack venture ecosystem. It brilliantly illustrates how so many pieces have to come together to enact systemic change. It starts with governments, with the tech transfer officers at universities, the R&D budgets that are invested into the innovation ecosystem. Then you have the LPs, the angels, accelerators, incubators, and the venture capitalists all working together. As the tide rises, all boats rise together. Every single piece of the stack needs to work together towards greater inclusion and belonging and representation in the ecosystem.

When we think about Newton's role in that, we think about who is not in the room: in our cohort of learners, we want to fully integrate pieces of the venture ecosystem. We are very explicit about including public servants. We are outreaching to civil servants to tell them, "You play a pivotal piece in the very start of this innovation economy." The decisions that governments make determine how big the pie actually is—not who gets a slice of it yet, just how big the pie can grow. Integrating the end-to-end venture ecosystem is a way for us to work together to get there faster.

15.7 *Wehmeier, Teare: Data Collection and Analysis*

Tom Wehmeier (Atomico)

Gené Teare (Crunchbase)

*Tom Wehmeier,[270] partner and head of research at Atomico,[271] and respon-
sible for the annual State of European Tech[272] report, and Gené Teare,[273]
Crunchbase[274] senior data journalist, discuss the role of data in improving
diversity in the tech and venture landscape. Taking the call for "more data"
among many investors seriously, we go into the details of what we already
know and how data can indeed drive change.*

Interviewed January 2021

WHY DATA MATTERS FOR D&I IN TECH

Johannes Lenhard (JL): *What role do you think data plays in moving the
needle on D&I in technology?*

Gené Teare (GT): Crunchbase was one of the organizations that led on
diversity data. From 2013 onwards, there was an active discussion around
female representation on engineering teams. In early 2015, we recognized
that with a global dataset of companies and founders in Crunchbase, we
could provide analysis on funding to female founders, and how that has
changed over time. In March 2015 we began to add gender to the data.
We analyzed personal pronouns to help with data analysis, getting to a
very comprehensive dataset within about two months, and wrote our first
report. That first report showed a big shift over that time frame. We found
that the percent of companies that had raised a first funding with at least
one female founder had increased from around 9% in 2009 to 18% by 2014.
Since then, we have continued to report how those numbers have shifted.

270. https://twitter.com/twehmeier

271. https://atomico.com/

272. https://2021.stateofeuropeantech.com/chapter/executive-summary/

273. https://twitter.com/geneteare

274. https://www.crunchbase.com/person/gene-teare

JL: *How important do you think this tracking is? What do we get from it in a secondary and tertiary process, as the tracking in and of itself doesn't change the needle, right?*

GT: For those concerned about funding to female founders, without knowing exactly what the numbers are, you could over-project, under-project, or misunderstand the trends. The numbers themselves do not shift the needle, but understanding the numbers does anchor the discussion. It also can lead people to act because they say, "Okay, this is worse than I thought it was," or "This isn't moving quickly enough, we need to do more." We have seen the data propel individuals to go out there and do something because they realize the numbers are not where they would like them to be.

Tom Wehmeier (TW): I agree. I think data assists in helping to understand the scope of the issue and the potential for solving it. If we are not familiar with the scope of the challenges that we face, we won't understand what levers we need to pull in order to shift the needle in the right way. I think data in general, whether it's around D&I or anything else, is such a vital component of telling stories and doing so in a way that is objective. In doing the work to source the data, then using that to drive a data-driven narrative is a really powerful mechanism to raise awareness to engage people and close those knowledge gaps. When measured over time, data enables us to track progress and hold different stakeholders accountable. The last piece is that it can be incredibly empowering. It becomes easier to speak up about when you have data to support and validate your experience. All of these things, when taken together, shape how data plays a role in helping various different individuals or organizations to try to move the needle in the right direction.

HOW THE STATE OF EUROPEAN TECH REPORT HAS CENTERED D&I

Erika Brodnock (EB): *Tom, you oversee the State of European Tech report yearly, covering funding and developments in the industry, as well as a large survey of more subtle attitudes among VCs and founders—including many questions on DEI. Why is the State of European Tech report such an important piece of work at Atomico?*

TW: I think it's a small contribution to the discussion. I look back to the first report we delivered back in 2015, and I think a very limited amount of data was focused around gender and diversity at the founder and operator level. Over subsequent years, we've grown the level of focus in the report. In 2018, we really doubled down the level of data, specifically pulling out and creating a chapter around diversity and inclusion. We also used that as the lead narrative into all of the media briefings following publication.

We are fortunate that over the years the report has become a high-profile piece of research that reaches a large audience of influential people—investors, founders, policymakers, LPs, and others. We have always been aware that it is a powerful tool and platform to influence the industry agenda. Take 2020 as an example, hundreds of thousands of people have engaged with the report;[275] 9,000 people attended the launch event. We rarely measure social reach, but beyond the launch itself, there was a huge amount of engagement too.

Given the reach and potential influence of our reports, we felt a sense of responsibility to put diversity and inclusion at the front and center of what we do. Some of the things we do as part of the research process gives us a means by which we can gather information and data about D&I that wouldn't otherwise be possible to collect at the scale that we can. Our survey, for example, features 5,000 voices from within the European tech industry. For multiple years now we have used that survey as a mechanism to collect interesting data around issues such as discrimination within the industry, or the extent to which companies that operate in the European tech industry are implementing different policies to drive positive progress around different aspects of D&I. Furthermore, we have some nice leverage in that when we have conversations with data partners that support us on the report, we can both ask them and push them to think through what data sets they might be able to share with their audience.

An incredibly important aspect is that it is a free report. It is open to anyone and each data point is exportable. The raw data, the charts, everything. This has been very deliberate, because we want it to be used as a resource that can be reused and recycled to create a compounding reach. It is a resource for anyone who wants to advocate for change. It has been great to see just how much people have taken that on, including the media. There are more than 500 media articles that we have tracked over the years that have a specific focus on D&I that reference back to some of the data in our reports.

---

275. This interview was conducted in January 2021.

However, we are still far from having anything close to all the answers, there are still mega hurdles in terms of collecting information about the state of what is happening. It is sobering to think that there might be people out there who think that what we do goes beyond what others do. Yet internally, we are there thinking this is only 5% of what it should be. It is amazing that we have people like Gené, with Crunchbase, who have for many, many years now been looking to address this too. As the diversity discussion has evolved beyond gender, Crunchbase has been at the forefront looking at ways to paint a clearer picture with data on different aspects of diversity.

COLLECTING THE DATA WE NEED TO DRIVE CHANGE

JL: *Gené, what do you think is the most important data that we can collect to change the landscape? Give some examples of things that you have already found and dive into some of the results.*

GT: At Crunchbase, we track companies as soon as they first raise funding, and then they start showing up on our reports. What is critical is that Crunchbase is an open platform that founders can access, to add themselves and their early funding rounds and become a visible part of the ecosystem.

In 2020, we added race and ethnicity to the dataset for the US market as part of our Diversity Spotlight data. People had been asking us over the years to look at the data with a race and ethnic lens. We had previously thought this was too difficult to address as race and ethnicity is sensitive data, and the meaning of race varies in different parts of the world. People would need to self-report at scale for it to be meaningful. We took the decision that, as a global database, it was too challenging.

In 2020, specifically in response to Black Lives Matter, we decided to add race and ethnicity to the data. We started with the US market, as it is a leading funding market. The process we went through for this data was interesting; we partnered extensively to get feedback and collect the data with organizations active in the Black and Latinx community, as well as investors. We worked with organizations such as the Black Founder List, Black VC, Stanford Latino Entrepreneurship Initiative, and All Raise, and the venture community.

After updating companies that were started by Black or Latinx founders, our findings confirmed what many were saying. "Within the US the funding to Black and Latinx founders is low, we think it's 1%, we think it's 2%"—everyone was collating their own datasets and coming up with those findings. We thought, given that Crunchbase has all this data, when we build it out we can do a comprehensive job and possibly show improvement on these stark statistics, whilst recognizing that we will miss some companies that will be added over time. What we found is that funding to Black founders was around or just under 1% over the last five years. When we looked at Latinx founders, that number was just under 2%. However, if you look at those two communities, Latinx make up 18.5% of the US population based on the US Census Bureau, and the African American community came in at 13.4%.

What's meaningful for us is that having worked with these partners, they don't need to recreate the dataset. They can take the Crunchbase data to then inform their own reporting on these issues.

EXPANDING TO EUROPE

EB: *I work with Extend Ventures, and we have published similar reporting for the UK. We are really interested in looking at the numbers across Europe. Do you have plans for that?*

GT: Yes, we would like to explore expanding our diversity data to Europe. For Diversity Spotlight we tag companies, not individuals, with "founded" or "led" based on race or ethnicity. By "led," we are focused on the CEO role at a company.

HOW RESEARCH TRANSLATES INTO PROGRAMS

EB: *Tom, how has Atomico used the research findings to enhance its thesis? What are the particular programs and investments that you're making now?*

TW: Atomico's founding thesis back in 2006 was, "Great companies can come from anywhere." And that is what we have learned. We have spent more time understanding the industry issues around D&I, that "anywhere" really means "by anyone in any location." The more we have spent time understanding this, the more it has reinforced and strengthened our conviction in that initial thesis, specifically, our resolve to back underrepresented talent in tech. It has been really influential in helping rethink every aspect of what we do, in terms of how we invest, also how we think about building our team as a fund.

To highlight a few specific initiatives that have directly come off the back of the work that we've done around D&I: we run an angel program and are launching our third cohort of angels. The first cohort was run in 2018. The primary motivation was to play a role in building a more diverse universe of early-stage angel investors in Europe. Assessing the numbers, we can see that, significantly greater than 90% of all angels and significantly greater than 95% of all investments involve white male angels, and so right from the outset of that program, D&I was embedded. Across the first two cohorts, 60% of the angels were women and 25% came from an underrepresented ethnicity. One of the core beliefs we held was, if we brought a more diverse set of people into the program, they would go back and invest into a more diverse set of founders. That group of 30 or so angels have made 150 investments across two years; 64% of those investments had a founder from either an underrepresented gender or ethnicity. It has been rewarding to see how research translated into a thesis, that translated into a direct initiative, that is now translating into amazing results in terms of helping to drive allocation of funding to a more diverse set of founders.

Ultimately, this is a long-term initiative for us, because our hope is very much that those companies that get backed with angel investments will mature and develop to become the next the companies that we back from our core fund. Also, from that program, the deals that we do are a direct reflection of the network that we maintain. It is therefore critical for us to ensure that we have a diverse network ourselves; inherent in getting to a more diverse network, is building a more diverse internal team. This has been reinforcing how we think about driving diversity into our investment team, as a direct means of driving more diversity into the investments that we make.

Some of the research we did highlighted the industry's dependency on warm introductions and the barriers to entry and blocks to network diversity this creates. Understanding that warm intros form a barrier to more diverse ways of capital allocation led us to roll out our Access Atomico[276] program. We scaled a program that runs permanently and allocates time from every member of our investment team to be available for people to apply to directly.

---

276. https://atomico.com/insights/access-atomico

More broadly, research has shown there is a lack of diversity at the GP layer in Europe at the early stages, which are formative moments for any young company gaining its first institutional check. That is problematic for us as a Series A investor, because clearly the companies that flow through to us are a reflection of the companies that get backed by the funds that invest before us. We created an initiative off the back of some of those insights to basically run a small fund-of-funds program. We are now making LP commitments to early-stage emerging fund managers with a clear focus on investing in underrepresented founders.

TURNING THE TIDE OF WARM INTRODUCTIONS

EB: *Tom, how are you selecting the angels? If the angels are selected from a warm introduction style network, surely that kind of perpetuates the problem, so is it open?*

TW: We start by going through our network to find candidates to go to our shortlist. We then leverage the network of the angels already on the program to make recommendations too. Though I would say that they are sought-out recommendations from our network, we are thoughtful in who we go and ask to supply those introductions to ensure that that field of people is diverse. There is also then the opportunity to openly apply. We have also been proactive in a data-driven way, to identify a potential diverse pool of candidates that we have reached out to ourselves, because we thought that they might represent interesting candidates for the program.

The search for potential angels has actually highlighted another problem that is not just at the founder level. Essentially, when you look at the founder level, then you look at the senior executive level across venture-backed startups, there is very high lack of diversity at that specific level. That matters given what we know about the flywheel of how those people go on to become the next generation of founders, and in having that profile. If you cannot break that lack of diversity at the senior executive level too, it just becomes cyclical and really hard to break.

FACING THE NEXT SET OF CHALLENGES

JL: *Where do you think we need more data for the future? Crunchbase started collecting data on women eight years ago, and on ethnicity relatively* *recently. What do we not yet know enough about, and what is another frontier that we can help push with data?*

GT: I spoke with BBG Ventures founders Susan Lyne and Nisha Dua, who focus on investing in consumer technology companies with a female founder. One of their findings is that their incoming deal flow in 2020 during COVID-19 for female founders increased. We spoke with other funds focused on female founders and confirmed this finding. That contrasts with our most recent report, demonstrating funding in 2020 to female-only founded companies was down, tracking closer to 2% than the previous year's 3%. That is concerning. We also cite a McKinsey report, which mentions 30% of working mothers may leave the workforce due to COVID-19. The concern at this point is: are we going to see stagnation or a step backwards for women in the workplace?

Tom, your point about the lack of diversity in the senior leadership level is an indicator that the next set of founders might not be as diverse as we expect. From my perspective, looking at the data in 2014, 18% of companies with an initial funding had at least one female founder. This includes female-only and female/male co-founded companies. The numbers have shifted a couple of percentage points to about 20% of companies in recent years. We haven't seen the same leap in the last five years that we did in the previous five years.

However, absolute funding has gone up considerably. In 2016, total global funding was around $170B. In the last three years, funding has almost doubled, closer to $300B per year on a global basis. Based on percentages, the pace of change has been slower. From an absolute number of companies founded by a woman and from an absolute number of dollars, however, the counts and amounts have grown compared to the previous five years.[277]

Tom made a point about networks being incredibly important. All Raise, which supports female founders here in the US, were concerned during COVID-19 that video conferencing doesn't quite replace the traditional networking function. The fact that people can't meet at events

---

277. Obviously, this trend has changed slightly since this interview; as Crunchbase reported, funding for female founders dropped dramatically in 2020[278] and again even further in 2021.[279]

278. https://news.crunchbase.com/venture/global-vc-funding-to-female-founders/

279. https://news.crunchbase.com/startups/
something-ventured-blockbuster-venture-investment-female-founders-funding-falls/

serendipitously, they feel, has impacted women because networks are incredibly important in this business.

TW: I agree. The things that would be most impactful is just building a more comprehensive coverage of some of the research and initiatives that we are already undertaking, whether that is building out coverage across regions, for gender or ethnicity. Also, being able to comprehensively map and understand the full lifecycle of a company. Not just in terms of their investments, but also be able to comprehensively look at things like exits and returns and IPO pathways. I think we need to be able to connect all of those different dots through the lens of gender or through the lens of ethnicity, and to start putting even more data on the table around the relative performance and returns from different founder groups. We are probably still at a point where we will still find amazing datasets that emerge from this level of research, but often, it's snapshots in time. I would love to have continuous longitudinal time series data across some of these areas that offers deeper coverage—then we would be in a really powerful position to tell the real story of what is happening.

But I would just say that every incremental 10% of improvement in the data that does exist is to be celebrated. It is not about trying to get to 100%. Every incremental report helps and is a valuable contribution to how we will eventually be able to create lasting and systemic change.

15.8 *Lewin, O'Hear: Tech Journalism and DEI*

Amy Lewin (Sifted)

Steve O'Hear (Zapp, formerly TechCrunch)

Media and journalism have always played an important role in agitating and facilitating the narratives, conversations, and movements that lead to change. Where DEI is concerned, we need to create systemic change at a variety of levels. This will only be achievable with sustained storytelling. Smart, sophisticated, strategic communication skills are essential for presenting a narrative in which systems are seen as open to change, controllable, and redesignable. We chatted with the tech journalists Amy Lewin[280] (Sifted[281]) and Steve O'Hear[282] (formerly TechCrunch[283]) to learn more broadly about diversity in journalism, as well as the perceived responsibilities of journalism in creating greater levels of diversity in the venture capital industry.

Interviewed March 2021

DIVERSITY IN THE JOURNALISM INDUSTRY

Erika Brodnock (EB): *Tell us about your world, tech journalism, and the issues around discrimination, equity, and diversity that you perceive to be there.*

Amy Lewin (AL): The journalism industry as a whole is not very diverse. Look at the number of editors of big publications that are women or people of color. Historically, tech journalism has been male dominated, especially on the gadget and big tech company side of things. I am very proud

---

280. https://twitter.com/amyrlewin
281. https://sifted.eu/about/
282. https://twitter.com/sohear
283. https://techcrunch.com/

of the fact that at *Sifted*, we are nine women and six men on our editorial team—and these are regular editorial contributors. It boils down to access to the opportunities you need to have to get into the industry in the first place. People need to have done an internship or several to get into journalism. Most media publications are based in London, if we are talking about the UK. It is not cheap to do an internship in London, as many of them are unpaid. The standard problems with diversity that you find across many industries are also present in journalism, which is partly the reason why we have the status quo as it is.

Steve O'Hear (SO): When I first entered the industry, I was taken aback. It was very stereotypical, with male journalists going to press events hosted by female PRs. I'm not sure that much has changed in gadget and consumer tech journalism. In the world of tech business journalism, however, the gender balance has slowly improved over the last decade. I am not sure it is so bad now in terms of regular reporters, but it gets worse as you go up the hierarchy, as is the case in many industries. Journalism is still heavily private-educated, Oxbridge, middle- to upper-class dominated to this day. That is strange, because in digital media, the proof is in the writing. I always tell other young journalists, if you want to be a journalist, just start writing.

EB: *Given how few people at Oxbridge are diverse in terms of ethnicity, social status, or socioeconomic class, what are your thoughts on diversity of that nature in journalism? Is there anything that could be done around tech journalism to open doors so that new people come to the fore?*

AL: Many internships are not being paid and most people need to come to London to do them. There is a great organization called PressPad, which got some money from Harry and Megan (the Duke and Duchess of Sussex) this week [in 2021]. They help people find accommodation while they are doing internships so that they can get the experience they need to break into the industry. We need media publications to be paying interns the London living wage, at the very minimum. We also need more examples of best practice around internship schemes. I run our internship program and every single time, I want the people who apply to it, and the people who are interviewed, and the people we select to be as diverse in all these different areas as possible. I still am clearly not spreading the word in the right places to get as diverse a pipeline of candidates as I would like, although we are getting a good mix. I would love to be able to speak to other people who run these schemes, who can say, you need to share it in these places or connect with this community. I do a lot of that legwork, but I know there is so much more to do. The answer is not easy to find. There is not a long list that says, "Contact these people, share it in these places."

EB: *There is also a disconnect from people to communities that have historically been overlooked where they do not know who to reach out to. There is this gulf in the middle that needs to be filled.*

SO: There is a pipeline problem, and it is hard to reach parts of society that you do not reach through your existing network. Journalism is terrible because there is an even worse hypocrisy. Journalists increasingly write about diversity and are supposed to be bastions of objectivity. Yet journalism is not made up of the people it serves, so how can it report on the important stories and/or in a representative way? How can it find the hard-to-reach stories if it cannot even find the hard-to-reach aspiring journalists?

EB: *Is there pushback on the fact that there is a pipeline problem? Are we suggesting that there are not enough good journalists graduating, or are they not graduating from Oxbridge and therefore not given the opportunity?*

AL: You do not need a degree from a red brick university to be a journalist. That is not a problem. A lot of journalists are very lazy when they are recruiting, and they will just email City University, which is the gold standard of journalism. They will say, "Anyone on your courses want our internship?" This is not the answer. You do not need a degree; you just need a passion for writing and to be really nosy.

JOURNALISM'S RESPONSIBILITY AND IMPACT IN TECH AND VC

Johannes Lenhard (JL): *Let us shift our views slightly away from journalism as an industry that has its own problems towards what tech journalism can do with diversity more generally in the venture world and in the technology startup world. Do you think there is a certain responsibility that journalists have with the DEI agenda, and a responsibility to advance this? What can you do as a journalist? Do you see that space for you?*

SO: One of the main reasons for journalism is to hold power to account. In any inequitable society, that means the power is concentrated with the privileged and not with the many. Tech journalism has a responsibility to hold diversity of companies and investors to account. I don't say this out of some sense of doing good. It is basic 101 journalism. At *TechCrunch*, we had a reporter that focused almost exclusively on diversity and inclusion. At the same time, we also had an editorial direction, which is that for any news story, we will consider the D&I angle. It is not just a separate topic.

AL: I see this as my responsibility and *Sifted*'s responsibility. I was the first employee at *Sifted*. Right from the start, I have tried to ensure that we focus on this and we do what we can to represent the startup ecosystem that we would like to see in our reporting. There is still a long way to go with that. It partly comes down to the criteria for inclusion that publications have. If your number one criterion is how much money has this company raised, then inevitably, you will not be featuring a very diverse set of founders. You have to change your criteria for inclusion. We focus a lot on what we call startup life, including hiring or organizational processes. Everyone has those kinds of jobs, and there is a much broader pool of people you could speak to, if you are writing about mental health at startups or about hiring and firing challenges. That is one practical method other publications can use if they realize that they are struggling to speak to diverse voices. You need to think about the reasons that you are not speaking to them in the first place, and do those barriers need to be there. There are other things you can do for events, such as making sure at the very least you have a "no manel" policy, meaning you must have a panelist who is a woman. If you want to go even further, include somebody who is underrepresented in another way on the panel. If you feel that you are struggling to find a woman for your panel, then your publication has issues, and you need to widen your network and range of sources. As Steve said earlier, you are not doing a very good job of reporting on what is out there if your network is in that state.

EB: *You both have done a huge amount of work with your writing and raising awareness around important topics, some of them with the D&I steer. Are you content with the impacts that you have? What, if anything, is missing to make you feel as though you are making a difference?*

SO: Do I make a difference? I don't spend too much time thinking about that, as it is hard to quantify. I get lots of lovely feedback, which can just boost someone's ego. Where journalists need to double down on making a difference is in two areas. There is a creep towards sort D&I washing, similar to greenwashing, whereby people exaggerate the company's D&I efforts or progress, because you get an incredible amount of PR. I find that at times disingenuous, and slightly creepy. For example, I am not sure that the first thing I want to read in a press release about a potentially amazing company is the D&I credentials of the team. I am going to judge the company on their product or the market they are attacking. That is what I do every day. PRs will come in where they have almost weaponized D&I, which I think is something to watch out for. The second thing that I struggle to grapple with is that the D&I agenda as a whole has fallen into a trap of importing US identity politics, which is quite easily hijacked by people that want to fight a culture war. I do not see coverage of D&I that starts with, why is it important to have a diverse and representative workforce? I would suggest that in a more traditional British progressive politics context, it is about social mobility as much as anything, which is making use of all the talent in society. It is about removing barriers so that talent can come through.

AL: *Sifted* is a place where people know they can find stories on D&I. However, we have not figured out how to make people care about diversity who do not already care about diversity. Often, I feel that we are sharing information with the people who already know it. I do not know how much we are changing hearts and minds or getting information to people who really need to think about this topic. More generally, we need more data. So often, you are writing a piece and you want to go and find stats on what is the percentage of founders who are x or what is the percentage of investment that went here. It is there for gender and it is coming for ethnicity in the UK, but not in Europe. As Steve said, then when you get to socioeconomic background, there is nothing. It is almost completely homogeneous—so many people who have been to private school, Oxbridge, and worked at an investment bank or consultancy. It is utterly ridiculous that a sector that only requires you to have a laptop to get started is full of people who have had such privileged upbringings. It does not need to be this way.

SO: The debate has largely been framed around identity politics, so it is not really surprising that socioeconomic status was not mentioned until about two years ago. If you start from a progressive position of wanting to advance social mobility, you would not miss that at all.

JL: *Social mobility is still not talked about very much. We made a specific point of having a conversation about socioeconomic class with an LP and GP, and the Americans do not recognize class in the same way Europeans do. There is still a distinct focus on gender and not much else in VC and LP conversations. In France, we cannot actually ask about ethnicity. In America, they do not think about social mobility.*

BRINGING INTERSECTIONALITY INTO VC REPORTING

EB: *At Extend Ventures, we showed that you are able to capture demographic information. One of the things that we found was that 42% of the money that is invested at seed stage goes to graduates of Oxbridge, Harvard, and Stanford. There is a flywheel that has been created. The thing that is overlooked is intersectionality and what it means to be four of the traits, such as if you are Black, trans, female-presenting, and working class. What could be done in terms of bringing that intersectionality to the fore, as well as raising the issue of social mobility and class?*

SO: VCs, especially in Silicon Valley, used to talk a lot about this notion of pattern matching. When you think about pattern matching on a personal level, that is almost confirmation bias meets unconscious bias, and within VC is promoted as a feature not a bug. I do not know how you deal with intersectionality in the context of pattern matching! Within journalism, you should also be making sure that you work hard to reach out to people that are not always featured. You should also focus on not just what you write but also the images that you publish, and other ways of making sure you do not miss the opportunity to represent the ecosystem fully.

AL: I do not have a good answer on intersectionality, either, but a lot of this comes down to journalists working harder. We need to ask more nuanced questions. If an investor says their team is 40% women, ask, is that the investment team? What percentage of your team are university educated? What percentage of your team have previously worked at a consultancy or an investment bank? Every time someone presents you with a stat, dig into that a little bit more. Continue to widen your network. Go to events, join Slack communities for people of color or women in tech. Use Twitter. There are many ways you can find different voices. When you are in a more senior position, be the person at your company who champions this, taking it upon yourself to educate other people or to share resources with other people so that they can get a better grasp of these issues. Make that part of the culture of your whole organization.

SO: It is really important to explain why it matters, not just that it does matter and how it is not happening. If the technology industry is not made more accessible to every part of society, then we are missing out on so much talent. We will all lose. It is not just about saying, "We need more diversity." It is going back to basics and saying why. As journalists, if we are not covering enough underrepresented groups, we are not giving them the same access to amplifying their mission or message, and we all lose out.

16 Conversations: The Power of LPs and Policy Makers

16.1 *Spencer, Henig Shaked, Tan: LPs and DEI*

Monica Spencer (formerly Mellon Foundation)

Darya Henig Shaked (WeAct Ventures)

Savitri Tan (Isomer Capital)

Many GPs cite LPs as being the real decision-makers, and therefore the "king-makers" of the ecosystem; they are the ones who stir the wheel in one direction or the other. Does this also hold true in respect of DEI? We sat down with Monica Spencer[284] (Andrew W. Mellon Foundation,[285] NYC), Darya Henig Shaked[286] (WeAct Ventures,[287] SF), and Savitri Tan[288] (Isomer Capital,[289] UK) to discuss findings against the "trade-off myth."

Interviewed January 2021

GPS AND LPS: WHO SETS THE RULES FOR DEI?

Johannes Lenhard (JL): *Let me start with a strong provocation from the research that I have done with venture capital investors. A lot of them, when I asked them about decision making and why they are doing certain things and not others, they said "Oh, it's the LPs"—so people like you three—that set the rules. How true is that when it comes to DEI?*

---

284. https://www.linkedin.com/in/monica-spencer-02b353/

285. https://mellon.org/

286. https://twitter.com/DariaShaked

287. https://www.wonderventures.com/

288. https://twitter.com/savitritan

289. https://isomercapital.com/

Monica Spencer (MS): My immediate reaction to that is: have they asked? I do think that things may not be priorities on the agenda because people are assuming they know what other people think, but have not actually taken the time to explore it. One of the things over time that we have worked hard in our conversations and in our work to address is this idea that maybe there is a trade off, and that managers feel they have to compromise investment results in order to accomplish a DEI goal. It has been very much the bedrock of our position to say that broadening the opportunity set, both theoretically, and in our experience, leads to better returns. Having more diversity around the table mitigates risks in helping teams to make better decisions and to identify issues proactively that might not be identified if they had a more monochromatic team. That is a very fundamental difference of view to what some folks used to say. As more and more people are talking about diversity and inclusion, they are realizing that there may be assumptions about what their counterparts think that are not quite accurate.

Darya Shaked (DS): The responsibilities of GPs and LPs to lead the venture industry into action, in this case, into a more diverse and inclusive social fabric and thus to better financial outcomes, is a complicated issue. I personally see it as a high priority and a mutual responsibility and believe it will take both groups of us to create enough pressure, to lead an accelerated change. Diversity in venture has historically improved in 1% more women for every decade and we can't afford waiting 400 years to achieve equality.

I also know that many in the industry tend to act only when pressured or when they feel at risk. a female GP told me that the only time she was ever asked about anything DEI-related by an LP, was in a board meeting, when a very young guy around a table of experienced men and women LPs, around the rise of the #MeToo movement, asked: "Am I going to be embarrassed by anything that is going on in your fund, which I invested the state's money in?" That was the first and only time that question was raised in her career. First, I felt bad for the women around the table that never had the courage or felt secure enough to raise a question in that sense, and I believe that is now much more common. Secondly, I realized that VC D&I actions started in Silicon Valley due to a liability concern, raised from LPs, and not as part of understanding their responsibility to maximize returns. So, we see LPs have an impact just by raising the question. Once LPs realize that the homogeneity problem is not only a liability issue but is also translated into the funds' financial bottom line, I believe they will be more outspoken about fulfilling their and GPs' responsibilities to avoid missing financial opportunities due to lack of diversity in the decision-making team.

I started my journey with the goal of pushing the industry into a more equal one, to make the industry more diverse from its original 90% male GPs and ~99% of capital managed by men. I believed that change had to start at the top. It is unfair and inefficient to leave this problem to struggling founders to solve. In 2018, I decided to start a fund of funds to become an LP, raise funds, and invest in the best and most promising diverse VC founders. I believed that once LPs raise the questions, GPs would have to act. We know now that when all criteria are similar, diverse VCs outperform.[290]

From what I see of the very few women who were able to make it onto the Midas List of the world's best 100 venture capitalists, they outperform because they attract a wider range of opportunities, they collaborate better, they evaluate opportunities differently, and they create added value in a wider scale, which is different than the majority of VCs. The women who made it to the top are inherently much better, and I decided to raise money and invest in female venture capitalists who left the biggest name VCs, such as Accel and Kleiner Perkins, to start their own funds, they will be over motivated and most equipped to outperform the previous fund; they will invest in a wider range of founders, and they will create a different story. It is a much bigger story, with more financial potential. Having more women starting new funds, diversifying the industry, and making innovation more inclusive will create more female success stories, more role models, and more money (and confidence) in HNW (high net worth) women.

I agree that LPs should be, as a first step, asking the right questions. We should be moving from a liability question to grabbing the financial opportunity that is left on the floor, still. When you talk to LPs, who are independent thinkers, family offices, or high-net-worth individuals, they are much more inclined and have strong conviction in the advantages of D&I focused investments, and are taking steps to enforce that thesis. The problem is still with institutional LPs who are slower and late adopters. I

---

290. https://hbr.org/2018/07/the-other-diversity-dividend

see the non-institutional LPs making that progress and leading the way in creating that change.

Savitri Tan (ST): I think you're right, Johannes, many GPs do make certain decisions because of an LP's influence, but that makes things sound very passive. I don't think GPs only do something about D&I when an LP tells them. When it comes to D&I in Europe and pushing forward the agenda to a) invest more diversely, and b) to have more diverse investment teams, I believe that some of these decisions are motivated by the interests of some partners in VCs and junior members of their firms, who have really been motivated to band together, highlight D&I issues, and create data-driven reports to show the status quo when it comes to D&I. I'm thinking of Diversity VC, which was set up in 2017–2018 to highlight D&I gaps in VC. I believe it now has a chapter in the US.

I think it's important to look at a few areas to assess D&I: the first two are a little subtle, and the final one is direct. It's important, during initial meetings, to spend time digging into team background, plans for growth, and how the partnership thinks about who and which skills to hire for. As an LP in early-stage managers, in the same way a VC may invest in a pre-seed founder, you are making an investment based on potential, thought process, and confidence to build effectively and attract different backgrounds and opinions around the table to make what already exists more robust. The second is in scrutinizing the VC's decision-making process, how they evaluate companies and founders, and where they look for dealflow. It's also important to ask direct questions to the VC. I think that many LPs, even institutional ones, may ask questions about D&I, but to work and make a conscious effort towards making a difference, this "question asking" has to be systematic and part of the process. Isomer is a 50:50 male to female ratio, we are a mix of different nationalities, span a wide age spectrum, speak a number of languages, and all had different career routes into becoming an LP, so asking questions around D&I may come more naturally.

THE "DEFAULT TO YES" APPROACH

Erika Brodnock (EB): *Monica, we were really impressed with your "default to yes" approach to all of the diverse managers that contact you. What has your experience of operating in that way been, and do you know of any other LPs that are doing similar things?*

MS: It is enormously time-consuming, but it is also very generative, and certainly has opened up a new network for me and has led to a number of lessons for us in our investment process. For context, our mandate on diversity extends primarily to underrepresented minorities, which as defined in the US Census data is Black, Latinx, and Native American. That is a particular focus of our diversity initiatives and of our "default to yes" approach to meetings with GPs. I do not think that anyone on our investment team intentionally imposes barriers—"Oh we only want established funds, we only want funds run by white men." We're understanding the implications of some of the traditional checklist items, such as: What do you expect your GP to commit to the fund? How do you think about how they are going to finance the startup expenses of the firm, and a GP commitment, if they do not come from a background where they were a successful partner at an established firm before they start the fund? Thinking through things like that, thinking through who are like-minded investors.

I do feel an extraordinary momentum building here, and where we had this "default to yes" approach starting a couple of years ago on new managers, there are now many other groups who are taking a similar approach. I was on a call a week ago with a bunch of endowment and foundation investors specifically interested in meeting diverse managers; there were 160 limited partners on that call. More and more people are eager to build a network here, because it aligns with their values, it aligns with their program goals, it aligns with pressure they may be feeling from stakeholders. A lot of groups are very eager to identify new managers. The tricky part is many endowments and foundations, and many of my peers are highly selective. I may have a "default to yes" on the initial meeting, but I am not going to have a "default to yes" on committing the capital. How can we be helpful to all of those managers that we are meeting with, in order to build capacity in the sector generally, even while we maintain being pretty selective with our investment program? It is a huge help to have a network of 160 limited partners who are interested, because part of the value that we can provide in those meetings is just listening to the managers tell their story, understanding where some of our traditional metrics and approaches might be unintentionally narrowing the aperture for new groups, but also helping them think about what their story is, and helping them craft a story that is going to be appealing to prospective investors. The other part we can do is to further introduce them to other LPs, and knowing what other groups are eager to build capacity makes the introductions that much more valuable.

EB: *My follow-on question on your approach, Monica, is whether there are specific things LPs need to abolish to stop emerging fund managers that are also diverse from being unable to raise?*

MS: I do not know that I would say there is a particular metric I would abolish. I do think that there are reasons why these have been established over time as good markers for important qualities you are looking for in a manager, but you have to go back to first principles and say, "Okay, why do I care about the GP commitment?" I want to know that the general partner is aligned with me, and that they are more focused on delivering investment return than capturing fees, and current income, right? I want them to be focused on generating gain over income, because that is what my priorities are. That is what the GP commitment is reflective of. Rather than saying, I need a hard and fast number for that, or I need it to look a certain way, I go back to first principles and say, "Okay, how can I understand the motivations of this new group?" That they are aligned with me, and that they are mostly focused on generating gain, and they are not focused on their own current income. You just have to think of a different way to answer the question. There is another example, when you think about follow-on financing for venture-backed companies. If you are early stage, a lot of the markers of success are who came in after you. If you are early stage, and you focus on diversity of founders, it is much more difficult for those companies to get follow-on financing. This is well established in the literature. What other metrics are you going to use to understand the success of those companies, if the founders for a variety of reasons, largely related to systemic bias, have had trouble raising funds? Again, you have to go back to first principles to understand why we are looking at this metric—to see if there is a different way you can get to the same answer.

DS: I agree, if you go back and think through the metrics and missions, you will have a better understanding of the ways those actually work together or against each other. You have a chance of preventing your focus from narrowing down. There are many examples, where people—even governments—meant to invest in one way but created rules that resulted in the opposite direction or in an inefficient way. Several institutional investors have a ~$50M mandate to invest in diverse emerging managers.

But their procedures direct those funds to a familiar, old, homogeneous advisors firm, which was approved by one or two state boards decades ago and is given a mission to invest in diverse VCs. These firms are expensive and with a relatively low ability to source for that mission in comparison to other newer entities, who are diverse and have that knowledge and networks, but haven't been historically approved. And so the mission of the mandate is expensive and inefficient but it is almost impossible, or nobody has the motivation to change the procedure and go through the two boards again.

Another example is when a government establishes a committee to invest in unique tech funds that allow citizens to participate in the innovation cycle. The requirement of experience for a committee member is twenty years of investment experience in venture. Twenty years ago, there were almost no women in VCs. Just making that condition for committee members excludes women from participating in the process of deciding where those public funds will go, preventing female GPs from being recognized for their potential and receiving those funds. Again, going back and discussing those metrics would eliminate many biases and blind spots in decision-making processes.

CONCRETE MEASURES THAT CAN STRONGLY ENCOURAGE DIVERSITY

JL: *Let us go into one more specific thing that I have seen LPs do: make GPs report the numbers. That is something that you do at the Mellon Foundation and that the Princeton endowment does, but not everyone is there yet. What are other measures that you could take very concretely, either, again, that you already have taken, and that you in whatever way use to put pressure on managers to invest more diversely and become more diverse themselves?*

MS: I am glad that you brought that up. I do think that as we have thought about collecting the metrics, we have always couched that as a component of an ongoing conversation. We have been very clear with the managers that it is not to publish them, or berate them publicly in any way about them, as it is to measure progress over time. We want to see: How are things progressing over time? Is this a priority for you? Where are the missteps? If you lose ground, it is not like we are going to kick you out of the portfolio because you have lost ground; we want to understand what the issue is that came up and how you are addressing it, and how that is going to lead to better metrics over time. We have always couched it in the context of a conversation.

We have also always felt it was important in that conversation to hold ourselves to a high standard. In hiring for our team, we have made a big effort to be more diverse in the sources of candidates who come through, and to be very public about showcasing the diversity of our own team. In that way we have more credibility, as we sit down with managers and say, "We want you to think about your investee companies and their diversity, and we want you to think about it in a holistic way." Demonstrating that we are doing the same puts us in a different conversation.

ST: I think I answered some of this before, but we see quarterly reporting and informal updates as an essential part of measuring progress across all areas of a manager's work. We want to understand how things are going. It's that classic case of "show your work, it's not all about the answer." Do you notice that a lot of your deals come from the same sources, how can you change that? How are you hiring for talent within your firm and how are you proposing to train up that person? You ran an initiative to encourage more diverse founders to seek investment, how did it go? We ask these questions, not to beat a manager over the head, but to understand the full context of their work and progress. And it is important to do this formally, through reporting, LPACs, and AGMs, but also to ask these questions informally and to catch up with managers to see how things are going. We operate an open-door policy with our managers, there are no assigned point people that a manager absolutely has to speak with first, who acts as some kind of gatekeeper to the team. Having trust and flexibility makes understanding the full context that a manager is operating in a lot easier.

As a team and as a fund of funds, we have always been open about hiring for different points of view and backgrounds, so that we can work with our managers in a holistic way. There are absolutely those in the team with institutional backgrounds and asset management experience, but we have exited founders, tech startup operators, those who worked in seed funds, and those with experience of working with startups in Africa and Asia. Demonstrating that we value a range of backgrounds and experiences is powerful for our GPs to see—we're in this together and learning too!

JL: *Did you want to talk about any other measure that you are thinking of taking or already are using in order to go on that level of change?*

MS: One of the things that, as an LP, we are in a very good position to do is share best practices. Having couched this survey effort as the beginning of a conversation, we started to get inbound questions like, "Oh, gee, you asked us if we had a DEI policy, we actually do not, but what have you seen from others? How should we think about putting one together?" Or, "Our team is really eager to have someone come in and talk about unconscious bias. Do you have a recommendation for a firm, a speaker, or a curriculum that would be helpful to our team?" And because we can compare across not just VC, but a wide array of investment managers, we can say, "Look, we do not know any other VCs that have hired a great consultant in workforce diversity, but we do know of this other firm that has a much larger employee base. They have been super successful with this group; you might talk to them. Here is a list of three others." Trying to be a resource has also come out of those conversations.

ST: I agree with that point on best practices. Of course, we can share things based on our own experience and what we see others in our portfolio doing, but we've also started to bring some of our portfolio together to learn from each other directly and connect to share contacts. We've also been running community events, for our portfolio but also for the wider VC ecosystem in Europe, where we organize around a topic that VCs tell us that they are interested in—we've had talent and diversity, sustainability, amongst other topics—and try to bring in domain experts to talk about these areas and take questions from the group. That's been a great way to share and enhance collective learning efforts.

DRIVING CHANGE IN THE MARKETS AS LPS

EB: *LPs are often believed to have lots of choices as to where to put their money. How much do you use that choice to drive change in the markets, personally?*

MS: It is hard to say—I have to be pragmatic. Looking after a $7B foundation portfolio sounds like a big number, but in investing markets that are trillions of dollars globally, there is only so much change that I can be responsible for. I am trying to be influential, trying to share best practices, and being very mindful of when we add a manager to our portfolio, how are they helping our metrics? Or are they not? It's a super important role that we can have. If every investor had the same approach, things would move very quickly. These things happen glacially, and then all at once, because people are watching, particularly the events of the last year [2020] and some of the notable successes of venture-backed companies, like the examples that Darya had, that are led by women and underrepresented minorities. We are on the precipice of a sea change, where we are going to be at the all-at-once part of the change, but no one person can influence that particularly. Other than trying to make sure that you are investing in line with the institution's values and trusting that history will bend toward justice.

DS: Monica and I are on the two furthest away edges of the scale, she is a part of a huge foundation, managing large sums of money; it is a lot of pressure, and a lot of metrics. I am a free spirit, I manage $10M to date of my money and funds that I raised under the social-financial thesis that my LPs are aligned with. Even though my AUM assets under management is not even a fraction of what Monica is in charge of, I feel I have significant ability to make a difference. Not only in my capacity as an activist and a speaker, writing opinion pieces, going on panels, etc., but I talk to GPs daily from Israel, Europe, and the US. I have the privilege of asking, "Who are the founding partners?" If they are all white men, I make sure they understand I am not a believer in a group of all-male, homogeneous GP teams. I tell them that once they have a diverse founding team, I'd be happy to talk to them again. It is OK if it takes 18 months or more, I see it as my responsibility to let male GPs hear it from me directly. I personally would not invest even if the funds brought in a female GP, a female partner, if they can fire her. LPs invest in funds they believe in. In the changing landscape, having an all-male founding team leaves too big of a blind spot, which will not maximize return potential and will not move the industry forward. GPs should know that when all other factors are similar, diversity outperforms homogeneity.

I know some LPs that refused to even ask their GPs about their diversity efforts; they used to say, "I will not ask difficult (D&I) questions because I will be called a troublemaker and may lose my allocation. The GPs can find other LPs from Europe, they don't need me," basically saying, "I'm not strong enough to create that change." I was thinking, "Oh my god, you are one of the biggest LPs in America. World-known GPs are bragging about having you as an LP. If you do not think you have enough power to lead change, nobody has enough." Plus, this is not really maximizing returns, as such a fund will see a limited dealflow, and will have less ability to DD and see the potential of a wider range of solutions for a wider range of clients. But today, after long conversations, these LPs realize the responsibility they have and they promise to ask those questions in their own way. But the questions will be raised once you realize the power that you have to make that difference, and the GPs that are confronted with this will have to prepare a good answer and eventually also act on it.

MS: I do not think we disagree at all. I just have a more pragmatic view—there are a zillion other LPs out there who are happy to not raise questions, and so I have to be cognizant of that. At the same time, the power of a long-term partnership, and of asking the questions of the managers in our portfolio, on an ongoing basis gives us a different kind of leverage, right? We say, "Look, we have worked with you for 15 years. We have been asking these questions. We have seen modest progress. We want to understand what is blocking you. We think it is terrific that you have hired your first female partner, and we want to know how you have changed your processes internally to make sure that she is successful in that role." You cannot just send a survey and publish metrics; you cannot be viewed as trying to call people out who are your partners. We are trying to make everybody better. We understand that we have the same challenges ourselves on our own team, and among many of our grantees. We are fighting all of these issues on many levels. We feel like some of that experience we ought to be able to bring to bear to help the managers in our portfolio.

ST: In some form or other, a fund of funds structure lends itself towards diversity as a way to maximize coverage and optimize for returns. As LPs, I think to answer this question, it goes back to not underestimating your own power and influence. Even with smaller funds like Isomer, we are one of a very, very tiny number of fund of funds that are 100% venture capital focused and do not shy away from investing into emerging managers. The decision that we make to invest, and then the long-term partnership journey that we embark on with managers to help them build their firms, have a ripple effect. Early decisions as a result of questions and challenges will become ingrained as processes in the future funds of these managers, so asking questions, monitoring over time, and working together with managers from their earliest years makes a huge difference in how they approach raising and managing their next funds.

NEXT STEPS FOR THE ROLE OF LPS IN DEI

JL: *Looking forward, what do you think is still missing to go to the next level? What are the next steps not only for you, but for the industry as a whole, for the role of an LP?*

DS: I see many brilliant and accomplished women struggling to raise money. It is a lot about perception. LPs (still the majority are men) tend to invest more and bigger checks in emerging managers that look like their younger selves, just like direct investors having a "gut feeling" when it comes to startup founders. An experienced female GP told me she received a $100K check from an LP who invested a million dollars in her male colleague, who had no investing track record.

There is still a difference in LPs' perceptions and unconscious biases. When comparing emerging GPs' journeys to raise their first funds, a survey conducted by First Republic Bank showed that it takes a male GP on average 11 months to raise $35M, and only 20% of them had investing experience, while female GPs raising their first fund took 16 months to raise $30M and 80% of them had investing experience. It is still harder for women to raise money, and it is up to us to keep pushing. We are all part of the process. We now have a female vice-president, and so we are moving in the right direction. Perceptions will eventually change; returns will continue to prove diversity outperforms homogeneity, and institutional LPs will follow the money and social-economic changes.

MS: That is right. It is mostly from here building momentum. One thing that we are very mindful of doing is highlighting successes. For example, among the larger managers—not so much in VCs who do not have quite so much infrastructure—but if there is a really terrific vice-president or principal who is diverse in some way, we always make an effort to establish a relationship with that person at the GP early, and to make sure that the leadership is aware of our interest in that person's career. There are a lot of opportunities to highlight and spotlight successes that shine a light on the good work that people are doing. For some reason, people tend to have a "don't ask, don't tell" policy on their diversity efforts. Maybe this goes back to where we started and the GPs saying, "Oh, we are just doing what the LPs tell us to do." It is because people are not having an open conversation, and mostly that they are not shining a light on the successes. Those kinds of stories go a long way in terms of communicating the missed opportunities, as opposed to being stuck in this liability mitigation backwater, where GPs are worried about being called out for a lack of diversity.

ST: I like your line on highlighting success, but it's also worth highlighting examples of learning and gradual progress as well. Highlighting that everyone is on a journey can be really useful. It is so easy to look at the glossy media story and think that a firm has nailed diversity or, worse, to overinflate what is going on behind the scenes. One, it might not be true, and two, it probably took a ton of mistakes to get to a good place. We've become brilliant as an industry about talking about diversity, the big hurdle of asking questions about D&I is largely gone when it comes to LPs asking managers. However, there is a tendency for us to think about D&I in "obvious" terms, particularly gender and ethnicity, but the conversation has to move forward from this and we must adopt a more intersectional approach to be able to measure real progress or we risk further marginalizing many groups. It is all very well, being able to ask managers about their approach to diversity, but we must also ensure that that conversation is happening at home in our own funds too, and that we are practicing what we may outwardly preach.

16.2 *Gauron, Skoglund: Goldman Sachs*

Suzanne Gauron (Goldman Sachs)

Anna Skoglund (Goldman Sachs)

Change in the venture capital industry is happening at a glacial pace. We sat down with Suzanne Gauron[291] and Anna Skoglund[292] of financial industry veteran Goldman Sachs[293] to explore what they are doing to support the wider industry in acknowledging the well-researched divides, but more importantly, what they are doing to funnel money into the gaps in access

291. https://www.linkedin.com/in/suzanne-gauron-b9200568/
292. https://www.linkedin.com/in/anna-skoglund-15a7b151/
293. https://www.goldmansachs.com/

to capital for diverse entrepreneurs. We discussed Black Womenomics, One Million Black Women, Launch with GS, and much more.

Interviewed April 2021

PROGRAMS THAT MANDATE DIVERSITY AND CLOSE GAPS FOR BLACK WOMEN

Erika Brodnock (EB): *In 2019, Goldman Sachs announced that it would no longer support IPOs for businesses without diversity on their boards. What led to that decision? What has been the reaction of your clients?*

Anna Skoglund (AS): The fundamental role of boards is to ensure the right corporate governance of enterprise. We believe that a more diverse and inclusive approach to corporate governance is going to lead to better decision-making. That is the thesis behind that. The reaction was broadly positive, but I am puzzled by the fact that we did not see our peers follow. Our peers did not say, "We will also do this and not take companies public unless they have one or more diverse board members." Diversity can be gender, ethnicity, sexual orientation. You can define it in various ways.

EB: *The "One Million Black Women" initiative filled me with hope because "when Black women win, everybody wins" is so powerful. Was that an internal phrase? If so, what are the reasons behind that belief and what are the program's aspirations?*

Suzanne Gauron (SG): We try to ground everything we do, whether it is Launch With GS, or One Million Black Women, in data. The data says that Black women as a group are one of the most disadvantaged communities in the United States. The wage gap is the broadest between Black women and white men. We are looking at the wage gap between white men as the 100% bar. We show the gap there, as opposed to between Black men and Black women. We summarize this in our Black Womenomics paper, where we show that at every life point, Black women are disadvantaged, whether it is in medical care, maternal mortality, access to education, and access to credit. If we are able to close gaps for Black women at any of these points, everyone else will be lifted up by that. Those are fundamental problems in all of our communities that we are addressing by measuring how much progress we can make for this most disadvantaged group that have not been given the recognition they deserve as our caregivers, employees, and stakeholders. One Million Black Women was a way of expressing the problem that was very specific. It also builds on a lot of work that we have done in the past, because we have been doing research on topics around women and inclusion for over a decade. Black Womenomics builds on the back of Kathy Matsui's work in Japan, which was groundbreaking at the time. You can hear echoes of her work on women's labor participation in Japan in that idea that if Black women win, everybody wins. Our 10,000 Women program is where we saw and could measure the impact of increased financial security for female entrepreneurs and the effects that that had on their immediate families, extended families, and entire communities.

Johannes Lenhard (JL): *Is there any specific data that you have when it comes to the tech ecosystem?*

SG: What One Million Black Women will do is be more broad-based on problems that cut across sectors. In Launch With GS, we focus very deeply on entrepreneurship, and venture capital, which is all deeply ingrained in the tech community. We can not claim ownership of any of the research. The research in the US is very similar to that in the UK, where people of color are less than 1% of all venture capital funding in the US. For gender, it is well below 3%, which is what you are seeing in the UK. Most of all venture capital teams in the United States do not include a person of color. The number of Black female venture capitalists is incredibly limited, and that is the least represented group that there is. There are steps being taken, especially in the seed stage, to address this. There are a number of innovative firms—a few of which we work with personally—who are taking a point of view on reaching out and making their investment thesis around investing in companies with underrepresented networks at the pre-seed and seed stage. We are seeing progress there, but there are still some places where the bridging of the capital is not there yet. The number of Black women who have raised a Series A or Series B in the United States is extraordinarily low. It is something that everybody should be concerned with. We have not seen a consistent approach yet from what I would call broad-based venture capital as to how we are going to address bias in assessing companies entrepreneurs as they progress into Series A and Series B.

EB: *There is a point at which the companies will fall off because they go back into a toxic market, and there is no chance that they can reach escape veloc-*

ity, unless we can fund them all the way through the lifecycle. Do you see any way of addressing that?

SG: I used to run our private equity and venture capital business and we were limited partners in funds. The ultimate answer is that the institutional investors who allocate capital to venture capital have to require a change, and they have to hold their managers accountable. People have tried to address this from both ends. One is to fund new managers that are disproportionately diverse from the beginning. The other is to pressure your longtime, very rich, all-white teams to change. There needs to be a continuum that meets in the middle, where you are asking the same questions of everyone. You allocate to a variety of strategies, some of which have no gender or diversity lens in them, but they are required to be thoughtful about D&I in what they do. We are just starting to see that but still not consistently from investors. Unfortunately, the problem with venture is there is a supply and demand mismatch, where the VC itself has been in the preferred seat because there is more demand than supply for top-tier ventures. The additional stakeholders are going to make a difference there around companies who require more awareness from people on their cap table, and social media and scrutiny.

IS VC STILL WAITING FOR SOMEONE TO TAKE A STAND ON DIVERSITY?

JL: *Do you see a point when Goldman Sachs is not going to invest in a VC fund because they are not equipped with the processes that you just described? At the moment, we have not met anyone who would say, "We do not write checks to people if they do not fulfill certain criteria."*

SG: People are waiting for someone to take a stand on that. You have to be able to measure it. We see many people collect data and collect insights, because we could not say, today, what is best in class and what is a passing grade. We need to arrive at a place where we can say this is the minimum standard. It is hard because there are many levels. There are the investment partners who allocate capital and there is the overall organization and who they are employing. It is the companies that they are seeking to invest in and what they require from those companies. You could come up with a lot of different answers depending on how you trade-off between those levels. We have some very thoughtful, very aware white male VCs and we want to figure out how to measure that in a way that would make sense.

JL: *We do know that adding 10% more women to decision-making roles in venture capital creates up to 2% of revenue or profit per year, and 10% more profitable exits over time. There is no more data that we need here.*

SG: I agree, but I think the structural challenges of having capital that can not leave means that the levers to create change are relatively limited. From the limited partner side, venture capital is a high returning asset class and so it introduces different incentives for different limited partners on how much they want to push when they look at their other asset classes, where they may have more ability to make change more quickly in public companies, for example. It is not a reason not to continue to push, but it is one reason why people have largely focused on newly established managers, which is some of our work as well. It is easier to partner with people from the beginning who have this belief and have a demonstrated commitment, than to turn the Queen Mary.

AS: There is no doubt in my mind that more diverse company leadership and corporate governance and input is going to lead to better outcomes. I also think that if we are saying that it is easy to do it, we are underestimating the actual effort, consistency, and frameworks that are required to drive sustainable change. This does not mean that we should not set ambitious targets and that we should not hold ourselves accountable, but we are not going to do ourselves a service if we gloss over the daily effort and tracking to make this work. Throwing money at things is not necessarily going to drive some of the changes that need to happen at the fundamental level of building sustainable companies. If the company fails, for whatever reason, and they are just in very small numbers, then the failures as a percentage becomes a bigger number than it actually is. Statistics is famous for being able to show everything you want. In a small sample set, it becomes more vulnerable. There is no doubt that this is the right thing for business, but achieving sustainable change and healthy growth in some of these companies needs to be done in a measured and thoughtful way. We could take two steps forward and one step back, but even worse is one step forward, and two steps back.

SG: I have been in finance for 20 years and have seen the efforts to try to change bottom-up, top-down, from the middle. In my experience, the two things that are different over the last couple of years with our initiatives is one, the CEO has made this a cornerstone of how he is operating our company. It is not an adjunct or championed by someone else. He is seeing this as part of the scorecard of how he is assessed and what his impact will be on the firm. The more managers and leaders who do that, the more it expresses that core thesis that it is accretive to business performance. People used to say, "What is the business case for diversity?" The business case for diversity is performance and stakeholders. With initiatives such as One Million Black Women, we are engaging with our community and society in a deeper way. This is about facing our responsibilities as a leading financial institution, but it is also about the world that our employees live in and experience every day. This has been very profound for me with One Million Black Women in better understanding the people I work with, and what life is like for them or others in their community.

THE MOVEMENT IS (SLOWLY) HAPPENING

JL: *I am a bit wary of when a finance professional steps forward and says "I care about this. Here is an initiative." I do not see billions of pounds on the table and this is not really going to do anything. Unless the LPs come in who do change something, the VCs do not have any incentive to do something differently. Their model has worked very well. White men investing in white men; there is nothing wrong with that and it works perfectly. They are making billions of pounds; why would they change anything? There needs to be some kind of a radical implosion, or explosion.*

AS: Some of them really are trying to change. They may not go as far as you would like them to, but it is part of their investment decision. It goes all the way up to the CEO. It is important for the CEO in these various funds to champion it, because it sets the tone. I also have some sympathy for why it is going slowly, because careers in this industry are made over decades. It takes a long time to grow as a professional. Whether change is moving as quickly as you or I would like to see, I am sure it is not, but I feel a movement. It is gathering pace and that gives me hope that we are going to continue to drive change.

JL: *The bottom line is going to take a moment.*

AS: I do think it is going to take some time. It might accelerate, but I doubt it is going to be a straight-line progress. This is hard to do and it is made harder by the incumbency of the certain business models which have been working perfectly fine, to your point. It is a reality that we have to deal with. We have to be pragmatic and realistic as well as ambitious. I do not want to be discouraged just because I am not seeing linear progress.

SG: People embedding this in their core businesses is really important. We interrogate ourselves about this at Goldman Sachs. We do not want to create new businesses, in order to say we did this; we want this to be part of how we run our growth equity business and manager selection business. In the limited partner market, some of the largest investors in the world have a very real commitment to making this change. Yet all of the governance structures and incentives that have been put in place to make them do their job correctly and manage their portfolios well, prevent them from affecting this change. You are in this armed standoff where governance is saying, "You can only invest in certain things in certain ways," while they are being asked every day, "Why are you not helping the world advance?" People are coming to a point where they are going to have to choose a third way. You are going to have to change your governance in certain areas in responsible ways, so that you can drive capital to things that you want to succeed. Until you do that, we will all be sitting here repeatedly asking the same question. This is one of the reasons we chose to focus on venture capital and private equity, because you can be very successful at a relatively limited scale of assets, which is not true in most other asset classes. We felt that with a small group of committed and like-minded investors, we could start to make change in this asset class. The problem, however, has a lot more zeros than just in venture.

WHAT'S MISSING FOR THE INDUSTRY TO TAKE THE NEXT STEP

JL: *If both of you have to name one thing that we need in the next 12 months, in order to take us to the next step, what would that be?*

SG: There has been enough change in the last ten years that the face of entrepreneurship and the face of successful venture is no longer a white guy in a hoodie who went to Stanford. Yet, the stories of successful women and people of color who have created companies are still treated as one-off anecdotes. We need a much more consistent drumbeat of telling the stories of a variety of people who have created companies. There are twenty other options besides talking about Elon Musk every day. These people have not only built companies, but sold them, and are very wealthy. Yet, people write about Bumble as if it is the only company where a woman has ever IPO'ed.

AS: The underlying fiduciary duty of these LPs is to make sure that they have been awarded. This is an experience-based business. People know what has worked in the past, and therefore, there is a safe rail around that. To drive the change in corporate governance and fiduciary duty framework and allow for "new things," we need to be highlighting, recording, and measuring success stories. This shows that this is not just a once in a blue moon outcome, but instead is systematic. This will give comfort to the system that this is the right thing to do, even if we intuitively know it is.

EB: *If we say that we need more data when there is data that is being ignored, are we buying into the problem? We will give them more data and people will still say, "We need more data." There is no incentive to ever have enough data to change this. The incumbents are saying, "If we change this, we are the people that are going to lose out." They are not seeing the pie as being made bigger. They are seeing someone coming to steal their pie. Unless we say that there has to be a new way and people see that the new way makes the pie bigger, I am afraid we will never get to a place where there is enough data. There is a constant reliance on new data when there is enough data available to make the right decisions already. Are we just kicking the can down the road?*

SG: When I talk to CIOs, I most commonly get asked, "What is everybody else like me doing?" We quote the statistics every day, but people like to be in the pack. As a CIO, you are looking to your peer group of CIOs. Somebody needs to stick their neck out as a CIO and implement it themselves. What people will believe most is that Yale made 8.1% last year in part because of this change, and the CIO is also being celebrated. Therefore, CIOs are getting questions from their boards about why they have not done that as well. Sadly, somebody has to be the first one to take the career risk, and then that single data point will change a thousand hearts and minds.

JL: *The idea of fiduciary duty in Europe is not as prevalent because the legal structures around it are different. It is an American excuse. There is an interesting argument in what Anna just said because the statistics are* *pointing to the fact that if you are not thinking about a diverse investment partnership, then you are violating your fiduciary duty.*

AS: Exactly. As soon as you have someone who is generating better returns because they are doing this, then there will be a FOMO shift.

SG: This goes back to the measurement. If you could measure the three things, then you can say you have over or underachieved your fiduciary duty. Coming to a collective measurement is equally hard on this topic as it is on ESG [environmental, social, and governance], and that is one of the reasons you do not have collective will on these things. The conversation is also slightly different by jurisdiction as well, which creates further challenges when you have capital from all over the world and you are investing all over the world. How do you come to an agreement on that? It is not an excuse by any means. That is one of the reasons we started in the US: start here and chip away, come to agreement on certain things, have outstanding questions, and then grow from there.

GOLDMAN SACHS'S PLANS IN EUROPE

EB: *My final question is around the activity flow that we see in the US. What are your plans for Europe, and what can be done to ensure that the UK does not end up being left behind in this?*

SG: We expanded the Launch program and it was always part of our plan from the beginning. We want our program to have the same footprint as our firm over time. There is no worry that the UK would be left behind. Our program is an investment program and the investment opportunity in the UK is very strong. That is part of why we are here and are focused on both companies and funds in the UK. Your statistics express the mirroring of the US. In the UK, the gap to be closed and access to capital is almost exactly equal. With adjustments for the local tech ecosystem and engaging in the right ways to know the important entrepreneurs and investors, we think the playbook applies in both places. We have some really exciting returns and ideas to pursue.

AS: Our first launch was very successful in the US, but we all collectively felt we did not get the momentum we wanted in Europe. We have a real opportunity now because the climate and the focus on this has increased. The key thing for us is going to be to find businesses that we want to invest in and come behind, because there is nothing like making a couple of investments. They have been very successful in the US and in Asia. Seun Toye-Kayode, vice-president and Launch With GS EMEA lead, has come on board and she is going to drive that here on the ground. She is going to give this momentum and we will start seeing some real action.

16.3 *Borlongan, Manku, Miczaika: Policy*

Kat Borlongan (Contentsquare, formerly La French Tech)

Gurpreet Manku (British Private Equity & Venture Capital Association)

Gesa Miczaika (Auxxo Female Catalyst Fund, German Startups Association)

Kat Borlongan,[294] *Gurpreet Manku,*[295] *and Gesa Miczaika*[296] *represent the who-is-who of tech policymaking and influencing in Europe. What can the world learn from European best practices in this respect? Where are we still lagging behind and where is there most potential to do better? We speak about quotas, the state as an LP investor, and maternity and paternity leave. The biggest issue: while the state has a lot of power, it is often slow to decide and use that power. But if it does, it has massive potential to—with the right policies—push DEI forward in the tech world.*

Interviewed January 2021

DEFINING DIVERSITY OBJECTIVES IN POLICY

Johannes Lenhard (JL): *What does diversity mean from a policy perspective? Is it about systematic disadvantages for some groups, or it about active discrimination? What is the objective for policymakers?*

Gesa Miczaika (GMi): The objective of DEI policy is to leverage the strengths of each group, if we are talking about diversity. Studies (e.g., in

294. https://twitter.com/katborlongan
295. https://www.linkedin.com/in/gurpreet-manku-75aaa339/
296. https://twitter.com/gsapzr

HBR[297] or by McKinsey[298]) have shown that diversity in all areas leads to better outcomes, and on all levels.

Gurpreet Manku (GMa): If you think about where diversity matters, our context is investment managers/firms and the portfolio companies they invest in. The question is about representation and whether the makeup of those firms actually reflects the society in which we operate and live. From our perspective, there has been a lot of focus on the lack of women in venture capital, and a lack of money going into female-founded businesses. We always point to the stats that 51% of the population in the UK is women. There is an increased focus now looking at ethnicity as well. When you look at the composition of the industry from an ethnicity perspective, there are few statistics, and what do you compare this to? The UK, or perhaps to London, where a number of firms are based? In March 2021, the BVCA [British Private Equity & Venture Capital Association, where I work] and Level 20 published the results of a survey[299] of private equity and venture capital firms in their membership, [which showed that ethnic representation in the industry still needs work].

Kat Borlongan (KB): From a policy perspective, what is important to say is also what diversity is *not*. It is not social correctness. It is not charity. If we look into the very specific context of where we are [in 2021], in the middle of the economic and health crisis, it is one of the smartest strategies we have to make sure that France, that other countries, recover well. If you look at the recovery plan[300] that is dedicated to startups in France, you will notice that a lot of it has to do with making sure that the best entrepreneurs can come from all across the country, especially as we want to invest in a new generation of startups that are coming up today. It is true that we have a lot of great entrepreneurs that have PhDs, come from the elite schools, McKinsey, and so on, but we also really believe that they can and should come from the suburbs, the inner cities, or the countryside,

297. https://hbr.org/2017/03/
     teams-solve-problems-faster-when-theyre-more-cognitively-diverse

298. https://www.mckinsey.com/featured-insights/diversity-and-inclusion/
     diversity-wins-how-inclusion-matters

299. https://www.bvca.co.uk/media-and-publications/news/bvca-press-releases/details/
     Gender-diversity-is-improving-in-private-equity-and-venture-capital-but-work-is-still-need
     ed-on-ethnicity-representation-new-report-finds

300. https://www.tresor.economie.gouv.fr/Articles/2020/09/15/
     launch-of-the-french-recovery-plan

amongst the refugees, the urban poor. For the French tech team inside the Ministry of Economy, diversity is about making sure that we can have the best talent regardless of where it comes from.

INVITING UNDERREPRESENTED COMMUNITIES INTO TECH

Erika Brodnock (EB): *On the minimum level, one goal for diversity, inclusion, and equity in tech would be to get more people to start thinking about entrepreneurship, VC, and technology. How would you achieve this?*

KB: I can tell you what we have done and what we are working on in France. It is great to have these intentions, but the truth is that when you actively try to recruit from communities that have been estranged from tech, you come across a whole bunch of problems. I know because we ran a recruitment campaign for a program that we created called French Tech Tremplin. We created it last year, and it is essentially designed to mimic the advantages that an entrepreneur from underprivileged communities might have, had they come from a well-to-do background.

There is a boot camp and originally €17K in funding. They are paired with a great founder in the country and if it works out, they move on to the second phase where they get 42K of non-dilutive funding. They are placed in one of the best incubators and accelerators across the country. They have that cohort support throughout the year. You launch something like that, and you are super proud of it. The overall budget for the program is €15M, and we were really excited about the fact that we can have hundreds of applications.

When we launched it, nobody applied for a long time. We did paid advertising and we launched this massive campaign on underground trains. We realized that even when people did see it, and they were interested in it, a lot of them just thought, "That is not for me, because I look nothing like the tech entrepreneurs we hear about." We had to suddenly start really investing in a lot of outreach and awareness programs. We started pairing and funding a lot of grassroots organizations to work with us.

When we started a second attempt, we worked with people representing the communities we were targeting and deployed them as our recruiters on the ground. They were reaching out to people that they knew via phone calls, and to anyone that had exhibited some form of entrepreneurial interest. We then put them into the boot camps as early as possible. It was during the boot camps that they realized whether or not entrepreneurship, or tech entrepreneurship more specifically, was really for them. It really is about building the pipeline and sending the right messages and not being this ivory tower that is far from everybody else. It is really about working with the communities themselves that have these entrepreneurs as a part of them.

PROMOTING VC AND TECH IN EDUCATION

GMa: This is about how you can open up access to the industry. I am talking broadly here in terms of whether it is becoming a VC investor or an entrepreneur. I would go back to education, as I do not know how much is currently taught about financial literacy or entrepreneurship at schools. Some people may not agree with me, but I do think it would help to start early when promoting career opportunities in finance, business, and entrepreneurship. You might not necessarily follow a straight path into entrepreneurship, and may take a different route first before you decide to set up a new business, and before you decide to go and work for a venture capital or other investment firm. You should still know that that career opportunity is there for you. We are thinking quite hard about how you get the message out to people still in education, from schoolchildren to graduates.

To promote career opportunities to younger people, you would need a broader program involving other stakeholders and industry participants. For example, Initiative 7 in the Rose Review of Female Entrepreneurship[301] is about accelerating the development and rollout of entrepreneurship-related courses to schools and colleges. It will be interesting to see how this initiative develops, especially as there is quite a bit we can do virtually nowadays.

On the point around schemes and trying to look for diverse talent, it is really important to get out and look beyond your firm's typical and traditional networks. There are a lot of networks and communities in the UK, and London in particular, including YSYS and SEO London, and VCs have been collaborating on events and resources for female founders. It is important that venture capital firms reach out to groups beyond their normal networks to explain what they do and what career and investment opportunities can look like. Diversity VC has been running a very success-

---

301. https://media.natwestbusinesshub.com/XyEBYqU6QyKTQ5ilzaMX

ful internship program called Future VC,[302] and they have lots of applicants that apply each year. That is an example of a really good program that is reaching out to individuals from different backgrounds.

GMi: I have been discussing the topic of education here in Germany, too. Bringing coding courses and entrepreneurship courses into schools nationwide, as part of the standard curriculum, would really help in this respect. Another way to get more people to start thinking about entrepreneurship is showing as many as possible diverse role models who are successful entrepreneurs. I have this podcast[303] here in Germany, where I interview a very diverse group of female founders. One example is a female founder who is really successful but has an anxiety disorder. I want to show that even if you have a condition, or if you have any kind of package that you bring along, it is still possible to become a successful entrepreneur.

There are also ways that don't focus on formal schooling and education we should think of. I am a venture partner at Entrepreneur First, and they would also accept you to the program if you dropped out of school or if you did not go to school at all. They want to find talents who are extraordinary compared to their peers. I liked that, because we do have several founders who did not actually go to university and went through the program.

KB: There is one really important component that we have to keep in mind. Entrepreneurship is expensive. It means quitting your job and plunging into some form of deep uncertainty for up to 18 months, at least, to get something out into the market or start raising. While the cultural aspect of it is important, you also have to make funding accessible to people who do not look like the people that normally would be lining up to meet VCs, or have friends that they went to school with who can send them the right intros. Those things happen at such a systemic level and as governments, those are the times that we really need to step in. Those are the times when behavior change policies aren't enough.

We were talking earlier about how it is different in the US. In the US, you have this big barrier between discussions about race, and then discussions about class. In Europe, and it is certainly the case in France, you cannot dissociate them. The discrimination is rooted in both and they have

302. https://futurevc.com/

303. https://www.thepioneer.de/originals/tech-briefing

such a difficult history of immigration, so if you are not looking at social justice, free education, or proper health care, then the idea of diversity just seems bogus.

SUPPORTING GENDER DIVERSITY WITH POLICIES FOR PARENTS

JL: *How can policy help to specifically support women to take a step into entrepreneurship? What is a better way of doing parental leave policy, for instance?*

KB: Parliament recently voted to increase paternity leave in France. We went from 11 to 28 days; 25 of those 28 days are entirely paid for by social security, i.e., by the state directly. That is a win for us. We are excited for what that means. It comes into effect this July, which, while it could be sooner, is a big move. Eighty-five percent of single households in France are run by women, so while paternity leave is important for families that are affected by it, there is also the other issue that has to go beyond simple policy and also has to do with facilities such as daycare. We spend a lot of time talking about funding VCs and discrimination, and at the end of the day, when you speak to a lot of people who are struggling to become entrepreneurs, it is something as simple as their daycare was booked out. They need to take public transport for an hour and a half to a different area to drop off their kids and lose three hours of the day during which they can possibly think about launching their company.

GMi: There are studies (for instance, one study in German[304]) that show that childcare is one of the main drivers for female entrepreneurship. Just granting better quality and quantity of childcare would really help, and then also the parental leave policies. In Germany, you can take one year, and the government pays a specific percentage of the wage that you used to have. Mostly it is women who would take the parental leave. I do not have a perfect solution for this, but I would like those parental leave policies to have more parity in terms of having both parents join in on that.

GMa: There is a lot of variation in terms of maternity and parental leave policies[305] in the UK. Corporations have a big role to play to voluntarily go beyond the minimum statutory requirements if they can, as the impact

---

304. https://www.ingenieur.de/karriere/selbststaendigkeit/
   warum-gibt-es-in-deutschland-so-wenige-gruenderinnen/
305. https://www.gov.uk/maternity-pay-leave

can be significant. Governments can create the framework for people to take leave, particularly shared parental leave, but then individuals need to feel that they can take this, including men. I have two men working on my team that both recently became fathers at the same time. They are now taking parental leave (in addition to their paternity leave), which is great. That is what you need to really move the dial on this particular point, you actually need to see people taking leave if they want to, particularly senior leaders, both men and women.

KB: Yes indeed, it is a very good thing to do that very visibly. My boss is the minister for digital affairs, and he had a baby right when he started, about a year and a half ago. I remember him telling his staff, in the first few months in office, "I am not going to come into the office until 11 o'clock for the next few days because I split the duties with my wife on taking care of the kids." He goes into these ministerial meetings, stands up and very vocally says, "I need to go home. It is my shift with the baby." They seem like small things, but coming from people such as these ministers in very public meetings really helps to set the standard.

GMi: Not only should the men be good role models with this respect, but there should be more female role models who decrease the time of their parental leave. In Germany, the culture is more, "You are going back to work after three months? How? Why do you have kids?" It would also help to show that it is totally possible as a mother to go back to work after a short amount of time.

THE DIVERSITY FAILURE WITHIN ROLE MODEL ORGANIZATIONS

EB: *Speaking of role model organizations in the state and setting examples, in many European countries the state is also an LP. That comes with a lot of power over GPs, but also a massive status as a role model organization. Unfortunately, often they fail to take this responsibility seriously; for instance, the European Angels Fund (EAF) investment portfolio is 95% white men. How does that need to change?*

GMi: It needs to change quickly. They should have quotas to crowd in as many females and non-white investors as possible. This is my personal opinion. It is not only the EAF, but the state as an LP. There are also state funds in Germany like Coparion, KfW Capital, and HTGF, and they should ensure that there is also a diverse group of general partners.

GMa: At a LP level, the biggest state investor in the UK is the British Business Bank and British Patient Capital. When it comes to due diligence on the funds that they are investing in, they do include questions around the makeup of the team and D&I policies. They have templates that firms need to complete on a regular basis and have adopted the ILPA DDQ[306] on D&I. What we have been doing here in the UK, whether it is ourselves, Level 20, or Diversity VC, is collecting and publishing information on the number of men and women and other genders in investment and non-investment roles within venture capital and private equity firms.

In 2021, we (the BVCA) have been surveying firms on gender and on ethnicity,[307] which is often difficult to get. Just publishing the information in itself is the catalyst for conversation, because we have set targets of around 20% of senior women in senior roles. It does not feel that high, but because of the way these firms are structured (as partnerships), they have founders who own the business and are likely to be in place for quite a long time; it can take these firms a bit of time to change the makeup of the senior leadership team. What we are seeing is that there are more women certainly coming in at more junior grades, and mid-level grades. The next point is just to what extent they stay in the industry and move up into those senior roles. Interestingly, investors do have a lot of influence here. They are funding these firms and if they are asking questions around diversity, firms will need to respond.

EB: *I am not sure if questions are enough at this point in time and I am also quite concerned about the fact that most of the hires are made at junior levels and then people have to work their way up for firm in a way that their male counterparts just do not need to, or indeed if it is on the ethnicity side, their white counterparts do not need to. I struggle with the ethnicity data being difficult to obtain when we have done some research in which we have been able to obtain it.*

KB: Information around ethnicity is not just difficult to attain, it is also illegal. It is a different approach where France, at least administratively and legally, does not recognize race. This term, widely used by Americans, tends to be considered offensive by the French. In France, race is a word

---

306. https://ilpa.org/due-diligence-questionnaire/

307. https://www.bvca.co.uk/media-and-publications/news/bvca-press-releases/details/
    Gender-diversity-is-improving-in-private-equity-and-venture-capital-but-work-is-still-need
    ed-on-ethnicity-representation-new-report-finds

that is more appropriate when discussing dogs or cows, but when it comes to human beings, there is only one race, which is the human race. The word diversity in English is not used the same way in France. When we say "diversity" in France, what we really mean is, equal chances, meritocracy, and socio-economic justice; our policies reflect this. For example, we choose to orient affirmative action or, what is referred to in French as "discrimination positive," based on economic needs: preferential admissions in our top schools are given to the brightest kids from the poorest neighborhoods, regardless of the color of their skin.

On gender balance, one of my favorite projects in France is the SISTA charter; it is a collection of commitments. It includes things such as measuring gender balance in portfolios, reporting data annually, or recruitment practices such as rethinking existing processes, like the language of job descriptions and interview questions, or setting up office hours. This was developed a little less than a year ago by a nonprofit called SISTA, which was founded by some of the most amazing female entrepreneurs in France. It was done with the government, so I am pretty sure that a good 95% of all of the GPs in France have signed it; the French government has as well. We are after all a massive investor; we invest €1.3B into startups directly or indirectly via our fund every year.

DRAFTING THE MOST HELPFUL DEI POLICIES

JL: *If you could do any policy to increase D&I in tech and venture capital, what do you think is the most needed and the most effective for right now?*

GMa: This is a hard one because if you want change, you need people to buy into that change and make that change happen. If you force it, you do not always necessarily get the right result, but where we are heading to is actively encouraging transparency and targets. Once you start measuring diversity in your team/investments and tracking progress, you are more likely to implement policies and change to improve upon those metrics—"what gets reported gets done."

KB: This is a tricky one, because then you have to decide if you look at the entire pipeline. If we are talking short term, such as trying to inject more diversity over the next five years, then I am going to have to go with policies of not necessarily imposing quotas but obliging a lot of VCs to actually be transparent about their pipeline. How many women or people from diverse backgrounds did they actually meet in the first place? How many have they actually invested in? What numbers? What is the average ticket invested in a company launched by a woman or co-launched by a woman? We should be making that just as normal as performance and a general standard, which is something that LPs can do. It is a policy that the state can put in place as an LP, but it is also something that LPs themselves can start doing.

GMi: I like what Kat did, talking about long run and short run. For the long run, the part about bringing entrepreneurship to schools is definitely my favorite. In the short run, I would really like to have more data available about how successful non-white, non-male teams are with their startups. There are several studies, such as one by the Boston Consulting Group,[308] who found out that female founders generate a high return on investment, have fewer write-offs, and take less time to exit. I would really like to have more and broader studies that really show that investing in diversity is good for you as a VC also.

308. https://www.bcg.com/publications/2018/why-women-owned-startups-are-better-bet

PART IV: NEW IDEAS

17 Radical Changes from outside the System

We had originally planned to write a book of the three parts you've seen so far: an introduction and outline of the history of VC, the experiences of investors and operators past and present, and best practices that could be used to inspire systemic change henceforth. By the time we concluded the last set of interviews and compared what was being said by the capital allocators with those who continue to fruitlessly seek capital as underrepresented GPs, innovators, and entrepreneurs, we instinctively knew that we weren't done.

Harking back to our original mission—to create a practical guide on how to change the venture capital industry—we needed to cast our net further afield and reach out to people who we originally thought may not have the power to fundamentally change the tech industry, because they were working either outside or alongside the traditional power structures. In hindsight, it appears that the tech industry as it is may well serve the existing power structures a little too well for it to be radically changed *from within*. Change by insiders is limited in terms of the scope of what they can achieve without being cut down and out. A clear example is that Black-led funds are emerging across the globe, yet there are less than a handful that have closed more than $30M for their first funds, with much of the investments in charitable or impact funding buckets. By comparison, the average first-time VC fund size[309] in 2021 was $85M in North America and $110M in Europe; in their recent report,[310] BLCK VC concluded that Black GPs on average raise funds that are 46% smaller than this average. We are far away from a level playing field. What we heard were often excuses: we want to do things differently, but change will and must take time to actualize.

---

309. https://pitchbook.com/news/articles/
pe-vc-first-time-fundraising-pandemic-recovery-charts

310. https://www.dropbox.com/s/ducejd5jpjnopiv/BLCKVC%20State%20of%20Black%
20Venture%20Report.pdf?dl=

The conversations in Part IV: New Ideas represent what we term the "radically different"; they moved us on from diversity to inclusion, from capitalism at all costs to sustainable growth, and from "mirrortocracy" to fair advocacy and allyship, while renewing in us a sense of hope for the future. We speak to academics, non-profits, founders, bankers, and big tech companies. What we have to conclude: it is very likely that this "radically different" future for VC will rest outside of the existing confines of the "as is" venture capital ecosystem.

The first section[§18.1] in this part of the book looks at the often neglected "I" in DEI: inclusion. In the first conversation[§18.1] in this section, we bring together people fighting for more inclusion in a variety of ways across ecosystems. Grace Lordan, professor at the London School of Economics and Political Science (LSE), has more than a decade of inclusion research under her belt, and is the founder of LSE's Inclusion Initiative.[311] She outlines her work for the next ten years—providing evidence-based research to ensure that people are hired, promoted, and rewarded based on their skills, talent, and ability rather than their networks. Kate Pljaskovova and Bibi Groot founded and work at Fair HQ,[312] a London-based inclusion consultancy that aims to put research into best practice via a tool that enables employers to assess their level of inclusivity and take steps towards continually improving. Having worked with countless investors and, most importantly, founders of startups, the two share some very practical insights of how to move from "skin deep diversity" to true inclusion. Lolita Taub details how she defied all expectations of a Latina from a lower socioeconomic background, while adding insights from her experiences as a Latinx operator, investor, and newly minted GP on the US West Coast. Her new fund, Ganas Ventures,[313] turns the VC model upside down by starting and ending with historically overlooked communities on the investor and decision maker side, as well as on the side of the founders they back.

Katja Toropainen rounds up this inclusion section with a series of applicable steps[§18.2] for anyone wanting to delve into becoming more inclusive. Formerly part of the core team of one of the world's biggest startup conferences, Slush,[314] Katja contemplated leaving the tech indus-

---

311. https://www.lse.ac.uk/tii

312. https://fairhq.co/

313. https://techcrunch.com/2022/03/08/lolita-taub-ganas-ventures/

314. https://www.slush.org/events/helsinki/

try because she was so disillusioned with the inherent lack of diversity. Instead, she founded the non-profit Inklusiiv,[315] through which she aims to ensure that there is practical advice and tangible actions available to anyone who would like to create a more diverse and inclusive ecosystem.

> *In addition to changing our behavior to become more inclusive, we need to change how the systems and structures work. This means figuring out ways to make the systems more fair and inclusive in terms of how we hire people, how we decide on promotions, and how we share responsibilities.*

The next section[§19] looks specifically at access to capital. The fast-scaling, exit-focused VC track has worked well in creating unicorns. The resultant flywheels have focused on blitzscaling unicorn founders—in an ever repetitive mode benefiting the same kind of proven investor and founders. So how do we begin creating these flywheels for diverse and overlooked founders, particularly when they don't have a standing start?

Harvard Business School professor Laura Huang, who is also the author of *Edge: Turning Adversity into Advantage*[316], shares insights[§19.1] from her research with us. From questions about bias from VCs to the structural inequality that has been holding overlooked funders back, Laura has some ideas about what works to help founders turn adversity to advantage and what VCs can do to get more capital flowing to historically overlooked groups.

Next we spoke with Village Capital,[317] who have been shaking up and disrupting the traditional VC model since their inception in Atlanta in 2009. Their focus on impact and equity is clear and inherent—just under 50% of their portfolio are female-led companies. Their focus on changing the structural inequalities seen in VC today lean on a "nothing for us without us" approach that sees them working with allies such as the Black Innovation Alliance[318] (BIA) to create solutions *with* the communities they seek to serve, rather than for them. We spoke to[§19.2] Heather Matranga, Ben Younkman, and Dahlia Joseph from Village Capital, and Bianca St. Louis from the BIA. Innovative reapplication of multi-ethnic savings plans for capital allocation, collective community action, and

---

315. https://inklusiiv.com/
316. https://www.penguinrandomhouse.com/books/600457/edge-by-laura-huang/
317. https://vilcap.com/
318. https://blackinnovationalliance.com/

reinvestment into their ecosystem to create a flywheel are present in their thesis, and we are excited to see where it leads, and indeed who will follow suit.

Next[19.3] we turned to Hadiyah Mujhid, founder and CEO of HBCUvc[319]—a training ground for VCs at historically Black colleges and universities—for her thoughts on mobilizing the next generation of venture capital leaders to increase access to capital for historically overlooked communities. Hadiyah believes that the success of traditional VC leaves clear and replicable clues for all communities wishing to emulate the creation of flywheels. Much of what is there rests and relies upon networks, therefore, the key to success is diverse groups not only being able to leverage their own networks, but also connecting them to the existing VC networks.

> *Those tight networks and relationships (which are usually anchored in universities) that exist in traditional VC, we also have them in our program. ... It is important for us that we are not creating separate but equal. We are not creating a separate silo of networks in this VC network that will operate independently. It is important that we build strong bonds with the community of existing networks.*

For the last conversation[19.4] in this section, we sat down with the creator of the Female Founders Alliance (FFA), Leslie Feinzaig. When FFA started, it was as a Facebook group that solved Leslie's own gripe of often being the only female in the room without peers to support her. She did not expect it to grow to more than 25K members and to become one of the biggest communities of female founders, nor to be able to spin out an accelerator and a fund (recently rebranded as Graham & Walker[320]) that have gone on to successfully lead and broker deals for other female entrepreneurs.

Similarly to Hadiyah, Leslie is now able to seed the next generation of potential investors. This, in our opinion, is what makes them radically different. Diverse fund managers being able to demonstrate a track record of successful investments could eliminate some of the first-fund barriers faced when attempting to obtain future LP commitments.

---

319. https://www.hbcu.vc/
320. https://grahamwalker.com/

The prospect of companies being funded differently, and as a result behaving differently, led us to our next section[20] on different kinds of founders and how they can be supported. A new wave of entrepreneurs and enablers are thinking slightly out of left field by balancing sustainability with still creating significant returns—to their investors *and* their wider communities.

Frustrated with the industry status quo, the co-founders of Zebras Unite[321] collectively wrote their manifesto, "Zebras Fix What Unicorns Break,"[322] in 2017. Two of those co-founders, Mara Zepeda and Astrid Scholz share their vision[20.1] for a more sustainable breed of companies, and how they plan to educate and influence existing investors rather than raise a fund themselves.

Evgeni Kouris, founder of New Mittelstand,[323] and Ines Schiller, founder of Vyld,[324] are keen to hold onto the old traditions of medium-sized (or family) businesses, while simultaneously adapting to the pace of startups. We sat with them[20.2] to explore this approach, which is centered around combining the best traditions of medium-sized companies—which have historically been the backbone of the European economy—with the lean agility and redesign principles of startups, in order to create a new economic future for Europe. As Evgeni explained to us:

> *What is missing in Europe is this diversity oriented and bottom-up way of doing entrepreneurship. We call it New Mittelstand because it is a new way of old business, a new definition for the 21st century. We are open to learning from startups and learning from all kinds of methods to do radical innovation, but you cannot forget your roots.*

From one backbone to another, we found that immigrant entrepreneurs are pulling outsized weight[325] in contributing to economic success to their respective countries across the globe. We caught up[20.3] with

---

321. https://zebrasunite.coop/

322. https://medium.com/zebras-unite/zebrasfix-c467e55f9d96

323. https://www.newmittelstand.org/

324. https://www.vyldness.de/

325. https://workpermit.com/news/
more-half-us-startup-unicorns-founded-immigrants-20220801#:~:text=Immigrant%
20founders&text=Al%20Goldstein%20(born%20in%20Uzbekistan,OpenAI%20and%
20The%20Boring%20Company)

Manan Mehta, founding partner at Unshackled Ventures,[326] to learn more about how they are leveraging the largely nascent talent of immigrants, who often struggle to obtain work permits to build lives and careers in the countries they have the potential to add so much value to.

Unshackled not only provides funding for immigrant-led startups, they also provide immigration support, with more than 150 successful applications under their belt, and the full Y Combinator-style experience of investor and mentor access throughout the 10–15 year startup journey. The model is truly fascinating, and portfolio founder Kesava Kirupa Dinakaran joined our conversation, crediting Unshackled with their role in his success.

While this volume is mainly concerned with VCs, the final section[§21] focuses on "other" players who can help produce radical differences (and are perhaps our best bet to do so). For the last few radically different ideas, we spoke with allies working in research, as funders, and as a collective of enablers, without whom we all acknowledge the struggle for equity would be considerably harder.

Given the relatively tiny number of startups that are able to success-fully raise VC each year, and the global shift in entrepreneurs wanting to solve problems in a more sustainable way, it felt remiss not to ask: is the VC track the right course for all startups? While we don't seek to allevi-ate any of the responsibility on the VC industry to actively become more diverse and inclusive, our conversation[§21.1] with Aunnie Patton Power sought to dispel the myth that VC is the *only* way to successfully seed and scale a startup.

Aunnie was able to shed some much needed light on some of the alter-native sources of funding available to entrepreneurs, from venture debt to equity-based finance and more. Most exciting was her take on using alter-native funding vehicles to broaden access to wealth creation on both the company and investor sides of the landscape.

> *You can start to imagine products that allow a larger set of indi-viduals at the company side to participate in wealth creation, as well as a larger set of individuals at the investor side. We are pry-ing it open from both sides. There is opportunity to build com-panies that are sustainable and that are integrated into communities. By doing so, you have better staff, a more incen-*

---

326. https://www.unshackledvc.com/

tivized workforce, better ties to communities, and better ideas about what communities need.

Our next conversation[§21.2] took us back into the belly of the beast and an unlikely, but welcome, source of future LP commitments: big tech. Usually created by VC themselves, big tech companies are not usually known for advancing DEI agendas—yet Twitter has been radically reshaping its DEI policies internally and externally, while setting clear examples for other enterprises to follow. One such effort is centered around being a LP that injects capital into VC funds led by overlooked GPs. In our conversation with Twitter's (now former) Chief People and Diversity Officer Dalana Brand, as well as Director of Corporate Development and Strategy Peter Lenke, we learned the tech giant's plan for aligning DEI with the heart of Twitter's strategy through 2025 D&I goals,[327] and their responsible investing efforts to create a more level playing field for diverse investors and founders.[328] Peter Lenke explained further:

> *People look at large brands, because they provide a real proof point and a stamp of approval. That signaling gives excitement and motivation for others to step up and make tangible commitments—writing checks, supporting through partnership, and a whole host of other ways.*

Maya Ackerman is a professor in artificial intelligence and machine learning at Santa Clara University and founder of music-generating startup WaveAI.[329] Maya began investigating the lack of diversity in tech based on her own experience as a founder trying to fundraise. Very quickly, she started poking well-researched holes[330] in the bad data we keep citing and has consistently produced powerful data-driven research with infinitely more precise insights ever since. This interview[§21.3] is a must-read for anyone interested in using data to drive change through the industry.

---

327. https://careers.twitter.com/en/diversity.html

328. This interview took place in July 2021. Since Elon Musk's acquisition of Twitter (and Dalana Brand's resignation) in November 2022, it's unclear whether the discussed DEI agenda will continue as planned.

329. https://www.wave-ai.net/

330. https://www.scu.edu/illuminate/thought-leaders/maya-ackerman/bias-in-venture-capital .html

But we need to tackle both bias against female investors, and bias against female entrepreneurs. Not first one, then the other. We need both male and female investors to take responsibility for and actively work on reducing bias in venture funds allocation.

Taking on the task of putting research into action and tackling the biases head-on is Nicola Corzine, the executive director of the Nasdaq Entrepreneurial Center.[331] She is responsible for the Center's strong focus on equitable entrepreneurship, more recently through the Venture Equity Project,[332] which commissioned the creation of the ecosystem history maps provided by Terry Irwin[§9.1] and featured in Part I of this volume. In this conversation,[§21.4] Nicola shares what she feels can be done with research, teaching programs, and community to move the needle for diverse entrepreneurs accessing the capital, connections, and contracts they need to thrive.

Building on the theme of collective responsibility, our final interview[§21.5] of the book was with a collective of allies who are open about working on themselves first, and then working to support and deliver DEI-focused initiatives throughout the tech and VC ecosystems. Ed Zimmerman (tech lawyer and LP at First Close Partners), Mitch Kapor (Lotus founder and former GP, also featured in Part III[§14.4]), and Eddie Kim (cofounder of scale-up Gusto[333] were joined by female fund managers Maya Horgan Famodu (Sub-Saharan-Africa-focused Ingressive Capital[334]) and Marie Ekeland (Paris-based 2050[335]). This conversation offers a clear demonstration of the power of allyship in creating positive outcomes for all. Not for the faint of heart, there are a few expletives in this interview, but it cuts to the heart of what needs to be done to create radical change.

What we learned by adding this final part to the book is possibly the most important takeaway for us: many of the established players—investors, LPs, policy makers—*within the system* are willing to change, but their style of change is incremental. This kind of change has so far led to very few tangible differences in terms of who controls and who receives VC capital. Our hope is really with the kind of people we talked

---

331. https://thecenter.nasdaq.org/

332. https://thecenter.nasdaq.org/vep/

333. https://gusto.com/

334. https://ingressivecapital.com/

335. https://2050.do/#

to in Part IV: academics with a different kind of overview and insight, operators and builders who push *new* flywheels from the bottom up, and some unlikely allies in big tech, law firms, or non-profits. Our hope is that the recent developments—COVID-19 in particular, and the ongoing tech-market correction—don't further put pressure on these new avenues for change. What we mustn't do is go back to business as usual—that will just lead to further reproduction of the existing power structure.

18 Conversations: Beyond Diversity to Inclusion

18.1 *Lordan, Pljaskovova, Groot, Taub: Inclusion*

Grace Lordan (London School of Economics, The Inclusion Initiative)

Kate Pljaskovova (Fair HQ)

Bibi Groot (Fair HQ)

Lolita Taub (Ganas Ventures, Operator Collective)

In this wide-ranging conversation, we bring together people fighting for more inclusion in a variety of ways across the pond. While Grace Lordan,[336] professor at the London School of Economics, sees research and evidence-based interventions as core weapons to raise awareness and best practice, Kate Pljaskovova[337] and Bibi Groot[338] founded and work at Fair HQ,[339] a London-based inclusion consultancy to put research into best practice every day. From the US West Coast, Lolita Taub[340] adds further practical insights from her experiences as a Latinx operator, investor, and newly minted VC.

Interviewed February 2021

THE WORK OF FAIR HQ

Erika Brodnock (EB): *Kate, can you tell us a little bit about why you started Fair HQ?*

Kate Pljaskovova (KP): Prior to Fair HQ I had a previous business targeting the gender pay gap that focused on empowering women to negotiate

336. https://twitter.com/profgracelordan
337. https://twitter.com/kpljaskovova
338. https://twitter.com/ASBGroot
339. https://fairhq.co/
340. https://twitter.com/lolitataub

in the corporate environment. We worked with more than 1,800 women across businesses including Sky, Spotify, Dell, and PwC. In doing so we discovered that by helping businesses to change their negotiation processes in pay and performance reviews, etcetera, they became much more effective in ensuring fair practices, and offering fair rewards to not only women, but anyone that comes from a nontraditional background.

I started looking into what has been done in the overall D&I space and how much money was being wasted on things that did not work. How could we better understand how businesses are performing? What does "good" look like when it comes to diversity and inclusion approaches internally in business processes, policies, representations, and the behaviors that are present in the organization? Then pairing that data with scientific evidence and making suggestions as to what companies can do to improve their behaviors, processes, policies, and the outcomes that it has on the different people in those organizations and ultimately, what outcome that has on their business performance. That is what we are trying to do. We connect the data, the recommendations, and create a holistic strategy for businesses that will effectively help them become more successful. We do that very systematically.

THE WORK OF THE INCLUSION INITIATIVE

Johannes Lenhard (JL): *Grace, can you tell us about the motivations behind starting the Inclusion Initiative and what it is?*

Grace Lordan (GL): I believe that in order to have productive, creative, and innovative teams, we have to have different types of people around the table where ideas collide. That is where we get great outcomes. I say that I hold a belief simply because most of the evidence on inclusion is from lab, experiments, and correlation studies. From an academic perspective, proving that by offering more evidence across all the levels, the macro level, and the individual level, and establishing causality at that level is interesting to me.

The second reason is that I have spent ten years now studying what makes people successful. One of the things that has come through in that research is that it goes beyond their skills, talents, and ability. I have studied discrimination explicitly. I have been looking more recently on the flip side of that and thinking about privilege as something that gets people ahead unjustly. I want to spend the next decade of my life trying to rectify that and making sure that people do get ahead based on their skills, talents, and ability, and we rewrite some of the other things that have been getting people ahead at the moment.

The last thing that I find fascinating is that we roll out a lot of D&I interventions in companies and we never check if they work, and people become fatigued with diversity initiatives. Being able to gather an evidence base that does not just say "this is what works," but also takes into account context as well, is extraordinarily important. Firms are on different journeys, there is a different distribution of culture; if I am a toxic firm, some things are going to be effective for me that will not be effective in firms that sit further up the culture distribution curve. The honest approach to D&I will say, "We think this is going to work and we are going to evaluate whether it does work. We are going to report back to you whether it works today, in a month, in a year, and be really honest."

I am really concerned about the fact that there are talented people who are from underprivileged backgrounds who are not getting to where they need to be for reasons that have nothing to do with the skills, time, and talent that they possess.

THE WORK OF COMMUNITY FUND

EB: *Lolita, to come full circle here, can you tell us a little bit about how and why you started the Community Fund?*

Lolita Taub (LT): I'm an unlikely VC fund manager. Yes, I have 14 years of experience under my belt as an operator and investor, and have produced over $70M in tech sales and made 60+ investments in and out of Silicon Valley. But as a kid, people used to tell me I would not amount to anything because of my socioeconomic condition (poor), gender (female), and ethnic make-up (Latina). Yet, I persevered, for my family and for all those others underestimated in my community. And, in October 2020, I co-founded and launched the Community Fund, a $5M fund investing in early-stage community-driven companies, with my partner Jesse Middleton.

My earlier experiences put me on track to thinking: as a businesswoman of color, I want to serve my community, and I see opportunity in founders that the industry overlooks who would otherwise produce outsized returns. I needed to become a check-writer and invest in underestimated founders. I kept working because I needed to pay the bills, but I started thinking about how I could break into venture capital. After my MBA and many hurdles and hoops, I slowly found a foothold in VC: Backstage Capital and the support of Arlan Hamilton came first; being an Indie.VC scout and a NextGen Venture Partner next. Last year, my husband and I launched the Startup-Investor Matching Tool, which connects underestimated founders with investors. Around the same time, Jesse Middleton reached out asking me whether I wanted to co-found a fund that would invest in the best (but underestimated) founders, and here we are.

HOW RESEARCH LEADS TO ACTION-BASED POLICIES

EB: *Business, entrepreneurship, and technology seem to be concentrated. Power seems to be concentrated in small, homogeneous networks at the moment. How can the power of research be mobilized to create systemic change?*

Lolita Taub (LT): Often, status-quo and biased investors tell underestimated founders[341] that they will not invest because their markets are "niche," "too small," and not capable of producing unicorns. That's just not true. The investors spewing these statements simply don't see or appreciate the market potential. Research and stats on the market sizes that are represented by underestimated and underrepresented communities are needed ASAP to highlight the money-making opportunity to invest in these markets.

Bibi Groot (BG): That is a great but also very challenging question. The power of research is to start thinking systemically and strategically about what are the small wins and the small changes that we can start implementing in our systems, in our businesses, to create larger scale changes. Culture is a collection of everyday behaviors. If we start by changing and embedding better everyday behavior, you will create systemic change over time, and you will create more diversity in themes. The only way to go about it is to start thinking from the process perspective inside businesses. How can you encourage, for example, younger or more junior employees to have more access to senior leadership teams? How can you encourage them to have a seat at the table? How can you share information better

---

341. Lolita defined an underestimated founder as "a founder that has the potential to build a successful company, a unicorn, but is overlooked by investors because she or he does not fit the stereotypical cisgendered-white-male-Ivy-League-drop-out-who-worked-at-a-FAGMA-co-founder mold."

across the business so that everyone gets insight into how decisions are made and that everyone gets a voice in the direction of the company? How can they participate in that decision making?

There is a body of great research on why these things are important.[342] We do not yet have very strong evidence on how to make it work, especially because every company is so different, and context has a huge impact on the effectiveness of interventions. We know the threads that we need to start pulling from the research. There is a lot of opportunity here to start embedding change not as these huge culture initiatives; let us just start targeting really specific things inside companies that we know have an effect, such as making sure that people are part of collaborative workgroups, they can access the resources they need, we have meeting formats where minority voices are heard, and it is not just the loudest person in the room talking. Let us start seeing if we can create compound change with small wins.

GL: I fully agree that we need to move to action-based policies. Rather than doing research and talking about why inclusion is actually good for business, given that we have the evidence from the lab, we have the evidence from the macro, we should take a risk. I do not like using the word "risk" here, because I do not feel that it is a risk. We should move forwards, make the changes, and take care to evaluate those changes, and then highlight that they actually work for business. That is the first part.

OUTSIDE PRESSURE IS HELPING DRIVE CHANGE

GL: The second part of it is to really show to firms that their image matters for their profit and loss and for their shareholders, that customers are starting to care more. Shareholders are starting to care, coming at it from a different angle will make firms not only take action inside, which at the end of the day is just one firm, but also will make them start managing their supply chain, which is a really powerful mechanism.

---

342. van Knippenberg et al (2020) Synergy from Diversity;[343] Herring (2017) Is Diversity Still a Good Thing;[344] Nishii (2013) The Benefits of Climate for Inclusion for Gender-Diverse Groups[345]

343. https://behavioralpolicy.org/wp-content/uploads/2020/08/Synergy-from-diversity-Managing-team-diversity-to-enhance-performance-1.pdf

344. https://journals.sagepub.com/doi/abs/10.1177/0003122417716611

345. https://journals.aom.org/doi/10.5465/amj.2009.0823

More and more international firms are asking for D&I evidence from companies and other teams that approach them for business. That is really effective. Monitoring what those diverse teams actually bring when they walk through the doors is really effective. If we think of the different groups of people in society, we do still have this group in society who are loud, who talk about a meritocracy as if the meritocracy is truly measuring merit.

That is why when we make these changes to our supply chain, and we start evaluating what happens when we do have more diverse and inclusive teams serving us as clients, we will really help move the needle on what actually is and is not a meritocracy. I believe that we are not in a meritocracy at the moment; that privilege is what advances people unnecessarily. If we move towards making changes now and evaluating them, and pushing that evidence out into society, what are the effects of having diversity at the table that is included? It will be really powerful, and the firms that do not follow should suffer creative destruction.

EB: *We are starting to see the sea change coming from lots of organizations; NASDAQ and Goldman Sachs have come out publicly recently that they are going to stop supporting companies and firms unless they have diversity at the table.*

KP: We have seen that when a lot of VCs right now are raising funds, LPs are asking them about the diversity numbers of the fund, portfolio, and pipeline. As a result, they are starting to put these measures in place from the outset. The third-party requirement is forcing their hand. This is then trickling down to their portfolio companies. VCs are wondering how they can support portfolio companies as early as just a couple of founders, to ensure that they are building diversity and inclusion into their DNA. It's an opportunity to get it right from the start.

Just a few months after launching Fair HQ, we started to confirm some of the data from the research that when you have low representation of women in leadership, you also see lower levels of inclusion for women across the business. What about people of color? What impact does representation have on inclusion for them? Meritocracy does not yet exist, even though we want it.

EMPATHY AND THE OUTSIDER PERSPECTIVE IN LEADERSHIP

JL: *How much have your own backgrounds influenced the work on inclusion that you are doing? Do you think it is feasible to expect those in power who are white, male, and from privilege to be able to empathize with what it is like belonging to an out group?*

LT: Coming from poverty, being a five-foot, three-quarter-inch-tall Latina, and being consistently underestimated has certainly informed my thoughts and approach to inclusion. As a human with a heart, I don't want others to be dismissed because they don't look a certain way or come from particular social circles. As a capitalist, I don't want to let financial opportunities fall through the cracks. There's generational wealth to be created in including a myriad of intersectional humans and investing in them. That last bit about generational wealth can have white guys embracing all types of people. Green is green. For money, I do believe that white privileged males can and will work through their bias and become more inclusive.

GL: A lot of diversity and inclusion focuses on gender. When we focus on moving women forward in organizations, or getting women more access to venture capital, we talk about female role models, because the role model needs to be able to identify with the group that they are bringing along. That first wave has really done incredibly well for women, because women are 50% of the population and about 45% of the workforce. There are a lot of voices there. If we rely on our background, in order to be able to identify with the people whose barriers we want to break down, we always end up being in a world that excludes.

I come from a working-class background, in a small city in Ireland, so I have access to some privilege and there are other aspects of privilege that are not there for me. I cannot experience what it is like to go through life as a Black woman. It becomes very important to listen to people who can tell me that story and tell me their experiences and obstacles. Then I can help them, not in the sense that I am a hero, but we all have to start helping each other at this point. We cannot think of an insider versus outsider hypothesis. If you take that to the extreme, the idea of the privileged white man, that we always think as the people who have the most in society, because that is what the statistics tell us, then there is a role for them stopping and listening to people who they see are not getting ahead in the data at the same pace as the average.

Any human being who holds any position in an organization can stop and listen to the obstacles that people are telling them that they are facing, and believe them, which is really important, and not doubt the words that are coming out of their mouth, even if they do not apply to them. Together, we need to think about creative ways to work together towards equity. If I am helping other groups bring down their obstacles, and they are helping me bring down my obstacles, or helping another group, then we advance towards the idea that we are all moving forward based on our skills, talents, and ability, and there is a collective.

One of the questions that I have about the gender revolution in professional work is whether women who actually get through and who get to the top, because they have been outsiders, recognize the need to stop and think about other people who are facing obstacles, learn about those obstacles, and bring those obstacles down. I worry that is not the case. I say that because when I speak at events for women, lots of women turn up. And when I am invited to talk to people about racism, or when I am invited to LGBTQ events, it is not the same people.

Once we remain segregated in this insider-outsider group mentality, we will not get that final convergence. Coming from a working-class background in Cork, when I grew up, I was not aware of it. I lived in a neighborhood where all the kids played together, we were all working class, they did not have lots more than me. Only two of us went to university, I never thought about it all the way through it. It only became salient to me when I went to university. And when I was actually now networking with people who did not have to also work 30 hours a week. At different points in our life, we become aware that we are an outsider, and that we have less in common with the people that surround us. Understanding those experiences of different groups has become extraordinarily important to me. Over the next ten years, it will be the root of my work: going forward and admitting that I cannot understand fully what the person has gone through, but I can listen, learn the obstacles, and hopefully be part of a movement that brings those obstacles down.

EB: *Grace, do you feel that your background as a working-class woman enables you to empathize a little bit more, because when you have had one type of disadvantage or outsider experience, you then realize how other people are feeling? If that has impacted the way that you are able to behave,* *how might people who have never had an outsider experience be able to gather that empathy for people in the circumstances that they are not in?*

GL: The answer is definitely yes. At the same time, when I talk to people, and they tell me about an experience, I will say to them, that has never happened to me, but if I was in that situation, I would have hated it. I get it. We do not know the counterfactual if I had been born incredibly wealthy, but I might have bigger blinkers than I have now.

We need a different type of manager going forward, and a different type of leader in society across all levels where there is power. We do need active listening and leaders who want to know about each other's experience. I met a senior manager, who spoke about the fact that he learned for the first time that a very senior managing director in this very big investment bank had been subject to racism when he was driving his car in New York, in Manhattan. He lives just outside New York, has a fantastic house, has fantastic experiences at work, his team love him—absolutely ideal life on the outside, but every time he drove into Manhattan with his children, he was being pulled over, in his Volvo, and how crushing and embarrassing it was for him. For that particular person who never had any experiences like that, it is so important for him to listen and hear that story and know about the experiences that the people on his team are having.

The first step is the obstacles that you can actually bring down. That empathetic ear is going to become much more important for managers, because that connection, particularly at a junior level, to be able to discuss with somebody something that they can not necessarily identify with, I do think it takes the mental health burden off of people in work where they can actually be more productive. Aside from doing the right thing as human beings and showing the person that they are actually cared about, it also has positive effects on productivity.

I do not think it is possible for everybody. There will be people across all types of demographics that will not be good at empathy, and perhaps you can learn it, but if they are not willing to learn maybe managing is not going to be for them and bringing along talent is not going to be for them. As we go forward, the role of the manager who actually leans in and wants to learn about people who come from different backgrounds and have different experiences, and not get uncomfortable with the negativity, is hugely important.

I noticed one of the flaws people regularly have is that they always want to put themselves in the story and say, "Oh, I identify with that, or I had this." You need to realize it is okay that somebody had a terrible experience that had nothing to do with you and your role in listening to the story is really to make sure that that does not happen in the future. If they are highlighting obstacles, your role is to be part of enabling them to bring those obstacles down and move forward. How you teach that, I do not know. That is going to become, at the professional level, the most important skill set leaders can have.

HOW TO ENGAGE LEADERS RESISTANT TO CHANGE

BG: We have been looking into how to overcome diversity resistance and how to engage majority men. It is more anecdotal, more qualitative research. Some of the ways that you can engage people who have been in positions of power quite comfortably is to encourage perspective-taking.[346]

We need to start creating this conversation in this space where people start listening to each other's stories. There are some really good techniques for learning how to actually engage with someone else's story and not making it about yourself, and being curious about someone else's experience.

It is also a promising idea to turn the conversation about diversity on its head. Instead of setting targets for increasing representation of women, people of color, or other underrepresented minorities, why not set the target for a maximum of 70% homogeneity? Striving for a maximum 70% people of the same gender, ethnicity, cultural background, generation, or educational background makes it less about "fixing the minority." This way, the traditional majority may feel they can still be part of the conversation. We need to create a conversation where everyone has a voice. Traditional majority men, most of the time, feel that they do not have a space to talk because they feel like they have been the perpetrator of this lack of diversity and inclusion. We need to start from a radically different space.

Unfortunately, unconscious bias training sometimes leads to pointing fingers, saying you are all biased and this is all of these terrible things that you are doing. It is obviously very important to be aware of unconscious

---

346. Galinsky et al (2015) Maximizing the gains and minimizing the pains of diversity[347]

347. https://www.scholars.northwestern.edu/en/publications/
    maximizing-the-gains-and-minimizing-the-pains-of-diversity-a-poli

biases, but we know from the research that being aware of your biases is not enough to actually change behavior in the long term. Let us avoid having these pointing fingers. Let us create more open conversation for people's experiences with perspective-taking, empathy, and active listening interventions. There are a lot of training programs and small wins that we can start building into our one-to-ones and our leadership and manager trainings.

KEY PRACTICES

EB: *Could you share any easy-to-implement, yet key, practices people can do to make their organization fund or portfolio more inclusive?*

LT: Would you ever ask your money manager to irresponsibly put all your eggs in one basket? No, you wouldn't. You'd want to ask for a diversified portfolio to optimize returns. Well, the same applies in the world of GPs and LPs. Diversification in fund portfolio investments and team makeup are key to achieving outsized returns. Fund managers need to keep this in mind and hire their teams and wire money to startups accordingly. I recommend that funds pick the best founders and the best investors, not based on homogeneity and comfort, but on what will increase the chances of honoring our fiduciary duties to our limited partners (of making them the most money we can). Because let's be clear: optimizing for outsized returns is not possible in a portfolio of homogenous companies, founders, and investors.

KP: Strategically, a fund has three areas they need to focus on. First is internally. What is the makeup of their team? And how do the different demographic groups in that team feel about the opportunities and decision-making they have access to? The second is the diversity in their pipeline, developing an understanding of how they are sourcing companies they invest in. How are they measuring their funnel? The third is how they are supporting their portfolio companies to be inclusive and diverse.

We have found that internal leadership is the most important area. If all partners are all white men, it is very likely that the founders invested in are also white men.[348] The second really important thing is the investment pipeline. VCs are extremely dependent on recommendations from other founders, if your founder base is all privileged white men, a broad

---

348. https://www.emerald.com/insight/content/doi/10.1108/GM-11-2019-0222/full/html

and diverse pipeline is unlikely. VCs need to actively reach out to different communities rather than saying there is a pipeline problem. It takes work to do that. What we have seen is in sourcing and analyzing companies, VCs tend to look at the deck, what school founders went to. If we apply a blind process as we do in hiring for firms, and start by looking only at the potential prospects of the business while removing the demographic information on the founder(s) from the process, that is going to be super effective. Research has also shown[349] that women are asked very different questions. Implementing structured conversations with the founders and writing their answers down will help to overcome this issue. Some funds are doing quite good work around this.

BG: In terms of inclusion when it comes to access to information and decision-making, from our perspective of the day-to-day behaviors, some really easy practices are making sure that your meeting times reflect different people's availability during the day, that you record all of your meeting notes, and that there is a shared knowledge base that people can access.

Another inclusion practice is ensuring that tasks that are not promotable tasks, such as taking notes, organizing the office party, or organizing a birthday cake for a colleague, are rotated between team members. From the research,[350] we know that women are asked to help out with "non-promotable tasks" much more frequently than men. But not necessarily because they're simply more helpful: women tend to face backlash when they say "no" to such tasks, while men do not. By rotating some of these non-promotable tasks, or by making some of the tasks important criteria for promotions, you are actually creating more equal spread of the stretch assignments and team tasks that also need to happen.

There is an interesting recommendation [in *Inclusion Nudges for Leaders*[351]] to also use checklists to define who you are going to assign to a stretch assignment, because managers tend to have their top two or three go-to people that they think of when they have a new, exciting project. By not checking yourself, in that moment, when you are making these decisions, you are creating this self-fulfilling prophecy where the same people

---

349. https://lbsresearch.london.edu/id/eprint/1196/

350. https://www.aeaweb.org/articles?id=10.1257/aer.20141734

351. https://books.google.ca/books/about/Inclusion_Nudges_for_Leaders_in_Organisa.html?id=D6JxzgEACAAJ&redir_esc=

get opportunities and then because they have these opportunities, they are able to advance more quickly. There are some very practical tips on how to create checklists, where you make sure that every week you write down in detail: "Who are all of the people who are available for a stretch task? What is the importance of the task? Who are you considering? Is there anyone else that you should consider that could add something to that specific task?" Those are some really practical ideas to make sure that you are considering everyone equally and fairly for access to opportunities.

The same thing applies for promotions and making sure that people have access to the leadership team. There is definitely interesting research on pairing up[352] senior team members with more junior to create these informal social networks, especially as we know that minority candidates or employees have different networking approaches[353] as well. They are slightly less broad networking approaches than for the traditional majority. Let us make sure that we create these opportunities for people who might not have had access or who might not feel much belonging with the organization as their divisional majority counterparts.

352. https://www.nationalacademies.org/our-work/
    the-science-of-effective-mentoring-in-stemm
353. https://journals.aom.org/doi/10.5465/amr.2015.0399

18.2 *Toropainen: Inclusion Best Practices*

Katja Toropainen (Inklusiiv)

We spoke with Katja Toropainen,[354] *founder of Inklusiiv*[355] *and former chief program curator at Europe's biggest tech conference, Helsinki-based Slush,*[356] *about tech and VCs embracing inclusion. Katja provides best practices, examples, and case studies for both tech and VCs focusing on diversity and inclusion in company culture. She highlights how embracing continuous learning and development and setting strong targets with good metrics are a key starting point on this journey. This is one of the most applied conversations in the volume—worth diving into for anyone who wants to take inclusion seriously.*

Interviewed January 2021

HOW TECH INSPIRED A MOVE TO DEI

Johannes Lenhard (JL): *Not too long ago, you were running speakers and programs at Slush. Now you are leading a DEI-focused community you founded. How has the tech world that you have been steeped into for the last years treated you so far? What has driven you on?*

Katja Toropainen (KT): I started learning more in-depth knowledge about diversity and inclusion (D&I) challenges in tech during the years that I led the curating of speakers and programs at Slush, the biggest startup event in the world. I wanted to learn more about D&I to understand our responsibility as event organizers to showcase diverse content and speakers. Had we not paid attention to D&I, our speaker lineup would have been almost exclusively white and men. I dove straight into the rabbit hole of finding more and more information about the history of

354. https://twitter.com/katjatorop

355. https://inklusiiv.com/

356. https://www.slush.org/events/helsinki/

diversity in tech, as well as diversity and inclusion best practices. It was devastating to realize how different turning points and decisions in the history of tech had led us to where we are now.

I started Inklusiiv as a non-profit to bring change, first as a movement that in the long run can have a lasting impact. After my years at Slush, I was pondering that I would probably want to leave the tech industry unless the industry got more diverse and inclusive. So, I decided I wanted to be part of the change and I chose to work in the D&I field. We are striving for an industry free of sexism, racism, or other forms of discrimination or harassment, where women and underrepresented founders, operators, and investors feel valued and appreciated.

It's shocking to discover data and research that reveals the lack of funding for underrepresented founders. These same biases affect what kind of companies we build and what sort of products and services we design. The tech industry is still representing our world from a narrow point of view, with over 90% of funding in Europe going to all-male founding teams[357] and the whole industry being extremely male-dominated.

My work with Inklusiiv, and being part of the Atomico Angel Programme, has given me more optimism because I've found supportive communities involved in building a more inclusive tech industry and got to know so many other people dedicated to advancing diversity, equity, and inclusion (DEI). Important reports such as the State of European Tech[359] by Atomico and Slush and the Nordic Startup Funding Report[360] by Unconventional Ventures bring to light invaluable new knowledge, while communities and networks for angel investors that work towards investing in and supporting more female founders, play a key role. Moreover, I feel very humbled and empowered to be able to work with people and companies committed to driving DEI topics forward.

Change takes time, but with time and more and more positive results, it starts to happen. I truly believe that in the upcoming years, the tech industry will become more inclusive towards underrepresented groups of people.

---

357. The State of European Tech: Diversity & Inclusion.[358] Automico, in partnership with Slush and Orrick, 2020.

358. https://2020.stateofeuropeantech.com/chapter/diversity-inclusion/

359. https://stateofeuropeantech.com

360. https://www.unconventional.vc/report/

DIVERSITY WON'T LAST WITHOUT INCLUSION

Erika Brodnock (EB): *What is your definition of inclusion and how important would you say it is? Is it something that is still underdeveloped in the tech industry, because everyone is so focused on diversity?*

KT: Where diversity focuses on hiring diverse talent, inclusion makes sure that people will want to stay in organizations. Without inclusion, diversity will walk away from the organizations, and in the worst case, even from the whole tech industry.

According to the US-based research by Accenture and Girls Who Code[361] in 2020, 50% of women in tech leave the industry by age 35 and 37% cite the non-inclusive work culture as the primary reason. The percentages are even worse[362] for women of color and women who belong to sexual or gender minorities. The importance of inclusion has been constantly highlighted by various research pieces and reports, for example, in the annual McKinsey report[363] investigating the business case for diversity. In the 2020 report, there is, so far, the strongest argument for inclusion; it's something that every business needs to commit to truly flourish.

According to Deloitte research,[364] combining diversity with inclusion efforts leads to better business outcomes. They found out that organizations with inclusive cultures are three times as likely to be high-performing, six times more likely to be innovative and agile, and eight times more likely to achieve better business outcomes.

Inclusion is about creating a sense of belonging. Like other DEI experts, I also agree with the emphasis that inclusion is about taking those daily actions while understanding that you can never be done or ready. Inclusion really is a lifelong journey of learning and developing practices and processes.

In terms of teamwork or organizational environment, we define inclusion as the work environment where everyone is treated fairly and respectfully. Individuals across the company have equal access to opportunities and can really fully contribute to the organization's success.

---

361. https://www.accenture.com/_acnmedia/PDF-134/Accenture-A4-GWC-Report-Final1.pdf
362. https://www.fastcompany.com/90558017/
    half-of-women-who-work-in-tech-do-this-surprising-thing-by-age-35
363. https://www.mckinsey.com/featured-insights/diversity-and-inclusion/
    diversity-wins-how-inclusion-matters
364. https://www2.deloitte.com/us/en/insights/deloitte-review/issue-22/
    diversity-and-inclusion-at-work-eight-powerful-truths.html

Inclusion fosters psychological safety and a sense of belonging, welcoming new ideas and making sure that everyone's voices are being heard. Some barriers of inclusion are, for instance, unconscious biases, lack of representation, and privileges. Building inclusion is also not just a one-person job but requires effort and commitment from everyone in the organization.

Within the tech startup and VC ecosystem, or within any industry, the most important thing to understand is that most of the DEI challenges are structural. In addition to changing our behavior to become more inclusive, we need to change how the systems and structures work. This means figuring out ways to make the systems more fair and inclusive in terms of how we hire people, how we decide on promotions, and how we share responsibilities.

CONCRETE STEPS TOWARD INCLUSION IN ORGANIZATIONS

JL: *Can we go into some concrete ideas for what startups can do to focus on inclusion and where is it particularly important?*

KT: In any company or organization, to create tangible change, there needs to be a stringent way of figuring out priorities and setting up measurable goals. Otherwise, change doesn't last. At the same time, I believe that we still need plenty of awareness-building, learning, and education around the topic of DEI. But in order to do something concrete, we need to move from awareness-building to action.

For instance, while it's great that unconscious biases are now much more widely acknowledged, acknowledgment by itself does not make a lasting impact. We need to focus on the processes and structures in the organization, such as recruiting or leadership principles, that are affected strongly by unconscious biases. By changing these structures to more inclusive ways, we can truly make a difference.

Great concrete ways to take on this work includes things like measuring employee and leadership demographic diversity and running employee surveys to find out about their engagement and viewpoints. Based on these tangible insights, it's possible to find priorities for improvement and measure development and success in inclusion practices.

Figuring out the DEI path for any organization can be really challenging as there are a lot of different aspects to focus on. Many companies have good intentions but don't know what to do or where to start. That's where DEI experts can provide value in helping them to learn and find ways, in collaboration with their team, to figure out specific priorities and steps forward. At Inklusiiv we prefer to host workshops and trainings, led by our experts, with a limited size of team. We've seen how inviting the people in teams to co-create the inclusion processes leads to better results: more tangible goals, and clearer actionable steps.

CASE STUDIES AND RESEARCH ON INCLUSION

The positive side of things is that there are plenty of best practices on how to include DEI in every function of an organization, including product management, marketing communications, engineering, and leadership. Where there's people, there's a need for inclusivity.

One real-life case example is told by Kjartan Slette, co-founder of a Norwegian growth company Unacast, on the stage at Slush 2017.[365] They were a company of 20 people when their co-founders realized the lack of diversity in their team. In just six months, they did a complete turn-around. The number of women in their team went from 17% to 36%, of which 31% were in engineering. Before that, they had no women in their engineering team. When asked about how they did it,[366] their answer was quite simple: commitment. They realized they had a problem, they wanted to improve on it and worked hard to make the change happen. There are plenty of different actions they took, ranging from internal discussions and changing the hiring process to sharing their story publicly, revising the company's culture, and many more. Of course, nothing happens in the blink of an eye, but the solution itself is easy—if you want to make it happen, commit to the work.

Another Nordic tech company, Spotify, is well-known for investing in diversity, equity, inclusion, and belonging. They launched their diversity data report in 2018[367] and are actively publishing new D&I articles and data on their HR blog.[368]

Excitingly, DEI is becoming a necessary leadership competency. Leaders who want to stay relevant during the 21st century need to develop

365. https://www.youtube.com/watch?v=aRlWJ5X1r7l
366. https://www.unacast.com/post/
   we-stopped-talking-about-diversity-and-did-something-about-it
367. https://hrexecutive.com/spotify-gets-real-about-improving-workplace-diversity/
368. https://hrblog.spotify.com/

these competencies to be able to continue leading. Some traits of inclusive leaders are, for instance, the awareness of one's biases, prejudices, and privileges. Inclusive leaders are also committed to diversity and inclusion topics and able to discuss these matters.

Deloitte has been publishing research about inclusive leadership[369] and the conclusions are clear: inclusive leadership has a direct impact on team performance. In any company, the leadership needs to be committed to learning about D&I and driving this culture forward. The research also highlights the importance of curiosity in understanding how different people's diversity, experiences, and backgrounds could work together in the best possible way.

THE INVESTOR ROLE IN BUILDING DEI

EB: *Would you say that this also applies to the world of investors, and do you have any best practice examples to share for them?*

KT: Investors and VCs have a crucial role in building a more diverse and inclusive technology industry. They have the opportunity to, first of all, affect improving D&I inside their own team and organization. In addition, they hold the power to affect who is building the future companies and getting funding. In addition, as investors and board members, they have the possibility of making sure D&I is prioritized in their portfolio companies and helping them to build these crucial skills that are required to build future successful companies.

Historically, white men have built tech and VC companies for themselves—for other white men. This means that their perspective is deeply anchored in the structures and cultures, making the challenge of inclusivity systemic.

Tech and the VC industry need more people who understand the specific challenges of this ecosystem when it comes to DEI. Our ecosystem needs to be better at listening to underrepresented people and educating ourselves on effective allyship. To become an ally, any investor can be more intentional in embracing DEI by educating themselves and by reading content by women, people of color, and other underrepresented groups. Learning about the structural privileges we have is important. To become an ally means also taking action and actively using one's own

---

369. https://www2.deloitte.com/us/en/insights/topics/talent/
    six-signature-traits-of-inclusive-leadership.html

position and power to drive change. For instance, a white investor can educate themselves more about the privilege of being white—free from structural racism—and use that privilege to make the industry more equitable for all. Many investors say that they would love to fund more underrepresented founders or diversify their deal flow. The solution for VCs is pretty simple: hire more women, people of color, and people from underrepresented groups to your investment team—especially as partners and general partners. That's the solution. The common challenge for investors seems to be commitment. As said before, D&I issues take work and long-term commitment. For instance, it might take efforts to diversify one's personal networks and learn more about DEI. Like with Unacast, changes in team structures and practices take time and effort. My best advice would be to start this work early enough. If you have built, let's say, a very homogeneous team of 10 people, you might already have difficulties attracting more diversity in your team. Funds such as Backstage Capital by Arlan Hamilton and Ada Ventures by Check Warner are leading the way, building funds with diversity and inclusion in mind since the beginning.

IMPROVING INCLUSION IN THE TECH WORLD

JL: *Looking forward, when it comes to specifically inclusion in the tech world, what is missing? What do people need to focus on next?*

KT: What seems to be hindering development is the fear that makes people or companies say that they are already diverse and inclusive, pretending they are there already. We should normalize and acknowledge that no one is there yet, no individual, organization, or even society itself. Acknowledging this will enable us to begin the real work. Understanding the problem and complexity of this also requires a lot of societal knowledge. This is why intersectional knowledge both from business and, let's see, humanities and sociology is important. Diverse understanding of society is key. In addition, we should be learning more about intersectionality within diversity, our privileges, and allyship.

We humans are imperfect and filled with unconscious biases, stemming from societal structures and biases. We just all need to acknowledge that and commit to this lifelong journey of learning, getting better, and making progress—that's the solution. There are no easy, quick fixes that solve everything. Or if there were, those would have already been adopted by most organizations.

19 Conversations: Building New Flywheels

19.1 *Huang: Founder Adversity*

Laura Huang (Harvard Business School)

Laura Huang[370] is a professor at Harvard Business School and has been researching topics right at the heart of DEI in venture capital and technology companies her entire academic career. She has published widely on how female and male founders are treated differently when pitching to VCs and the role that gut feeling plays in the investment process, among other things. We talked about implicit bias among VCs, what needs to change to overcome it, and the disparity of education in the tech ecosystem, which is reproducing another kind of elite.

Interviewed via email March 2021

PROBLEMS WITH DEI IN THE INVESTMENT PROCESS

Johannes Lenhard (JL): *You have been involved in pathbreaking work on the relationship between VC investors and (female) founders, and are published widely in top journals. Translating this back into concrete insights for VCs and founders and their everyday work: what are the biggest findings when it comes to identifying problems in the investment process with a specific focus on DEI?*

Laura Huang (LH): One of the largest problems in the investment process is the impact of implicit bias—the perceptions people hold of others based on internalized biases and stereotypes. Effectively communicating with and winning over investors is one of the most imperative skills to the development of a founder's career, and getting funding from VCs is heavily reliant on how the investors perceive the founder. However, as a result

---

370. https://twitter.com/ProfLauraHuang

of implicit bias, many investors have an unconscious idea of what a successful entrepreneur looks like. Based on common stereotypes, this image typically reflects a young, white male entrepreneur. This is the root of the problem, as this puts female founders at a disadvantage from the get-go: they simply don't look that part of a successful entrepreneur.

From this initial disadvantage, internalized implicit bias continues to have a negative impact on female founders by manifesting itself through investor-founder communication. In my research,[371] I have found that while investors are more likely to pose positive, promotion questions to white male founders, they are more likely to pose negative, prevention questions to female founders. This disparity in communication, based upon the investor's initial perception of who "fits the bill" of a successful businessperson, allows white male founders to discuss their business in a more positive, attractive way while female founders are left to grapple with defending their pitches from negatively tinged questions.

For example, take a founder who is seeking investment from a VC in order to scale a company that has struggled with generating revenue in the past. If the founder is a white male, he is more likely to be asked questions that allow him to highlight the positive aspects of the company, such as discussing the total addressable market or emphasizing the potential for high-market return on investment for the VC. However, if the founder is female, she is more likely to be asked questions that require her to defend the company's issues, such as explaining the current lack of investment or discussing the barriers to past revenue generation.

As you can see, these positive and negative spins on communication can have a huge impact on the investment process—founders who are able to engage in positive communication are significantly more likely to land a successful pitch with a VC than founders who engage in negative communication. Therefore, implicit bias and perceptions are incredibly influential in investing and can shape the entirety of interpersonal relationships from the start of a conversation. In relation to DEI, this has negative implications for how female founders operate within the world of business. If female founders are put at a disadvantage just based on their gender and appearance, how can they effectively position themselves to compete with their male counterparts?

---

371. https://laurahuang.net/research/

HOW VCS CAN OVERCOME BIASES AND INCREASE DEI

JL: *Turning from the problems to possible solutions, have you come across any best practices which VCs could embrace and use in order to overcome the issues you identified in the investment process? What do VCs need to do better to increase DEI in the space?*

LH: First and foremost, we must remember that even though VCs are large financial institutions with significant influence, at the end of the day, they are organizations comprised of a group of people. As I've discussed in my research, people have the natural tendency to internalize stereotypes, make snap judgments, formulate their own perceptions, and make judgments. However, this can become problematic if people with a lot of power, such as partners at VC firms, foster and unconsciously act upon implicit biases that negatively impact minority and female founders. At its core, this is a deeply human problem based on perceptions and negative attributions. Although my research and book focus on addressing those at a disadvantage—learning how to flip negative perceptions and turn adversity into advantage—I also believe progress can be made if those with the advantage are willing to make a change.

I believe there are a number of actions VCs can take if they want to solve the major problems that currently stand in the way of a more diverse and equitable investing landscape. First, VCs can make an impact by hiring partners from diverse backgrounds. VC partners typically fit the archetype of the wealthy, white, male investor, which means that most of the decision-making power is given disproportionately to members of that group. If the partners of a VC firm were more diverse, meaning if there were a greater balance of women and people of color given a seat at the table, then the biases of the entire decision-making organization would not skew so significantly in the direction of favoring one particular population. Additionally, VCs can counter implicit bias and stereotypes within their organizations right now through the implementation of diversity, equity, and inclusion training courses as a requirement for every single investor meeting face-to-face with founders. These courses can help train their current executives to unlearn implicit biases and approach investing in a more effective, open-minded fashion that benefits both the founder and the VC.

HOW THE EDGE PRINCIPLES CAN HELP ENTREPRENEURS

JL: *In your book* Edge: Turning Adversity into Advantage, *you draw learnings from both your own and other people's experience as an overlooked and underprivileged person. What are the top three learnings that specifically an entrepreneur can take from* Edge? *What are concrete best practice for entrepreneurs to take on to do better?*

LH: In my book, I describe what I like to call the "EDGE Principles"—the four steps to honing your own unique edge. The acronym stands for *Enrich*, *Delight*, *Guide*, and *Effort*. I believe they are the top learnings that any entrepreneur should take from *Edge*.

- *Enrich* calls upon the individual to identify your own basic goods—the greatest value you have to offer. What is your greatest strength that sets you apart from others? At the same time, you must be able to recognize your weaknesses as well. From this holistic understanding of both your strengths and weaknesses, you understand the cards you bring to the table and can operate within that parameter.
- *Delight* is the idea that you must pleasantly surprise key stakeholders in order to make others more intrigued by you and/or your services. Delight can come in many forms, such as micro interactions or company-wide policies. For example, a founder of a small clothing business can delight customers by offering them a free gift with their purchase. This gift both pleasantly surprises the customer and gives them incentive to return to the store in hopes of more delightful interactions.
- *Guide* calls upon the individual to reframe others' potentially negative perceptions into a positive view. For entrepreneurs, this is an incredibly effective tool that can help them grow and manage a startup. First, you must recognize the reason why others have a negative view of you, your product, and/or your business. Then, you must understand the positive perceptions you want people to have in place of the current negative perceptions. From here, you must formulate an action plan that can reframe people's perception of your business to highlight the positive and downplay the negative. Guide is not about denying or changing yourself, it is about embracing yourself and your brand completely and purposefully highlighting the positive aspects. Essentially, you must figure out a way to tell people about who you are rather than

letting them rely on their own personal assumptions and snap judgments.

- Finally, *Effort* is the classic "hard work" that is touted to everyone as the key to success. I include it last in this acronym because I believe hard work alone won't carry success. However, hard work is a very necessary component to success and will carry you to the finish line if you can master the first three skills. After enriching, delighting, and guiding others' perceptions of you, effort is where you have to show up and perform the hard work you promised to from the start.

GUT FEELING VS. HARD DATA

JL: *In some of your work, you talk about the role of "gut feeling" in VC investment decisions (also in contrast to the relative lack of impact of "hard data"). Isn't the impact of such "soft factors" a convenient excuse for VCs to keep investing in and hiring an un-diverse set of founders and next-gen investors? Could a "professionalization of the industry" (e.g., with data) help get over this kind of self-reproducing behavior?*

LH: That is an interesting idea, and my first instinct would be to question what kind of data we would use to "professionalize the industry." We have to remember that, as in interpersonal relationships and current investing processes, hard data and statistics can also be manipulated by the personal biases of the people programming, coding, and analyzing the data. With that said, even if it were possible to completely randomize, redact, and present founders/startups as anonymized datasets, I am not sure if the industry would be accepting of this kind of change. At the root, entrepreneurship and investing are deeply human, people-facing industries. However, the only way you can remove the impact of the aforementioned soft factors is by removing all interaction between VCs and the founders, as these soft factors are the result of gut feel, internalized biases, and quick perceptions. Would any VC be willing to make a major investment into a company without having substantial face-to-face interactions with the founder and startup team? I would imagine it would be hard for a firm to part with a large sum of money to invest in a company without having any interaction whatsoever with the leadership team.

With all of this said, would I like more attention paid to the hard data founders present in their VC pitches? Yes, as this is often the "meat and potatoes" of the investment pitch. However, the problem won't be solved by doing a complete 180 and focusing solely on data. Instead, the duty should be placed upon VCs to see the value in DEI and put measures in place to prevent implicit biases on part of their partners from negatively impacting investment decisions. There are a number of actions VCs can take to promote DEI, as I discussed above already. In summation, I believe we can tackle the lack of diversity in entrepreneurship by calling upon VCs to change their business practices that currently have the most negative impact on diversity in investing.

BEST PRACTICES FOR FEMALE FOUNDERS

JL: *Most recently, you have been working on female founders and their networks, and how that affects their chances of success. What are you learning from that (ongoing) research? What concrete "best practices" would you advise female founders to proactively engage in based on these findings?*

LH: As I continue to work with female founders and their networks, the greatest defining feature that always pops out to me is the disparity between how male and female founders are treated in business. It seems that women in business tend to get the short end of the stick, especially when communicating with VCs. With that said, I've also found that these same female founders are also incredibly intelligent and talented businesspeople, which makes this disparity all the more concerning.

Regarding best practices, the first thing female founders need to understand is that they have power over how others perceive them. As I discuss in my book *Edge: Turning Adversity into Advantage*, we are able to guide others' perceptions of us to view us as how we want to be recognized. Relating back to the investment process, female founders can guide communication with VCs to parry unproductive discussion topics. It is difficult to change the communication style of the investor, simply because investors hold the power. However, female founders can work proactively to identify red flag statements from investors that indicate negative implicit bias, and then reframe the discussion within their retort. Essentially, female founders must master the art of noticing prevention questions, and then phrasing their response in a way that reframes the initial statement as a promotion question and then answering in a positive fashion.

For example, imagine a situation in which an investor asks a female founder how her company can be attractive if it currently is underperforming in revenue generation. If the female founder is able to recognize this communication pattern, then she can answer this prevention question in a promotion-based nature that reframes the conversation and makes the business appear much more positive and attractive than before. She can respond by acknowledging the investor's concerns, but then asking him to look at the issue from another perspective: "Though we don't have significant revenue stats as of right now, we are a scrappy startup that is prepared to take on the market as we grow and scale even further. In fact, our total addressable market is [amount of money] and we expect our revenue margins to exponentially increase as we continue to build out our product and push our new and invigorating advertising campaign. In fact, let me tell you more about our new and innovative marketing approach ..." From here, the female founder has not only gained control of the conversation, but can now direct it to highlight the positive attributes of her business. And this tactic doesn't have to focus on an advertising campaign, but can redirect the conversation to anything such as product development, partnerships, and the management team.

Essentially, I advise female founders to gain a comprehensive understanding of communication styles and implicit bias. From here, they can go on to utilize what they've learned in the workplace.

INEQUALITY IN EDUCATION AND ACCESS TO TECH AND VC

JL: *Lastly, what is a big area of interest for you that is not understood well enough yet when it comes to increasing DEI in the tech/startup/VC ecosystem? Where are the crucial blind spots you will be working on next?*

LH: I think another crucial blind spot that currently plagues the industry is understanding how inequality in education impacts the tech/startup/VC ecosystem. In this country, there is a significant disparity in the quality of education students receive based upon the socioeconomic status of their family. If you are only enrolled in the public education system, then the quality of education you receive is solely based on the family in which you were born as well as the geographic location of your home. This tends to create a racial divide in which students of color, who are more likely to be born into low-income neighborhoods, receive a lower quality education in comparison to their white peers. This goes on to follow low-income students throughout their professional careers, as they lack access to the resources and capital necessary to thrive in school, gain acceptance to a higher education institution, and ultimately land a job in tech or entrepreneurship.

This has always been an issue I've been passionate about—in fact, my first job out of college was as a math teacher in a low-income neighborhood in Maryland. If we want to increase DEI in the tech/startup/VC industries, then we need to start empowering underrepresented populations at an early age. As such, I am in the process of founding Project EMplify, a non-profit dedicated to helping underprivileged students develop integral soft skills, bridging the gap between what is taught in school and what is needed in the workplace. Project EMplify's mission is to combat socioeconomic inequality by giving disadvantaged students access to the resources necessary to become competitive in the professional workplace, including a book donation program, mentorship program, and workshop series. I look forward to working with our first cohort of students and working towards making the future professional working environment more accessible and diverse.

19.2 *St. Louis, Matranga, Younkman, Joseph: Village Capital*

Bianca St. Louis (Black Innovation Alliance)

Heather Matranga (Village Capital)

Ben Younkman (Village Capital)

Dahlia Joseph (Village Capital)

Village Capital[372] has been doing things differently in the VC world since they started in Atlanta in 2009. They have always been strongly focused on impact and equitable access—with a lot of success; almost 50% of companies they have invested in or that went through their programs are run by women. We spoke to four representatives of the Village Capital team

---

372. https://vilcap.com/

(Heather Matranga,[373] Ben Younkman,[374] and Dahlia Joseph[375]) and the Black Innovation Alliance[376] (Bianca St. Louis[377]) about the structural issues in the VC model that prevent access for people, their work to overcome some of these problems, and their overall focus on "process innovation," i.e., radically rethinking how VC works.

Interviewed September 2021

CHANGING THE VC MODEL OR MAKING A NEW ONE?

Johannes Lenhard (JL): *If we want to really have diversity and inclusion in this industry, do we need to change the model of venture capital and rethink the structure of GPs and LPs more generally?*

Bianca St. Louis (BS): We need to not look to those stakeholders as the only people in the conversation. We need to think not just within the realm of the venture ecosystem, but also to who supports the work of enabling the next generation of entrepreneurs. We need a more holistic conversation, asking: what does it mean to support diverse entrepreneurs?

Heather Matranga (HM): We cannot expect a one-size-fit-all funding model to work in all circumstances. We cannot take this old model and use it to solve structural inequities that have existed for a long time. We need to be more creative about deploying capital, not only in terms of what structures we are using, but also in terms of who is managing that capital, where it's directed, and who is making the decision on how to deploy capital. For example, the traditional fund model worked for a particular type of investment focus and type of company, but it has limitations for supporting very early stage companies and aligning incentives for fund managers.

JL: *What are other non-traditional funding channels, and who are the other stakeholders that need to be elevated?*

BS: I am of Haitian descent, and we have a practice in the Haitian community called *sou-sou*. It is a money pot, like a savings club. Some new FinTech companies are leveraging similar models. There is this desire to

---

373. https://www.linkedin.com/in/heathermatranga-47583623/

374. https://www.linkedin.com/in/younkman/

375. https://www.linkedin.com/in/dahlia-joseph/

376. https://blackinnovationalliance.com/

377. https://www.linkedin.com/in/biancast/

reinvent the wheel, versus leveraging the work that has already been done, just slightly differently. How do entrepreneurs already interact with funding and information? We need to step back and look at where the gaps between the currently powerful system and other systems that people are already engaging with are. Many times, these are accelerators. We need to understand where the people that you are looking for are and why they are within those systems. How can we overlay some of the current structures to find that middle ground to close the gap?

Ben Younkman (BY): The decision-making process of how venture capital is deciding how to allocate their capital and what their criteria are is opaque. Increasing transparency is a step in the right direction to helping people understand what they need to come to the table with, to be attractive to that individual funder.

BS: Programs that have a sheer level of honesty remove a lot of friction. The best entrepreneurs have quality information, and they have great access. Mentors are giving them the truth. People are currently so mindful about not "looking bad" that they may not be telling the truth and not enabling the entrepreneurs. People that are leading the accelerators and managing entrepreneurs can help fill in the gap.

JL: *Coming through the initial gap does not necessarily mean that you are able to then become the unicorn. That is another question in and of itself. Do we want to create unicorns, just led by a more diverse set of founders? Or do we want to focus on something else, for instance, more sustainable zebra companies? Do we want a secondary, alternative system, or just to make the current system more inclusive?*

BS: We need to get more participation for companies to grow, whether that is mentorship, capital, or something else. It is analogous to saying to a young child, "Good luck. See you when you graduate and I have all this money waiting for you here. Good luck getting there." What does it look like to be invested throughout the lifecycle of these founders? Is it participating in the entrepreneur support? Is it being in conversation with a different ecosystem player? I do not think it requires a second system, what we see are massive gaps that illuminate the opportunities.

SUPPORTING THE ORGANIZATIONS THAT SUPPORT DIVERSE ENTREPRENEURS

JL: *Dahlia, at Village Capital, in collaboration with the Black Innovation Alliance (BIA), you just launched Resource,*[378] *a project to focus on minority founders. Can you tell us about it?*

Dahlia Joseph (DJ): Resource was born out of COVID. We all know that COVID disproportionately affected the BIPOC community systems like health care, education, finance, housing, all of which were meant to protect us and our wellbeing, and that really let communities of color down. We also saw that in the venture space and entrepreneurial space. There tends to be a lot of focus on entrepreneurs, which is great. Yet there was not a lot of support for organizations that support those entrepreneurs. It is all a system—if one is unhealthy, it can trickle down. Village Capital and Black Innovation Alliance came together to address that problem, specifically around unclear practices. When it comes to running accelerator and incubator programs, there tends to be many siloed resource networks. There tends to be secretive conversations and inequitable funding.

BS: These entrepreneur support organizations (ESOs) are the front line of defense—listening to the entrepreneurs and supporting them on the late nights. As we think about Resource, we wanted to create a community of support, and be a resource for them along this journey because it has a deep impact on the entrepreneurial ecosystem.

JL: *We know much of VC is about having the right relationships; is one part of Resource about making the connections that can help strengthen people?*

DJ: A big part of this program is Village Capital and BIA being connectors to both stakeholders and entrepreneur support organizations that would not necessarily have the opportunity to connect with such large funders like JPMorgan Chase or UBS. The funders in this program play a big part in building this network together, and they also have the opportunity to engage not only with the ESO but also the ESO's network—their startups, entrepreneurs, and community. We act as a bridge between the two.

BS: We also do not rely on the same networks. If success is being a white male VC from Stanford, then we are failing to include others. What are the different pathways to success? Once we start to invest in different path-

---

378. https://resource-initiative.com/

ways and different resources, we create a different conversation around success for entrepreneurs.

HOW VILLAGE CAPITAL HAS IMPROVED ACCESS

JL: *At Village Capital, DEI has been at your core from the very beginning. What are the ways you have increased access for diverse founders and funders?*

HM: Our mission at Village Capital is to go big—to reinvent the system to support the entrepreneurs of the future, which are the entrepreneurs that have lived experiences, are impact oriented, and want to solve some of the most pressing global problems. We cannot continue to maintain the status quo, and we really have to re-evaluate the way that the system works. The current system is not supporting the types of entrepreneurs we want to support.

Our core innovation is a process innovation. Rather than just thinking about who or what we are supporting, we look at how we are supporting them and how we are investing. One focus was peer selection—where we democratize entrepreneurship and increase access, by changing who makes the decision. We facilitated that process for ten years and made over a hundred investments that way. A few years ago, we looked at whether the hypothesis that peer selection would lead to more equitable and inclusive decisions was true. We did a data-driven evaluation with an academic partner from Emory University, and the top line message is that entrepreneurs are well suited in forecasting which of their peers will be successful, and they do so in a way that does reduce bias. They are evaluating the companies according to the company's merit, and less about the demographics of the founders. It is not perfect and there is more work to be done; bias is not completely eliminated, only mitigated.

We are also pushing ourselves in continuing to think about ways to improve the way capital is allocated. We have launched other research studies, some around capital structures. What investment tools and structures can improve inclusion? Can we tweak the way that investors evaluate companies? Will that lead to more inclusion? The ecosystem needs a lot of testing and experimentation to push the status quo and, ideally, scale those solutions to mainstream investors.

HM: Peer selection has lots of benefits. It is also pretty resource intense and is risky in the eyes of many institutional investors. There has been friction in getting them on board. The more fundamental question is, is there a different process than what currently exists to reduce and mitigate bias?

IGNORING DIVERSITY LEAVES MONEY ON THE TABLE

JL: *Many GPs and LPs say, "I have one thing to do in this world. That is not to fund diverse entrepreneurs, but it is to make money." Erika and I argue that by not funding diverse entrepreneurs, VCs are losing out on financial returns, in fact. Would you make a similar argument?*

HM: Yes. For traditional LPs and investors, investing in diversity is not about what makes you feel good, but because you are leaving money on the table. It is an uphill battle to make that case to those who rely on pattern recognition. The way we have tackled changing the investing process is not inclusion for inclusion's sake, but so that you are identifying the highest potential company that is going to make you the most money. We continue to point to success stories and do the work of demonstrating through data that more inclusive companies and diverse founders are leading to higher returns. We have done a study[379] that demonstrates that, on average, for every dollar invested in a woman entrepreneur, they outperform in terms of revenue generated for the company.

BY: How can you improve network access for these entrepreneurs? Can you improve the visibility of different companies and how they are being evaluated? We have created something called Avoca, which tries to connect people and investors who care about a particular theme such as gender, sustainability, or something else. We want to cluster those investors and highlight entrepreneurs that might not have visibility yet. To do this, we must be really intentional with partnering with people who have deeper networks, like the Black Innovation Alliance or Female Founders Alliance. That helps us improve our pipeline, and then we can highlight how these entrepreneurs have great ideas. We are much more intentional about our sourcing process and expand that network to be as inclusive as possible to get the best ideas, not diversity for diversity's sake.

---

379. https://impactalpha.com/social-enterprise-leveling-the-investment-playing-field/

NEXT STEPS FOR MOVING THE INDUSTRY FORWARD

JL: *Is there anything that you have not tackled yet that is an important piece to move the tech ecosystem as a whole and that you are looking to as an important lever going forward?*

HM: When one part of the system is unhealthy, it infiltrates the whole. One big missing piece of the system is policy and regulation from the government side in the US and abroad. For example, the US passing the ability for individual investors to invest in companies through crowdfunding can be massively impactful, help launch innovative businesses, and create more access to capital. More research needs to be done, but there is a role for government and policy to play.

BY: Another challenge that impact faces is a unified way to measure and track. It is also not incentivized by investors. There is an attempt with ESGs [environmental, social, and governance criteria], but it is a big challenge that we are trying to explore. This needs to happen to move us to an inclusive and impact-focused investment community.

HM: The other piece is the people who control money. If we are demanding more of where our money is going and more of our institutional investors, you will start to see more systemic change. With the Black Lives Matter movement and protests against police brutality, there was an awakening among many institutional organizations in the US who are making commitments to support racial equity. This has resulted in many Black-led funds raising more capital. In ten years, we might see, as a result of what is happening now, a number of diverse founders getting more capital and scaling businesses. This leads to more success stories.

19.3 *Mujhid: Overlooked VCs*

Hadiyah Mujhid (HBCUvc)

Hadiyah Mujhid[380] is the founder and CEO of HBCUvc,[381] a non-profit mobilizing the next generation of venture capital leaders to increase access to capital for communities historically overlooked. In our conversation, Hadiyah shares how HBCUvc is developing, connecting, and mobilizing the next generation of venture capital leaders in communities where entrepreneurs face barriers: they run (educational) programs, build inclusive networks with existing communities, and help VCs jump over "wealth barriers" with their own pool of capital. All of these initiatives empower a new generation of Black, Latinx, and Indigenous VCs to take HBCU culture into VC.

Interviewed February 2021

BRINGING HBCU CULTURE INTO VENTURE CAPITAL

Erika Brodnock (EB): *Hadiyah, you are educating VCs around the HBCU [historically Black colleges and universities] ethos. Can you tell us how that is different from traditional VC?*

Hadiyah Mujhid (HM): When we are thinking about developing the next network or next generation of investors, we do anchor in HBCU ethos, which is not a formal ethos. It is a unique American experience, where people throughout the diaspora can go to a place and participate in educational and professional opportunities, and at least in the United States, do not have this invisible layer of racism, or this invisible layer of being the diversity token. It is one of the few environments outside of your home environment where these multi-layered identities that you have, such as being Black, are not something that you see as a barrier.

---

380. https://twitter.com/hadiyahdotme
381. https://www.hbcu.vc/

In that sense, HBCU culture is very affirming. It is also encouraging and inspiring, and it facilitates the environment for students to thrive. It shows the vastness of the diaspora and the diversity of Blackness. It shows the students that there is not one way to be Black. It encourages freedom and liberation.

When we say that we are rooted in the culture of HBCUs, especially when we teach venture capital, we want our next generation of Black, Indigenous, and Latinx venture capitalists to be rooted in their own cultural competencies—not to run away from that—and to come to the table understanding that those cultural competencies are the value added.

CONNECTING THE HBCU COMMUNITY TO TRADITIONAL VC NETWORKS

Johannes Lenhard (JL): *Venture capital is a relationship business, both when it comes to recruiting into VC, but also when it comes to investing. It is based around university friends, company networks, etc. What are you doing specifically to build up a new, much more diverse, Black VC network—in a sense, a second pillar that in and of itself functions?*

HM: Those tight networks and relationships, which are usually anchored in universities that exist in traditional VC, we also have them in our program. Those connections and those relationships are already there. We do not have to recreate that. It is important for us that we are not creating separate but equal. We are not creating a separate silo of networks in this VC network that will operate independently. It is important that we build strong bonds with the community of existing networks.

One of the ways that we do that is by teaching them just how important the existing relationships that they have within their HBCU community are. We start with how they are formed and allow them to leverage the ways that they built these relationships. Once you show them that informal relationship building is happening, and show the ways that they are doing it, it provides a pathway for them to intentionally create those networks. They have the blueprint to build strong relationships with this existing ecosystem, which is rooted in networks.

EB: *What are the practices and programs that you use to build up the network? There are so many new networks forming at the moment, particularly for Black and Brown founders; are there good practices that you would*

*share about some of the things that you have done, to enable strong founda-
tions?*

HM: You have to create the unicorns. At the same time, there is still work
to be done while the unicorns are being created. After there is the awareness of just how important relationships are and the intentional drive to
create more of them, we then create opportunities for these relationships
to happen. Before COVID, it was in-person retreats, where we put people
in the same room, and they did not have the distractions of their day-to-
day, and they could really get the opportunity to get to know each other.
You spend three days in this beautiful location and get to know up and ris-
ing Black VCs with different backgrounds. How do we create those opportunities to put everyone on equal footing, just to build strong friendships?

With COVID, we still want to create these experiences and we are moving along alongside society as we learn how to create new relationships
without in-person interaction. We are still creating these opportunities for
people to connect, but it looks very different, whether it is through various
tools like Zoom, or other networking tools.

BUILDING INCLUSIVE NETWORKS BEYOND THE HBCUS

EB: *Are you using the Kauffman Fellows Program,[§15.6] for instance, to support Black VCs, to get their foot in the door and to build networks? I completely appreciate that there is the opportunity to create a network within
the HBCU community, but I wonder if that recreates the same thing too, in
that if you did not go to a HBCU as an entrepreneur or as a VC, you could
end up locked out. It would be the same Harvard-Stanford network, but just
for HBCUs only, and even though lots of Black people go to HBCUs, there are
still millions that did not. How do you incorporate the rest of the ecosystem,
as well as ensuring that you do not end up just recreating the same problems?*

HM: Our HBCU program is one of four programs. Our HBCU students or
participants in our program are only a third of the people that we support
across all programs. Second, in the program itself, we teach the systemic
issues of venture capital. There is an awareness that because of these
siloed communities, we have created limited opportunities. Now that you
know that they exist, and being rooted in inclusiveness, how do you break
out of these in use? You informally created these communities, now how

do you break out of this to intentionally build relationships outside of just your neighbors within reach?

EB: *How do the programs work? What do they look like?*

HM: Each program is slightly different, but we are anchored around teaching modules. We have foundational classes that we teach, a lot of them are educational and a lot of them are soft skills—such as, how do you build a relationship intentionally and, at the same time, leave room for serendipity? For the HBCU program, which runs throughout the academic year, there are scheduled classes and activities where relationships can be built not only within the community, but also with existing partners and leaders in the industry.

Our summer program is open and is not HBCU-specific. It is anchored in more of an apprenticeship model, where you are placed in a paid internship program at a firm, but you spend two weeks full-time in an immersive experience that brings these fundamentals upfront—the foundations and histories of VC, the soft skills, the motivations of a VC (which is something that we have to teach). There is a classroom-style curriculum to it, as well as a component where every opportunity or every interaction is adopted, building a line of relationships.

SECURING GP COMMITMENT WITHOUT PERSONAL WEALTH

JL: *One thing that is complicated when it comes to becoming a VC is the commitment of GPs. In order to start a fund, you need both a track record and cash. You basically need to be wealthy. What can you do about that with your programs?*

HM: There are a couple of things. There is absolutely the ability to develop your own track record and your ability to show that you can find entrepreneurs, who will go on and generate the returns that VC deems worthy. Traditionally, building your own track record came through you using your own wealth to demonstrate that first. Within the past 10 years, we have seen that shift slightly, where people have shown that they have the opportunity to access these entrepreneurs without using their personal wealth.

In traditional VC, I would use my own personal wealth as a demonstration that I have done this, but then go out and raise larger capital. The end factor was that I was always managing someone else's money. We are ultimately seeing LPs just want that return. If you are able to show that you have that potential of a return, what we have seen are some LPs becoming a little bit more lenient on how much the GP commits. We are also seeing the development of other programs where you can develop your track record without using your own capital—maybe it is just developing an entrepreneur support company. I have seen people develop their own portfolio of companies that they support without using money.

One of the ways that HBCUvc is very specific about doing this is that we have created our own fund or pool of capital that our fellows could use after developing their own track record and give entrepreneurs a stipend through this fund. It creates a financial relationship with entrepreneurs, and then they work with entrepreneurs to develop that relationship to support them to grow.

HOLDING THE INDUSTRY ACCOUNTABLE FOR REAL CHANGE

EB: *What is next for HBCUvc? What is the next barrier that you are hoping to not just attack but to fundamentally change?*

HM: In the last five years, there has been a lot more awareness of the impact of the industry and how racial inequities exist within the industry. What we have seen as a result—which is all good—is a lot of programs that are similar to ours, who are helping to develop this pipeline of investors who were overlooked. However, I do not think it is the total solution. When you look at the people who are leading these efforts, a large percentage of us are coming from the communities who are impacted by it. We are trying to solve a problem that we did not create.

There is a huge amount of work for the institutions that have created the structure, to truly understand the barriers and take serious actions to remove them. Right now, there is a whole system that is to this day upholding barriers that prevent talented people from entering the industry and prevent talented entrepreneurs from receiving funding to grow their business. The industry has to take a serious effort in going beyond diversity-speak about the barriers and commit to serious action to eliminate that. When I think about what is next for HBCUvc, it is important for us to shift the culture for the institutions to understand how complicit they are and for them to drive serious action to remove the barriers.

EB: *It is one of those age-old issues that I fight against on a day-to-day basis. I am constantly asked to help companies to shift and restructure the way in*

which they are built and the way in which they operate. But they never want
to pay me a fee.

HM: The lack of understanding of how that perpetuates the issue they
want to stop is ridiculous.

EB: *What you have said there is interesting, around the fact that you do not*
want to be responsible for solving the problem that you did not create. How
does that stack up and what has your experience been of situations like this?
What would you say would be the best way out of this? What is the solution?

HM: It is asking us for a solution. We do not own the solution, because
we did not create the problem. We care about the solution because it has
impacted us and we are tired of living like this. We are going to keep fighting for it, because we are fighting for our own survival. In the United
States, one of the strongest impacts in the capitalism system is slavery.
Using Black bodies and Black laborers to create the system and build
wealth. The United States' capitalism system was first built on stolen land.
We took the assets from Indigenous peoples, and then we stole people
to build up the land. Some of the guidelines around capitalism have
changed, but I do not think that many people understand that this concept of the devaluation of Black and Brown bodies in their labor still exists.

We are formed as a not-for-profit organization. We are not operating
to create a profit, but it also does not mean that money is irrelevant in
how we operate. We have full-time staff that need to be paid, they need to
feed their families, and all of our staff identify as being Black or Brown.
When we talk to our for-profit partners, we talk about this commitment in
both a time commitment and an awareness, this intentionality to learn, to
improve, but also a financial commitment to support this organization to
make a change.

It is interesting how after explaining the history to the institutions,
around 50% of the time we get pushed back on the financial push. It is
mind-boggling to see that. One of the largest firms we have been in conversations with has said, "We are in alignment with your mission, we want
to change." We say, "Great, are you able to make a financial contribution?"
They say, "No."

EB: *I am not surprised at all. I would also not be surprised if that was an*
institution that put up a black square on Instagram. I too am tired of the
performance. You do not get to pretend that you do not understand that

it is wrong to ask people to work for free. We shall—even if not overcome yet—write it down.

19.4 *Feinzaig: Female Founders Alliance*

Leslie Feinzaig (Graham & Walker, Female Founders Alliance)

Leslie Feinzaig[382] started one of the biggest communities of female founders, the Female Founders Alliance.[383] At its core is a simple principle: you are stronger together. Over the last few years, it has developed from a mentoring and sharing community to running an accelerator and a VC fund, Graham & Walker,[384] all with a focus on female entrepreneurs. Leslie is hopeful and is seeing the fruits of her and others' hard work, but she worries about the increase in women leaving the workforce and the lack of support when it comes to childcare and parental leave policies.

Interviewed February 2021

BANDING TOGETHER TO COMBAT GENDER BIAS

Johannes Lenhard (JL): *In 2017, you founded one of the biggest startup communities for women, the Female Founders Alliance (FFA), which currently has 25K+ members. What motivated you to do that and what aims did you have with it?*

Leslie Feinzaig (LF): I do not have a founding story like other companies or startups. It was not as if I woke up one day and decided to build this. It was more that I was going through all the motions of growing my company—find a co-founder, raise some capital, and hire people. In the process of it, I hit a wall, and I started this community as a way to help myself.

---

382. https://twitter.com/LeslieFeinzaig
383. https://femalefounders.org/
384. https://grahamwalker.com/

Gender wasn't something that I had ever felt held me back before. Throughout my early career, the idea that I was having a different experience than my peers because I am a girl, or because I am a mom, or because I am Latina, or whatever—it never occurred to me at the time. With the benefit of hindsight I realize that I was wrong, of course gender had an impact. I spent decades internalizing what turned out to be gendered feedback—that I was too emotional, too quiet, too loud, too aggressive, etc.—and just assumed that there was something wrong with me that I had to keep working at fixing.

That changed in the context of trying to raise capital. The impact of gender was no longer quiet, it was obvious. I was the only woman in the room so much of the time. The reasons I got rejected were very often clearly stemming from gender bias. And what's more—it was not fine anymore to be treated differently. It was demoralizing. It was minimizing. And it was a waste of time while I was getting my startup off the ground.

What's now the Female Founders Alliance began as a small Facebook group. I started adding all the women that I met along the way. It was what I needed for myself at the time—a group of peers that tacitly agreed to lock arms, help out, and figure it out together. And it turned out a lot more women needed it too. Four years later, with a lot of work, it is a much bigger thing.

JL: *Now, after several years of running and growing the community, what do you think it does for female founders? In what way is it something important for them, and how is it concretely helpful?*

LF: We run a private online group that is super active and for founders only. No investors, no employees, no media. It's much easier to be authentic and vulnerable when you're not being evaluated. We run programs to match founders one-to-one with investors, media, and subject-matter experts routinely through the year—we broker hundreds of these meetings annually. This is a big part of the secret sauce: to broker relationships that result in the startups' advancement. And we run a very successful accelerator. You can learn more and join the community at femalefounders.org.[385] It is free and accessible to scalable startup founders everywhere.

---

385. https://femalefounders.org/

BEST PRACTICES FOR FIRST-TIME FOUNDERS

JL: *Are there two or three best practices for underrepresented founders to succeed?*

LF: In my experience, the biggest challenges are faced by first-time founders that are also outsiders to venture capital and tech. Picture a more traditional founder: a software developer or a product manager from Stanford or Google or Facebook, or a hot growing startup that "fits the type" and is well connected to angel investors. Underrepresented founders who also don't have those mainstream credentials and that network are the ones who have it hardest.

So if you are some version of that founder, what do you do?

The short answer is you have to prove yourself first, and build out your network. One way to do that is to try working for a well-known startup for a while, and develop your idea on the side. That way you add to your experience on how startups work, add to your credentials, and add to your network. This is especially doable these days when so many startups are hiring remotely, you don't actually have to move to Silicon Valley to get that experience anymore.

If you don't have the time or ability to do that, then you have to build those same proof points through your startup itself. The first and most effective way to do that is to gain traction with your company. Get real customers that love what you offer, even if your product has to be a very minimal version of what you want it to be. Focus on growing that customer base reliably. Real results are hard for any VC to argue with.

Simultaneously, you have to build your reputation among possible investors. Meet them before you need their money, and keep them updated so that they can witness you delivering results and will be more ready to invest in you when you ask.

Finally, it is so important to surround yourself with a community that is supportive, authentic, and tangibly helpful. It helps on so many levels! You get to share the ups and downs, and get advice from others who know the space. You get access to resources and introductions—a huge help in building that network of investors, or access to that network, from your own peers. Because most investors won't know you, so a referral from another founder is the next best thing. We need more mechanisms by which those first-time founders get taken seriously, and these referral networks are an incredibly powerful and grassroots approach to solving that problem together.

JL: *Have you seen any that work well?*

LF: That is what our accelerator does. We look for founders nobody else believes in. We admit first-time founders who have achieved traction on their own, and we put a stamp of approval on them a little bit, and we teach them how to play the game and talk the talk. This is specifically our accelerator, which is much smaller than our community. We have done it three times, graduating eight startups per cohort. It is tiny, if you compare it to Y Combinator, which is graduating 300 startups a year. I am doing eight, but we really take care of those eight. Our most recent cohort graduated in December, and half of them have already closed their rounds, collectively raising $7M.

Our approach is to teach founders how to pitch venture capitalists properly, drill down into their business model to help them be defensible when investors dig deeper, and exhaustively have them practice formal and informal investor interactions, over and over again, until they're super confident. We teach them how to run a fundraising process so that it is successful. On the other side of the program is our investor community, we help legitimize these startups for our large investor community. We tell the investors, these are founders you should talk to, and since the accelerator is so selective, and so much goes into picking the cohort, they believe us. By the end of the program, we put the founders in front of close to 200 VCs and angel investors.

THE LATEST HIT TO WOMEN'S SUCCESS IN THE ECONOMY AND IN VC

JL: *What are the biggest challenges ahead of us right now, maybe thinking about the next five years, when it comes to inclusion? What can we do about it?*

LF: Coming out of the pandemic, the biggest challenge I see is women's participation in the economy, which just took an unprecedented hit. We had been very slowly but consistently making progress, increasing awareness of issues, talking about things, improving them. That is not where we are anymore, by almost any measure. Many women, moms especially, have left the workforce entirely. In my space, the proportion of venture capital invested in women dropped substantially—it is now more unequal than it was when FFA got started. It is going to take a real effort to claw back out of what we just went through.

JL: *Do you have any big push that you would like to see over the next 12+ months that would really help with the issues you're seeing around women's participation in the economy?*

LF: Parental leave, support for childcare. Equitable parental leave is really important. We need to start supporting dads and other parents the same as we do moms. I went to the London School of Economics and I did a senior thesis; twenty years ago, I was arguing for equal paternity-maternity leave before it was cool. We need bigger support for new parents. I would love to see real innovation in the childcare space.

20 Conversations: Supporting Different Kinds of Founders

20.1 *Zepeda, Scholz: Zebras Unite*

Mara Zepeda (Zebras Unite)

Astrid Scholz (Armillaria, Zebras Unite)

Central to the need for change in venture capital is the need to think more holistically about the impact of companies, including their footprints on the environment and influences on the societies they have been designed to serve. Historically, this has tended to be more of an afterthought, rather than purposefully built into the creation of venture-backed companies that strive for hockey stick growth at all costs. We caught up with Mara Zepeda[386] and Astrid Scholz,[387] two of the founders of the Zebras Unite[388] movement, to explore the possibilities of another way. We learned how they have built a founder-led, cooperatively owned movement of 6,000 founders across six continents, who are creating the culture, capital, and community for the next economy.

Interviewed June 2021

THE ORIGIN OF THE ZEBRA STARTUP

Johannes Lenhard (JL): *The first time I came across Zebras Unite was in the 2019 New York Times article,[389] where you and the other founders stepped forward with a very unconventional message to the VC and startup community, saying that the system they built does not work for most people;*

---

386. hhttps://twitter.com/marazepeda

387. https://twitter.com/ajscholz

388. https://zebrasunite.coop/

389. https://www.nytimes.com/2019/01/11/technology/start-ups-rejecting-venture-capital.html

we need to rethink how this whole world is structured. What motivated you to do that and what brought you to that point where you believed we needed to do something differently?

Mara Zepeda (MZ): Before starting Zebras Unite, we were founders ourselves and we had experienced the problem from the side of being an entrepreneur. We saw how limited the capital was, and we all hit a wall that many founders do. All four of us Zebras Unite founders are systems thinkers. Rather than bemoaning how frustrating our situations were and rather than taking it personally, we then began to ask ourselves if perhaps this is a failure of the system itself. Reframing the question gave us a more expansive and wider lens through which to examine existing capital. We came to learn that it does not serve most entrepreneurs and we desperately need alternatives.

Astrid Scholz (AS): One thing to remember is that the four of us were all successful leaders and achievers in our respective domains before becoming entrepreneurs. In my case, I had a great track record raising money for my ideas from philanthropic sources, and all of a sudden I hit a wall when talking to VCs. I was the same person, my salesmanship was the same, but the milieu I found myself in had changed. This was borne out in the questions I was being asked that had no bearing on the quality of the business we were building, our traction, or our potential. The questions were easily recognizable as being in service of the prevailing pattern matching in the VC industry.

JL: *Let's actually go back for a moment: what exactly is a "zebra" and what does it have to do with diversity and inclusion?*

MZ: In 2017, we penned this manifesto, "Zebras fix what unicorns break,"[390] in opposition to what we saw with unicorn companies that were generally looking for a massive, outsized return that benefits a small number of investors. They are focused on hockey stick growth at all costs. They tend to be very engineering heavy, and they will marginally throw crumbs at some philanthropic cause, but they are not interested in community benefit and shared prosperity. We know what the unicorn is.

With zebras, we see a completely different psychographic of founder. These are founders that were not interested in getting exorbitantly

---

390. https://medium.com/zebras-unite/zebrasfix-c467e55f9d96

wealthy and they were motivated instead by shared prosperity and having both profit and purpose. They tend to work at multiple altitudes. On the one hand, their company might be solving a specific problem. They are also systems players and working on systemic solutions as well. They are mutualistic and cooperative. Rather than have a dominant monopolistic market share, zebras are interested in how they cooperate with one another, or with the communities they serve, in order to have strength and advantage through cooperation, not competition. Unlike a unicorn, a zebra is real. We see a lot more zebra companies in the wild than we do unicorns, which is a fantasy animal that occurs once in a blue moon.

AS: We often get asked this question about how zebras relate to diversity and inclusion. That's a bit of a red herring, if you can pardon that metaphor. Zebras come in many different stripes, and we observe that the types of founders that tend to either be systemically excluded from mainstream venture capital or are actively charting a different course for capitalizing and growing their companies from the get-go tend to be led by people that have live experiences and insights that differ from white, cisgendered males educated at a few elite universities. So zebras are to startups what all the other ice cream flavors are to vanilla—see what I did there? VC: vanilla capital.

FUNDING DIVERSITY IN THE STARTUP WORLD

Erika Brodnock (EB): *Thinking not just about the entrepreneur-side of things but also about the money, what funding alternative do you want to provide and how does that link with increasing diversity in the startup world?*

MZ: If we want to see more diversity in entrepreneurship, we need more diverse funding mechanisms that align with the needs of diverse founders. Diverse founders very often are not coming from the same pattern-matching structures that venture capital is pattern matching, which is largely affluent white men with educational privileges. When we think about the psychology of diverse founders, they have a different relationship to money. Many are not motivated by hoarding, but by sharing, and are interested in giving back to the community that has helped them to succeed. They have a reciprocity and mutuality mindset, and many are interested in creating community and place-based impact. What we are attempting to do is ask about the founders' values and design capital that aligns with those values.

People have asked us if we are going to start a zebra's fund, but often when investors want to make social impact, there is an egotistically driven idea of starting funds to be the savior of the industry. We are more interested in how we can influence how funds are created, so that investors have some more creative ideas for how to deploy their capital in ways that achieve different types of returns and serve different types of founders. Much of our work is about education and meeting with investors to say, "What if you make some recoverable grants over in your philanthropic arm? What if you design your capital stack to include revenue-based financing?" We help navigate them towards a capital stack that itself is more diverse. To diversify founders, you must diversify the capital stack. To diversify the capital stack, you must educate investors about why it is in their interest and that it is not that hard. Eventually, we will likely have a fund. Currently, if we decided to start the capital fund we would raise a million dollars, and it would be the hardest million dollars to raise. Instead, we are in talks with $100M funds to help them think about how to diversify their portfolio. It is a far greater use of our time.

HOW THE NEXT GENERATION IS CHANGING DIVERSITY

JL: *Can VCs be rescued? Is the current way of thinking about diversity and inclusion the right thing or do we need more radical systems-level thinking? How do you teach that?*

MZ: The tokenization of Black and Brown communities and women to try to shoehorn them into ventures-style returns is not in alignment with anything. They are slowly beginning to realize that there must be a better way. I have hope because demographically, history is on our side. The next generation of people coming up will not tolerate this extractive, winner-takes-all model of making very few very wealthy. Every single young person that I know is not only not interested in it, but they have the discernment to judge people that are in it for rapacious, capitalistic wealth hoarding. When you look at what they want from employers, when you look at the environmental catastrophe that they are facing and how many of these companies are enabling that, and when you look at the way that they have been raised in the shadow of Black Lives Matter and Indigenous rights movements, the next generation will be a forcing mechanism for a number of these VCs.

We are in this bridge generation. We are trying to say things like, "We are trying to save you from yourselves." It is profound to see investors that do reach this place of enlightenment. When many of them already have philanthropic arms, it is just a question of having both sides of the house speaking to one another. (The Omidyar Group[391] provides an example of how capital can be deployed all the way across the financial system and how grants can be used to catalyze entrepreneurs.) The question now is, how can philanthropic money work towards more social impact companies? How can those companies receive different types of investments? I do have hope. A lot of it must come from trust building and relationship building with these investors, which takes time, but it is certainly not from telling them "you are idiots." That is not a winning proposition. Building sincere relationships with investors, recognizing how little exposure they have to the founder experience and to diverse perspectives, and bringing them along from a place of compassionate accompaniment are the best things we can do.

AS: An institutional investor I respect likes to point out that there is no accreditation or license for VCs, literally anyone can become one. There is no code of conduct or any kind of proof that you know what you are doing. And it shows! How few VCs have actually been operators themselves and have built companies? So there is a huge opportunity for learning, education, and seeking more authentic relationships with the entrepreneurs that do not look like them. Similarly for the LPs, the people who invest in VC funds and other vehicles: many wealth and asset owners literally cannot relate to the founder experience, and so there is again an opportunity to educate and craft experiences that help them relate. One of the things I liked to do, back in the days before the pandemic, is have people play an interactive board game I created where they navigate a stylized course from idea to Series A in the persona of an entrepreneur who is not like them. The visceral reaction people have to the journey of, say, a Black entrepreneur, or a [Native American] woman along the same path as a white man, is truly enlightening. People get shout-out-loud enraged about the injustice of the system, and I do think there is potential in creating these sorts of visceral learning opportunities.

---

391. https://www.omidyargroup.com/

LEVELING THE PLAYING FIELD

EB: *Quite a few people have said to us that they do not want to be the charitable case. They want access to the same amount of money and opportunity. It is not just about giving them something, it is also about giving them the same as all the white men with Stanford degrees have had for many years. How do you address that?*

MZ: It is not so much that philanthropic capital needs to go to the diverse founder, instead it is that they need to be participating in the ecosystem and field building. Philanthropy could go to education, cooperative models, or advocacy campaigns so that pension funds are freeing up capital. Philanthropy can be a very powerful lever towards systems change in the ecosystem. It is not about giving the check to the founder, it is about giving the check towards organizations that are working at a systems level, so they can start to bridge the blood-brain barrier between. Philanthropic capital can be creating different conditions for more entrepreneurs to succeed. The psychographic founder that we tend to serve is not coming from the place of what is in it for them, growing a company and then exiting. The people that are part of our movement recognize that users, employees, and community are creating value. If you think about value creation in a multi-stakeholder way, traditional venture capital does not serve you because you cannot include those stakeholders easily, other than giving them nominal amounts of equity.

If you come at the value creation, you can say the value is created with this group of people, and the capital that I would need to go and pursue should be in alignment with the values those people have. Venture capital does not do that. We need people that are pushing the Sequoias and the Andreessen Horowitzs of the world. However, the expectation is that if they get the venture capital, then they have a billion-dollar exit. We can have a much higher number of Black women that are receiving venture capital, and then need to create the conditions to ensure that they are able to get the billion-dollar exit, so they can tell us a success story at the end of the day that aligns with LPs expectations. To do that, you must create the market conditions for a Black woman to have a $3B exit. That is where Zebras Unite wants to help and would like to play. Yet, every dollar of venture capital you are taking, you are making a promise that you are going to 10X or 100X that. For every one success story, you have 99 failures. We are asking, how can 100 entrepreneurs succeed on their own terms with the capital that they need? If you have a venture mindset, you are saying, "I believe that I am the one who is going to make this exit, and I don't care if the 99 others get left in the dust." The zebra mindset is just a different one that says systemically, for the sake of our community's economic development, the environment, and the next generations, we need to figure out how more people can succeed at this game on their own terms. It is a different mindset.

THE FUTURE OF ZEBRAS UNITE

JL: *What are concrete next steps that you are taking as Zebras Unite?*

MZ: We have over 25 chapters in cities from Amman to Mexico City. Each one of those chapters is rejecting the Silicon Valley status quo. We are excited to see that there are entrepreneurs and investors that are taking a stand and saying, "Keep the Bay at bay. We do not need Silicon Valley to come and infect our entrepreneurial communities." I am excited about the cultural wisdom that is going to come from our chapters because each one is so unique.

In terms of innovation, we are working with investors that are thinking holistically about much more meaningful systems change to address this larger sub ecosystem of problems. We are finding those investors, philanthropists, and people that think on a systemic and holistic level, rather than band-aids. Here in the US, the wealth gap for Black and Brown entrepreneurs is just so extraordinary. The Inclusive Capital Collective[392] (ICC) is an initiative that is being incubated under Zebras Unite. It includes 100 BIPOC fund managers in the country, and we are incubating a co-op of them inside of Zebras Unite. The thinking is that this cooperatively owned infrastructure will then start to generate generational wealth in these communities, because rather than be a non-profit, they will be a co-op, which will then allow them to own the means of production of their own capital. We are very interested in layering alternative ownership structures on to these new innovative models so that people are not just bucketed and non-profits.

AS: The Inclusive Capital Collective is also a great illustration of how we are going about mobilizing more capital to founders of all different stripes. Rather than creating our own fund, we are building distributed infrastruc-

---

392. https://www.inclusive-capital.us

ture to serve hundreds of, in the case of the ICC, mostly BIPOC, fund managers and entrepreneur support organizations. Instead of slowly building from our own Fund One, to Fund Two, to Fund Three, we can thereby support a range of types and sizes of innovative capital vehicles and their managers, and create leveraged opportunities for them. We believe we can mobilize larger volumes of capital faster this way, and plan to do a lot more of this sort of collective design of capital and entrepreneur support ecosystems all over the world. Stay tuned!

20.2 *Kouris, Schiller: New Mittelstand*

Evgeni Kouris (New Mittelstand)

Ines Schiller (Vyld)

Evgeni Kouris[393] and Ines Schiller[394] believe there is huge potential to build a new, sustainable economic backbone in European economies, in the form of medium-sized (or family) businesses: New Mittelstand.[395] We sat with them to explore this approach and the New Mittelstand vision, which is focused on combining the best traditions of medium-sized companies with the agility and futuristic redesign principles of startups.

Interviewed June 2021

A TRANSFORMATIVE INITIATIVE FOR MEDIUM-SIZED AND FAMILY BUSINESSES

Johannes Lenhard (JL): *You had your own startup before New Mittelstand (NM) was founded. What motivated you to start this organization?*

Evgeni Kouris (EK): It started in a personal crisis, which was related to the meaning of venture capital. I had idealized the startup ecosystem as I went and moved to Berlin in 2012. I quit both my careers as a musician

---

393. https://twitter.com/ekouris

394. https://www.linkedin.com/in/inesschiller/

395. https://www.newmittelstand.org/

and a consultant of BCG. At the time, the startup path and innovation with venture capital seemed like the ways to create a better future and innovate radically. To some degree, it was right, but the problem that I encountered there is that you may start with great purpose and vision, but venture capital is not necessarily helping you to get there. It rather requires a lot of experience to not divert from the original path. Money has a lot of influence. Venture capital structures are very clearly exit and monopoly oriented. So, in the unlikely event that your startup succeeds, the result is only advantageous for a few people involved: "win-lose principle." I started looking at other models of entrepreneurship that do not require this kind of exponentiality and can scale and be successful long term for many people: "win-win principle."

Erika Brodnock (EB): *What is the ethos you are following and how is that connected to a new way of being and of doing business?*

EK: The ultimate question for us is, do we have our own vision for the European way of doing entrepreneurship? The Silicon Valley startup methodology was not invented in Europe. It is very successful so far. You can see the Asian adoption of that mindset too. If you look in Europe, and especially Germany, what is going on here? We always talk about family and middle-sized businesses or "mittelstand," which are the backbone of the economy. In the US, there are only two kinds: large or small—grow or go. It is different in Europe. You have three types of companies, and the ones that are providing most of the jobs are the middle-sized ones. They are also driving industrial innovation. The 2019–2020 numbers showed rapid decline over the last 15 years in radical product innovation, in this field where you would typically expect that innovation to happen. Startups were completely overhyped. So, there is a major issue with the traditional family businesses that needs to be addressed. Otherwise, we will lose that edge that normally was driving the German or European economies. That is one of the reasons why I initially founded the transformation initiative, New Mittelstand. It quickly became a community and movement of like-minded entrepreneurs who define themselves as New Mittelstand. It has been my complete focus since then.

The startup has become a zebra on its own. We are a for-profit and for-purpose company, even though many people expect these initiatives to become non-profit. We want to set an example of doing things differently here. We want to find a new way of doing a family business ourselves.

What is missing in Europe is this diversity oriented and bottom-up way of doing entrepreneurship. We call it New Mittelstand because it is a new way of old business, a new definition for the 21st century. We are open to learning from startups and learning from all kinds of methods to do radical innovation, but you cannot forget your roots. What values do we want to maintain? Diversity, freedom, democracy, and all the values that we really love. They are just unique and have a lot of history. We cannot forget these while moving into this radical technology innovation, evolution, or disruption. This is the challenge. As we used to say, it is about keeping your roots intact, while still having the wings to fly into this new future. This is really challenging for traditional companies, especially the ones who have been around for generations.

JL: *Ines, from the perspective of a startup founder, what does NM do differently and how does that reflect your "ethos"? What is attractive in NM for you?*

Ines Schiller (IS): When I started Vyld, I was not only thinking about the "what"—a radically sustainable product (our ocean-saving tampons made from seaweed)—but also about the "how"—the way we do business to bring this "good" product into the world, because for us the end does not always justify the means. We wanted Vyld to be able to grow and thrive in the same healthy way that we want our seaweed to, integrated in regenerative circular systems that are non-exploitative and designed to last. So I did a lot of research on alternative ways of doing business and, besides other inspiring sources like the steward-ownership model and the feminist business approach by Jennifer Armbrust, NM and the zebra startup movement are very promising and empowering vehicles for us to incorporate these values into our company's DNA. We can use them like templates without having to (re)invent everything ourselves. I appreciate the work of Evgeni and the others very much, as they do a great job illustrating the fact that there are already alternative ways of doing business that actually work. I think it's very helpful that they are doing this as living examples!

BRINGING DIVERSITY TO THE NEW MITTELSTAND MOVEMENT

JL: *How are you addressing what kinds of diversity are in the New Mittelstand sector?*

EK: In the German language, diversity is narrowly defined and we want to look more broadly. We consider New Mittelstand to be a positive vision for entrepreneurship in Europe. We need to find ways to do things where we have natural advantages in Europe and need to learn from what US and China ecosystems have done very well. What are our advantages traditionally? We have a lot of cultural diversity, which we need to leverage to our advantage. For example, in my VC-backed startup Gamewheel we started communicating in English from day one. Five years later, we have traffic from all over the globe, but not many people from traditional family businesses understand our site because it is in English. I thought, why do we always start in English? We have very different languages here in Europe and very different cultures. Startups are monocultural vehicles to great monopolies. Cultural diversity is more hindering, because it is more expensive, legally, culturally, to scale. You need different teams on the ground, and you need different models. Startup business models require a high degree of standardization. Family businesses, on the other hand, are regionally rooted. Yet they also experience a "family innovator's dilemma." They have an advantage of being regional, but they have the disadvantage of family-driven monoculture, because they traditionally try to find a successor from the family itself. Over the generations, this creates tunnel vision for the way of thinking and culture. This is not enough.

With New Mittelstand standards, we want to combine the best of both worlds. How can you be closed and open at the same time? How can you be focused on a particular type of culture or portion of the market, while still radically innovating? How can you find other things where your unique cultural DNA could be of value? How can you combine that with technology or startup innovation? This makes European innovation challenging and tough because you need so many discussions to decide. There are bottom-up structures, which are sometimes inefficient. We need to figure out how to leverage these structures and make it more effective for people. That will be our biggest advantage. After the internet economy that many European companies have missed, there will be a purpose economy. A new generation will require us to be more purpose oriented and have a triple bottom line, such as with UNSDGs Sustainable Development Goals.[396] This new generational demand will be in favor of companies who embrace their culture, the DNA, the history, and also care about the next

---

396. https://sdgs.un.org/goals

generation. What do I do to make the next generation look good for the next generation after? This is where Europe can shine, or the diversity culture can shine.

JL: *Ines, what role does diversity (of different kinds) play for you?*

IS: As a female and usually white-passing founder, I experience the consequences of a lack of diversity in the industry on a daily basis. Our economy suffers a lot from overemphasizing the importance of typical startup business models, but it loses so much by ignoring the vast majority of business models, ideas, founders, geographies, etc. This monoculture in business is as unhealthy as it is in nature. As a trained marine and field guide, I see the dramatic impacts that biodiversity loss has on our natural environment. I think we can really *not* overrate the importance of diversity for healthy systems—businesses or societies are not different from ecosystems, in fact as we are part of nature, our systems collapse in the same way that ecosystems do from biodiversity loss. We focus so much on "more of the same" logic, e.g., founder's profiles coming out of the "good and right schools," the "well-balanced, senior teams," and "proofs of concept," that we prevent ourselves from true innovation. But we are facing existential problems on this planet, and we will not solve them by following the same logic that brought us here. We need to think way more holistically and integrate other perspectives if we want to tackle this crisis complex. I call it a complex because for me the same mindset that enables gender inequality and the oppression of womxn enables the unpunished exploitation and destruction of nature. A very hands-on example in our own business is the way we talk about our products—usually they are called "feminine hygiene products" and marketed towards women, but not every womxn menstruates, not everyone who menstruates is a womxn, and periods are nothing that needs "hygienic" treatment, they are just natural. That's why we use the more inclusive terms, menstruators and period products. Language matters indeed!

MITTELSTAND ALTERNATIVES TO VC FUNDING

EB: *How do you propose funding this new way in this new system? How does it differ from the traditional way of VC funding?*

EK: For many family businesses and Mittelstand companies, independence is one of the biggest motivating factors, which they have successfully kept for generations. Some never leveraged a lot of external capital or they have kept their shares mostly in the family. They try not to raise external funding and dilute the shareholding in a way that it becomes uncontrollable or less controllable by the family. They are well funded and are very independent in the way they do things. We are looking into what we call "qualitative investing"—it requires a different capital structure, and investor and founder profiles. Jointly with our partner organization Zebras Unite,[§20.1] we are working towards acceleration of alternative capital structures for such a qualitative economy. Investing in zebra startups is, on the one hand side, purpose oriented and on the other hand side it is profit oriented. Zebra founders are focused on balancing the social, monetary, and environmental aspects, and hence zebra investors expect less exponential growth and more positive impact.

JL: *Ines, what role does venture capital play for you? Are you already engaging in alternative ways of funding?*

IS: We are just at the beginning and far from being a Mittelstand company, and as we have an innovative, R&D-heavy product, we need outside investment to come to a point where we can grow organically. That's why we are looking exactly for this type of "qualitative investment" that Evgeni describes, one that is in line with our regenerative business approach. In general, I think it's really urgent for investors, but also the economy as a whole, to understand that the VC hypergrowth model, with its reliance on fast, blitzscaled[397] growth, is just not a good idea on a finite planet. To be very clear, for us as a profit-for-purpose company, the VC model just doesn't make sense. We don't want Vyld to be a vehicle for investors making tons of money, but instead a tool for realizing our vision and creating positive impact. The decision-making power should not be coupled to the amount of money someone put into the company, it should always stay within the company. That's why we're using the steward-ownership model, which prohibits absentee owners from making decisions that are contrary to the actual company purpose (like extracting a lot of money that could be used for more impact). This is not an easy way and there are still many open questions like whether there is even enough of this mission-aligned capital out there for a R&D-heavy enterprise like ours, but we

---

397. https://hbr.org/2016/04/blitzscaling

are willing to take that risk as following the conventional VC logic would just feel like a poor compromise.

OVERCOMING NEGATIVE CONNOTATIONS AND CONSERVATIVE VALUES

EB: *Purposeful can sound charitable. What are the impacts of making it seem as though it sits in the philanthropic social bucket? How can we shift away from the negative connotations that some from capitalist back-grounds associate with philanthropic investment?*

EK: Qualitative investing is when purpose and profit orientation are balanced. Patagonia is a famous successful example, the company is profitable and purpose oriented. They accept less monetary growth to maximize the positive impact and to focus solely on company purpose. Many new generation founders want to combine profit and purpose orientation, and do not see that as a contradiction. New Mittelstand is a natural evolution of family business culture—the oldest way of doing business in a sustainable and balanced way. Balance is a core value to create a win-win economy rather than trying to get everything out of the company and maximize on profits.

We share the successes of these family businesses or so-called "hidden champions" in our online magazine, and this helps other entrepreneurs and investors see that there are other ways to be successful. About a half of global hidden champions came from Germany. They generate millions and sometimes billions and generate many jobs in Germany and globally, while not many people know much about them. We want to help them become more open and collaborative. We want them to talk about their successes and show that they are also funding new initiatives that will follow their footsteps. We want them to create internal startup-like initiatives and work with external startups. Many are going in this direction, and they are not investing on classical venture capital terms. New Mittelstand firms are often interested in qualitative zebra investments, where they expect a moderate positive return on investment over time. In the current economic context, this is quite attractive.

Traditional family businesses are leaner and often focus on profitability from day one. They still need to have capital and partnership to scale. Frosta, a New Mittelstand company focusing on frozen foods, is in a third generation of their business. They have been financing sustainable packaging development since the beginning of the century. No one wanted to

pay a premium price for it ten years ago, so the company struggled financially for a long time. Normally, in venture capital, they would stop, but
they kept going. Now, they are leading sustainable packaging with their
plastic-free products. These are the typical New Mittelstand stories we
share, which inspire. We are searching for good entrepreneurship that is
purpose driven and it does not matter where you come from. You do not
need to have gone to a good school, have an MBA, or a good network. It is
about doing the right things in the right way and having something special there.

EB: *Sitting on the other side of the fence, they do matter. As a Black female
entrepreneur that does not have the "elite" (Oxford, Cambridge, Harvard,
Stanford) degree, I am treated differently. In an ideal world, it would not
matter. There is a mindset and education shift that needs to happen on the
part of the people that are doing the overlooking. What are your thoughts?
The world you have outlined is an ideal one in which I could thrive, not
because of the color of my skin, but because of the quality of my business.
How do we get from here to there?*

EK: There are two verticals we are building based on the New Mittelstand
vision: an online magazine and a transformative community. The online
magazine helps us share the stories about diversity, radical innovation,
and sustainability. One of the issues in traditional Mittelstand is lack of
female leaders: according to a recent study, only about 11% of management and board members are female. If you consider origin and cultural
background, you will end up with almost no representation at all. We want
to grow and support the next generation that is taking charge on an even
broader definition of diversity. It may take some time because it is about
succession, and it takes years for existing families to rethink that and to
make this decision. Jointly with Zebras Unite, we are working on alternative capital structures and to share inspiring stories of zebra entrepreneurs, relevant to transforming existing businesses.

Traditional family offices are often still very conservative. That money
does not support the purpose-oriented narratives their brand identities
indicate. We think this is inconsistent. So, the other vertical is focused on
transformation with help of our community. The next generation wants
more diversity and sustainability, new digital experiences, etc.—all this
requires evolutionary and radical change at the same time. We developed
a transformational framework to help next generation leaders to find ori-

entation and necessary guidance, and share experiences in various circles and collaborate. We treat the culture of a traditional family firm as a product of entrepreneurship and apply new agile and iterative methods to develop it further. Often, we need to experiment in radical ways and there is an increasing interest to do that. But there is also an open debate. How far do we want to go? Some family businesses are going back to their roots in a negative sense, saying, "We do not want radical change, because we calculated it is not going to be good for us." This debate is difficult, but we need to have the debate and move it into transformative action. This is the value our community creates and our positive impact.

JL: *This is where politics comes into the conversation.*

EK: If you ask Mittelstand companies and family businesses, what is the biggest hurdle for them to do innovation? They will say bureaucracy. The second-biggest issue is access to talent. In changing the way the capital is allocated, we need to figure out ways to do that without increasing bureaucracy. We need to direct the capital to the right people based on quality rather than traditional benchmarks and historical numbers. There is never going to be enough historical numbers, if we do not change radically and take some risks. I hope that these independent capital owners will be more likely to take risks, because at the end of the day, they want to say they did something good with it. Even if the business does not work, the purpose was still right. This is the balance of purpose with profit. The question is, what is the right ratio?

20.3 *Mehta, Kirupa Dinakaran: Immigrant Founders*

Manan Mehta (Unshackled Ventures)

Kesava Kirupa Dinakaran (Luminai)

Unshackled Ventures[398] is working to support immigrant entrepreneurs in the US. Immigrants, historically and across geographies, have started and grown businesses that build enormous opportunities for employment; yet, immigrants face many challenges, particularly in the US, when it comes to their ability to work. Visa hurdles on top of everyday discrimination, as well as potential language and cultural barriers, make it far too difficult to start new businesses without assistance. We spoke to Unshackled's founder Manan Mehta[399] and one of his portfolio-company founders, Kesava Kirupa Dinakaran,[400] who came to the US at 19 and started Luminai[401] (formerly DigitalBrain), a customer-service automation platform, in 2020. Kesava's story, intimately intertwined with Unshackled's mission, is the perfect example of how important it is to help immigrant founders overcome the administrative barriers they face.

Interviewed February 2021

THE ORIGINS OF UNSHACKLED VENTURES

Johannes Lenhard (JL): *Manan, your investment thesis is completely focused on immigrants. How did that come about? Why do you focus on that specific, outstanding niche, and why do you believe in fostering this specific kind of diversity?*

---

398. https://www.unshackledvc.com/

399. https://twitter.com/mananm

400. https://twitter.com/kesava_kirupa

401. https://www.luminai.com/

Manan Mehta (MM): Eight years ago, I attempted to start my first business with a co-founder who had an H-1B visa (a work visa for the United States). I am native-born and raised here in Silicon Valley—little did I know that his H-1B would shackle him to his employer. Nine months into tinkering and moonlighting, immigration became a major hurdle. His inability to transfer his visa made it much harder for us to raise outside capital and for him to work full-time. It was truly a chicken and egg problem that cost us too much time.

Over the past eight years, some of these dynamics have shifted, but the fear of not having work authorization to work on a startup is very frightening for a lot of immigrant entrepreneurs. It was through my journey as an American-born citizen that I was free, but as an entrepreneur with a co-founder on a visa, I had to learn that immigration affected me too. I had never thought about it once in my life up until then.

Every night we would go to these co-working spaces—a prime example of the type of entrepreneurial talent our country attracts. After hours, you would see so many immigrants working. You could smell ethnic cuisines heating in the microwave, hear countless numbers of non-English languages, and you could tell this was not their full-time day job. What I came to realize was that this population of entrepreneurs were immigrants, and it was significantly larger than the population of native-born people working at night.

It makes sense, immigrants who have left their home country by choice are inherently more entrepreneurial than native-borns. These people are often more ambitious, have more drive, and more purpose. Immigrants are the most financially successful entrepreneurial group in the United States (more than 50% of tech IPOs have an immigrant founder). I do not think that has changed. In fact, one of the richest people in the world, Elon Musk, is an immigrant. This is something that is very appealing when you are talking about venture capital and creating upside.

Unshackled is not a not-for-profit: we invest in people who truly want to make both an economic and social impact. It is important that we align with them on both those philosophies. It was that intersection that brought us to start Unshackled.

WHAT IT TAKES TO SUPPORT IMMIGRANT FOUNDERS

Erika Brodnock (EB): *My parents are immigrants, and listening to this from the perspective of being first-generation, it is incredible, because I* *know how much they struggled. What do you do at Unshackled to support immigrant founders?*

MM: Many immigrants come with ambition, not with money. For immigrants who leave their home country by themselves, accessing the networks of influence is extremely hard. Our goal at Unshackled is to be a scalable source of friends and family capital, who will take the full risk with founders financially. We are very fortunate that our investors are comfortable with taking the full risk. We have shown there is a strong population of entrepreneurs who could use this support and accelerate with it.

The second thing we do is provide immigration support. I've learned in the United States there's a difference between immigration and being an immigrant. Immigration can be solved in time, with a thoughtful strategy and government filings. But being an immigrant is a lifelong journey. Unshackled unlocks the immigration journey early on to support entrepreneurs during the ten to fifteen years it takes to build a startup. Over the last six years, we have done 150 filings on behalf of our funders. We are excited to share that 100% of our founders have secured work authorization and/or a green card through our efforts.

The third way we support immigrant founders is through access to influential networks and resources. Our team helps immigrants indoctrinate themselves into these ecosystems where people are described as "adverse selection." We show how these immigrant founders are a net positive. As a result, our ultimate role at Unshackled is being the strongest and fastest on-ramp to the highway of venture capital. Kesava is a prime example of how fast an immigrant can move if given a chance.

HOW UNSHACKLED BROUGHT A KNOCK-OUT ENTREPRENEUR INTO BUSINESS

JL: *Kesava, let us talk about your story of being an immigrant founder. Can you share your experience of when you arrived? What have you been building and what were some of the biggest challenges?*

Kesava Kirupa Dinakaran (KKD): I grew up in the southern part of India, where most of my family are all coconut farmers. There is a good thing to it, which is you get to drink coconuts all day and live on a farm. But the other side is everybody follows a very standard path: finish high school, get married, have kids, live on the farm, life moves on. I have seen people go through that path, and I thought I was going to do something similar to this world around me.

When I was 11 years old, I stumbled upon the Rubik's Cube and started getting really good at solving them. I walked into my first ever Rubik's Cube competition, and I was surrounded by CEOs, musicians, artists, engineers, and doctors. I was blown away for the first time, and I realized I did not have to follow the same path that my family took. I realized if I continue to participate in this community, then I will see that there is so much more to do. I ended up breaking multiple Guinness World Records and was the captain of the Indian National Team. From 11 to 17, that is all I did.

Because of the Rubik's Cube community, I was introduced to a high school called the United World College. It is a high school that brings together people from 70 different countries to work on international peace and understanding. I went to this high school surrounded by people my age wanting to really change the world. Through this journey—from a very traditional family where, unfortunately, a lot of them still struggle to survive, to the Rubik's Cube, to a full scholarship at the high school, to cycling across countries from Europe to Asia—I realized that anything was possible.

My journey continued when a foundation from the US flew me out for a ten-day summit called Three Dot Dash. After I finished, as someone who loved technology, I wanted to visit Silicon Valley. In April 2019, I came out to the Bay Area for five days. I crashed at a friend's room at Stanford, and I was blown away. I thought, "This is my type of people."

When I was back in India, I realized, "What am I doing here?" This is where we hacked the system. My mentor set up a fellowship so I could come to Silicon Valley on a tourist visa for two months. In that short period of time I learned so much. I ended up rejecting a college scholarship so I could continue learning and working on projects in Silicon Valley. Then, I completely ran out of money.

Every weekend, there are hackathons in Silicon Valley where you could end up making $5K building a product. At one of these, I met my now co-founder, Dmitry Dolgopolov. While we could code and build websites over a weekend, our immigration status denied us from high-paying jobs. Instead, we ended up hacking these hackathons and living off of it for six months.

At one point, the company that sponsored a hackathon said they liked one of our products and asked if we could ship it to them. They wanted to sign an annual contract. That was the only customer that was willing to sign a sales agreement and it got us into the whole startup bug. At one point, we realized living off of hackathons is not the most sustainable way of life. It was time for us to raise money. We had zero connections in Silicon Valley and were just trying to make our way through it. We sent about 200 emails to investors we followed on Twitter, got three responses, and all three passed immediately. We thought, "This is crazy. We have a story to tell and they were not even willing to listen."

This is where the crazy stuff happened. Unshackled had a form on their website to be considered, and we thought, "Who is going to look at a form? This makes no sense." But the site promises that they will definitely get back to you. We ended up filling the form. Two days later, one of the people at Unshackled got in touch.

The first meeting with Manan was the first time I felt respected. I felt that he was listening to me. At the end of the call, they were very sincere and said, "You are the kind of people who we bet on." Over the next three weeks, we met and discussed the business. Finally, on February 13, we got $250K. Where I am from, that is more than my family has ever made in their life. It was quite wild. That put us in a place where we could rely on a community of founders and people. Unshackled was there to support us, but we were still on our journey of figuring out what we wanted to do.

This is when things start moving. Unshackled is a signal for other people in many ways. We had applied to an accelerator called Y Combinator (YC) and we did not get an interview. The second time we applied with a slightly different idea, and we got an interview. They never asked us about the idea itself. They said, "You moved from India to Silicon Valley at 19—how? This makes no sense." That evening they said, "We like you guys. We would like to fund you, but we think your idea should change." We iterated, learned, and went to Manan and Nitin, who told us to jump into it with the new product in customer support.

The catalyst for raising a seed round was primarily because of Unshackled. We put together a document on Notion of 100+ investment firms, and they connected us to each one of them. This is what we mean by breaking into venture capital. In a matter of three weeks or so, we raised $3.5M to grow the team. Now we are six people and living this dream we have always wanted to live. The timeline was less than a year, as a result of initial access and our hunger to move fast. I came here on a tourist visa, then my status switched to O-1, which is something I never would have thought to be possible without the team at Unshackled. Changing my immigration status was a big relief because now I can keep growing the dream and not have to worry about anything related to me being here.

THE ACTIONS UNSHACKLED TAKES ON BEHALF OF IMMIGRANT FOUNDERS

EB: *Manan, what is your biggest challenge with immigrant founders? How do you deal with visas and other policy issues that could potentially stop you in your tracks from unearthing such incredible talent?*

MM: We just went through the Trump administration, and if we can get through that, we believe we can get through a lot of immigration changes. During this period of challenging rhetoric, there was a boom in immigrants seeking more help from stable platforms. We still had 100% success on immigration after four years of Trump. The policy, the rhetoric, and the politics of it served as tailwinds for the Unshackled thesis. It accelerated us—the "why now?" became clearer to people.

That being said, the biggest challenge that we will always face is finding people like Kesava. We *know* there are more people like him and know there are similar stories. How do we become that first email and not the email after 200+ emails? By getting to a point of further reach, it gives somebody like Kesava a little bit more inspiration. Our responsibility at Unshackled is to share the example to immigrant entrepreneurs, so that more immigrants will try a little bit harder to break into the venture ecosystem. Our responsibility is to match the aspiration of wanting to start a company with the inspiration of doing it. Regardless of our funding, this gives entrepreneurs a much higher jump-off point.

The challenge for us is always can we serve and scale the market efficiently enough? Can we deliver our promise on a daily basis? Thus, we have to truly amplify entrepreneurs' time and resources at the stage they need it the most.

21 Conversations: Finding Allyship in Unexpected Places

21.1 *Patton Power: Alternatives to VC Funding*

Aunnie Patton Power (Impact Finance Pro, University of Oxford)

Not all startups need or should seek venture capital funding; instead, the majority of businesses shouldn't buy into the fast-scaling and exit-focused VC rhythm. In her research and writing, Aunnie Patton Power[402] has focused on all the alternatives out there, many of which can further enable diversity in the ecosystem. From venture debt to equity-based finance, Aunnie shares concrete ideas of what other sources of funding startups can resort to in a detailed sneak peek of her recent book, Adventure Finance.[403]

Interviewed July 2021

WHAT ALTERNATIVE FINANCING ADDRESSES

Erika Brodnock (EB): *You recently published*[404] Adventure Finance, *a comprehensive guide and casebook on how companies can raise financing outside of the traditional venture capital model. Why did you write the book?*

Aunnie Patton Power (APP): Realistically, venture capital does not work for 99% of businesses, and particularly businesses that are founded with any definition of diversity. One reason is this need for exponential growth, which is not sustainable. Specifically, it is the need for VCs to perceive the possibility of exponential growth.

---

402. https://twitter.com/aunnie

403. https://www.adventure.finance

404. This interview took place in 2021; Adventure Finance was published May 28, 2021.

In my experience working with startups and VCs for the last 13 years, I've seen that women and other people who have been underestimated in their own lives are less likely to have the hubris to be able to talk about becoming the next Facebook. They are coming into business models with much more realistic scenarios for how they are going to grow a business. That is not what VCs are looking to hear. They will not find a $50M market interesting. Nor would they support someone planning to build a company to address a need for a niche population that the VCs never interacted with. There is also the exit piece, which is about needing to grow to a point to sell. Not all founders are interested in selling their business. Even if they are willing to sell parts of it, they are not interested in being up against an artificial deadline of seven to eight years, depending on what the VC fund looks like. VC was designed for tech-enabled, asset-light, highly scalable companies, which has morphed into the only type of risk capital that is available for early-stage businesses.

Most early-stage businesses are not these types of companies, and they do not get funded. The market failure is that VC is risk capital; risk capital is not venture capital equity. There are so many more options. People think they should close a business instead of questioning whether the capital is right or not. It is a chicken and egg conundrum around the industry, where you need funders who can do different types of financing and you need founders who understand different types of financing, what they need, and what will be best for them. You also must consider the element of society and communities. How are we designing funding systems and enterprises that are creating value for communities outside of the small number of funders and founders who benefit from venture capital?

Johannes Lenhard (JL): *How are alternative funding mechanisms and practices accelerating the openness of the industry? Are they changing the availability of funding towards people who are overlooked? What plays the biggest role?*

APP: It is a combination of the process and the product. You can have an inclusive product that works for a lot of founders. However, if you do not have an inclusive process, then you are not going to be able to attract the deals. In addition, if you have the most inclusive process in the world, and you are using a product that is not going to work for these diverse founders you have pulled into this process, you will also not get to the end goal. It is about designing how you find, source, and diligence deals, as well as how you structure them, to be able to really embed inclusivity and diversity. How do you bring in deals? How would you think about the merits of those deals? How do you decide to fund them? What type of structure do you offer them? It is not just about being a venture capital fund that can offer venture debt now, nor hiring a Black analyst or a Latina associate. It is about, what are founders feeling when they walk through the door? Are you providing a product that makes sense for what they want to build?

I work a lot with female founders. They want an investor who offers them the type of investment they need and the type of support they need. That is not necessarily forthcoming from traditional VCs. For example, in regard to structured exits, one thinks about, how do you continue to own this company? How do you repurchase this equity? How does the founder maintain a lion's share or a large percentage of the ownership? There is a shift from the funder's perspective around portfolio construction that is not betting on one to two businesses with the rest failing. By shifting that portfolio construction to having a higher hit rate from a returns perspective and having more liquidity earlier on in the process, you can invest in companies that are going into markets that do not require exponential growth. You are able to then work with companies that have normal growth expectations for companies that are risky and are looking for this type of upside. You can still provide very similar IRRs [internal rates of return], but you are able to engage with these companies. Adopting a portfolio construction is one piece of it, but it is also important to figure out how you go out and find deals from creating sourcing opportunities, use peer-based decision making, make sure that your ICs [investment committees] are diverse, or make sure that your scouts are diverse. All of those different pieces coming together is where I see the early-stage funding becoming genuinely interested in diversity and not at a superficial level.

HOW FOUNDERS CAN BENEFIT FROM ALTERNATIVE FINANCING

EB: *What are the key benefits of that for the founders themselves, especially those who have been traditionally overlooked?*

APP: This is exciting. If you can help founders hold on to more of their business longer, you can create or expand the ownership base. You can think about employee ownership, and even community ownership; we can focus on wealth creation for more than just a couple people. We can use structures such as redeemable equity, where the founders can repurchase the shares, and then they themselves will hold more of that wealth. If they create something over time, then they will have more of that wealth.

Taking it further, you can have founders purchasing shares and employees owning them. With this employee ownership scheme, employees are incentivized to continue to create value in this company. Now you have wealth creation, not just at the top. This creates opportunity. From the other side, with crowdfunding and other types of large, distributed ownership, there is also an opportunity for more retail investors and individuals who feel locked out of the traditional VC market or startup market. You can start to imagine products that allow a larger set of individuals at the company side to participate in wealth creation, as well as a larger set of individuals at the investor side. We are prying it open from both sides. There is opportunity to build companies that are sustainable and that are integrated into communities. By doing so, you have better staff, a more incentivized workforce, better ties to communities, and better ideas about what communities need.

EB: *This also opens the gamut to solving the problems that most need to be solved and that are not currently being solved.*

APP: This has so many layers and it takes both the process and the product. It is not just about funding a few more underrepresented founders. It is about critically thinking and asking, what does this capital allocation look like? What are these business models from the wealth creation and accumulation perspective? We have looked more at changing people from beneficiaries to producers and consumers, but have not yet made that last jump from producers and consumers to wealth creators.

JL: *Crowdfunding can have a radical potential when it comes to providing a different type of funding to startups. Is this something that can benefit stakeholders who have been overlooked and unable to participate?*

APP: Calling it crowdfunding undersells it. I like to say crowdsourcing or community-driven finance. Crowdfunding can sound like preordering a shoe. Community-driven financing is going to be incredibly powerful. Thinking about investing, one of the most powerful structures are platforms (e.g., AngelList) that allow traditional investors to do the due diligence pre-screen, and then put them up for a co-investment by individual investors. This is powerful because it is not just relying on viral social media. If you can have co-investment opportunities, beyond just equity, and allow individuals to invest small amounts of money into a diverse portfolio, you are investing in regenerative agriculture. There are so many ways to do civilian community ownership schemes. Local communities can borrow from financial institutions and then turn that into a source of dividend income down the line.

We have always just assumed that masses cannot do it. We need to revisit those assumptions. Companies can be owned by employees and be able to utilize their employees and larger community to be able to attract capital that is engaged with that company. There are many ways in which we can think about how the resources that communities have must help small businesses and developments, beyond just money. We underestimate that opportunity.

HOW TO THINK ABOUT DEBT

EB: *Everyone wants equity finance, but debt financing is usually not an option for digital businesses because they lack the required security assets. How has that changed, and what are the key factors that will make a debt journey successful for an entrepreneur? How suitable is that for historically overlooked founders?*

APP: We need to understand exactly what we need to fund, then we need to be able to assign the right types of debt to it. Three different types of debt stand out as options that should be in most founders' toolkits.

The first is trade finance: supply chain financing, invoice factoring, or purchase order factoring. These are increasingly facilitated by FinTechs. What they allow you to do is to access working capital, which is terrible to fund with equity, because you are trading ownership in your business for short-term capital needs. Instead, you can use your customers or FinTechs to facilitate payments from your customers. It is short-term expensive financing, but it can be incredibly valuable, particularly for companies that are asset light now.

Revenue-based financing is the next step. It is a complement to traditional equity and more and more VCs will start using it. It also pushes companies to create revenues. By focusing on the internal financing and then monetizing that for growth, revenue-based financing has a lot of opportunities. It is a relatively short-term option, but then we can look at mezzanine financing, particularly for SMEs [small and medium-sized enterprises], which few organizations understand how to do. We need more of them. It has small amounts of collateral, but it also has a fixed interest rate with a profit share. Those three tools are starting to be more accessible, but they are for very specific cases.

Specificity is a bonus for founders, and founders need to better understand their needs as an entrepreneur, as opposed to going on raising an equity round, and then figuring out what to do with the money. We have seen that go wrong so many times. They need a better understanding of the type of capital that fits for the specific type of spend, and then go out and search for that. This is where debt becomes interesting, because that can be customized very specifically. There are even asset-based financing options that are starting to be much more attractive for SMEs, which are often developed by FinTechs and specialist institutions, as opposed to traditional banks. All of those are very tailor-made to the type of spend or the type of assets that you are funding, which creates more discipline.

WILL ALTERNATIVE FUNDING CHANGE THE GAP IN ACCESS TO BIG MONEY?

EB: *Having funding alternatives is great and it will allow many companies to raise money that would not have been possible otherwise. But, does it democratize access to big money? I mean, do you think that any of the alternatives are going to fund the next Amazons and Googles? Or are we saying that we are going to carve out a new way because the old way is not working, but the old way will continue, and white males will be over there getting VC funding while women and other diverse entrepreneurs will get smaller pots?*

APP: This is a good question. Do we want more Facebooks and Amazons? I do not think we do.

We do not need a separate type of capital for underrepresented founders. We need to redesign our system. VC still has a place. More of those founders need to be women and underrepresented. I live in South Africa, where there has been a big push for Black Economic Empowerment. Yet if you create three Black billionaires, there are still 50 million people that are suffering. I do not think there should be billionaires, and I work with billionaires. Billionaires should not be part of how society works.

There is room, however, to make female founders and underrepresented founders create big companies. I do not see those as mutually exclusive. There should not be an A and B track. We do not want it to be white guys running VC funds continuing to do what they want, and we create options for everyone else. This will unfortunately continue for a while. We are still going to be polluting and destroying the environment, even though we know we need to save it. Funds need to start walking the walk around diversity. Businesses should be founded by the people who have the good ideas—and not just [the ones who] look like a specific type of founder.

21.2 *Brand, Lenke: DEI at Twitter*

Dalana Brand (formerly Twitter)

Peter Lenke (Twitter)

Big tech companies are not usually renowned for their DEI perspectives, and are even less known for driving radical change in this or any other space that could backfire and harm advertising revenues. Twitter has been trying to do things differently not just when it comes to their AI team but also to their DEI efforts, including by directly funding VCs led by overlooked GPs. We spoke in 2021 with two of the people responsible for pushing these efforts at the tech giant, Twitter's Chief People and Diversity Officer Dalana Brand[405] and Peter Lenke,[406] director of corporate development and strategy, responsible for Twitter's investments in VCs.

---

405. https://twitter.com/DalanaBrand
406. https://twitter.com/P_Lenke

◇ **IMPORTANT** *Back in 2021, when Twitter was on a different path, we were impressed by the action the tech corporation had taken to increase diversity in the industry. Shortly after the Elon Musk acquisition in late 2022, Dalana Brand resigned from her position. We can't say for sure what the takeover and changes in staffing mean for Twitter's future, including its DEI efforts. Despite that, this interview is a record of the work that was being done at the time.*

Interviewed July 2021

TRANSPARENCY AND ACCOUNTABILITY AT TWITTER

Erika Brodnock (EB): *At Twitter, you openly communicate about your strong commitments to DEI. What are the core pillars of this commitment?*

Dalana Brand (DB): Transparency and accountability. We are adamant about making sure that we go on our inclusion and diversity journey in the public eye. Twitter's mission is to serve the public conversation; our work around inclusion and diversity is no different. We release quarterly blogs[407] stating our progress. We always have these conversations internally, on a quarterly basis at a minimum. I share this information with the board of directors. We are constantly having conversations about what we are doing, what progress we need to make, what the opportunities are, and the challenges.

Transparency does not just mean when things are good. It is also when we have things that we need to work on. By having that conversation[408] with our Tweeps [Twitter employees], and with our broader communities that support us, we can bring people along in the journey and help make progress faster.

The other is accountability. It is not just talking about it. We are also putting several mechanisms in place to make sure that we are meeting the objectives that we stated,[409] and that we are holding managers, leaders, everyone at Twitter accountable for inclusion and diversity to those goals and objectives as much as possible.

---

407. https://blog.twitter.com/en_us/topics/company/2022/
     inclusion-diversity-equity-accessibility-report-our-global-approach-April-2022
408. https://blog.twitter.com/en_us/topics/company/2020/
     inclusion-and-diversity-report-may-2020
409. https://careers.twitter.com/en/diversity.html

TWITTER'S DEI BEST PRACTICES

EB: *Which three best practices are working well to drive DEI internally? What are practices other organizations may have avoided in the past, but should be adopting?*

DB: We were one of the first, if not the first, companies to compensate our Business Resource Group leaders—employees who connect with people around the globe and are championing all the inclusion and diversity efforts that we have as a company. Business Resource Groups or employee resource groups are the foundation and the backbone of the work that we do with inclusion and diversity, and they have been doing this on a volunteer basis up until last year.[410] We listened and took feedback, and one of the biggest barriers we found was that those individuals who we count on and rely on so much were doing this as a side hustle. They were not able to fully commit in the way they wanted to. We decided to compensate them by recognizing that they are doing two jobs at the company. We wanted to place a value on the work that they were doing, because it makes a difference.

We have highlighted and profiled the work that they are doing, including through our quarterly Inclusion and Diversity blogs and journalistic pieces.[411] We have raised this work in terms of awareness with their managers, so that it gets included in their performance management conversation or talent planning discussion. The work that the Inclusion and Diversity folks are doing, as well as the Business Resource Groups, are company-building activities. Those activities essentially make the company better, and it now gets recognized by the managers.

We also train managers on how to lead those individuals in a very inclusive fashion, such that people are getting the recognition and credit that they deserve. When you think about the people in the organization that you place tremendous trust and responsibility in, in terms of driving your goals and initiatives, you must make sure that you set up the infrastructure, and the support system to allow them to do their best work. The third thing we have done is try to meet people where they are—managers, in particular. This inclusive journey in the organization cannot be done just at the top of the house, or with a diversity and inclusion team off to the

---

410. This interview was conducted in 2021.

411. https://www.axios.com/
      twitter-brg-business-resource-group-fbecbca9-b629-40c9-a9b9-b89bd84261be.html

side. We must embed it in all the People practices and all practices across the organization.

To facilitate that process, we have inclusion and diversity business partners [dedicated members of HR/I&D assigned to specific teams to support hiring and other processes with a diversity-focused lens] that are embedded within the business, that support managers and leaders go along this journey. Training[412] can be the standard toolkit or a team building activity or something else. We want to meet people where they are at because we are trying to change the hearts and minds of individuals. You cannot do that with a standard program, you have to tailor and customize your offerings and solutions based on the needs of those you are trying to serve.

LEADING THE WAY IN BACKING NEW VENTURE FUNDS

EB: *Peter, you just supported the writing of three checks to Black-led VCs.*[414] ALIGN LEFT *Why did you get involved in the VC funding space?*

Peter Lenke (PL): I'm part of the Corporate Development and Strategy team. We do all the mergers and acquisitions, a lot of strategy work, partnering with our Product and Engineering and business teams, to drive forward roadmap strategy and pressure test how it relates to Twitter's overall vision. We also have the ability to do investments directly into private companies and VC funds.

As Dalana has explained, our D&I efforts span the whole company, so also implicates us at Corp Dev. We have been acquisitive over the last couple years, onboarding hundreds of "acquired" employees. These acquisitions tend to onboard very senior technical people, often product and engineering team members who come in and lead core initiatives and are elevated in the organization. Corp Dev took a step back and wanted to make sure that we are accretive and not dilutive to Twitter's stated 2025

---

412. You find example of the training in Twitter's annual diversity report: [413]

413. https://careers.twitter.com/en/diversity/annual-report-2020.html

414. The funds themselves published extensive press releases when the investments were announced; MaC VC's press release can be found here,[415] Female Founders Fund's announcement came through *TechCrunch*,[416] etc.

415. https://macventurecapital.com/
mac-venture-capital-raises-a-110m-inaugural-fund-to-invest-in-founders-building-the-futur
e-we-want-to-see/

416. https://techcrunch.com/2021/07/13/
female-founder-fund-closes-third-fund-with-57m-for-female-bipoc-founders/

D&I goals[417] in terms of both the makeup of the team, but also the geographic makeup of where people are located. We looked at our processes as well as the pipeline in terms of where our deals and activity come from. We realized that if we are spending time with the same funds up on Sand Hill Road, the companies we are spending time with are going to look the same. We are proactive about our pipeline, and have worked with, especially in the first half of [2021], funds that are funding Black, Latinx, women entrepreneurs, and diverse founders and teams. We have both an explicit mandate on funding those types of founders and an implicit mandate, given who the GPs [VC partners] themselves are. We have met a huge pool of these emerging funds to really align with Twitter's company-wide goals of being proactive around our Corp Dev pipeline. As a result, we have taken the step of backing a select number of those funds with dollars, and we have used that as both a tool to provide visibility as well as partnership with those funds. That's how the LP commitments came about.

Johannes Lenhard (JL): *What do you envision the changes you are currently making will look like in 12 months? How can others replicate the efforts that you have started?*

DB: From a cultural perspective, one of our main objectives is to write the playbooks that other companies are going to follow. We are very intentional about wanting to make sure that we are not just creating radical change for *our* company, but for the industry as a whole.

PL: We have seen a select few organizations on the venture investing side using dollars to back diverse founders and teams as well. The Apples,[418] Paypals,[419] and Bank of Americas[420] of the world have come in alongside of us or have been active in public in backing other venture funds. People look at large brands, because they provide a real proof point and a stamp of approval. That signaling gives excitement and motivation for others

---

417. https://careers.twitter.com/en/diversity.html

418. https://www.apple.com/newsroom/2021/01/
apple-launches-major-new-racial-equity-and-justice-initiative-projects-to-challenge-syste
mic-racism-advance-racial-equity-nationwide/

419. https://www.prnewswire.com/news-releases/
paypal-invests-50-million-in-black-and-latinx-led-venture-capital-funds-301161730.html

420. https://newsroom.bankofamerica.com/content/newsroom/press-releases/2021/01/
bank-of-america-announces-investments-in-40-private-funds-focuse.html

to step up and make tangible commitments—writing checks, supporting through partnership, and a whole host of other ways.

M&A and investment are important mechanisms here because they both drive real dollars and opportunity. Investment provides dollars of support, to hire team members, build technology, and scale business; while M&A provides dollars in returns, to founders, teams, and investors, which provides proceeds for valuable hard work and potentially wealth creation. M&A can also open new opportunities and roles inside the buyer's organization for people to thrive. Both can be high-leverage opportunities.

PL: We have all seen the metrics out there in terms of the types of teams that are being backed by venture investors. This goes full circle to the teams being acquired via Corp Dev mechanism at large corporations. If you are not proactive, thoughtful, and intentional around the types of teams in the Corp pipeline, then the problems will be perpetuated. This is the beginning of the process. We are excited about writing checks and will continue spending time with those funds that are just starting to chip away at the problem.

BUYING AND INVESTING IN DIVERSE COMPANIES

EB: *People who are running funds at firms need three Cs in order to succeed: capital, connections, and contracts. Nine times out of ten, if you have contracts and connections, the other does follow. Does Twitter have any policies in place that awards procurement-based contracts to diverse companies as well?*

DB: Yes. We look across the entire company and look for ways to embed inclusive and diverse practices within the organization. Procurement is no different. We have a wonderful team that partners with finance and our inclusion and diversity team to make sure that managers, leaders, and others are contracting and giving opportunities to the communities that we represent, and that use our platform and service in those contracts. We will continue to evolve and grow, but we are incredibly proud of that.[421]

---

421. You can find more detail on the procurement process in Twitter's March 2021 report[422] as well as earlier reports, e.g., from 2020.[423]

422. https://careers.twitter.com/en/diversity/annual-report-2020.html

423. https://blog.twitter.com/en_us/topics/company/2020/ Inclusion-and-Diversity-Report-March-2020

JL: *You are making a case for diversity for the VCs and the LPs, from the perspective of the exit. You are saying that you want to ultimately buy and invest in diverse startups at Twitter, but instead of waiting for the VC industry itself to move forward, you are directly going in there pushing them.*

DB: We recognize our responsibility as an organization that has a strong voice, is represented in tech, and has an incredible following, to be at the forefront of driving that change.

PL: Corp Dev work is just one pillar of Dalana's full company-wide initiatives. Every team has a part to play. Historically, you would not be talking to a Corp Dev team member on a D&I topic. We all must make sure our pipeline is robust when we are vetting opportunities, making investments, and thinking about how they are additive to Twitter as a whole, not only from a narrow technology and product standpoint, but from the full person.

JL: *Can you talk a little bit about both the challenges and immediate other opportunities that you are thinking about to make the VC and tech ecosystem more diverse and inclusive, to create radical change over the coming years?*

DB: Tech changes when it is required to do so, and when information becomes more widely accessible. Pay equity[424]—making sure that employees in equivalent roles are compensated equally—has been a conversation for a long time. You are starting to see more transparency laws come out and more conversations about equity and parity happening within organizations. Increased pressure for more transparency, whether that is through laws or regulations[425] or by public sentiment, drives a lot of the efforts around inclusion and diversity broadly. Our goal is to make sure that we are not doing it because we must, but because those are our core values and principles. We hope others will follow from that perspective.

PL: So much of what fuels the venture ecosystem is around connection, relationships, and founders that have previously exited. With some of these funds that we have backed, as well as others, you see founders that

---

424. https://twitter.com/d_lux_brand/status/1374774028779491330?s=20
425. https://www.natlawreview.com/article/
    patchwork-pay-transparency-laws-continues-to-evolve

are then having successful exits, and they will be the angel check writers or repeat founders that can continue this path. Getting this flywheel going is tremendously important and takes time. These venture-backed companies take a long time to build, scale, and exit, but we are hopeful that the needle is moving in the right direction.

21.3 *Ackerman: Data Activism*

Maya Ackerman (WaveAI, Santa Clara University)

Maya Ackerman[426] is at first sight an unlikely activist in the space of DEI in startups; AI professor at Santa Clara and founder of a music-generating AI startup herself, she turned to investigate how bad the lack of diversity really was some years ago based on her own experience as a founder trying to fundraise. Very quickly, she started poking well-researched holes[427] in the bad data we keep citing, and has maintained a steady production of power-ful weapons with more precise data and insights ever since.

Interviewed June 2021

MACHINE LEARNING FOR INVESTORS

Johannes Lenhard (JL): *You are a computer engineer and an expert in artificial intelligence and computational creativity. How did you start to think about AI and startups in VC?*

Maya Ackerman (MA): I started a startup through some of my work in computational creativity, particularly in helping people to write songs. On the side, I am an opera singer. I did some research on the automatic com-position of vocal melodies to help me write songs. After three years, it became clear that this was to be a company so we could share this knowl-edge with other people. [The company became WaveAI.[428]]

I have had plenty of shocking experiences, as far as biases, that left me extremely perplexed. You never know if it is your gender, and I am an academic so I would never take a sample of one as a serious data set. One of my students wanted to build models to help VCs make decisions. I

426. https://twitter.com/ackermanmaya

427. https://www.scu.edu/illuminate/thought-leaders/maya-ackerman/bias-in-venture-capital
.html

428. https://www.wave-ai.net/

thought, why not? Let's pick a little team. We ended up having a team of three students to build machine learning models to help investors make intelligent decisions. We then wanted to look at race and gender, and once we tapped it, it all started oozing out. It is crazy. It is awful. It is shocking.

DATA AND BIAS EXPOSURE

Erika Brodnock (EB): *How important would you say the data and the right kind of data still is in this field? Do you think we know everything there is to know already? Is there more to learn?*

MA: It is strange to realize how misguided the whole field is, to the point that you think it is on purpose. This level of ignorance can hardly be accidental. Given how many smart people are in venture, there is no way that I am the first one to think about it. They keep looking at totals. For example, they may say, "female-only founding teams dropped from 2.7% in 2019." This is important information. But, it is easy to attack it with the "pipeline problem." A critic may argue that not enough women are trying to raise money, and this is why such a small percentage goes to them. We need a better way to expose the bias.

Instead, let us not talk about totals or the percentage of total funding allocated to women, let's talk about averages.

On average, if a man and a woman go to raise, how much is each one expected to raise? This is not complicated mathematics. You see the big gaps in the research I did,[429] and I can show you the charts.

A woman raises at least 10 times less under most circumstances. How do we go about justifying it? It does not matter how many of them there are, and the pipeline problem becomes irrelevant. Then we can look at education, prior exits, and gender. The data still shows it. The amount of bias we are dealing with here is at a different magnitude than people like to recognize. Another issue with looking at totals is if you look at the total amount of money going to women, at early stage versus late stage, you see an even smaller percent of the total pie is going to women in late stage. Then we say, let us make sure we help there. That is super ignorant, because there are fewer people at the late stage. Instead, if you just look at averages for women, there is about a 35% discrepancy at the late stage and a 65% discrepancy at the early stage.

---

429. https://www.scu.edu/illuminate/thought-leaders/maya-ackerman/bias-in-venture-capital
.html

CURRENT SOLUTIONS AND MISUNDERSTANDING BIAS

JL: *You looked at the impact of COVID on funding, particularly for female founders. What did you learn from that? What are the nuances that people had not understood before?*

MA: The COVID analysis seemed to suggest that things just got worse. There were the same problems that we had before, but worse. It is even harder for women to raise funding than before.

JL: *Are the strategies for change drawn from your analysis focused on gender and race?*

MA: Current solutions are not designed around what is happening. I have a very controversial view around the birds of a feather analysis, where we say investors like to invest in people like themselves. This narrative needs to either be significantly altered or dropped. It is causing a lot of problems. Firstly, it seems to suggest that we need to solve the VC diversity problem before we solve the entrepreneurial problem, which means that we are looking at decades in the future, and it is shoving the problem aside. Secondly, women are biased against women. There is a study by the UN[430] showing that they are less biased against women than men, but it is still very significant.

People are not born with sexism, but it is something you learn from society. Men and women learn to discriminate against women in certain contexts. This is not criticism of female VCs. Many of them are doing a fantastic job, particularly in efforts to reduce bias, and we definitely need more of them. The issue is about how bias works. We all soak it in from culture. All of us need to work to overcome it. By saying we just need to hire more women, men think it is not their problem. They hire a woman and then she is responsible for the diversity investments, which have a tiny fraction of the money. This is a fundamental misunderstanding on how bias works and how bias needs to be resolved.

But we need to tackle both bias against female investors, and bias against female entrepreneurs. Not first one, then the other. We need both male and female investors to take responsibility for and actively work on reducing bias in venture funds allocation.

---

430. https://www.undp.org/press-releases/
     almost-90-menwomen-globally-are-biased-against-women

By contrast, we look at bias in academia. I am a computer science professor where there is plenty of bias against people like me in this space, but there are male professors who actively work to recruit women. That is part of the reason why we are making some progress in that space. In some spaces, female professors are twice as likely to get a job, because there was so much effort to try to correct the bias.

There are other problems with the current solutions. A lot of venture firms have an explicit mandate to invest in women, and when you look at the details of the mandate, they say to invest in companies that have at least one female founder. Companies that have at least one female founder typically outraise companies that do not have a female founder. The key aspect is who is the CEO. If a guy is a CEO, this company that had the female co-founder was already doing better and they do not need help. They do not need diversity investors. Right. This misunderstanding on the details is causing money that is supposed to help to not help anybody.

THE CHALLENGES OF EXAMINING RACE

EB: *Let us look at ethnicity. How is that a bigger issue? What is preventing you from looking at it now yourself? What do you expect to find there?*

MA: We have done some preliminary analysis and there are so many pieces. First, this is not about white and non-white people. This is a complex issue. And we need to be careful to not overgeneralize. For example, here in the US, people from different Asian countries get treated very differently when it comes to fundraising. We started looking specifically at Black founders. The problem is that we ran it on data that was not complete enough. The data seemed to suggest that the problem is of a similar magnitude to gender discrimination. Again, it might be even worse, and it might manifest differently. We need big numbers. There is no data. There is a lot of missing data. We do not know if the percentages are correct. We are trying to build our own.

It is so tricky because we need to classify ethnicity based on pictures, for example. We are using other people's algorithms. It is a very complicated thing. A lot more people can be working on this. They are scared, because you can share some information, and then investors can try to misuse it. The ecosystem is so biased, and we are hundreds of years behind in the venture space. Trying to do something positive is so complicated and you must be so careful. There are researchers who want to work on this who do not because they are scared.

IMPROVING AN INDUSTRY THAT'S DECADES BEHIND

EB: *Why do you think we are so far behind in the venture space?*

MA: There is so much power in there. If we look at how progress is made, for example, in women's rights, it's gradual. Venture runs the world to a large extent. There are more gates because it is such an important space. From a sociology perspective, I am not sure how this has manifested. Female doctors or professors, there was resistance to it, but eventually we got there. Now it is the government and businesses, and they do not want us there.

JL: *What are some of the big unanswered questions? What is next?*

MA: Let us start with the assumption that we do not know anything. I spent a year doing research on this and many things that are taken for granted in venture are just flat out wrong. We need to do analysis for each race carefully. We need to do intersectional analysis very carefully on large data sets. We need to then understand, how does my bias manifest against women in female CEOs versus male CEOs? There is some research and people who are doing good work, but just not enough basic questions are getting answered. If you want to design solutions, you need to understand what is happening. The way it is going right now, we are just relying on the passage of time more than anything else. Certain things may take a very, very long time—and perhaps may never be fixed through a passive or poorly-informed approach. I do not know if there is enough will to really correct it, and if there is enough will to fund research like this.

EB: *What are some of the biggest structural issues that you found through your research and the lack of funding for it that prevents real change from happening?*

MA: It is an incentive issue. The people in power who are extremely powerful and wealthy, and they do not want things to change. I can easily see for decades, they are going to pay lip service to it and they are going to throw these little funds together, treating them as a charity. Things will go on as they did, most likely. Government is powerless against them; they have laws that prevent discrimination lawsuits, and they are not allowed to do anything that would hurt their bottom line. They can claim that diversity investment can hurt their bottom line, and there is nothing anybody can do about it. In venture, they can have any reason under the sun, and there is just completely no retribution. Somebody in power needs to be willing to take a stand. I do not know if anybody has power against these people. In the States, at least, it is all about money. That is where the money is at. I am sure they have more arms in the government than anybody else, so good luck changing any laws. One hope is to do the research and come up with very pragmatic, narrow ideas to start to untangle the discrimination. Even that is turning out to be trickier than I expected, which is surprising me. There are mechanisms that make this complicated, but it is more promising than hoping for something else.

21.4 *Corzine: Nasdaq's Non-profit*

Nicola Corzine (Nasdaq Entrepreneurial Center)

Nicola Corzine,[431] *the executive director of the Nasdaq Entrepreneurial Center,*[432] *has been leading the Center's activities since its inception in 2015. She is leading the Center's strong focus on equitable entrepreneurship and shares in this conversation what can be done with research, teaching programs, and community to create improvements on both sides of the Atlantic.*

Interviewed February 2021

NASDAQ ENTREPRENEURIAL CENTER'S PRIORITIES FOR EQUITABLE ENTREPRENEURSHIP

Erika Brodnock (EB): *As the director of the Nasdaq Entrepreneurial Center, could you tell us when and why it was established? What exactly do you do there?*

---

431. https://twitter.com/ncTheCenter
432. https://thecenter.nasdaq.org/

Nicola Corzine (NC): I was brought on as the founding co-executive director in 2015, to lay the strategy for an independent non-profit supported and funded by Nasdaq. It truly changed the landscape of access to education and resources in the field of entrepreneurship.

Over the years, the Nasdaq Foundation has been making intentional investments in business plan competitions and mentorship programs across the US. At every single inflection point, Nasdaq always felt there was so much more that could be done because of the network and because of who they stood for in the world, but they did not want to run it directly themselves. For all the right reasons, they felt it should really exist as a standalone mission.

I was fortunate to be able to come in, figure out that strategy, build the operation, articulate what we stood for, and look at the entire landscape. I have an amazing team that makes this all easy, day in and day out. I work beside funders and foundations to really make a change in access and equity through this field.

Johannes Lenhard (JL): *How has that research that you have undertaken shaped and influenced the position that Nasdaq has, specifically when it comes to listing companies going forward?*

NC: Entrepreneurship has been fairly well-studied in academic settings, but not so much at the practitioner layer. In many ways, entrepreneurship is one of the least patient industries, so the ability to slow down and look at the science to inform the art has not been the typical outcome. Case in point, if you think of the investor euphemism, "Within the first few minutes, I knew whether or not I was going to make an investment." What was actually driving that consideration? If we are talking about "gut" being the gateway to acceptance, then what is actually happening behind the scenes? What is that gut? How do we scientifically explain what gut facilitates and what it does not, and perhaps more importantly, who is getting lost in that process?

To maximize inclusive innovation economies, sometimes the lessons to be learned come from not so obvious places. Take for example the public markets, where in recent years you've seen public sentiment drive greater responsibility and outcomes at an ESG [environmental, social, and governance] level of public companies. There is a recognition that all companies must drive towards greater social impact for their sustainability and the world.

Just to be clear though, we are learning from public markets, but maintain separation of church and state: we are not Nasdaq the entity, but the Nasdaq Entrepreneurial Center, a public non-profit. We're incredibly fortunate to have Nasdaq as a foundational donor and one of our greatest sponsors and champions. We were very pleased and proud of their moment earlier[433] in 2021 when they facilitated intentionality around tracking board diversity with a lens towards really showcasing an index of great companies that were born with diversity in mind. Nasdaq also has the first female CEO of a financial institution of its kind. Adena Friedman is someone who is passionate about DEI; she is passionate about it being the driving force of the future of work, of economic opportunity and prosperity for all, and really pulling forward all communities in that conversation.

What we need to do from a research lens moving forward for the Center is create an environment where change is more than a moment, but generational. That's the kind of longitudinal commitment that a non-profit such as ours is not only tasked with in its mission, but ultimately uniquely capable of driving a coalition of support towards achieving.

So, let's take the lack of funding that flows to Black and Brown founders, as an example: less than 1%. We get super clear as to what are the barriers that persist around that systemic ecological challenge, and then we take a step back and say, "What else is getting lost in that construct?" While the conversation is often critical about venture, that's not the only environment where minority entrepreneurs are left behind in the capital allocators arena.

A great example of that in some regards could be found with the stimulus funding of the PPP [Paycheck Protection Program] program in the US, which did not flow at a diverse layer to all of the businesses that it aimed to serve. Was that bias that lived at the financial institution layer of banks? Perhaps in part. Probably more likely, in part, there was a lack of understanding or actionable research that could inform policy on how banking relationships and selection differ with different constituents and stakeholders in communities. The end result: the capital did not flow to the businesses that the government aimed to support.

In some ways it's understandable: entrepreneurship by its nature of being wants to do, wants to build, wants to fix. But this triggers a very

---

myopic approach that focuses on one specific issue area, and ultimately does little to fix the root cause of the problem. So, by not being patient in really understanding all the stakeholders involved in the problem, we end up contributing to the problem, because we just want to get in and either throw money at it, or make it better and get back to work. Only by slowing down to speed up can we really address a systemic, intentional, longitudinal change in an environment that continues to hit these kinds of barriers and obstacles along the way.

THE IMPORTANCE OF PRIORITIZING THE INDIVIDUAL

EB: *In that vein of slowing down before you speed up, what are some of the key evidence-based programs and initiatives you have developed at the Center? Which of those are you most proud of? Have you been seeing any results that you would like to showcase?*

NC: Contrary to popular belief, we are less focused on businesses and much more at the individual, human, flourishing layer of entrepreneurship. When we look at the detrimental outcomes, like the recent passing of Zappos founder Tony Hsieh, entrepreneurs are really dealing with the fact that there is perhaps no lonelier journey than the journey they're on. If in fact, our job is to protect and value the system surrounding the entrepreneur's journey, then we need to make sure that we are standing up a whole system of support around the individual. Businesses will go and flux, ideas will come and go, but the individual is probably going to go do this more than one time. How do we really build up strong, intentional entrepreneurs that can continue to go down this path and realize their maximum potential to inspire the next generation of entrepreneurs?

We have framed more of a responsive support system, amplified by near peers. We do not focus on any one industry, geography, or environment, we actually find that there is greater trust and greater confidence that comes by being in a room of learners from different industries. Their ability to lean in and see new opportunities in front of them from different perspectives is infinitely more likely. That is amplified because of the diversity that the Center has had at its get-go. With 51% women and 70% minorities, there is not a class or a workshop or a learning environment where diversity and diverse thoughts, perspectives, backgrounds, and ideas are not always surfacing.

Since everything that the Center does is free, we are building up a pay-it-forward mechanism where even inside of the environment, they have to commit to supporting one another. That is perhaps the ultimate "aha" we've learned along the way. Great mentors, advisors, and industry experts are amazing to inspire and guide, but nothing can beat near-peer amplification. We found, for better or worse, that the best way to facilitate learning can come by being inspired by front-of-the-class learning. Yet, the most intentional outcomes happen when you are learning from someone who has just gone through a problem ahead of you. That builds up trust, and it builds up confidence in really intentional and transformative ways.

We believe entrepreneurs need to define their own paths of success. It is not for industry to define it; it is for themselves. Most of the time, it is not just financially driven. With our 35,000 entrepreneurs that we have now worked beside, seven out of ten times there is deeper motivation going on, there is an intention of wanting to better a community, wanting to provide societal outcomes that are our driving factor as well. If we can find these motivations, we can get them the tactical and practical help that they need at a subject matter layer of expertise, but also make sure that they have got someone betting on them as a leader, and an individual.

It is ironic in some ways that in the industry, we celebrate only the successful having access to business coaches. Yet the ways in which it can make the biggest difference is early on in the trajectory of an entrepreneur. We have chosen to give that earlier on in the journey, and what we are seeing are much greater outcomes, again, at that self-efficacy level, and certainly at that confidence marker.

Confidence of a founder can drive the best outcomes; one of the KPIs that we care about is whether we are building more confident founders who can drive towards figuring things out, because they are the ones that have to do it. They have to believe in themselves above all else, if they are going to make it.

LACK OF TRANSPARENCY HOLDS THE INDUSTRY BACK

JL: *What lessons have you learned over the years as an investor, what has changed, and do you feel we need to see more progress urgently?*

NC: When I first started, the Angel Capital Association (the equivalent of the National Venture Capital Association) was not even imagined. Angel investing was almost a dirty word of sorts among VCs. Now accelerate to where we are: we know the volume of dollars flowing into seed stage deals at an angel versus venture level are typically three to one—some reports show even higher. The number of businesses that are supported by angels far outweigh the number of deals that will ever get funded by venture because of the nature and the way in which the deals look at exit and liquidity.

Band of Angels is the oldest angel investment group in the United States, celebrating a tremendous history and record. I was very fortunate to have the first year working beside an individual who is recognized as largely being the original angel investor in American history, Hans Severiens. Hans was always one to say to me, "We invest in people that we want to be invested in, and the friendships and relationships of what they stand for far outweigh any returns we are going to get." What I did not appreciate was how in tune one had to be to connect with individuals, and the questions that matter versus the ones that don't.

Hans and every other investor that was part of Band were senior operating individuals, founders of the most notable companies in Silicon Valley: Hewlett Packard, Symantec, the list goes on and on. I had them as my mentors and my guides, helping me understand what talent looked like and what innate qualities must always be present. I learned why credibility was the number one reason that founders got funded, and why if you showed for a moment that you did not have that credibility within you, we were going to turn away from that deal in a heartbeat.

But that's not the narrative that entrepreneurs are told—if anything, quite the contrary! On the one hand they're told, "put up a chart, claim you are a billion-dollar unicorn company," that is all that is needed. Obviously, when you start to try to get an understanding as to what that number means, it all crumbles away like a pie, and the entrepreneurs are left shaking in their boots. The investors walk away going, "We are not going to fund you, you do not know what you are talking about." The truth is, the industry largely has told entrepreneurs "you need to play this game," but then we don't share the rules. So how can they really be set for success?

INSPIRING OPPORTUNITY THROUGH CAPITAL

When I come back to the untapped talent that is not yet being funded, with our Black and Brown founders in this country and across the world, what I realized is, nobody ever said, "There is this game, here are the rules. This is how you do and do not play it if you want to succeed." We are starting to get better within the industry. We are starting to realize the unfairness of the game, or perhaps the cheating that goes on behind the game.

There still remains some uncertainty that lives behind the magic of the industry, and this uncertainty is, "What is that gut?" If I go back to that earlier comment, of knowing if you are going to fund a founder within two minutes. Why are we making that determination? Is it purely pattern matching? If it is, shame on us.

Another thing I definitely say about the industry is we are celebrated in some regards, and yet we get it right one out of ten times: everywhere else, you would have been fired decades ago, if you ever got it right one in ten times.

To a certain degree, our job within venture is to inspire more opportunities for future entrepreneurs to lean in, because we are not always going to get it right. If you can find entrepreneurs who are going to build great legacy and build more entrepreneurs of the future, then you are investing with a healthy return. There are two axes that matter: the right time to exit, and the amount that is returned to you upon exit.

Angel investing is perhaps a more honorable field to a certain degree, because it is one's own money rather than other people's money. You get a better sense of truth when it comes to what drivers matter. More often, we would see entrepreneurs that we would love to fund when we know they would be making a 3X return in a five-year period. The jobs that were being created, the opportunities and innovation that were being born, and the inspiration for future innovation to come from those types of moments was highly valued. The time span of these returns was both justified and good. I would not mind getting a 3X return in that kind of time period every day of the week.

IMPROVING ACCESS TO CAPITAL

EB: *If you were president for a day, what would you mandate? What is the one thing the whole ecosystem could do to improve access to those who are currently being overlooked?*

NC: We always said the one market you can never change as an entrepreneur is how many hours there are in a day and what you can do in one day. Prioritizing your time and knowing where to lay your efforts is one of the entrepreneur's greatest challenges. I wish there was an environment from which we could all agree on what could and should be tracked when it comes to fair performance for our entrepreneurs.

It is a declining environment for entrepreneurs because we have changed the goalposts a thousand times in the field. Once upon a time, the American Dream stood for something radically different than what it does today. As the daughter of an immigrant entrepreneur, and having started three companies in the US and abroad, I know like many what the opportunity to dream means. I believe, like many, that all ideas should be valued, that the opportunity to be a part of the entrepreneurial economy should be within reach of all, and that we all suffer when that doesn't occur.

Eight out of ten times when I meet an entrepreneur, they say to me, first and foremost, I am not a "real" entrepreneur. When I lean in to ask them why, they say because I do not look like—and I do not mean to pick on Elon Musk or Mark Zuckerberg or any of them—but they say because I am not like that. My ideas aren't that big. I've always felt the term "incremental innovation" has limited our potential to recognize the exponential growth afforded by community entrepreneurs. I'd like to re-imagine that scale and appreciation of impact made possible through all entrepreneurs.

I realized that we have let the narrative of entrepreneurship be shaped and shifted by media more than we have by policy, and we celebrate only those that produce a certain kind of result, as mandated by a market cap or some other experience, above and beyond what entrepreneurship actually stands for. If I was president for a day, I would come in and create a fair standard that prioritized the true meaning of entrepreneurship, and had us all take a step back and realize entrepreneurs are amongst all of us. They are all equal. All ideas are valuable in the world, and innovation is a currency that we all must contribute to.

21.5 *Zimmerman, Kapor, Kim, Horgan Famodu, Ekeland: Allies*

Ed Zimmerman (Lowenstein Sandler, First Close Partners)

Mitch Kapor (Kapor Capital and Kapor Center)

Eddie Kim (Gusto)

Maya Horgan Famodu (Ingressive Capital)

Marie Ekeland (2050)

Building on the notion that we need a collective of people with the power, resources, and potential to create systemic change in the venture capital ecosystem, we spoke to a who-is-who of key players who openly celebrate their allyship towards diversity and inclusion: Ed Zimmerman[434] (tech lawyer and LP at First Close Partners[435]), Mitch Kapor[436] (Lotus founder and former GP), and Eddie Kim[437] (co-founder of scale-up Gusto[438]). They were joined by female fund managers Maya Horgan Famodu[439] (Ingressive Capital[440]) and Marie Ekeland[441] (2050,[442] in a demonstration of the power of allyship in creating opportunities and fruitful outcomes for all.

Interviewed April 2021

SEEING DISCRIMINATION AND RACISM AS AN ALLY

Erika Brodnock (EB): *To the three men in this (virtual) room: what was the lightbulb moment that put you onto the DEI movement?*

---

434. https://twitter.com/EdGrapeNutZimm

435. https://firstclosepartners.com/

436. https://twitter.com/mkapor

437. https://www.linkedin.com/in/edawerd/

438. https://gusto.com/

439. https://twitter.com/mayahorgan

440. https://ingressivecapital.com/

441. https://twitter.com/bibicheri

442. https://2050.do/#

Ed Zimmerman (EZ): White people ask me this question and I often bristle about answering because I believe part of why they—particularly able-bodied, straight, white people—are asking is because they would like to make sure that I can check a box that they do not check so that they are relieved of any obligation to themselves participate in diversity, equity, and inclusion. There is an extent to which they are looking for an excuse. Years ago, when my father passed away from lung cancer, everyone asked, "Was he a smoker?" I feel that there's a similarity between those two questions; people wanted to say, "If you are underrepresented then it makes sense that you are doing DEI work," just like you don't really have to worry about lung cancer unless you smoke ... In other words, it's not actually their problem.

My older sister was in a wheelchair. She looked very different and interacted with the world in a way that was very different. She was six years my senior and I have very vivid memories, as well as palpable anger, at the way she was treated and disrespected. She was stared at and pointed at, and people crossed the street to avoid her. I saw some of that same behavior with friends in college who were Black. We went into an elevator together and a woman grabbed her purse, and I knew that she was not clutching her purse because I was there. I would say that, certainly through high school, I was probably about as racist as the next person in my neighborhood, and about as xenophobic as the next person in my neighborhood in Brooklyn.

I started actually acting on things in college and going to a couple of marches and engaging more. As a practicing lawyer, I did some things that were tangible steps forward in favor of diversity, equity, and inclusion in the '90s. In '94, I asked for permission to be pro bono outside counsel to a dance company that was led by a Black, HIV-positive, gay dancer and choreographer. I worked for free on a project about AIDS, which was a pretty controversial project. I have been pro bono counsel to that arts non-profit for the last 27 years. In '95, I asked the firm if I could host a gathering and a dinner, when I went on campus to my alma mater, for all of the leaders of the student organizations like Lambda, Black Law Students Association, and Asian Pacific American Law Student Association. We as a law firm had never done that before. To them, drinks and dinner were great, but bringing people back to the firm, when the firm was not particularly ready for them, was less effective. It was the right idea, but there was so much more work that needed to be done, and I lacked any economic power or oversight within the firm as a young associate still making my way.

IDENTIFYING AS AN OUTSIDER AND UNDERSTANDING PRIVILEGES

Mitch Kapor (MK): In my childhood, I skipped second grade and went directly into third. This left me almost two years younger, and that was really disastrous socially. It cemented my identity as an outsider that I had all the way through high school. I was convinced that I was the least popular child that ever went through the Freeport public school system.

Fast-forward a couple of decades and unexpectedly, in my early 30s, I found myself running a wildly successful tech startup, Lotus, that was experiencing explosive growth. In that situation, as we have seen from all of these other companies like Google and Facebook, the founders get a get out of jail free card. There's no adult supervision. The founders can do whatever they want. Some try to send rocket ships to Mars, I was interested in making Lotus be the kind of employer that even a misfit like me would feel comfortable in.

Freada and I[§14.4] began working together there. She was hired to make Lotus the most progressive employer in the US. We were not a couple then. We were professional colleagues and worked on many projects around building a highly inclusive and diverse corporate culture. That was in the '80s. In the '90s, we got together as a couple. By osmosis and proximity, I moved into a different world than the world that I grew up in. Frieda has been doing DEI work for four decades. She is a pioneer and co-founded the first group in the US on sexual harassment, and has been on top of issues of intersectionality when it comes to gender discrimination. We have dozens of colleagues who are people of color, and our scholarship programs serve low-income communities of color. Through dozens and hundreds of encounters and relationships large and small, I began to have a better understanding of the day-to-day experiences of people who, just by virtue of the color of their skin, face barriers, discrimination, and microaggressions. There is a whole range of manifestations of systemic racism that is part of day-to-day life.

With Freada's framework with which to understand this and do something about it, I have over time had my own evolving process. I was not racist in an overt way, but I certainly had a very large number of unexamined assumptions about who is likely to succeed and who was not in tech and startups that amounted to racist beliefs. It is a continuous and often painful process of reassessment. I was, in hindsight, overly focused on ways in which I had been excluded, which were real. I went to Yale as a lower-middle-class kid in the late '60s, early '70s, which still reeked of privilege. I knew that Yale was not the kind of place that was made for people like me. Yet, until the last decade, I was not paying attention to the advantages I continuously derive from being white, male, and Ivy League educated. A lot of the work that I have done has been in understanding that I have gotten boosts through means that I cannot take any credit for. There is a fundamental injustice around that. It is just wrong.

LISTENING TO THE EXPERIENCES OF THE "ONLY" ON THE TEAM

Eddie Kim (EK): A couple years after co-founding Gusto, we had raised our Series A round of financing and were hiring software engineers as fast as we could. We had an engineering team of eight, all men and one woman. I went on vacation for a couple weeks and, to my delight, by the time I came back we had hired another three engineers. In my first weeks back, I had a one-on-one meeting with Julia, the only woman engineer on the team. She told me that while it's great that we're growing our team so quickly, she wanted to share with me her experiences being an "only" on the team. Over the next few weeks, I asked a lot of questions about diversity and inclusion as we went on late-afternoon runs together up and down Embarcadero Street in San Francisco. I cared about Julia a lot and took our conversations to heart.

Our conversations gave me more questions than answers, and I started to do more research in this space, particularly on gender diversity in software engineering. I had a lightbulb moment when I stumbled across a chart published in an NPR article titled "When Women Stopped Coding."[443] The chart plots the percentage of college graduates who are women in certain majors over time. The four majors plotted were medicine, law, physical Sciences, and computer Science. From 1965 to 1985, all four plots look about the same: they start around 10% and make their way up to 35%, indicating that the fields are getting more gender diverse. Three of the lines—medicine, law, physical sciences—continue upward to nearly 50% by 2010! But the line for computer science takes a different trajectory starting in 1985. Instead of continuing upward, the percentage of women majoring in computer science takes a sharp turn *downward*, settling to a

---

443. https://www.npr.org/sections/money/2014/10/21/357629765/when-women-stopped-coding

multi-decade low of around 17% in 2010. When you take into context other societal and cultural trends happening in 1985, it becomes very clear that systemic and societal issues played a large part in making the field of computer science difficult for women starting in 1985. It really opened my eyes to how *systems*, not just individuals, play an important role in creating more inclusive and equitable environments in the technology industry.

LEARNING TO EMPATHIZE AND UNDERSTAND

EB: *People who have been through some adversity or feel as though they did not fit in themselves are much more inclined to have empathy towards other out groups. Ed, do you think that your sister plays a fundamental part in your ability to empathize with other groups now?*

EZ: I worry that my experiences with my sister made me more empathetic to people other than my sister. She is no longer with us, but I am sure that it did. I am sure that watching who was kind to my parents (and who was not) played a role. I am sure that seeing my parents struggle and get the short end of the stick also played a role. There was further intersectionality because my sister was bisexual. My mother was bisexual, and also bipolar. There was a lot going on. I lived upstairs with my aunt and my grandmother, and my sister and my parents lived downstairs. My aunt was also disabled. I grew up in a house where there were four women, two of whom were disabled and two of whom were bisexual. My wife and I got together when we were 18 years old. We met on August 28, 1986, during her first day of college and my first day of my sophomore year. She has made me a more empathetic and better person. I have spent the last decades striving to meet what she saw I could be in a lot of ways.

MK: My own experiences and all of the work that I have done to move myself forward into a better, happier, more impactful state, has all really opened the door to understanding other people's experiences in a way that would not otherwise have happened. This is particularly true for the young people we met in a scholarship program we started for UC Berkeley undergraduate about 20 years ago. We became very close to some of those kids and were surrogate parents to them. I worked to understand that, despite enormous differences in every possible dimension, these kids wanted nothing other than what I wanted. Put simply, I wanted to be who I was and not have to become somebody else. I wanted to have a shot and an opportunity to make something of myself, without sacrificing myself.

I understand these kids from low-income communities of color who had really struggled and managed to get into University of California, Berkeley, race blind, also wanted that. But there were structural barriers in their way. I believed we have to do something about this. It was not an intellectual conclusion. It was a deep-seated moral imperative.

FORGING A NEW PATH: BUILDING CONFIDENCE, FIGHTING BIASES, AND TAKING PRIDE

Johannes Lenhard (JL): *Maya and Marie, you have grown up female in this world of technology. Have male or other allies influenced your careers?*

Marie Ekeland (ME): I believe I would not have had the same career if I had not been a female. I started in the VC industry in France in 2000, which was really the beginning of the industry. We had zero playbook apart from just looking at what was being done in Silicon Valley. I was the only woman in the boardrooms for 15 years or so. My French VC colleagues were really looking at Silicon Valley role models. There were no women at all. I never had any female role models to look up to, in my practice. In addition, I was raised in Vancouver and for a while I had been working in New York. I was not impressed by the US culture, because I had partly experienced it.

I am a mathematician and computer scientist by background. My way of thinking was always focused on the question: how can I be the most useful possible? What are the problems that I can solve? This was my way of getting into the job and trying to find my own way of doing it. That has really played a role in my being able to innovate in the VC world, and to find my own way of doing things and to step up. There was freedom because nobody was expecting anything from me, because they had not seen any female French VCs before. I was the curiosity. The good thing is when you are in that position, and you are ambitious and focused on solving problems, and you are efficient in doing that, people remember you. This helped me in adapting the job to what I thought was good for me.

There were three important moments. The first one is that I seeded the biggest French success to date in 2006. I stayed on the board until three years after the IPO. That company is Criteo; the founder is called JB (Jean-Baptiste) Rudelle. He moved to Silicon Valley at some point, and I met him regularly in San Francisco. I remember a particular evening where we were having dinner, and he said, "Marie, when do you start your fund?" I had never thought about it before. I thought, "He thinks I should do it.

He is an entrepreneur, and he sees that in me. He is a good entrepreneur, and he feels that I should spread my way of practicing this job." I eventually ended up building my own fund, two years after. This was the moment when I started thinking about it and started building confidence in doing so.

Number two is in my way of management or being on the board, and in my practice, I was encountering things that were linked to people. One of my founders is Arabic. In France, racism is mostly around Black people and Arabs. He had been suffering from racism since he was a kid because he lived in "the ghetto." He ended up being a rapper and becoming a tech entrepreneur. He is a self-made man. He was an activist as well, and he would point to me, saying, "This is not normal." He was the one discovering what was happening to me in boardrooms or in my own company. He helped me in understanding that these relationships actually were not normal, and that they were linked to biases that people were having and that I was tolerating them because I was not seeing them. He helped me react to these behaviors, because he had been fighting all his life for them. He transferred his knowledge to me.

Number three is being able to show what you have done. Whenever Ed would put me on a conference, he would say, "Marie is not presenting herself." He would do the marketing for me. I never realized before Ed told me that I was the first woman to have raised over $200M [for a] first time fund in Europe. He told me it could even be the case that I would be the first woman in the US. I had mixed feelings. Of course, I can be proud, but it is also so sad. The US industry has been around before the European industry for 20 years. How could I be the first one? I was learning to recognize that if I had achieved something, I should say it.

BREAKING THROUGH RESISTANCE, THEN MAKING CHANGES

Maya Horgan Famodu (MHF): In 2014, I tried briefly to raise a fund, and I mainly positioned it towards African investors and a few women angel impact groups. I got no traction and no interest. The people who ended up being interested at first were actually all males from the US. In my fund one, we have 40 investors and four women. It all started in 2016, I was trying to get a job within venture capital; I wanted to be an intern or work and start exploring the industry from that way. When I did not get a job at all, I launched Ingressive Capital as my fund one. Our first 15 fifteen investors were male from Nigeria and the US. Interestingly enough,

I would say male allies and those who truly took the leap of faith in our work, before I had the touch points and the credibility, were American and Nigerian investors and businessmen.

EB: *What do you think was the main contributor to the difficulties that you faced?*

MHF: I started it with little professional experience. I tried launching a $15M fund when I was 23, with about a year of work experience. Reasonably, I did not get very far with that background. However, when I did have investor relationships, knew how to source a good deal, knew how to launch client initiatives across the continent, what prevented me on the Africa side was the very ageist and patriarchal society. I was young, female, with an American accent; there was a lot of resistance at first. At the beginning, I had to either hire an older male, or bring my dad, who is a pastor and has no business experience, into a meeting and pretend that he was the boss, and I was the assistant, and I was speaking on his behalf. I did that for maybe the first two years of business, because I wanted to get the deal done. My thoughts were, "I know that I own the business, but I need to portray myself or the company such that we can get things done, because I am not going to fight that battle at first." I had my commitment and conviction. If I wanted to, at the beginning, change the narrative and the perception of African and American businessmen about how a young mixed-race woman could succeed, I wonder if I would have gotten as much traction as I did with just wanting to get this done however I needed to. I did not have time to deal with the bias, because I was trying to move ahead, however possible.

EB: *Thank you for being so candid about that. There is something to be said about doing whatever it takes to get where you need to go, and then changing it from the vantage point of having achieved that.*

MHF: Exactly. Within our fund, we are a strictly for-profits venture capital fund, but 64% of our team is female, and almost 40% of our portfolio companies are female founded and co-founded and 100% are Indigenous Black founders. While I did not focus on it on the front end, we are now financing the next generation of billion-dollar businesses, and they are all owned by people who are women or Indigenous. We are aiming to create unquestionable change, changing asset ownership and wealth creation such that this will never even be a conversation in the future, because the people that are making the decisions are fundamentally different.

BEST PRACTICES FOR ALLIES IN VENTURE CAPITAL

EB: *What are the most powerful best practices that you have already tried and used effectively to alleviate the pressure of overlooked founders, investors, and employees? What are the strategies that other people should adopt to ensure that they are able to broaden their hiring and leadership practices?*

EK: By far, the most important thing is to believe at your very core that funding and hiring people from non-traditional backgrounds is itself a strength that will turn into an unfair advantage for your business. At Gusto, we've learned that small business owners are incredibly diverse and come from very non-traditional backgrounds. Oftentimes, they started their business because they were so overlooked and rejected by others that they had no other choice but to do something on their own. If Gusto only hired people whom our society was designed for, we'd have a much weaker understanding of what our customers need and how they think. It would be like trying to understand the nuances of a poem when you don't speak the language well. But once you internalize that being non-traditional is a strength, you'll notice a lot of great things start happening: You'll start to see things that your competitors miss. You'll make better decisions. You'll have access to the long tail, which is usually where startups need to get their start.

MK: The most powerful best practice is to hold up a mirror to yourself and to take on your own assumptions and reexamine the whole basis of how you operate as an investor. For instance, in evaluating a founder, it is easy, without knowing it, to apply different criteria depending on who is pitching. You could say, "You do not have the track record," while in other equivalent cases, you say, "I'm going to invest in potential because I think this person could do it." The interesting thing is that any investor, including investors of color, can make that mistake unconsciously. You have to systematically go through and be willing to look at that and challenge yourself.

The second-best practice is to diversify your own network and ecosystem. In the wake of the murder of George Floyd [in 2020], so many partners in VC firms came to Kapor Capital and said, "I need to hire a Black general partner." To which I wanted to say, "Go look over in Aisle 12." Obviously, it does not work like that. Investors are known for having good ecosystems and they network all the time. They must start being intentional and conscious about diversifying those networks, which is a lot easier to do than hiring a partner, which is a hard decision and something you do infrequently.

The third is to not require a warm intro for founders. One of the most obnoxious things I have ever heard a VC say was from Marc Andreessen, who said, "If you are not smart enough to get a warm intro, you are not smart enough for me to invest in you." That was really offensive. When you do not let people whom you are connected with jump to the head of the queue, you actually get better results. It is a much fairer process.

The fourth best practice is to rethink what matters when you look at founders. There is still too much attention paid to pedigree, and a corresponding lack of attention to what Freada has called distance traveled—where somebody started in life, what barriers they have already overcome, and how far they have already come. That is a much better predictor, and there is a ton of research that backs up these strategies. There are more best practices, but these are a few key ones.

CHANGING THE INDUSTRY'S POWER DYNAMIC

JL: *What is the one thing that we need to fundamentally change and flip this power balance in tech and VC?*

MK: I am reminded constantly of a quote by the great Frederick Douglass: "Power concedes nothing without a demand." If we are going to change things in these many ways, we have to be willing to step up, be bold, take risks, and really to find ways to challenge the systems we find ourselves in. It is a constant, ongoing thing and there is no one magic formula. If we are really committed to doing the work, I think we can genuinely be hopeful that, over the longer term, systems can change, people can rise to the occasion, and we can all get to a better place.

MHF: We need to get rid of the belief that there needs to be a blueprint that came before that looks like us before we can go and enter the industry that we are pursuing. We have to understand and adopt the belief that we are the blueprint. We are defining the new spaces that we are pursuing, as opposed to looking into others for likeness, to be able to have permission to participate. In addition, we have to deeply understand the power of equity and ownership and its ability to support systems of oppression or to transform decision making on a global scale.

ME: We need to change the decision-making process. Finance is really all about machine learning. What you are doing is that you are investing on past data, and you are trying to optimize on past successes. This is one of the reasons that adding diversity at the GP level is hard, because we have to convince LPs, who only invest in people who do have a track record. People who do have a track record are usually white males. There is a bad incentive for GPs to try to hire people who are adding diversity, because there is the risk that they will lose LPs, because this is the way the investment decisions are taken. Yet we can adopt the idea from venture capital, where you do not have data for early-stage venture capital. It is all about pattern recognition. We really need to change the way we make these investment decisions.

EB: *You are 100% right. Many people say that we need the data to be able to make different decisions. However, there is a plethora of data, and Mitch's fund is producing an IRR [internal rate of return] of 29.1% by doing things differently and investing in diversity. How much data do you think we need before we start to see a shift in mindset?*

ME: On a personal level, people who are making the decisions are going to say, "I'm putting my money in this fund, which is run by three experienced white males who have been working together for the past 20 years, and not in this new team." When you start investing in diversity, you do not have that track record to reassure LPs. All you do have are studies to say, we are building the perfect team. The reason I could raise this $100M fund is because I had a track record. The reason I could build my own track record is because I came into the industry when there was no required track record to move up the ladder. Today, track records exist, and these are the people you are competing against. Massive amounts of money go to existing track records. There is an incentive, even if you are not in agreement with your partners, to stay with your partners, because that is a way of getting more money. If you break that, if you bring on new people, then you are running the risk that your current LPs will say there is too much change on the team. The risk reward is not good. You will get a reward to add diversity on performance, but if the risk you are taking on your fundraising is higher, you will not do it. The people who are making the institutional fund decisions are under a mandate, and it is very restricted and standardized. People have said to me, "Marie, I know you're a good investor. I just know it. I want to give you money, but can you do something normal?" They do not give me the money in the end because their model is in classic finance. If you want to move out of that, they do not have the responsibility for it. I believe change will come from LPs who have their own money and can take the risk. It will not come from traditional finance.

LP-GP RESPONSIBILITY AND ACCOUNTABILITY

EB: *We are seeing some LPs are starting to speak out about this and encouraging others to do things differently by acting themselves. How important are LPs going to be to drive change?*

ME: We are living a complete transition of the economy towards a more sustainable economy. It is a transition and disruption that is even deeper than what we went through with digital. The finance industry will need to acknowledge not only financial performance, but environmental and social performance. Most people do not have a track record in this respect, and I believe diverse GPs will stand out positively. Including these parameters in the investment criteria and this type of performance will help move money towards more diverse GPs.

EZ: We really need to understand the way in which we design systems to perpetuate the racism and bias that we have built in, even when we do not think we are doing it. For example, when we talk about the LP-GP dynamic, people have been talking for the last couple of years about the GP commit, and we have a very clear understanding of the wealth gap in America. When we say, in order for you to impress me, that you have "skin in the game," what we are really saying is, having "white skin in the game." We know that we have an enormous wealth gap. Yet, we ask the founders of a venture fund to commit a significant number of their own dollars into the venture fund to show that they are committed and that they are at risk. If I am worth $100M and I commit $1M, and someone else is worth $100K, and they commit $50K, they are much more at risk. If my fund fails, and I started out being worth $100 million, I am not that at risk. We (the venture/LP industry) have baked in the further entrenchment of a wealthy set of individuals who are able to start venture funds because of their wealth, not to mention that people with existing wealth typically have the friends and the contacts to further support that wealth.

For years, Beezer Clarkson and I have co-hosted a dinner to introduce underrepresented VCs to LPs of any stripe (meaning LPs who are overrepresented and underrepresented). In 2018, we conducted a survey. These survey respondents were only LPs who self-selected, in such that they would travel to New York to sit in a dinner with us and discuss DEI in venture and meet underrepresented VCs. Presumably, these are very forward-thinking LPs. We asked them what their typical capital commitment to a venture fund is: 47% said between $10M–$20M, 20% said greater than $20M, 0% said less than $5M. If you look at the stats on where diversity resided in the venture world at the time, that meant that none of these LPs who cared enough to meet underrepresented GPs could write a check into a fund of less than $30M or $50M. Few, if any, of these GPs could raise a fund of more than that, or of that size. Similarly, when we asked what sort of experience these LPs wanted from the VCs that they backed, 80% said they would invest in a first-time fund "if the GP has past institutional investment experience," 73% said they would invest in a first time fund if that fund was a spin out of a prior firm, 47% said they would do so if the GP was a successful angel investor, and only 13% said they would do so if the GP had not invested more than $10M before either as an angel or part of an institutional fund. If you think about the fact that our diversity statistics have been horrific, what that basically means is you had to be white to have done any of those things. We should make it *"potential-cratic,"* because meritocracy means, "Here is what I got on my SATs or ACTs that enabled me to get into Stanford and put me in proximity with other people who had wealth and who were going to have this career trajectory." It is very much *not*, "Here is what I did once I got to University of Maryland or Howard or Hampton or whatever." The problem is that we have to look into all of these things that we have just laid out and say, these are the trappings of and the perpetuation of systemic racism and systemic bias. We cannot apply these metrics to the people that we are trying to put in positions of financial authority.

We had a dinner a couple of years ago at my firm, during Black History Month. There were a number of white partners who believed we (as a community) can do better, and we need to do better. I think our firm is pretty progressive and forward looking, but we need to do better. One of the Black women at the dinner said that she left a prior firm because the senior partner in her group said, "I really like so and so, she reminds me of my daughter." She said, "Look at me and where I come from, I will never remind him of his daughter. I needed to go someplace else where that is not the way I get ahead." I was glad she felt that our firm was a place she could transfer to where she would receive greater opportunity, but her comment about her prior law firm is something I have heard many times about numerous places.

As for best practices, we need to shout vociferously, publicly, and frequently about the things that we see that are wrong. Then we need to follow up, apply metrics, and impact compensation. I recently had a conversation where one of my colleagues was on the phone with me. She is Black and very experienced. The person on the other end of the phone did not know her. I suggested that she and he introduce themselves to one another. He did, she did, and he said, "Oh, so then this isn't your first time doing x." She has 15 years of doing x. I called someone to complain about the fact that he had said that. I talked to her about it afterwards as well. He is not part of our firm. I do not care whether he intended or did not intend to be demeaning, I do not care whether he was disrespecting our firm, as opposed to disrespecting her. That was not okay. I realized that I may have impaired a relationship as a result of complaining about that, and I had to follow up to get someone on the phone to complain about it.

We have to call people out and we have to make them feel uncomfortable. We have to seek accountability. This is a particularly important use of the privilege that I have. Watching people complain about the calling out (itself) is really interesting. I know that it is off-putting, and exhausting. People complain, "We want to do this stuff with you, but you're so damn impatient." Yet, with 400 years, how much patience are we supposed to have? If more of us are publicly articulating what is wrong, and the fact that most of the bias—99% of the bias—is *not* implicit, and is second nature, that is very fucking different than implicit. Your racism, your sexism, or homophobia or transphobia, is second nature. It is not implicit. It is built in, build it the fuck out. Dock people their pay. Make sure it is part of the compensation process. Make sure it is part of the review process, pro and con.

CONCLUSION

22 The Present Isn't Rosy ... but There Is Still Hope

Since we met and started this project in 2019, it feels like the world has fundamentally changed. The impact of COVID-19 is still not fully decipherable; the markets, including venture capital funding, reached record heights in 2021[444] and then dipped drastically in 2022.[445] Russia's invasion of Ukraine continues to have far-reaching impacts on the global economy, as has the rise of central bank interest rates. A cost-of-living crisis has taken a stranglehold on those least wealthy in society, as everything from energy, to food, and fuel have risen in cost exponentially. Cryptocurrencies and the associated technologies of decentralization, or "Web3," have moved from a fringe interest to a mainstream phenomenon, and environment, social, and governance (ESG) principles have begun to make waves[446] in startup fundraising and VC.

What does all this mean for the aim of this volume, to increase diversity, equity, and inclusion (DEI) in venture capital and startups? The unfortunate truth is that the numbers of diverse entrepreneurs accessing capital have receded in the last two years. The overall share of female VC partners is stagnant at around 15% (in Europe[447] and in the US[448]), while women manage an even smaller share of money than these numbers would suggest (5% in Europe[449]). We still don't have a good overview of

---

444. https://www.forbes.com/sites/truebridge/2022/06/14/
    state-of-vc-2021-breaking-every-record/
445. https://news.crunchbase.com/business/
    global-vc-funding-decline-monthly-recap-april-2022/
446. https://sifted.eu/articles/venture-capital-esg/
447. https://europeanwomeninvc.idcinteractive.net/10/
448. https://pitchbook.com/media/press-releases/
    pitchbook-report-on-women-in-vc-finds-growing-number-of-female-checkwriters-could-bo
    lster-female-founded-startups-disproportionately-impacted-by-pandemic
449. https://europeanwomeninvc.idcinteractive.net/14/

how much money is being managed by Black GPs globally, though we do know that Black-led funds in the US represent around 3% of total funds,[450] and that Black fund managers are raising significantly smaller funds[451] (46% smaller) than the industry average; we know even less about any other overlooked group mentioned in this book. What is clear, however, is that we are a long way off—even further away than before COVID—from approaching equity!

While funding for mixed-gender teams has grown to over 15%[452] of total funding in 2021 (up from just 7% 10 years before), funding to all-female teams has shrunk to 2%[453] (down from 2.4% in 2011[454]), while 2021 happened to be a record-setting year for VC funding overall. The funding allocated to Black entrepreneurs has also fallen dramatically in 2022 so far (by at least 25% in the US,[455] for instance) at 1.2% of total VC dollars[456] (as of June 2022).

Two explanations for this lack of improvement are systemic: on the one hand, women were more likely to step back[457] during the work-from-home times of COVID and take the lead on caregiving responsibilities. On the other hand, much of the funding boom of 2021 has been deployed to later-stage funds, which are still much more likely to be managed by white men. To inspire some hope, the longer-term trend is slightly better: the number of rounds of funding received by female-only teams has risen slowly but steadily over the last decade according to Pitchbook data,[458] from only 3.7% of deals in 2011 to 6.5% in 2021, the highest percentage reached so far. Similarly, the deal count percentage for mixed-gender teams has risen in parallel, from 10.9% in 2011 to 18.8% in 2021.

---

450. Deloitte, the National Venture Capital Association, and Venture Forward, 2022.

451. https://www.dropbox.com/s/ducejd5jpjn0piv/BLCKVC%20State%20of%20Black%20Venture%20Report.pdf?dl=

452. https://pitchbook.com/news/articles/female-founders-dashboard-2021-vc-funding-wrap-up

453. https://www.bloomberg.com/news/articles/2022-01-11/women-founders-raised-just-2-of-venture-capital-money-last-year

454. https://pitchbook.com/news/articles/female-founders-dashboard-2021-vc-funding-wrap-up

455. https://techcrunch.com/2022/06/17/black-founders-are-seeing-a-decrease-in-funding-amid-economic-downturn/

456. https://news.crunchbase.com/diversity/vc-funding-black-founded-startups/

457. https://www.oecd.org/coronavirus/policy-responses/caregiving-in-crisis-gender-inequality-in-paid-and-unpaid-work-during-covid-19-3555d164/

458. https://pitchbook.com/news/articles/female-founders-dashboard-2021-vc-funding-wrap-up

Dramatically, however, we have also seen new research[459] undermining some of the core tenets of recent efforts to put more money in the hands of female VCs. So far, the assumption was that more money managed by female GPs would automatically lead to more female founders getting funding. While this might be true to an extent, taking female GPs' funding makes those female-led teams *two times less likely* to receive money from male investors, who control 95% of venture capital, in future funding rounds.[460] As a result, a team's chance of building a successful VC-backed business is in fact smaller if they take early-stage funding from female VCs, while there is no pipeline of diverse funding that sees that startup through to escape velocity. While no comparative study exists for Black founders and Black investors, or any other of the groups we address in this volume, we fear similar biases might hold true.

This finding sheds new light on what we should ask for to increase DEI in VC and tech. The authors of the research paper, who are based out of the INSEAD international business school, have a proposal: we need more *inclusive* money rather than homophilic money, meaning investment teams that have a balance of genders rather than, say, six men and one woman, or the reverse. The insights from our panel on allyship[§21.5] become particularly crucial with this in mind: we need men, especially white men, to step forward and take decisive action, as they currently hold the majority of money in their hands, and the data clearly shows that startup success is more likely[462] when the teams behind them are diverse (see Boston Consulting Group[463] and McKinsey[464] for more evidence on this front).

In the event we continue to see levels of investment in diversity recede rather than advance, we will need to think at a more senior level. Given

---

459. https://pubsonline.informs.org/doi/full/10.1287/orsc.2022.1594

460. Snellman, Kasia and Isabelle Solal. "Does Investor Gender Matter for the Success of Female Entrepreneurs? Gender Homophily and the Stigma of Incompetence in Entrepreneurial Finance." *Organization Science*,[461] 2022.

461. https://pubsonline.informs.org/doi/full/10.1287/orsc.2022.1594#d6892339e1

462. https://www.emerald.com/insight/content/doi/10.1108/JBS-06-2012-0020/full/html#idm45599070538480

463. https://www.bcg.com/publications/2018/why-women-owned-startups-are-better-bet

464. https://www.mckinsey.com/business-functions/people-and-organizational-performance/our-insights/delivering-through-diversity

that data shows[465] that diverse fund managers can identify investments traditional fund managers overlook, we need to create funds focused on diverse founders that span the entire lifecycle of a company. Currently, there are mostly smaller pre-seed and seed funds run by GPs from overlooked backgrounds.

There are three fundamental levers we believe will be crucial in changing the way investments are made, all of which were touched upon in Part III: Best Practices and Part IV: New Ideas:

- **LPs must allocate money with DEI in mind.** Well-versed portfolio theory states that resources should be spread across a variety of categories and managers to minimize risk. We also know that investing in diverse VC teams has financial benefits. To this date, however, most LPs appear to be stuck in legacy relationships and haven't taken decisive action when those funds continue to invest homogeneously. This must change dramatically so that money is distributed more equally across a larger diversity of managers. LPs are arguably neglecting their fiduciary duty in not taking DEI more seriously. Lawsuits may follow.

- **GPs need to acknowledge their biases and change their investment behavior.** A first step to overcome common human bias—preferring or being more likely to trust people who are similar to yourself—is to recognize it. This can be a lot to unpack when it comes to VC, but there are clear starting points for investors:

  - Make it easy for people to pitch you without a warm introduction. For example, have a form on your website which you check regularly.
  - Run serious office hours, open to everyone, where you allow for pitches and track outcomes. If there are no investments made from office hours, either stop running them or commit to making an investment from the next one.

465. Ibarguen, Alberto. "America Is Growing More Diverse. Investors Are Far Behind."[466] *Barron's*, 2021; "Beyond Good Intentions: Why Diversity Is Vital In Investment Decisions."[467] Aon.

466. https://www.barrons.com/articles/
america-is-growing-more-diverse-investors-are-far-behind-51638833895

467. https://www.aon.com/unitedkingdom/insights/
why-diversity-is-vital-in-investment-decisions.jsp

- Undertake effective DEI training[468] and actively diversify the funnel of startups that you monitor.

- **We all need to work together to create new flywheels.** We are still hopeful that some of the existing ecosystem whales and lions will be willing to push for change, but at the same time, new players may have an easier time writing different playbooks and building new flywheels. Our conversations with the Zebras Unite[§20.1] and New Mittelstand[§20.2] founders made this very clear in particular; with a different ethos and a new kind of startup idea in mind, change follows. LPs need to take a chance on these players that come from alternative backgrounds, without a track record, and who are unable to pay a large GP commitment. There is a strong role here to be played by state-funds, like the European Investment Fund, the British Business Bank, or KfW Capital, who can take "risks"—evidence has shown these investment decisions are actually less risky[469]—under the banner of "inclusive development." It is important that these institutions lead from the front and make these important decisions now. At the same time, we need established managers to be friendly: sponsor new ecosystem players, take personal responsibility for their success by co-investing with them and forming syndicates, or by writing LP checks (like the Screendoor GPs-turned-LPs[470] or LocalGlobe[471] in the UK, who are heavily invested in Black Girl Fest[472]).

Notably, this list does not include continuing to put the DEI responsibility on the few Black female VCs and CEOs; it does not include continuing to ask for more DEI data[473] that only serves to stall real action; it does not include hiding behind charitable, DEI-focused side funds. It's time to stop talking and start wiring checks to diverse funds and founders. If you look at your portfolio and there is only one type of diversity, as in you have invested in either one white woman or a few men of color, there is a problem that requires your urgent attention. Single dimension diver-

---

468. https://behavioralscientist.org/
the-open-secret-of-what-works-and-what-doesnt-for-diversity-equity-and-inclusion/

469. https://neuroleadership.com/your-brain-at-work/
why-diverse-teams-outperform-homogeneous-teams/

470. https://www.screendoorpartners.com

471. https://localglobe.vc/

472. https://www.linkedin.com/company/black-girl-fest/

473. https://sifted.eu/articles/vc-diversity-data-excuse/

sity in 2022 just isn't good enough. The 30% Club[474] taught us that to make seed change and truly feel the benefit of diversity, the diverse talent in the room need to feel as though they belong and have a voice. That tends to be best achieved when there is a quorum of 30% or more.

23 Final Reflections

We began this project in 2019 with a rush of hope and exhilarating energy amid what was supposed to be our "real work"—Erika was running her startup Kinhub (then Kami) and Johannes was writing an academic book on VCs. We saw a big opportunity to combine our knowledge and networks to raise awareness, elevate voices, and finally define the agenda for concrete action. The first interviews, focused on broadening the definition of diversity, were eye-opening for us. The problem was even bigger than we had thought, and so much of it was hidden behind the industry's closed doors.

After the initial push, things began to slow down as interviewees were sourced and scheduled, and the pandemic brought new concerns and changes to the industry. A new series of wins were the wind behind our sails that we needed to make it through the dip; we were able to connect with people we thought would be out of reach, like Mitch Kapor,[§14.4] who we reached via Twitter, and who was incredibly kind and giving. Success usually reproduces itself, and the next phase of interviews flew by, propelling us through the VC world.

The second phase of interviews focused on people who had launched initiatives and taken action *within* the system's predefined parameters. We heard from many of the people on the VC, LP, and operator sides, learning that much of what we thought had revolutionary potential from the outside turned out to be localized, small-scale, or merely cosmetic. To complete the interview series and meet the promise we had set out with—to create a handbook on how to fundamentally change an industry—we decided to cast a wider net. We reached out to people who we thought had *less* power and influence because of their position outside of the "power centers" of tech. We connected with people like the founders of Zebras Unite and the New Mittelstand; we spoke to investing orga-

---

474. https://30percentclub.org/

nizations embedded within companies; accelerators who aren't copying Y Combinator, such as Village Capital;[19.2] and individuals who thought (and acted) fundamentally differently about what needed to be done, like Ed Zimmerman[21.5] and Nicola Corzine.[21.4] Looking back at these conversations, we believe that in the long run, they hold the biggest promise. Building new flywheels—being true disruptors and contrarians—holds a lot of hope. How quickly and in what way exactly this hope will materialize into systemic change remains to be seen.

For us as interviewers, co-authors, and now also great friends, the journey of researching and writing this book was a phenomenal one indeed. We started with almost opposite experiences—very practical from a founder's perspective versus very abstract from a researcher's point of view, and as a Black mother and entrepreneur versus a white male academic. But bringing these experiences *together* to work on this book can serve as an example of what we have learned the industry needs more of: starting with a diversity of viewpoints and integrating them inclusively into the design, process, and end product. Whether this is for a book or for an investment decision, weaving the tapestry *together* is what we need much more of.

About the Authors

Erika Brodnock is a multi-award winning serial entrepreneur and philanthropist. Following her MBA, she was Research Fellow at King's College London, and is currently finishing a PhD at the London School of Economics and Political Science. Through her work at the intersection of technology and wellbeing, Erika specializes in building products and services that disrupt outdated systems. Erika is co-founder of Kinhub (formerly Kami), an employee wellbeing platform focused on enhancing equity and inclusion in the future of work. Erika also co-founded Extend Ventures, where she leads research efforts that aim to democratize access to venture finance for diverse entrepreneurs.

Johannes Lenhard is a researcher and writer based in London. Following his PhD at Cambridge, he has spent the last three years researching the ethics of venture capital between Europe and the US during his postdoc. His first book, "Making Better Lives"—on homeless people's survival in Paris—was published earlier this year. He regularly contributes to journalistic outlets, such as Prospect, TechCrunch, Vestoj, Aeon, Tribune, The Conversation, and Sifted. Most recently, he is the co-founder and co-director of VentureESG.

About Holloway

Holloway publishes books online, offering titles from experts on topics ranging from tools and technology to teamwork and entrepreneurship. All titles are built for a satisfying reading experience on the web as well as in print. The Holloway Reader helps readers find what they need in search results, and permits authors and editors to make ongoing improvements.

Holloway seeks to publish more exceptional authors. We believe that a new company with modern tools can make publishing a better experience for authors and help them reach their audience. If you're a writer with a manuscript or idea, please get in touch at hello@holloway.com.

Printed in Great Britain
by Amazon